starting out:
open games GLENN FLEAR

R0061399036

01/2012

MAN CHESS

...s plc www.everymanchess.com

First published in 2010 by Gloucester Publishers plc (formerly Everyman Publishers plc), Northburgh House, 10 Northburgh Street, London EC1V 0AT

British Library Cataloguing-in-Publication Data

A catalogue record for this book is available from the British Library.

ISBN: 9781 85744 630 2

Distributed in North America by The Globe Pequot Press, P.O Box 480, 246 Goose Lane, Guilford, CT 06437-0480.

All other sales enquiries should be directed to Everyman Chess, Northburgh House, 10 Northburgh Street, London EC1V 0AT (tel: 020 7253 7887; fax: 020 7490 3708) email: info@everymanchess.com: website: www.everymanchess.com

Everyman is the registered trade mark of Random House Inc. and is used in this work under licence from Random House Inc.

EVERYMAN CHESS SERIES
Chief Advisor: Byron Jacobs
Commissioning editor: John Emms
Assistant editor: Richard Palliser

Typeset and edited by First Rank Publishing, Brighton.
Cover design by Horatio Monteverde.
Printed and bound in the US by Versa Press.

Contents

For the three people closest to me,
Christine, James and Nathan.

Bibliography

Books

4...Qh4 in the Scotch Game, Lev Gutman (Batsford 2001)

Beating the Open Games, Mihail Marin (Quality Chess 2007)

Dangerous Weapons: 1 e4 e5, John Emms, Glenn Flear & Andrew Greet (Everyman Chess 2008)

Danish Dynamite, Karsten Müller & Martin Voigt (Russell Enterprises 2003)

New Ideas in the Four Knights, John Nunn (Batsford 1993)

Play the Open Games as Black, John Emms (Gambit 2000)

The Complete Vienna, Mikhail Tseitlin & Igor Glazkov (Batsford 1995)

The Four Knights, Jan Pinski (Everyman Chess 2003)

The Giuoco Piano, Eduard Gufeld & Oleg Stetsko (Batsford 1996)

The Italian Game, Tim Harding & George Botterill (Batsford 1977)

The King's Gambit, Neil McDonald (Batsford 1998)

The Latvian Lives!, Tony Kosten (Batsford 2001)

The Petroff Defence, Gyozo Forintos & Ervin Haag (Batsford 1991)

The Philidor Files, Christian Bauer (Everyman Chess 2006)

The Scotch Game, Peter Wells (Batsford 1998)

The Two Knights Defence, Jan Pinski (Everyman Chess2004)

The Two Knights Defence, Yakov Estrin (Batsford 1983)

Winning with the Bishop's Opening, Gary Lane (Batsford 1993)

Winning with the King's Gambit, Joe Gallagher (Batsford 1992)

Reference

Encyclopaedia of Chess Openings Volume C, 5th Edition (Sahovski Informator 2006)

Informator 1-105

New in Chess Yearbook 1-92

Software

ChessBase 9

Deep Fritz 8

Introduction to 1 e4 e5

After learning the rules and then playing a few games, most chess players come to realize that there is a lot to be said for opening with 1 e4. The king's bishop and queen are then free to come into the game. Playing Black, similar thinking attracts one to the reply 1...e5 **(Diagram 1)** which, in addition, restrains White's attempts to build a broad centre with d2-d4. So it's no surprise that the following is a typical position that has occurred in countless games (in fact on my largest database 12% of all games start in this way) between players of all strengths.

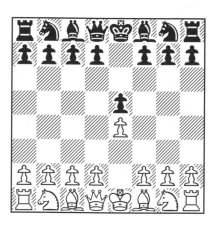

Diagram 1 (W)

Starting Out: Open Games

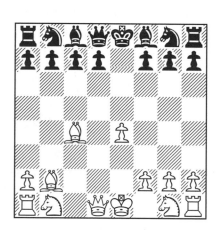

Diagram 2 (B)

A gambit variation

Once this position has arisen the players need to think about developing their pieces.

Even someone near the beginning of their chess adventure is aware of the need to get their pieces out, especially the kingside ones. A little later, the relative safety of the kings and the importance of the centre are appreciated, as they tend to determine who gets the chance to attack first and hit hardest. Our chess personality influences our approach: some players just aim to get their pieces out as quickly as possible; others try to soup up their activity with gambit play; whereas another method involves manoeuvring while aiming to carefully build up a strong pawn centre.

However, whatever the style or level of experience, there is something for everyone in the world of Open Games.

Here are some examples of the variety of positions that can occur.

Gambits

A gambit is an offer of material to accelerate development in an attempt to seize the initiative.

1 e4 e5 2 d4 exd4 3 c3 dxc3 4 Bc4 cxb2 5 Bxb2 (Diagram 2)

A line of the Danish Gambit. White has sacrificed two pawns in order to obtain a lead in development and attacking chances. Note in particular his threatening bishops.

Manoeuvring

1 e4 e5 2 Nf3 Nc6 3 Nc3 Nf6 4 Bb5 Bb4 5 0-0 0-0 6 d3 d6 7 Bg5 Bxc3 8 bxc3 Qe7 9 Re1 Nd8 10 d4 Ne6 11 Bc1 c5 12 Bf1 Rd8 (Diagram 3)

One of the main lines of the Four Knights Game leads to some tension in the centre. However, the main feature of the coming phase is manoeuvring by both sides, seeking superiority in the battle between White's bishops and Black's knights.

Direct confrontation in the centre

1 e4 e5 2 Nf3 Nc6 3 Bc4 Nf6 4 d4 exd4 5 e5 d5 (Diagram 4)

A sharp struggle ensues from the Two Knights Defence where both players aim to develop rapidly, but at the same time compete for control of the central arena.

Does this whet your appetite?

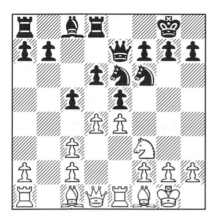

Diagram 3 (W)

A manoeuvring game

Diagram 4 (W)

Central confrontation

What are Open Games?

If you are an inexperienced player, or perhaps not that familiar with chess terminology, the expression 'Open Games' may give you the impression that I will be covering a selection of games where there is an *open board*; that is, examples involving several pawn exchanges and plenty of opportunities for lively piece play. In fact, although this may occur in a number of variations, Open Games actually refers to something more specific. After the moves 1 e4 e5, a certain number of encounters featuring top Grandmasters will continue 2 Nf3 Nc6 3 Bb5 (which is known as the 'Spanish' or, in certain quarters, the 'Ruy Lopez'), but most club players, and virtually all beginners, will vary on moves two or three.

I shall consider all of these non-Spanish systems to be the 'Open Games' and are the subject matter of the book in your hands. If you are contemplating playing the Spanish as White or meeting the Spanish as Black, then you will also need to pay attention to various Open Games as these can be tricky if you are not expecting them! Indeed, according to my statistics, 65.7% of encounters after 1 e4 e5 become Open Games rather than the Spanish Opening.

Many grandmasters have at some point played the positions resulting from 1 e4 e5, and some, such as myself, have continued to do so all their careers. There are just so many fascinating ideas! If you too are tempted by the Open Games, with either colour, this book will serve as an introduction and hopefully give you the confidence to try out some of these systems in your own games.

The scope and limitation of this book

My idea has been to introduce people to the types of position that occur, and to offer them a few ideas that should enable them to venture the Open Games, for either colour, with a certain degree of confidence. In the illustrative games and notes I have also tried to give an indication of the better ways of handling a system, based on my own experience.

As I have, admittedly, played these systems uniquely with Black, there is a natural tendency for me to point out some neat ideas for the second player based on my own repertoire. However, I have also highlighted some of those lines that have posed me problems in the past, so read carefully and you could find at least the basics of a robust system or two for White in these pages.

It's impossible for me to go into great detail as space is limited, so later on you may need to refer to more specific works, or an important database with a greater number of game references. Nevertheless, we all need to start out sometime and now seems to be as good a time as any. So let us begin...

Chapter One
The Quiet Italian

Introduction

Starting a chess game with a few 'natural-looking developing moves' makes common sense. That is perhaps why we see the moves **1 e4 e5 2 Nf3 Nc6 3 Bc4** and then, after say **3...Nf6, 4 d3 (Diagram 1)** occurring frequently at all levels of play.

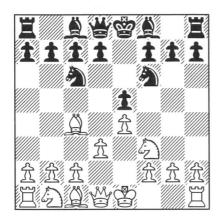 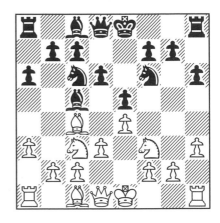

Diagram 1	**Diagram 2 (W)**
The Quiet Italian	Symmetrical chess

Basically, White seeks a quiet life with Bc4 and d2-d3 where there is a minimum of reliance on theory.

The bishop would seem to be well placed on c4, bearing down along the potentially vulnerable a2-g8 diagonal. Then, to follow up, and before getting involved in any complications, the move d2-d3 will enable the other bishop to emerge.

This scheme, which I will refer to as the *Quiet Italian*, is known for its solidity and enables White to have a stable foundation, both in the centre and in terms of development, and can be employed against both of Black's principal third moves, 3...Bc5 and 3...Nf6.

From White's point of view, the positioning of his queen's knight deserves some thought. If the knight goes to c3 it comes into play without further ado and clamps down on the d5-square; however, White's pawn structure then lacks flexibility.

The more modern way is to play an early c2-c3 and then prepare an expansion with d3-d4 (later in the game when White is better organized) or b2-b4. The queen's knight, in order to fit in with this plan, will need to manoeuvre typically via d2 and then either to c4 or perhaps to f1 and then g3.

White plays Nc3

What can we say about the following?

1 e4 e5 2 Nf3 Nc6 3 Bc4 Nf6 4 d3 Bc5 5 Nc3 d6

If nothing else one could remark that so far development has been straightforward. The same cannot be said about the further moves...

6 h3 h6 7 a3 a6 (Diagram 2)

...which reflect the fact that both sides are playing cautiously, being concerned about limiting opportunities for the opponent. You often see young children get this symmetrical position, or similar ones. Playing like this, they may avoid leaving anything hanging, but they invariably run out of useful moves and predictably enter the middlegame without a good plan.

Strategy

Rather simplistic. This type of opening lacks pawn breaks, so pieces come out to sensible squares to await developments. White tries to use his extra tempo to create pressure, whereas Black needs to find the right moment to break the symmetry.

Castling requires some thought by both sides, as allowing a pin in front of one's castled king is fraught with danger.

Theoretical

Not really; a few general principles and a sense of danger is more or less sufficient.

Game 1
☐ **E.Eliskases** ■ **D.Bronstein**
Mar del Plata 1960

1 e4 e5 2 Nf3 Nc6 3 Bc4 Nf6

After the other popular move, 3...Bc5, the sequence 4 d3 Nf6 5 Nc3 d6 6 Bg5 comes to the same thing.

4 d3 Bc5 5 Nc3 d6 6 Bg5

Instead, after 6 h3 h6 7 a3 a6 (as in the introductory text), it's important to be patient as there is nothing special happening as yet. There are no easy ways of expanding in the centre and both sides lack pawn breaks.

When I have had this sort of position as Black I try to break the symmetry fairly early. For example, after 8 Be3 (White's most testing move) I tried to play without castling short in the following game: 8...Bxe3 9 fxe3 (White has a nominal pull due to the open f-file, but this isn't such a big issue if Black is careful) 9...Qe7 (9...0-0 10 0-0 Be6 should lead to equality but isn't very ambitious) 10 0-0 Nd8!? (covering f7 and preparing to play ...c7-c6) 11 Qe1 c6 12 Nh4 g6 13 Qf2 Nh7 14 d4 Ng5 15 Kh1 Nde6 and I had safely achieved a position where there was some tension and chances for both sides, K.Roser-G.Flear, French Team Ch. 2005. Furthermore, after 16 Rad1 Bd7 17 b4, I was sufficiently confident to play 17...0-0-0!? with a complex struggle in prospect.

6...Na5! (Diagram 3)

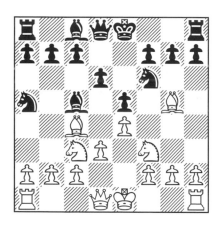

Diagram 3 (W)

The best antidote

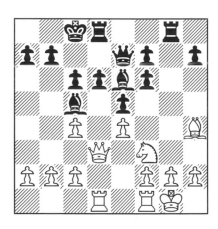

Diagram 4 (W)

The black king is safe

A notable move that deserves a diagram.

6...Na5! is recognized as the best antidote to the pin in this position. Black is not afraid of having doubled f-pawns if he hasn't castled kingside.

NOTE: As a general rule in chess, castling is a good way of tucking the king away – if (and it's a big 'if' that is sometimes forgotten) any danger to the king is less than it would be elsewhere.

In this position castling would be an error, as the pin would then become strong: i.e. 6...0-0? 7 Nd5 and Black has difficulties already. See Emms-Flear (Game 3) for a good illustration of a deadly pin in the Quiet Italian.

7 Nd5 Nxc4 8 dxc4 c6 9 Nxf6+ gxf6 10 Bh4

Keeping up the pressure on the h4-d8 diagonal. A famous game V.Korchnoi-D.Bronstein, USSR Ch., Moscow 1952, continued as follows 10 Be3 Qb6 11 Qd2 Be6 12 0-0-0 0-0-0 13 b3 Rhg8 and Black's position was the more promising, the g-file and light-squared bishop being important assets.

10...Rg8 11 0-0 Be6 12 Qd3 Qe7 13 Rad1 0-0-0 (Diagram 4)

With Black fully developed and White lacking threats the king can happily go to the queenside.

14 Rfe1 Bg4 15 Qb3 Qe6 16 Rd3 Rde8 17 Nd2

White reorganizes his pieces, but Black has had sufficient time to prepare useful counterplay.

17...f5!

Not just intending to trade off a doubled pawn. In fact, Black seizes the initiative.

18 Kf1

Otherwise 18 exf5 Bxf5 19 Rg3 allows 19...Qh6 and White is rather tangled.

18...Qh6 19 g3 f4 20 f3 fxg3 21 hxg3 Bh3+ 22 Ke2 f5! (Diagram 5)

And again! Black batters away at the centre.

23 exf5 Bxf5 24 Ne4 Bxe4

Leading to the win of a pawn, as White isn't in a position to cover the resulting isolated e-pawn.

25 fxe4 Rg4 26 Kd1 Qg6 27 Rf3 Rxe4 28 Rxe4 Qxe4 29 Qd3

White survives to an endgame, but not a particularly enticing one, though his active rook gives him some hope.

29...Qg6 30 Qf5+ Qxf5 31 Rxf5 Rg8 32 Rf7 h6 33 Rf6 Rg4 (Diagram 6) 34 c3

Perhaps 34 b3 Rd4+ 35 Ke2 Bb4 36 a3!? Bxa3 37 Rxh6 with some drawing chances.

34...Rxc4 35 Rxh6 b5 36 Rg6 b4

Generating a pair of central passed pawns.

37 cxb4 Rxb4 38 Kc2 Re4 39 g4 Re2+ 40 Kb3 Kd7 41 Bg5 Bd4 42 Bc1 e4 43 Bf4

Black was threatening ...e4-e3 shutting the bishop out of the game.

43...d5 44 Rd6+ Ke7 45 Rxc6 Rxb2+ 46 Ka3 Rf2 47 Rc7+ Kd8 48 Rf7 Bc5+

48...e3 is the most precise here.

49 Kb3 Rf3+ 50 Kc2 Be3 51 Bc7+ Kc8 52 Re7 Bg5 53 Rh7 d4 54 Ba5 d3+ 55 Kb2 e3 56 Rc7+ Kb8 57 Rc5 Rf2+ 58 Kb3 d2 0-1

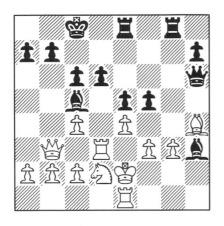

Diagram 5 (W)
Battering away at the centre

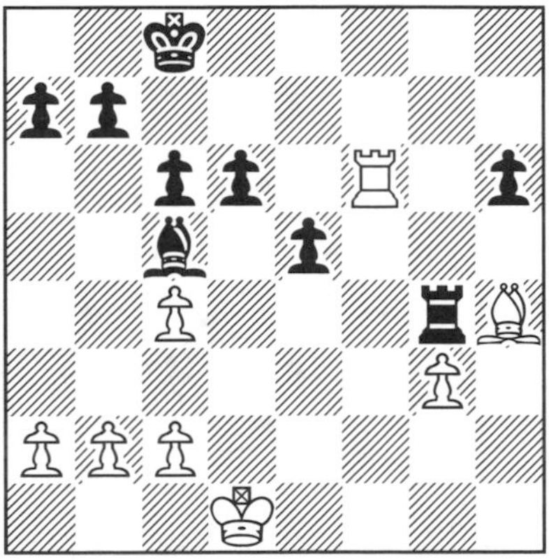

Diagram 6 (W)
White is unlikely to survive

Think before castling!

The following miniature illustrates the problem with 'castling into it'. Here this means committing the king early, followed by provoking the opponent to advance his pawns on that front. This doesn't mean that I'm against castling, far from it, but it shouldn't be a routine move. The general rule should be: think before committing your king!

Game 2
□ **V.Knorre** ■ **M.Chigorin**
St Petersburg 1874

1 e4 e5 2 Nf3 Nc6 3 Bc4 Bc5 4 0-0

Most players these days prefer another fourth move, but this isn't bad in itself.

4...d6

There is a case for 4...Nf6 in order to give himself the option of ...d7-d5, which is advisable in certain positions – see the notes to Game 3.

5 d3

5 c3 is more dynamic as White can then consider an early d2-d4 or even b2-b4, expanding and gaining space. I've also noticed that 5 h3 has been very popular here, as many people really have been determined to avoid the pin with ...Bg4!

5...Nf6 6 Bg5 h6 7 Bh4? (Diagram 7)

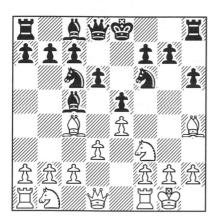
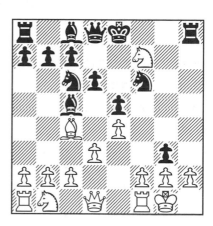

Diagram 7 (B)	**Diagram 8 (W)**
A careless retreat	Black has a very strong attack

This natural move is actually a mistake, but is still played by the unsuspecting to this day! We have an ideal scenario for Black: White has committed his king early and is inviting Black to attack!

7...g5!

The first world champion, Wilhelm Steinitz, may have been the first to have played this move (see below).

8 Bg3

Instead, 8 Nxg5 is already rather desperate, as after 8...hxg5 9 Bxg5 Rg8 10 h4 Bg4 11 Qd2 Nd4 12 Nc3 c6 White doesn't have much to boast about for his sacrifice.

8...h5

Pinning with 8...Bg4 is also tempting, when Black would certainly have a comfortable game. Then after 9 c3 there is a choice between several promising ideas: 9...Qd7 with ...0-0-0 in mind, 9...h5, or 9...Nh5 intending a timely hop to f4.

9 Nxg5

The alternative 9 h4 isn't fully satisfactory either: 9...Bg4 10 c3 Qd7 11 d4 exd4 12 e5 dxe5 (12...Ne4! 13 Bh2 0-0-0 would also be strong) 13 Bxe5 Nxe5 14 Nxe5 Qf5!? (simplest is 14...Bxd1 15 Nxd7 Nxd7 16 Rxd1 0-0-0 with advantage, as 17 cxd4 is strongly met by 17...Ne5!) 15 Nxg4 (15 Qa4+! Kf8 16 Nxf7 is less clear, as in Moun Moun Latt-Nay Oo Kyam Tun, Yangon 1999) 15...hxg4, and Black obtained a winning attack along the h-file in S.Dubois-W.Steinitz, London 1862.

9...h4

One point of Black's play becomes clear: White's bishop is trapped.

10 Nxf7

Otherwise White will find himself material down.

10...hxg3! (Diagram 8)

This leads to a very strong attack despite the lack of a queen!

11 Nxd8

After 11 Nxh8 Bxf2+!, Black seems to be better but not necessarily winning; e.g. 12 Rxf2 gxf2+ 13 Kxf2 Ng4+ 14 Kg1 Qh4, or 12 Kh1 Qe7 13 Bf7+ Kd8.

11...Bg4 12 Qd2 Nd4!

In chess, mating the king is more important than counting pieces!

13 Nc3?

Preventing ...Ne2+ but overlooking an even more deadly check. The only defence was 13 h3! (13 Nf7? Rxh2 14 Nc3 Nf3+! also leads to mate) 13...Ne2+ 14 Qxe2! (not 14 Kh1? Rxh3+! 15 gxh3 Bf3 mate) 14...Bxe2 15 Ne6 Bb6 16 Nc3 Bxf1 17 Kxf1, when White survives for the time being with two pawns for the exchange.

13...Nf3+! 14 gxf3 Bxf3 0-1

Mate is now forced so White resigned.

 WARNING: For those who like to castle at the earliest opportunity – underestimate potential action in front of your king at your peril!

White plays c2-c3

This is a more modern way of handling the Quiet Italian. White aims to retain a flexible structure and thus the option of expanding his pawns on the left-hand side of the board with b2-b4 or d2-d4. However, White also hopes to retain plenty of influence on the kingside and indeed in the first illustrative game (Emms-Flear, Game 3), circumstances dictated that White's chances lay there.

The following sequence of moves is typical:

1 e4 e5 2 Nf3 Nc6 3 Bc4 Bc5 4 c3 (Diagram 9)

White gives himself the option of playing d2-d4 next move.

4...Nf6

Developing naturally and getting ready for possible action in the centre.

5 d3

A restrained approach, putting off any direct confrontation until later. The consequences of 5 d4 are examined in Chapter Three.

5...a6

If White is going to play slowly then Black has time to do so too. The intention is to retain the bishop on the a7-g1 diagonal and drop back to a7 out of harm's way. If Black instead plays 5...d6 White sometimes expands with 6 b4 Bb6 7 a4, when 7...a6 is required anyway. White may well later gain time against the bishop on b6 with a4-a5 or even Nd2-c4. By playing 5...a6, enabling the bishop to hide immediately on a7, Black is also discouraging this plan.

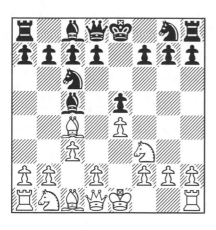

Diagram 9 (B)

Preparing d2-d4 – or not

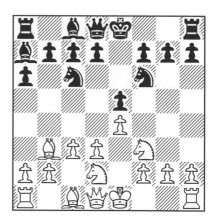

Diagram 10 (B)

A modern Quiet Italian

6 Bb3

A useful semi-waiting move. The bishop will no doubt have to make a decision soon, and White often plays this immediately before committing his other pieces.

6...Ba7

Another prophylactic move, as Black avoids any danger of his bishop being exposed to attack. In games where there is no immediate contact between the two sets of forces, both sides typically manoeuvre in readiness for a possible sharpening of the struggle.

7 Nbd2 (Diagram 10)

The queen's knight comes into play but won't stay on d2, blocking its own bishop, for long. The knight will sometimes go to c4 and then e3 from where it surveys some potentially interesting squares such as d5 and f5. Another common route is via f1 and then either to e3 or to g3.

Traditionally White follows up by castling kingside and then plays Re1 before Nf1, but these days the plan of leaving the king in the centre for now is popular. White obtains additional options as, with the f1-square free at present, White can play his Nf1-g3 manoeuvre before castling (thus not necessarily requiring the rook to come to e1). Sometimes White will not bother castling at all and aim to create attacking chances on the kingside against Black's castled king.

Strategy

White aims to keep his options open and be ready to react if Black tries to break out with an early ...d7-d5. In most lines early manoeuvring is common, with White's extra tempo offering him more leeway.

Black has to decide between ...d7-d6 and ...d7-d5 and to get the timing right for castling. He also needs to have some idea of how to generate counterplay.

Theoretical

There is not a great deal of sharp theory, but some lines require a certain amount of memory work, particularly when it comes to the subtlety of move orders. The most important aspect for both sides is understanding the whys and wherefores of the various manoeuvres.

Game 3
□ J.Emms ■ G.Flear
Southend 2009

---

1 e4 e5 2 Nf3 Nc6 3 Bc4 Bc5 4 c3 Nf6 5 d3 a6 6 Bb3 Ba7 7 Nbd2 0-0 8 Nc4!? (Diagram 11)

A tricky move that requires a vigorous response. For other moves see the next game.

8...d6?!

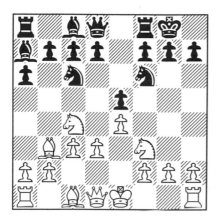

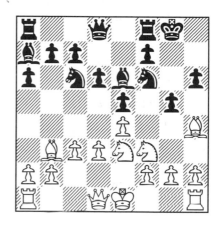

Diagram 11 (B)
How should Black react?

Diagram 12 (W)
Asking for trouble

Too routine. Here Black should react in the centre with the immediate 8...d5!; e.g. 9 Ncxe5 Nxe5 10 Nxe5 dxe4 11 d4 c5 (hitting back at White's centre) 12 Be3 Nd5 13 dxc5 Nxe3 14 fxe3 Qh4+ 15 g3 Qe7 16 Qd6 Bxc5 17 Qxe7 Bxe7 18 0-0 Bf6 is equal, M.Klinova-Qin Kanying, FIDE World Ch., New Delhi 2000.

During the game I was aware that 8...d5 was the right idea but wasn't sure what to do after 9 exd5 Nxd5 10 0-0 f6 11 Re1. In fact the right follow-up is 11...Kh8! (keeping away from any tactical ideas on the a2-g8 diagonal) 12 h3 b5! (challenging for the initiative) 13 Ne3 Nf4 14 d4 exd4 15 cxd4 Ne7, as in A.Tzermiadianos-H.Gretarsson, European Cup, Rethymnon 2003, and Black was fine.

9 Bg5

Now Black suffers because the pin is extremely annoying, to the point of poisoning his whole set-up.

 WARNING: Be careful about pins in front of kings.

9...h6 10 Bh4 Be6

It's risky to advance pawns in front of one's king in such positions, but 10...g5 may be a lesser evil as White's knight (on c4) is then further away from my king! Note that if the sacrifice on g5 then isn't clear, White could also retreat his bishop and aim to open lines with an early h2-h4. In such positions, this generally offers White an initiative *if he hasn't already castled*, as action on the wing puts Black's kingside defences under pressure.

11 Ne3 g5? (Diagram 12)

Asking for trouble, but I was short of ideas! Instead, 11...Kh7! followed perhaps by 12...Rg8 (when ...g7-g5 would finally be on) would avoid any serious damage.

12 Nxg5! hxg5 13 Bxg5

Retaining the deadly pin is worth a small material investment.

13...Kg7 14 Qf3 Nb8

14...Rh8 is well met by 15 Bxe6 fxe6 16 Ng4.

15 Nf5+

After 15 Bxe6, Black has 15...Bxe3 16 Qxe3 fxe6 17 Bh6+ Kf7 with chances to wriggle out.

15...Bxf5 16 Qxf5 Nbd7 17 h4! (Diagram 13)

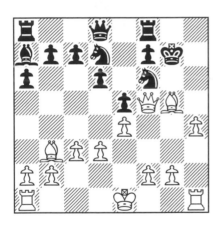

Diagram 13 (B)

White will play Rh3-g3

Diagram 14 (B)

White is winning

Preparing to bring up the next wave.

17...Rg8 18 Rh3 Qe7 19 Rf3 Kh8!? 20 Ke2!

Keeping the bind rather than winning material. Objectively, White would be doing quite well after 20 Qxf6+ Nxf6 21 Bxf6+ Qxf6 22 Rxf6 Rxg2 23 Ke2, but with opposite-coloured bishops and some activity, Black would have drawing chances.

20...Rg6 21 h5 Rxg5 22 Qxg5 Kh7 23 Rg3 Rg8 24 Qf5+ Kh8 25 Rxg8+ Kxg8 26 h6

The presence of the h-pawn is now the most serious problem for Black.

26...Kh8 27 Rh1 c6

Or if 27...Nc5 28 Rh3 Nxb3 29 Qg5! and White soon mates.

28 Rh3 Bb6

If 28...d5 the most incisive is 29 Rg3 threatening Rg7.

29 Rg3 Bd8 30 Rg7 d5 31 exd5 Nc5 32 dxc6 Nxb3 33 axb3 bxc6 34 g4! (Diagram 14)

The rest is just Black trying to mix things in mutual time trouble, but White maintains his iron grip on events.

34...e4 35 d4 e3 36 fxe3 Qd6 37 g5 Qh2+ 38 Kd3 Qh1

38...Qxb2 would be met by 39 Qf1! and White gets there first.

39 Kc2 Qe4+ 40 Qxe4 Nxe4 41 Rxf7 Bxg5 42 Kd3 1-0

Game 4
□ V.Bologan ■ V.Malakhov
European Club Cup, Kemer 2007

---

1 e4 e5 2 Nf3 Nc6 3 Bc4 Bc5 4 c3 Nf6 5 d3 a6 6 Nbd2

White sometimes reverses the order of his moves, but the main point is that Bologan intends to avoid (or at least delay) castling in order to retain additional options. This is the modern, and perhaps most challenging, way of handling the opening.

The traditional main line continues 6 0-0 Ba7 7 Bb3 d6 8 Nbd2 0-0 **(Diagram 15)**.

Many games have reached this position where White usually tries one of the three following moves:

a) 9 Nc4 Ne7 10 Bg5 Ng6 11 Nh4 Kh8 12 Qf3 (after 12 Nxg6+ fxg6!? and 12 Ne3 h6 13 Nxg6+ fxg6, Black accepts a compromised structure but obtains some activity in return) 12...h6 13 Bxf6 Nxh4 14 Bxh4 Qxh4 15 Ne3 Bd7, V.Sanduleac-G.Flear, Chamalières 2008, White has no particular problems at present, but the bishop pair gives Black long-term potential.

b) 9 Re1 (this enables Black to kick-start his counterplay) 9...Ng4! 10 Re2 Kh8 11 h3 Nh6! 12 Nf1 f5 13 Bxh6 gxh6 14 exf5 Bxf5 15 N1h2 Qf6 16 Qd2 Rae8 and Black is very active which more than compensates for his damaged pawns, K.Spraggett-M.Adams, French Team Ch. 2001.

c) 9 h3 h6 10 Re1 (now that the g4-square isn't available to Black) 10...Nh5 11 Nf1 Qf6 12 Be3 Ne7! (I was recently shown by Jean-Marc Degraeve that 12...Nf4?! is inferior due to 13 Ng3 g6 14 d4 and White has a small but persistent edge) 13 Bxa7 (or 13 d4 Nf4 14 Ng3 Neg6 15 Bc2 Nh4 16 Nxh4 Qxh4 17 Qf3 g6 18 Rad1 Kg7 19 Nf1 Ne6 20 dxe5 dxe5 21 Bxa7 Rxa7 22 Qg3 Qxg3 23 Nxg3 Ra8 and Black had more or less equalized, A.Areshchenko-K.Sakaev, Russian Team Ch. 2008) 13...Rxa7 14 Ne3 Nf4 15 Kh2 Ra8 16 a4 Be6 17 Bxe6 fxe6 (opening the f-file has its points, but here White is well placed to thwart any enemy activity and the black position is shown to lack vitality; instead 17...Nxe6 is very solid) 18 Ng1 Rad8 19 g3 Nfg6 20 Rf1 d5 21 Qe2 Nc6 22 Ng2 Rf7 23 h4 Rdf8 24 Rad1 Nge7, A.Karpov-A.Yusupov, Bugojno 1986. Black has nothing better to do than wait, while White can hope to improve and even consider a timely break-out with f2-f4.

6...Ba7 7 Bb3

In the case of an early ...d7-d6 the bishop will have to drop back anyway to meet the positional threat of ...Na5, and in the case of ...d7-d5 White may prefer not to capture on d5. So this actually constitutes a useful (semi-waiting) move inviting Black to show his hand!

7...0-0 (Diagram 16) 8 h3

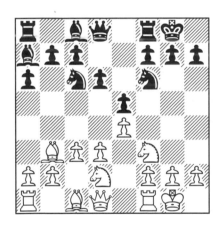

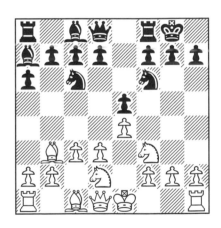

Diagram 15 (W)
The traditional main line

Diagram 16 (W)
Keeping the option of ...d7-d5

After 8 Nf1, Black should react actively with 8...d5!; e.g. 9 Qe2 dxe4 (9...Be6 keeps some tension) 10 dxe4 Ng4 11 Ne3 Nxe3 12 Bxe3 Bxe3 13 Qxe3 is equal.

8...d6

Here 8...d5 has been played quite often, and certainly has a positive side, but after 9 exd5 Nxd5 10 Ne4 White's knight on e4 is quite well posted.

9 Nf1 d5!

Only now that White has retreated his knight to f1 does Malakhov react in the centre.

10 Qe2 Be6 11 Ng3

Following 11 Bc2, Black could opt for 11...b5 gaining space and giving himself the useful option of ...d5xe4, d3xe4, ...Bc4.

11...dxe4 12 dxe4 Bxb3 13 axb3 Ne8

Black aims to use this knight to cover the f5-square.

14 Nf5 Nd6 15 g4!? (Diagram 17)

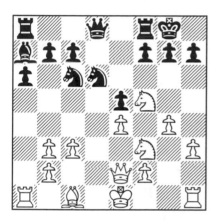 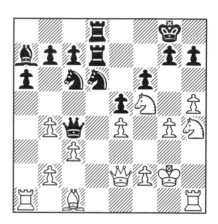

Diagram 17 (B)

White seeks attacking chances

Diagram 18 (W)

Forcing a queen trade

Supporting the knight with the g-pawn in this way makes it difficult for Black to contemplate exchanging on f5, since that would open the g-file, giving White attacking chances. One of the points behind delaying castling is that White gives himself this type of possibility.

More cautious is 15 0-0; e.g. 15...Qf6 16 Bg5 Qe6 17 Nxd6 Qxd6 18 Qc4 Rfe8 19 Rfd1 Qe6 20 Qxe6 Rxe6 21 Rd7 f6 22 Bd2 Re7 and Black had equalized in S.Tiviakov-P.Leko, Wijk aan Zee 2006.

15...Qf6 16 h4 Qe6 17 b4 f6 18 h5

White seeks attacking chances, whereas Black aims for solidity on the kingside and play in the centre.

18...Rad8 19 N3h4 Rd7 20 Kf1

White finally decides on the future of his king: the g2-square.

20...Rfd8 21 Kg2 Qc4 (Diagram 18)

The exchange of queens reduces the effectiveness of any white attack.

22 Qxc4+ Nxc4 23 g5!? Rd1 24 gxf6

After 24 Rxd1 Rxd1 25 gxf6 gxf6 White has great knights but they lack support and he has to be careful along the first rank.

24...Rxh1 25 Ne7+

Tiviakov analyses 25 Kxh1 gxf6 26 Nh6+ Kf8 27 N4f5 Rd1+ 28 Kg2 Nd2 29 Ng4 as unclear. Both sides have precariously-placed pieces.

25...Nxe7 26 fxe7 Re8 27 Kxh1 Bxf2 28 Nf5 Nd6

Perhaps Black could have played for more than equality with 28...g6! 29 Nh6+ Kg7 30 Ng4 Bh4 31 Bh6+ Kf7 32 Rf1+ Ke6, when he emerges with an extra pawn as e7 is set to fall.

29 Nxd6 cxd6 30 Bg5 h6 31 Kg2 hxg5 32 Kxf2 Rxe7 ½-½

The rook ending is drawish after 33 Rg1.

Game 5
□ S.Tiviakov ■ L.Bruzon Bautista
Calvia Olympiad 2004

---

1 e4 e5 2 Bc4

The move order in this game (via the Bishop's Opening) is not that unusual and usually transposes if Black plays both ...Nf6 and ...Nc6.

2...Nf6 3 d3 Nc6 4 Nf3 Be7 (Diagram 19)

Placing the bishop on e7 (rather than c5) has the advantage of leaving the bishop in the vicinity of its own king. Black thus reduces the chances of becoming victim to a kingside attack.

Another plan is to place the bishop as quickly as possible on g7! Here is a sample line: 4...h6 (this avoids an early Nf3-g5; remember if White is going to play 'slowly' with d2-d3 then Black can also take the time to make a useful prophylactic move) 5 0-0 d6 (consolidating the e5-pawn; as a general rule the centre needs to hold firm when intending to make a long-winded manoeuvre!) 6 c3 g6 7 d4 (attempting to quicken the pace, but the logical reaction is to keep the position closed and thus avoid giving White any targets) 7...Qe7 8 Re1 Bg7 9 Nbd2 0-0 (now Black has achieved his aim of getting his kingside sorted out with the bishop on the dynamic g7-square) 10 h3 Bd7 11 Nf1 Rae8 12 Ng3 Qd8, I.Kurnosov-E.Inarkiev, Russian Team Ch. 2006. With development completed Black can look forward to the middlegame with confidence in this position where chances are balanced.

However, the tempting 4...d5 seems premature, as after 5 exd5 Nxd5 6 0-0 Black has problems defending his e-pawn. For example:

Diagram 19 (W)
Black plays 4...Be7

Diagram 20 (B)
White awaits developments

a) 6...Bc5 7 Re1 0-0 8 Nxe5 Qh4 9 Qf3 Nf6 10 Nxc6 Ng4 11 d4 Qxh2+ 12 Kf1 Bd6 13 Ne5 (13 Ne7+ has been tested in some correspondence games; it's also good but more easy to go wrong!) 13...Bxe5 14 dxe5 Nxe5 15 Rxe5 Qxe5 16 Nc3 Qh2 17 Ne2 is better for White, his two pieces being superior to the rook and pawn, K.Shavana-M.Lyell, European Ch., Dresden 2007.

b) 6...Be7 7 Re1 Qd6!? (7...Bg4 hasn't worked well in practice, White having a big score after 8 h3 Bxf3 9 Qxf3 Nf6 10 Bb5!) 8 d4! (8 Nbd2 Bg4 9 Bb3 Nb6 10 Ne4 Qg6 was fine for Black in A.Delorme-J.Netzer, French Junior Ch. 1998) 8...exd4 9 Nxd4 Ndb4 10 Nxc6 Qxd1 11 Rxd1 Nxc6 12 Bf4 with a nagging edge for White, E.Gerbelli Neto-G.Cunico, Registro 1999.

5 0-0 0-0 6 Bb3 (Diagram 20)

Another example of this 'useful' waiting move as White wants to see where the black d-pawn is going.

TIP: In manoeuvring positions, improving already developed pieces can often be more important than rapid development.

Now Black has to decide what to do with his d-pawn.

6...d6

6...d5!? 7 exd5 Nxd5 is a more active approach, with which Black opens up the game at the risk of leaving his e-pawn weak. But note that here, in comparison with 4...d5 above, White has 'wasted' a move playing Bc4-b3.

Now 8 Re1 allows 8...Bg4 to be played under favourable circumstances: 9 h3 Bxf3 10 Qxf3 Nd4! 11 Qe4 (the point is that Black is not afraid of White capturing on d5: after 11 Qxd5 Qxd5 12 Bxd5 Nxc2 13 Rxe5 Bf6 14 Re2 Nxa1, both sides have chances) 11...c6! (a new idea) 12 Qxe5 Bf6 13 Qh5 Nb4 14 Qd1 a5 and Black had sufficient play for the pawn, I.Nepomniachtchi-A.Naiditsch, European Ch., Dresden 2007.

So the most challenging response is the prophylactic 8 h3, when Black does well to play 8...a5! **(Diagram 21)**, forcing White to make a decision about how to meet the threat of ...a5-a4:

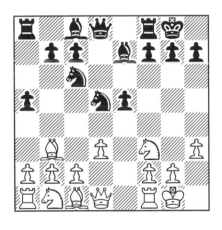

Diagram 21 (W)

An active approach for Black

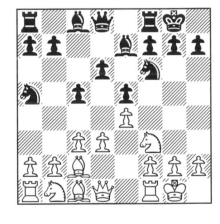

Diagram 22 (W)

Black gains space

a) 9 Ba4 can be met by 9...Nd4, as then 10 Nxe5 Nb6 gives Black interesting play for the pawn; for example, 11 c3 Nxa4 12 Qxa4 Ne2+ 13 Kh1 Bf6 14 d4 Bxh3! with a strong attack in A.Shirov-D.Mozetic, Tilburg 1993. Indeed, in the game after 15 gxh3 Qd5+ 16 Kh2 Bxe5+ 17 dxe5 Qxe5+ 18 Kh1 Qd5+ 19 Kh2, Black felt sufficiently confident to go for more than a draw with 19...Ra6!.

b) After 9 a3 Black could opt for 9...a4 10 Ba2 Kh8 (or 10...Be6!? as in line 'c') 11 Re1 f6 12 d4 (12 Nbd2 Bf5 13 Ne4 Qd7 is equal) 12...exd4 13 Nxd4 Ndb4 14 axb4 Qxd4 with dynamic equality, V.Kramnik-G.Kasparov, New York (rapid) 1995.

c) 9 a4 Be6 10 Re1 Bf6 11 Nbd2 Nf4 ensured easy equality in S.Tiviakov-A.Onischuk, Russian Team Ch. 2007.

7 c3 Na5

Chasing the bishop, as one often sees in the Spanish.

7...d5 is interesting, voluntarily losing a tempo – the point being that in an 'open' position the d3-pawn may (now that White has weakened it with c2-c3) prove to be weak. For example, 8 Qe2 (or 8 exd5 Nxd5 9 Re1 Bf6, and then White does best to avoid 10 Nbd2 due to 10...Nf4) and now:

a) 8...dxe4 9 dxe4 Bc5 is similar to some lines resulting from 4 d3 against 3...Bc5. However, Black has lost time to reach this position and one of the tempi forsaken is ...a7-a6, so White could now try and exploit this by 10 Ba4!? with a hint of pressure.

b) 8...Bg4!? (also an attempt at activating) 9 Bg5 (perhaps White could try to punish the bishop with 9 h3 Bh5 10 Rd1 and then Nbd2-f1-g3) 9...dxe4 10 dxe4 Nh5 11 Be3 Nf4!? 12 Bxf4 exf4 13 h3 Bxf3 14 Qxf3 Bg5, followed by ...Ne5, was pleasant for Black in S.Belkhodja-S.Karjakin, French Team Ch. 2006.

8 Bc2 c5 (Diagram 22)

Black gains space, not worrying too much about the d5-square which White will have difficulty in occupying with a piece.

9 Re1

If White takes time to expand on the queenside with 9 a3 Nc6 10 b4 a6 11 Nbd2, Black should react in the centre with 11...d5! as in G.Wall-M.Hebden, EU Championship, Cork 2005.

Alternatively, changing tack with 9 d4 can be met by 9...cxd4 10 cxd4 Nc6 11 d5 Nb4 12 Bb3 a5! 13 Nc3 b5 with adequate counterplay in L.Yudasin-Y.Grünfeld, Haifa 1995. Black's knight manoeuvring is an idea borrowed from the Chigorin Variation of the Spanish.

9...Nc6 10 Nbd2

The position is very similar to the Spanish Opening where White has settled for d2-d3 instead of the more ambitious d2-d4. The main difference is that Black hasn't played ...a7-a6 and ...b7-b5 (in the Spanish, where Black has played these moves, he gains some queenside space, at the risk of being put under pressure from an early a2-a4 by White).

10...Re8 11 a3 Bf8 12 b4 g6 (Diagram 23)

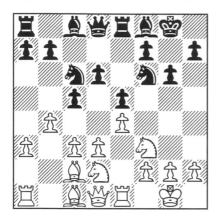

Diagram 23 (W)

A typical Spanish idea

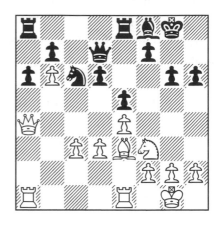

Diagram 24 (W)

Black is fine

Another typical idea from the Spanish: Black aims to bring his bishop to the g7-square where it gets out of the way of his other pieces! On a more positive note it will then be ready for any central play by White, as well as helping to cover the kingside.

Nevertheless, it seems even more appropriate to aim for an early ...d6-d5; for example with 12...a6 (aimed against b4-b5) 13 Bb3 (or 13 Nf1 d5!) 13...h6 14 Nf1 and now 14...d5.

13 Ba4 cxb4 14 axb4 Bd7 15 Nc4 h6 16 Be3

Tiviakov later suggested a possible improvement with 16 b5 Na5 17 Ne3, when Black lacks space and the knight on a5 is rather out of play.

16...Ng4 17 Bd2 a6

The threat of ...b7-b5 forces White to react.

18 b5 Na7 19 b6

But not 19 bxa6? due to 19...b5.

19...Bxa4 20 Qxa4 Nc6 21 Ne3 Nxe3 22 Bxe3 Qd7 (Diagram 24)

This simplified position is fine for Black, especially as the exchange of two pairs of minor pieces has reduced the significance of White's slight space advantage.

23 Nd2 d5

Black further frees himself, although White will now be able to use the c5-square.

24 Nb3 Rad8 25 Bc5 dxe4 26 dxe4 Qc8 27 Red1 Rxd1+ 28 Rxd1 Rd8 29 Rd5

It seems that exchanging off White's more active pieces represents the path to equality.

29...Bxc5 30 Nxc5 Rxd5 31 exd5 Ne7 32 d6 Qxc5! 33 Qe8+ Kg7 34 Qxe7 ½-½

34 dxe7? is bad due to 34...Kf6!. After 34 Qxe7 play could continue 34...Qxc3 35 g3 (or 35 h3 Qc1+ 36 Kh2 Qf4+ etc) 35...Qe1+ 36 Kg2 Qe4+ with a draw by perpetual check.

Game 6
□ H.Hamdouchi ■ Y.Gozzoli
French Team Championship 2007

---

1 e4 e5 2 Nf3 Nc6 3 Bc4 Nf6 4 d3 Be7

With Black opting to leave his bishop to help out on the kingside, there is less of a case for White to delay castling.

5 0-0 0-0 6 Re1

Making it more difficult for Black to consider ...d7-d5 which would now constitute a speculative (perhaps dubious is more to the point!) pawn sacrifice. Indeed, 6...d5? 7 exd5 Nxd5 8 Nxe5 Nxe5 9 Rxe5 must objectively be good for White.

6...d6 7 a4 (Diagram 25)

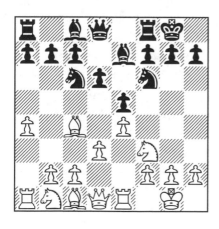

Diagram 25 (B)
Safeguarding the c4-bishop

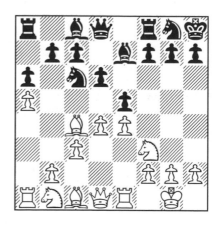

Diagram 26 (B)
A timely central reaction

White aims to keep his bishop on the a2-g8 diagonal.

7 c3 is the other popular move here, but after 7...Na5 8 Bb5 a6 9 Ba4 b5 10 Bc2 c5 we have transposed directly into a line of the Spanish where White has settled for the restrained d2-d3. Then 11 Nbd2 Re8 12 Nf1 Bf8 13 Ng3 Bb7 would be a normal continuation, when Black is ready to play ...d6-d5, so White does best to try central action himself with 14 d4, but after 14...cxd4 15 cxd4 exd4 16 Nxd4 g6 the activity of Black's pieces is sufficient to balance out his slightly inferior pawn structure, E.Mortensen-J.Emms, Copenhagen 1995.

7...Kh8

Black decides to move his king out of the firing line, while also hinting at where his counterplay is going to come from.

8 a5 a6 9 c3 Ng8

Now things become even clearer: Black shows his intention to follow up with ...f7-f5.

10 d4 (Diagram 26)

A timely central reaction before Black has had time to hit back. After 10 Qb3, Black can still follow up with 10...f5; e.g. 11 exf5 Rxf5 12 Nbd2 Nf6 13 Be6 Bxe6 14 Qxe6 Qd7 15 Qxd7 Nxd7 16 d4 exd4 17 Nxd4 Re5 and Black had equalized in V.Tkachiev-L.Fressinet, Cap d'Agde 2002.

10...f5!

Carrying on regardless! The main alternative is 10...Bg4 11 d5 (White gains space and time but commits himself, so Black now knows how to react; if instead 11 dxe5 Bxf3 12 Qxf3 Nxe5 13 Qe2 Nxc4 14 Qxc4 f5 15 Nd2 fxe4 16 Qxe4 d5 17 Qd3 Nf6 18 Nf3 Ne4 19 Be3 Qd6 20 Rad1 Rad8 21 Nd2, as in Z.Efimenko-V.Bologan, World Chess Cup, Khanty-Mansiysk 2005, Black has easy equality by capturing on d2) 11...Nb8 12 Be2! (after 12 Nbd2 Bg5 D.Sermek-N.Mitkov, Pula 2000, Black solves the problem of his potentially worst minor piece) 12...Nd7 13 Nbd2 f5 (hoping to counter White's centre with a quick reaction) 14 exf5 Bxf5 (the downside of play-ing an early ...f7-f5, when it is not possible to recapture on f5 with a pawn, is that White may be able to install a piece on the e4-square if Black isn't careful) 15 Nf1 Qe8 16 Ng3 Bg6 17 Ng5 (the knight has both e6 and e4 in its sights) 17...Bxg5 18 Bxg5 Ngf6 19 b4 Qf7 20 c4 Ne4 21 Nxe4 Bxe4 22 Bh4 Qg6 23 Bg3 Nf6, M.Sebag-L.Fressinet, Paris 2004. White has the bishop pair and a space advantage, but as Black's pieces are reasonably well placed any white pull is quite small.

11 dxe5 fxe4 12 Rxe4 Rxf3! (Diagram 27)

A positional exchange sacrifice.

Gozzoli had previously tried 12...Bf5, but after 13 Re1 dxe5 14 Qxd8 Raxd8 15 Nbd2 Bd6 16 Ng5 Rd7 17 Be6 Bxe6 18 Nxe6 Re8 19 Ng5, V.Baklan-Y.Gozzoli, Guingamp 2004, White had a small but enduring edge as Black is stuck with the inferior pawn structure for the duration.

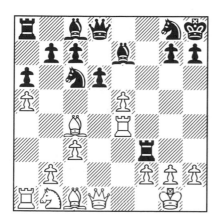

Diagram 27 (W)

A positional exchange sacrifice

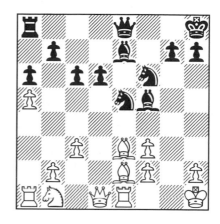

Diagram 28 (W)

White's rooks are ineffective

13 gxf3

After the unfortunate 13 Qxf3? Black has 13...d5, forking and winning material.

13...Bf5 14 Re1

In K.Maslak-J.Radulski, Olomouc 2005, White decided to return the exchange with 14 e6 Qe8 15 Kh1 Qg6 16 Nd2 Bxe4 17 fxe4 Rf8 18 f3 Ne5 19 Be2 Qxe6 20 Nf1 Nf6 but Black achieved a pleasant game.

14...Nxe5 15 Be2 Qe8

Black has been willing to offer the full exchange, as in return he has lively pieces and White has a compromised pawn structure.

16 Kh1 Nf6 17 Be3 c6 (Diagram 28)

On a crowded board, the advantage of an exchange is hardly noticeable, especially as the white rooks have little scope for activity.

18 Rg1 Qf7 19 Nd2 d5 20 Nf1 Rf8 21 Ng3 Bc8

White has covered his king, but Black's pieces are on alert and cannot be denied good postings...

22 Bd4 Bd6 23 b4 Ng6 24 Qd2 Nf4

...for example, the f4-square!

25 Rae1 Nh3 26 Rg2 Nf4 27 Rgg1 Nh3 28 Rg2

If 28 Rgf1, then 28...Nh5 could be interesting with Black's knights being more influential than White's rooks. Even after the most challenging 29 Bd1 N5f4 30 Be5 Bxe5 31 Rxe5 Qf6 32 Re3 Ng5, Black has adequate compensation.

28...Nf4 ½-½

Summary

Attacking chances can occur if either side castles into an awkward pin or allows the opponent a free hand in developing kingside pressure. The best way for Black to meet any attempted attack on the wing is a central counter, often involving ...d7(d6)-d5.

Otherwise strategic considerations are primary, with White's flexible plan involving c2-c3 and delayed castling being the most challenging for Black.

Chapter Two
Two Knights Defence

Introduction

1 e4 e5 2 Nf3 Nc6 3 Bc4 Nf6 (Diagram 1)

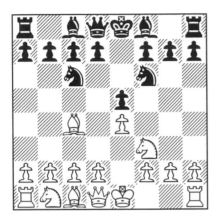

Diagram 1 (W)

The Two Knights Defence

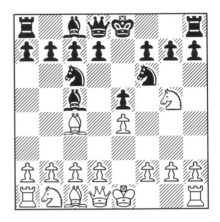

Diagram 2 (W)

Ignoring the attack on f7

Black brings out his king's knight as early as move three. For centuries this set-up has been called the Two Knights Defence, highlighting the particularity that Black has developed both knights before touching his bishops.

Thinking back a few years to my youth, I remember that this was actually my favourite Black opening! I would invariably get lively games with chances to seize the initiative.

Even to this day the Two Knights has a good reputation and many lines of the opening lead to complicated play. White's next move sets the tone.

4 Ng5!?

This, the most direct try, is covered in Games 7-10. The knight moves a second time in the opening but immediately bears down on the f7-square, which is often described as Black's Achilles' heel. So we could consider that White has invested a tempo in order to create a strong threat. Indeed, Black has to react forthwith to the threat of something nasty happening on f7.

In total contrast, the cautious 4 d3 was covered in Chapter One.

4 Nc3 is sometimes played by inexperienced players, but this is well met by 4...Nxe4!, as 5 Nxe4 d5 already equalizes, while 5 0-0 Nxc3 6 dxc3 leaves Black with the pleasant choice between 6...Be7 7 Qd5 0-0 with comfortable equality, or the ambitious 6...h6 7 Qd5 Qf6, when the onus is on White to prove that he has enough for the pawn.

The other move that deserves a close look is 4 d4 where White blasts open the centre. Following the natural reply 4...exd4, White can choose between 5 Ng5 (again hitting at f7, but this time with the centre open), 5 0-0 (getting on with development), and 5 e5 (where the threat to Black's knight gains a tempo in the fight for central control). These ideas will be developed in Games 11-16 below.

4...d5

The most natural reply: Black reacts in the centre, blocking the white bishop's sight of the f7-square, while at the same time opening lines for his own pieces.

Instead, the odd-looking 4...Bc5!? **(Diagram 2)** isn't an oversight at all, but introduces the wild Wilkes-Barre (or Traxler) variation. Although the Wilkes-Barre is occasionally played by strong players it is a rare visitor to over-the-board tournaments.

White can capture on f7 either way, winning material and disrupting Black's development, but in return Black gets a lead in development and serious counterplay against White's own soft spot on f2. For example, 5 Nxf7 Bxf2+! isn't clear at all.

The most challenging response is 5 Bxf7+ Ke7 6 Bd5; e.g. 6...d6 (or 6...Rf8 7 0-0 d6 8 c3 Bg4 9 Qb3 with chances for White to obtain an advantage) 7 d3 Qe8 8 Bxc6 bxc6 9 Be3 Qg6 10 Nf3 Bxe3 11 fxe3 Qxg2 12 Rg1 Qh3 13 Rxg7 Kd8 14 Rg3 Qh6 15 Qe2 was much better for White in V.Anand-A.Beliavsky, Linares 1991.

5 exd5 Na5

There are a couple of sharp options here: 5...b5 (Ulvestad) 6 Bf1! h6 7 Nxf7, and 5...Nd4 (the Fritz variation, named after a human not a computer!) 6 c3 b5 7 Bf1! Nxd5 8 Ne4, but in each case the complications are probably not quite sound for Black.

The most obvious move is 5...Nxd5 **(Diagram 3)**, recapturing the pawn, though this has been criticized by the majority of commentators over the last four hundred years or so! However, neither of the suggested refutations is completely clear:

a) 6 Nxf7 Kxf7 7 Qf3+ Ke6 8 Nc3 Nb4 enables Black to hold onto his extra piece after 9 Qe4 c6, while the complications following 9 a3 Nxc2+ 10 Kd1 Nxa1 11 Nxd5 Qh4! are also suspicious for White.

b) After 6 d4 Be6! 7 Nxe6 fxe6 8 dxe5 Bc5, Black certainly has some activity for the pawn, and then 9 Qg4 is critical. Martin de Zeeuw is responsible for the latest attempt at reviving 5...Nxd5. In this variation White should probably forget about winning a pawn and instead settle for a small edge with 7 0-0! Nxd4 8 Nxe6 fxe6 9 Qh5+ g6 10 Qxe5 Qf6 11 Qxf6 Nxf6 12 Bd3 as suggested by Karsten Müller.

The main line continues with the following moves:

6 Bb5+ c6 7 dxc6 bxc6 8 Be2 h6 9 Nf3 e4 10 Ne5 Bd6 (Diagram 4)

Black is a pawn down, but in return can count on a lead in development.

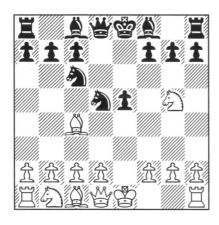

Diagram 3 (W)

A controversial variation

Diagram 4 (W)

The main line

White plays 4 Ng5

By forcing the pace White incites his opponent to enter complications. In the main line White grabs a pawn but loses the initiative, although there are various sidelines which involve White sacrificing material. Each tempo counts and the key to many variations lies in the weighing up of a material deficit against a lead in development.

In the first two illustrative games White deviates with 8 Qf3!? and 9 Nh3!? respectively; whereas in Games 9 and 10 he enters the main line, albeit with mixed results.

Strategy

Tactical play is quite important and the strategic aspects tend to involve maximizing the potential of one's pieces in open play.

Theoretical

Yes, there can be a fair deal of theory in certain lines, but much of this is quite old and well established. Once one has learnt the basic moves in such key variations, then a penchant for piece play plus a good eye for combinations is more important than following the latest theoretical developments.

Game 7
□ **F.Vallejo Pons** ■ **E.Inarkiev**
World Chess Cup, Khanty-Mansiysk 2007

1 e4 e5 2 Nf3 Nc6 3 Bc4 Nf6 4 Ng5 d5 5 exd5 Na5 (Diagram 5)

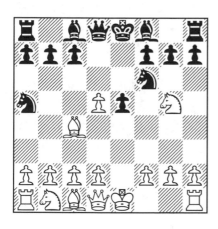 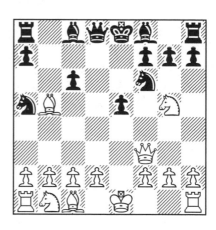

Diagram 5 (W)
Attacking the c4-bishop

Diagram 6 (B)
The Bogoljubow Variation

Black gains a tempo against the bishop on c4; on the other hand the knight is not ideally placed on the edge of the board. However, this is the move that is considered the most reliable by the World's elite.

6 Bb5+

6 d3 is almost never seen these days, as after 6...h6 7 Nf3 e4 8 Qe2 Nxc4 9 dxc4 Bc5 Black has excellent piece play and better development for his pawn.

6...c6

There has been some interest in 6...Bd7 7 Qe2 Bd6, with which Black hopes to castle quickly, keeping his pawn structure intact, and generate some play. This has surprise value, but personally I don't really like Black's chances. For example, 8 Nc3 0-0 9 Bxd7 Qxd7 10 a3 b6 11 d3 c6 12 b4 Nb7 13 dxc6 Qxc6 14 Nce4 Nd7 15 Qf3! and White has good play plus an extra pawn, A.Morozevich-I.Sokolov, Sarajevo 1999. Similar is 7...Be7 8 Nc3 0-0 9 0-0 c6 10 dxc6 Nxc6 11 Bxc6 Bxc6 12 d3 Re8 13 Be3, D.Marciano-G.Flear, Clichy 1995, although here Black almost has enough for his pawn. Pinski now suggests 13...b5!? but this needs testing.

7 dxc6 bxc6 8 Qf3!? (Diagram 6)

The Bogoljubow Variation is a dynamic alternative to retreating the bishop and one that has become fashionable again in recent years. White activates his queen before making a decision about his bishop.

8...Rb8

Several moves have been tried here, including the exchange sacrifice 8...cxb5!?, but the text move, which activates the rook, is probably best as capturing on c6 is now risky.

9 Bd3

White has tried other moves including the greedy 9 Bxc6+ Nxc6 10 Qxc6+; e.g. 10...Nd7 11 d3 Be7 12 Ne4 Rb6 13 Qa4 0-0 14 Nbc3 f5 with compensation for the two pawns as Black's pieces have great potential, B.Belotti-E.Dervishi, Arco 2002.

A recent try is 9 Be2 Be7 and now 10 b3!?, but after 10...0-0 11 Bb2 Rb4 12 c4 c5 13 Qd3, C.Matei-G.Berecz, correspondence 2007, Black has 13...Qc7 with adequate compensation.

9...Be7 10 Nc3 0-0 11 a3

The continuation 11 0-0 Rb4 12 Re1 Rg4 13 Nge4 Rf4 14 Nxf6+ Rxf6 15 Qe3 Rh6 was murky in I.Kurnosov-G.Kiselev, Krasnoyarsk 2007. Black's rook manoeuvre was quite remarkable and offers him attacking chances in view of White's slow development.

11...c5 12 b3 Rb6 13 0-0 Bb7

White may have an extra pawn in the bag, but Black's active pieces offer plenty of counterplay. However, when venturing these lines it's important to remember that the knight on a5 can become hopelessly out of touch, so it may be worth taking a time out from other plans to improve the prospects for this piece.

TIP: Whatever activity you have, never forget about your worst-placed piece!

Bearing this in mind, Inarkiev suggests the immediate 13...Nc6! followed by ...Nd4.

14 Qh3 h6 15 Nge4 Nh7 (Diagram 7)

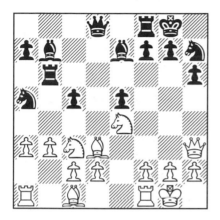
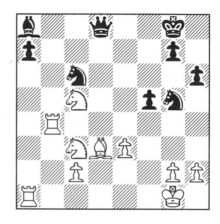

Diagram 7 (W)

Making way for ...f7-f5

Diagram 8 (W)

The queen is boss

Black keeps pieces on the board and prepares to counter with ...f7-f5. Otherwise he could consider 15...Nxe4 16 Bxe4 Bxe4 17 Nxe4 Qd4 18 Nc3 Rg6, but White's shell is hard to crack and in these cases simplification tends to favour the player with the long-term advantage of an extra pawn.

16 b4!?

Returning the material advantage in order to liberate his position. Inarkiev later felt that this idea should have been preceded with the moves 16 Qe3 Ng5 17 f3 Ne6, and only then 18 b4!?. In either case matters are far from clear.

16...cxb4 17 axb4 Bxb4 18 Ba3

White has solved his development woes, but the game is still complicated...

18...f5! 19 Bxb4 Rxb4 20 Nc5 Ng5 21 Qe3 Ba8 22 f4

22 Qxe5? is bad because of 22...Rg4 and wins, but 22 f3!, closing off the long diagonal to Black's bishop (and avoiding ...Rg4), is a solid positional move aimed at keeping control.

22...exf4 23 Rxf4 Re8 24 Rxb4?!

Imaginative, but it turns out to be inferior. Instead, 24 Qg3 Rxf4 25 Qxf4 Ne4 is considered as superior by Inarkiev in his notes, when he feels that Black should be able to equalize at best, whereas in the game he is favourite.

24...Rxe3 25 dxe3 Nc6 (Diagram 8)

Although the position remains complex, the queen proves to be superior to the pair of rooks in the play that follows.

26 Rb5 f4!? 27 h4 f3

The players trade blows in the fight to take control. This leads to further complications as neither player wants to back down!

28 N5e4?!

After 28 hxg5? Qxg5 White is in all sorts of trouble. However, I can't see much wrong with the consolidating move 28 Rd1, when things would have been less clear. Whereas now Black takes over...

28...Nxe4 29 Nxe4 fxg2 30 Kxg2 Qe8 31 Rab1 a6 32 Rb6 a5 33 R1b5 a4

The passed a-pawn forces White onto the defensive.

34 Kf2 a3 35 Ra6 Qc8 36 Rc5 Qf8+ 37 Ke2 Nb4 38 Raa5 a2 (Diagram 9)

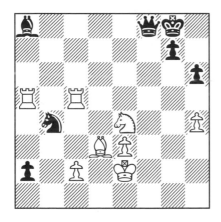

Diagram 9 (W)

White's last chance

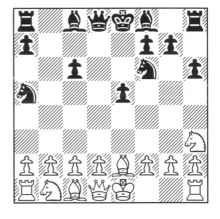

Diagram 10 (B)

The Steinitz Variation

39 Bc4+?

A time trouble error. Instead, 39 Rf5! Qb8 (rather than 39...Qxf5?? which loses tragically to 40 Rxa8+ etc) 40 Nc3 would make a fight of it.

39...Kh7 40 Rcb5 Bxe4 0-1

Game 8
□ V.Malakhatko ■ G.Timoshenko
Kiev (rapid) 2003

1 e4 e5 2 Nf3 Nc6 3 Bc4 Nf6 4 Ng5 d5 5 exd5 6 Bb5+ c6 7 dxc6 bxc6 8 Be2

White sometimes prefers 8 Bd3!?, which has the advantage of being less well analysed. 8...h6 9 Ne4 (the main point behind White's previous move) 9...Nd5 10 0-0 g6 11 Re1 Bg7 12 Bf1 0-0 13 d3 f5 14 Nc5 Qd6 15 Nb3 was more than comfortable for White in N.Short-I.Sokolov, London 2009, and it may be that 8...h6 is just too compliant. My recommendation is instead 8...Nd5!; e.g. 9 Nf3 Bd6 10 0-0 Nf4 11 Re1 Nxd3 12 cxd3 0-0 13 Nxe5 Re8 14 d4 c5 15 d3 cxd4 16 Nf3 Rxe1+ 17 Qxe1 Bf5 with enough compensation, P.Negi-G.Sargissian, Helsingor 2009.

8...h6

Black has open lines for his pieces which will ensure a lead in development. But will this be enough for a pawn?

9 Nh3!? (Diagram 10)

The knight retreats to the edge of the board, but keeps out of trouble! This line was attributed to Steinitz in the 19th century and revived in the modern era by US World Champion Bobby Fischer. Hence the line goes by the name of the Fischer-Steinitz Variation.

9...Be7

Another promising move is 9...g5!?, aiming to leave the knight on h3 locked out of play. Practical tests seem to confirm that it yields adequate play for Black; e.g. 10 d3 Bg7 11 Nc3 0-0 12 Ng1 (or 12 Be3 Nd5 13 Nxd5 cxd5 14 0-0 d4, A.Gretarsson-V.Yemelin, European Cup, St Vincent 2005) 12...Nb7 (both players try and improve their worst-placed pieces rather than mechanically develop) 13 Nf3 Nd5 14 0-0 Nd6 15 Ne4 f5 16 Nxd6 Qxd6, A.Grischuk-V.Malaniuk, Russian Team Ch. 2001.

The immediate 9...Bxh3?! 10 gxh3 is considered dubious for Black, and even played a little later is often risky at best. The structure is smashed and White may even lose the forward h-pawn, but in return he will obtain chances to dominate the light squares.

 TIP: When trading minor pieces to damage your opponent's structure, it's worth asking yourself if you will also have weaknesses as a result!

10 d3 0-0 11 Ng1

Alternatively, after 11 Nc3 Rb8 12 0-0 c5 13 Kh1 Nc6 14 Ng1 (again there is not much else to do with the knight: after 14 f4 Postny suggests that Black can play 14...Bxh3!? 15 gxh3 exf4 16 Rxf4 Bd6 17 Rf2 Nd4, and obtain very good compensation; here capturing on h3 seems fine as Black can follow up with some active moves) 14...Nd4 15 Nf3 Qc7 Black's general control gives him enough practical compensation for the pawn, E.Postny-O.Romanishin, European Ch., Dresden 2007.

11...c5 12 Nf3 Qc7 13 Nbd2 Rd8 14 0-0

If instead 14 b3, then 14...e4 would prove to be unpleasant for White.

14...c4 (Diagram 11)

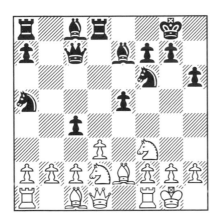

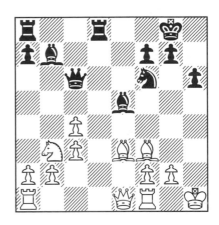

Diagram 11 (W)	**Diagram 12 (B)**
Opening lines	Black to play and win

Using the pin to open lines and prise away at White's structure.

15 Qe1 Bb7!

Activity rather than pawns – a typical theme in the main line of the Two Knights.

16 Nxc4 Nxc4 17 dxc4 e4 18 Nd2 Bd6 19 Nb3?!

In view of what happens White should have played the more safety-conscious 19 g3; e.g. 19...Bc8 20 Nb3 Bh3 21 Qa5 with a couple of pawns and a living king for the exchange!

19...Bxh2+ 20 Kh1 Be5 21 c3 e3!

A fine move, giving up a key pawn for attacking chances.

22 Bxe3 Qc6 23 Bf3? (Diagram 12)

The best try is 23 f3, although after 23...Nh5 24 Na5 Qg6! 25 Nxb7 Ng3+ 26 Kg1 Re8, Black's attack involving ...Qh5 will be tough to meet.

23...Qxf3! 0-1

A killer. Malakhatko was probably anticipating 23...Qxc4 24 Bd4 with chances. Now after 23...Qxf3 24 gxf3 Bxf3+ 25 Kg1 Ng4 White's king is in a mating net.

Game 9
☐ **V.Popov** ■ **G.Kiselev**
Krasnoyarsk 2007

---

1 e4 e5 2 Nf3 Nc6 3 Bc4 Nf6 4 Ng5 d5 5 exd5 Na5 6 Bb5+ c6 7 dxc6 bxc6 8 Be2 h6 9 Nf3

The normal retreat, which is considered to be the main line. Black now has the chance to gain time for development.

9...e4 10 Ne5 Bd6 (Diagram 13)

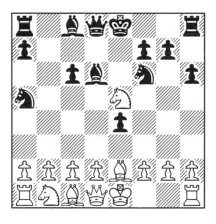

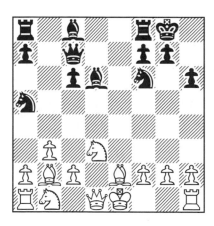

Diagram 13 (W)	**Diagram 14 (B)**
The main line	Is Bb2xf6 a threat?

11 d4

It seems that the main alternative 11 f4 has dropped out of fashion, probably as Black is considered to be able to obtain adequate compensation with normal developing moves; e.g. 11...exf3 12 Nxf3 0-0 13 0-0 Qc7 14 d4 c5 15 Nc3 a6 16 d5 Bb7

17 Kh1 Rad8 with sufficient pressure, especially against the d5-pawn, V.Bagirov-Y.Estrin, Beverwijk 1965.

11...exd3

Opening lines at this point is best as it suits the player who is better developed.

12 Nxd3 Qc7 13 b3

White can castle after playing the preparatory 13 h3; e.g. 13...0-0 14 0-0, but then Black has 14...c5! 15 b3 c4 16 bxc4 Nxc4, E.Sutovsky-O.Romanishin, Essen 2001, with adequate play.

13...0-0 14 Bb2 (Diagram 14) 14...Re8

Here it isn't in White's interest to capture on f6 as the broken pawns would then be less of a problem than the vacant dark squares. For 14...Ne4 see the next game.

Another move that ignores the potential threat of Bxf6 is 14...Bf5, as in J.Mestel-G.Flear, London 1986: 15 Nd2 Rad8 16 h3 c5 (a familiar theme – Black uses a minority attack to shake up his opponent, while at the same time finding a role for his worst-placed piece) 17 0-0 c4 18 Nxc4 Nxc4 19 bxc4 Qxc4 20 Bxf6!? (otherwise White doesn't have anything constructive to do) 20...gxf6 21 Bg4 Bh7 (no, thank you!) 22 Re1 Bc5 23 Qc1 Bd4 24 Rb1 Qxa2 with a complicated struggle where Black isn't worse.

15 h3 Qe7

A slightly annoying pin.

16 Nc3 c5 (Diagram 15)

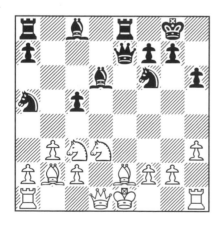

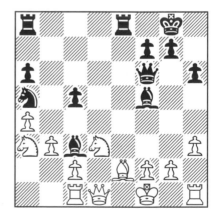

Diagram 15 (W)

A critical position

Diagram 16 (W)

White can hardly move

17 Nb5?!

An panicky idea, especially with his king stuck in the centre.

17 0-0! is better; e.g. 17...c4 18 Bf3 Bb7 (18...cxd3!? is an ambitious and somewhat murky exchange sacrifice; e.g. 19 Bxa8 Qe5 20 f4 Qc5+ 21 Kh1 dxc2 22 Qxc2 Bf5 23 b4 Qc8 and Black obtained enough compensation in K.Honfi-I.Polgar, Hungarian Ch., Budapest 1968) 19 Re1 Qd7 20 Bxb7 Qxb7 21 Rxe8+ Rxe8 22 Ne1 Rd8 23 Qf3 and White was able to consolidate his extra pawn in G.Swathi-C.Gokhale, Indian Ch., Nagpur 2002.

17...Bb8 18 Bxf6?

White exchanges a pair of pieces, at the cost of ceding the dark squares.

18...Qxf6 19 a4 a6

Or perhaps the thematic 19...c4.

20 Na3 Be5 21 Rc1

Also after 21 Nxe5 Qxe5 22 Kf1 Bb7 23 Nc4 Nxc4 24 Bxc4 Rad8 Black's pieces dominate.

21...Bc3+ 22 Kf1 Bf5 (Diagram 16)

White's forces can hardly breathe!

23 Nb1 Bb2 24 Nxb2 Qxb2 25 Bd3 Nxb3!

Crashing through.

26 cxb3 Bxd3+ 27 Kg1 Re2 0-1

Black's pieces could be described as slightly more effective than their white counterparts!

Game 10
☐ T.Radjabov ■ A.Naiditsch
European Championship, Warsaw 2005

1 e4 e5 2 Nf3 Nc6 3 Bc4 Nf6 4 Ng5 d5 5 exd5 Na5 6 Bb5+ c6 7 dxc6 bxc6 8 Be2 h6 9 Nf3 e4 10 Ne5 Bd6 11 d4 exd3 12 Nxd3 Qc7 13 b3 0-0 14 Bb2 Ne4

A natural leap to an influential central square.

15 Nc3 (Diagram 17) 15...Bf5

It may be better to support the knight with the f-pawn, when the option of ...f5xe4 tends to disrupt White's plans. For example, 15...f5 16 h3 Ba6 17 0-0 Rad8 18 Qe1

Rfe8 19 Nxe4 Rxe4! (here after 19...fxe4 20 Nc1 Bxe2 21 Nxe2 Black lacks bite) 20 Qd1 c5 21 Bf3, and just as White seems to be consolidating Black has a forcing line: 21...c4! 22 Bxe4 fxe4 23 Ne5 Ba3 24 Qg4 Bxb2 25 Qe6+ with a draw by perpetual check, Y.Yakovich-E.Tomashevsky, Russian Team Ch. 2006.

16 h3 Rad8 17 0-0

This position has been tested a few times and experience suggests that White can gradually improve, whereas Black lacks punch.

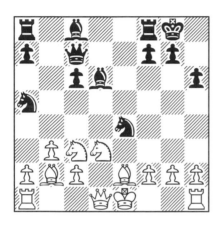

Diagram 17 (B)

Another critical juncture

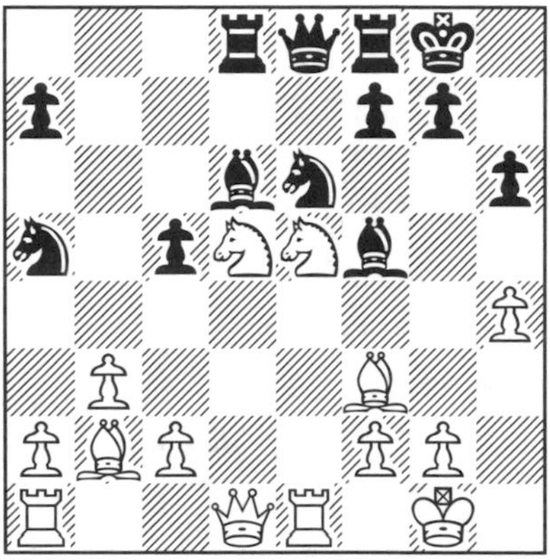

Diagram 18 (B)

Black is just a pawn down

17...c5!?

The standard idea, but with White being so well placed it's important to evaluate any potential weakening of the d5-square. 17...Rfe8 18 Bg4 Bg6 19 Nxe4 Bxe4 20 Qd2 c5 21 Qc3, as in E.Sutovsky-H.Jonkman, Israeli Ch., Tel Aviv 2001, was less compromising.

18 Bf3 Ng5?!

Surely Naiditsch should have tried 18...Nxc3 19 Bxc3 c4, as then 20 Bxa5 Qxa5 21 bxc4 Be6 would yield some compensation.

19 Nd5 Qd7 20 h4!?

Forcing Black's hand.

20...Ne6?

Again simplifying may not give full compensation, but 20...Nxf3+ 21 Qxf3 Nc6 would at least keep Black in the game.

21 Ne5 Qe8 22 Re1 (Diagram 18)

White's pieces have sprung to life and Black finds himself a pawn down in an inferior position.

22...Bb8 23 Qd2 Qb5 24 c4 Qa6 25 Bc3 Nb7 26 Nc6 1-0

The German GM was about to lose further material and clearly had had enough. 26...Qxc6 is well met by 27 Ne7+ Kh7 28 Nxc6 Rxd2 29 Bxd2 when White is the exchange and a pawn to the good, as well as having a dominating position.

White plays 4 d4

Whatever the objective pros and cons of 4 Ng5 many White players don't like the idea of losing the initiative in the opening. So 4 d4 has many followers, due to the fact that it opens lines in order to speed along White's development.

Strategy

The strategy depends on a number of early choices but the line 4...exd4 5 e5 d5 6 Bb5 Ne4 7 Nxd4 (Games 12 and 13) is perhaps the most challenging. There the battle for central squares requires a certain understanding and precision.

Theoretical

Yes, many lines require serious memory work in order to avoid a disaster in the opening.

Game 11
□ P.Peters ■ G.Flear
Montpellier 1985

1 e4 e5 2 Nf3 Nc6 3 Bc4 Nf6 4 d4 exd4 5 Ng5

White opens the centre and then bears down on the weak f7-point. However, Black can comfortably cope with the threat, so this line shouldn't be a problem.

5...d5! (Diagram 19)

A central counter is often the best reaction to precocious wing play.

6 exd5 Qe7+!

This check looks odd at first sight as Black blocks in his own bishop, but White is invited to make a major decision and, as we'll see, doesn't have an easy solution.

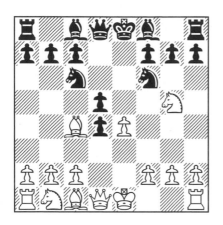

Diagram 19 (W)	**Diagram 20 (W)**
Countering in the centre	A provocative move

7 Kf1

There are two other plausible replies:

a) After 7 Be2 Nxd5 8 0-0 White has a lead in development, so Black has to play carefully. I recommend 8...h6; e.g. 9 Nf3 Bg4 10 c4 (10 Nxd4 Bxe2 11 Nxe2 0-0-0 would be awkward for White) 10...Nb6 11 Nxd4 Bxe2 12 Nxe2 (and now Black can't castle long, but after...) 12...Rd8 13 Nd2 Kd7! 14 Re1 Kc8 (...you would hardly believe it!) Black's position is the more comfortable, G.Murawski-F.Barglowski, Polish Team Ch. 2004.

b) 7 Qe2 gives Black the opportunity to seize the initiative in the queenless middlegame that follows; for example 7...Qxe2+ (or perhaps 7...Nb4!?) 8 Kxe2 Ne5 9 Bb3 h6 10 f4 Bg4+ 11 Kf2 hxg5 12 Re1 0-0-0 13 fxe5 Nxd5, J.P.Grondin-S.Barbeau, Quebec 2001.

7...Ne5 8 Qxd4 Nxc4 9 Qxc4 h6 (Diagram 20)

A provocative move. Black puts the question to the knight!

9...Qc5 is a sensible alternative, when Black should be fine after both 10 Qxc5 Bxc5 11 Nc3 Bf5 and 10 Qe2+ Be7 11 c4 (or similarly 11 Nc3 Nxd5 12 Nge4) 11...Nxd5 12 Ne4 Qc6 13 Bg5 Bxg5 14 Nxg5+ Kf8 15 Qe4, G.Sax-J.Smejkal, Budapest 1975. The only slight inconvenience in this line is that White can drop his knight back to e4.

10 Nc3

Sacrificing a piece! After the more modest 10 Nf3, Black has a choice between
10...Bd7 11 Nc3 0-0-0 12 Bf4 Qc5, as in K.Sorri-J.Norri, Espoo 1992, with adequate
compensation (White has to take time to castle by hand and will face various
threats on the light squares); and 10...Qc5 11 Qe2+ Be7 12 c4 Nxd5 where, compared to the previous note, the knight is less active on f3.

10...hxg5 11 Bxg5 Qc5 12 Re1+

One point behind White's play is that the black king is obliged to move.

12...Kd8 13 Qe2

The best try could be 13 Qf4 Be7 14 h4, when Pinski recommends 14...a5 15 Qe5
Ra6, but 14...Bd7 15 h5 Kc8 16 Rh4 Bd6 17 Qf3 Ne8, as played in J.Carleton-
J.Franzen, correspondence 1991, also looks promising for Black.

13...Bd7!

Instead, 13...Be7 14 d6 Bxd6 15 Ne4 wasn't so clear in Y.Fstrin-A.Lilienthal, Moscow
1946.

14 Ne4 Bb5! (Diagram 21)

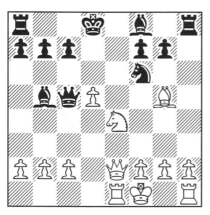

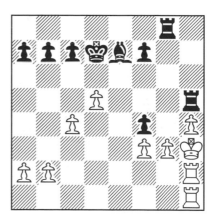

Diagram 21 (W)

White's attack is over

Diagram 22 (W)

Black is near victory

White's attack is defused without fuss.

15 Nxc5 Bxe2+ 16 Rxe2 Bxc5 17 Bxf6+ gxf6

Two pawns certainly don't compensate for the piece, though there is still some
work to do.

18 g3 Kd7 19 h4 Rh5 20 c4 Rg8 21 Kg2 Rg4 22 Rc2 f5

Breaking up the kingside is probably the simplest way to make progress.

23 Kh3 Be7

Threatening ...Bxh4 with mate in two in mind!

24 f3 Rg8 25 Rch2 f4 (Diagram 22)

White's kingside is undone and the full point is within striking distance.

26 g4 Rxh4+ 27 Kg2 Rxh2+ 28 Rxh2 f5 29 Rh7 fxg4 30 fxg4 Rxg4+ 31 Kf3 Rh4 32 Rxh4 Bxh4 33 Kxf4 Kd6 34 b4 b5 0-1

Game 12
□ M.Munoz Sanchez ■ A.Moreno
Quito 2003

---

1 e4 e5 2 Nf3 Nc6 3 d4 exd4 4 Bc4 Nf6

White employs a slightly tricky move order, but Moreno chooses the most reputable response by transposing into the Two Knights Defence. 3 Bc4 Nf6 4 d4 exd4 is the standard route to this position.

5 e5 (Diagram 23)

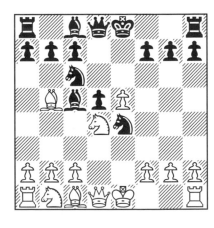

Diagram 23 (B)	**Diagram 24 (W)**
The Modern Variation	Ignoring the attack on c6

This is known as the Modern Variation. By attacking the knight, White hopes to gain time and disrupt Black's development. In reply, it is possible to move the knight to either e4 or g4 and then for Black to adapt his next few moves according to circumstances. However, I consider that the most principled, and probably best move, is to hit back immediately in the centre.

5...d5!

NOTE: In many Open Games Black can often catch up in development with a timely, and frequently precocious, ...d7-d5.

6 Bb5

The best response as 6 exf6?! dxc4 7 0-0 gives White an inferior sort of Max Lange (see Games 14-15). Indeed, Black can capture either way on f6 (with advantage!).

6...Ne4 7 Nxd4

Regaining the pawn with a threat.

7...Bc5! (Diagram 24)

Ignoring the pressure on c6 and creating threats of his own!

The plausible and fairly common reply is 7...Bd7, but this is slightly docile in that it gives White sufficient time to keep control after 8 Bxc6 bxc6 9 0-0 and then:

a) 9...Be7 is one passive move too far, as 10 f3 Ng5 11 f4 Ne4 12 f5 offers White interesting attacking possibilities.

b) 9...Qh4 10 Be3 Be7 is less one-sided, but after 11 f3 (or 11 Nb3 0-0 12 N1d2) White is better placed in his fight to control the c5-square than in the main line.

c) 9...Bc5 10 f3 Ng5 11 f4 Ne4 12 Be3 Bb6 13 Nd2 Nxd2 14 Qxd2 c5 (otherwise White plays Nb3 with a bind) 15 Ne2 d4 16 Bf2 Bc6 17 c4, G.Garcia-J.Friedel, Chelmsford 2001, and Black has one very good bishop, but one very bad one!

8 Be3

White's most precise move, reducing the importance of any counterplay along the a7-g1 diagonal. It also helps with the middlegame plan of clamping down on c5 and d4 which, if achieved, will leave Black's queenside looking rather forlorn.

Playing devil's advocate with 8 Nxc6?! Bxf2+ 9 Kf1 is very dangerous after 9...Qh4!, as Black has excellent play for the sacrificed material. Nevertheless, the position remains unclear; e.g. 10 Nd4+ c6 11 Nf3 Ng3+ 12 Kxf2 Ne4+ 13 Ke3 Qf2+ 14 Kd3 Bf5 15 Nd4 Bg6 16 Rf1 Qxg2 17 Ke3 cxb5 18 Qf3 Qxh2 with wild complications.

After 8 0-0, Black can again leave c6 *en prise* with 8...0-0! 9 Nxc6 (9 Bxc6 bxc6 10 f3?! also hands the initiative to Black because of 10...f6!, exploiting the pin along the a7-g1 diagonal) 9...bxc6 10 Bxc6 Ba6! and already has chances for an advantage; for example, 11 Qxd5 Bxf1 12 Qxe4 (rather than 12 Bxa8? Bc4! when Black wins very quickly – just look at White's first rank!) 12...Bb5 13 Nc3 Bxc6 14 Qxc6 Bd4 15 Bf4 Rb8 16 Nd5, K.Pitschka-R.Bräuning, German League 1989, and now 16...Rxb2! when Black keeps his material advantage in the complications.

8...Bd7

Necessary, as Black now needs to defend against the threat to capture twice on c6.

9 Bxc6 bxc6 (Diagram 25)

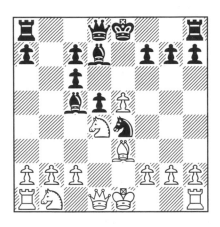

Diagram 25 (W)

A standard position

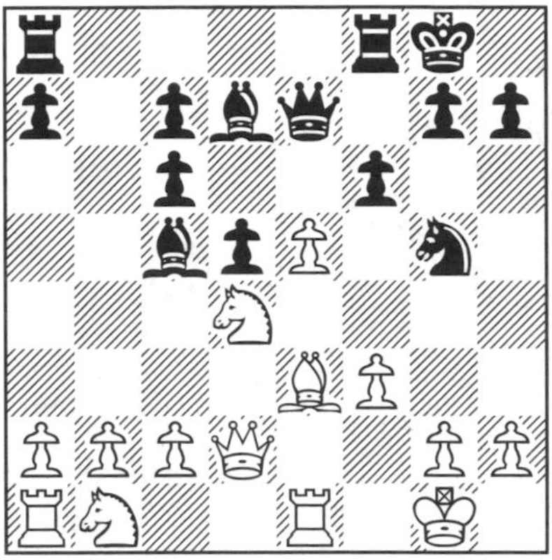

Diagram 26 (W)

Challenging the e5-pawn

With this structure Black's central pawns can be a problem for him if White is able to gain control of the c5- and d4-squares. Then his bishop pair may end up being rather impotent and his queenside majority would have little value. Black needs to act in a positive way to avoid slipping into a bind.

10 0-0

The superior 10 Nd2 is examined in the next game.

10...Qe7!

Delaying castling in order to play this useful move is definitely best here. The queen defends the c5-bishop, while also influencing events down the e-file.

11 Re1

After 11 f3 Black solves his problems with 11...Nd6! 12 Bf2 (12 exd6? loses a piece to 12...Qxe3+ and 13...Qxd4) 12...Nf5 13 c3 0-0 and is ready to rock, whereas White is handicapped by his backwards development.

11...0-0 12 f3 Ng5

Now there is no option but to place the knight on this slightly clumsy square.

13 Qd2 f6! (Diagram 26)

The right moment for this key move.

14 c3

This solidifies d4 but makes the task of developing the queen's knight rather diffi-cult. Instead, after 14 exf6 Qxf6 15 Bxg5, Black can capture on d4. So perhaps White's best idea is 14 Nc3 Bb6 15 Na4, when 15...Ne6 would seem to be about equal as White is unable to maintain a central grip of any worth.

14...h6

Over-protecting the g5-square is prudent, but the more ambitious 14...Rae8! is possible.

15 h4?!

A wild lunge that just leads to problems on his kingside.

15...fxe5!?

15...Nh3+ 16 gxh3 fxe5 is also tempting, with chances for an attack.

16 hxg5 exd4 17 cxd4 Bd6 (Diagram 27)

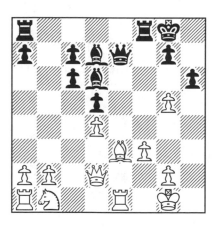

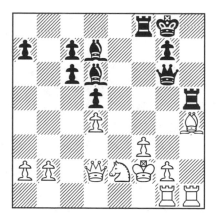

Diagram 27 (W)

Black is slightly better

Diagram 28 (B)

Black to play and win

Black has a slight lead in development and the safer king, so he is already thinking about being better.

18 Nc3

18 gxh6 plays into Black's hands after 18...Qh4, but exchanging off one of Black's dangerous bishops with 18 Bf4 comes into consideration, when a continuation such as 18...Qd8 19 Bxd6 cxd6 20 gxh6 Qf6 21 hxg7 Qxg7 22 Re3 Rf6 23 Nc3 Raf8 gives Black enough compensation for his pawn.

18...Qf7 19 Kf2 Qg6

A useful square from which to survey the kingside!

20 Rh1

Not 20 gxh6? due to 20...Bg3+.

20...hxg5 21 Bxg5 Rf5 22 Bh4 Rh5 23 Ne2 Rf8 24 Rag1 (Diagram 28)

White's pieces have all been called up to help with the defence, but it's not enough.

24...Qh7! 25 g3 Bg4! 0-1

After 26 f4, then 26...g5 is immediately decisive. Even the eccentric-looking 25...g5!? was possible; e.g. 26 g4! Rh6! 27 Qxg5+ Kf7 and White can't untangle.

Game 13
□ H.Nakamura ■ M.Hebden
Gibraltar 2008

1 e4 e5 2 Nf3 Nc6 3 d4 exd4 4 Bc4 Nf6 5 e5 d5 6 Bb5 Ne4 7 Nxd4 Bc5 8 Be3 Bd7 9 Bxc6 bxc6 10 Nd2 (Diagram 29)

Challenging Black's active knight.

10...Qh4!

Keeping the tension is Black's best option here.

I fell for a nasty trap when faced with this position for the first time: 10...Qe7? (bad!) 11 Nxe4 dxe4 12 e6! fxe6 (what else? – note that the bishop on c5 is tactically exposed; e.g. 12...Bxe6? 13 Nxe6 fxe6 14 Qh5+ and White wins a piece) 13 Nxc6! Bxc6 14 Qh5+ g6 15 Qxc5 and Black's pawn structure was a wreck in V.Okhotnik-G.Flear, Mont St Michel 1992. The fact that there were opposite-coloured bishops was only a minor solace for my arduous defensive task ahead.

Instead, 10...Nxd2 11 Qxd2 0-0 avoids any tricks, but 12 Nb3 gives White the more comfortable game as his bind on the central dark squares is hard to challenge. After the further 12...Bb6 13 0-0 f6 14 exf6 Qxf6 15 Nc5 notice the relative value of the two majorities. White has a solid 3 vs. 2 on the kingside, whereas Black will struggle to make anything of his queenside.

11 0-0 Bb6

Avoiding any tactics against the slightly vulnerable bishop.

12 N2b3

After 12 Nxe4 Qxe4 13 Re1 Qg6 14 Nb3, White would seem to be making good progress on the queenside, but then Black can make something of his 'active' queen: 14...Bg4 15 f3 Bh3 16 Qd2 d4 17 Bf4 c5 and Black had good play in M.Illescas Cordoba-J.Campos Moreno, Alicante 1989.

12...Qe7 13 Re1 0-0 14 f3 (Diagram 30) 14...Nc5?!

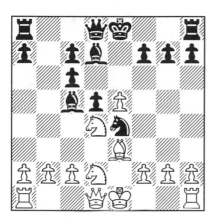

Diagram 29 (B)

Challenging the e4-knight

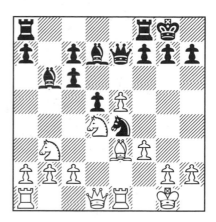

Diagram 30 (B)

What now for Black?

I don't like this move, as it gives White the opportunity of clamping down on the queenside. Instead, 14...Ng5 15 Qd2 h6 is possible, with a tense middlegame ahead. However, the most dynamic is 14...c5!, when after 15 Ne2 Black has an interesting choice between 15...c4, 15...d4, or even 15...Nf6 – in each case he should have adequate play.

15 Nxc5 Bxc5 16 Nb3 Bb6

Or 16...Bxe3+ 17 Rxe3 f6 18 Qd4 and Black lacks counterplay.

17 Qd2 Rae8 18 a4 f6

The standard method of hitting back at the centre, but White doesn't have to capture on f6...

19 e6!

Now White seizes the initiative.

19...Bxe6 20 a5 Bxe3+ 21 Qxe3 Qb4!

The only way to fight back.

22 Qxa7 Bf5 23 Rec1 Bxc2!

After the quieter 23...Qf4 24 Qd4, White's a-pawn would be a strong trump card.

24 Nd4 Bd3 25 Nxc6 Qxb2 26 Qd4 Qxd4+ 27 Nxd4 (Diagram 31)

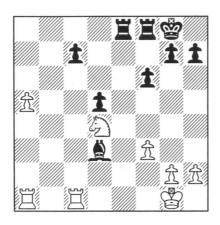

Diagram 31 (B)

The a-pawn is very strong

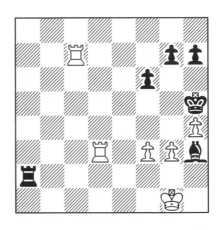

Diagram 32 (B)

White should win

The smoke clears. White is a pawn down, but his passed a-pawn and more rele-vantly placed pieces means that it is Black who has the problems to solve.

27...Bc4 28 a6 c5 29 Nc6 Re6 30 a7 Rxc6

Although Black is worse whatever, this is the best practical chance. The obvious-looking 30...Ra8? loses after the forcing continuation 31 Rcb1! Rxc6 32 Rb8+ Rc8 33 Rxc8+ Rxc8 34 Rb1! and 35 Rb8.

31 a8Q Rxa8 32 Rxa8+ Kf7 33 Ra7+ Kg6 34 Re1!

Activating the second rook.

34...Bd3

The defensive try 34...Kh6 35 Ree7 Bd3, can be met by 36 Rac7 Rxc7 37 Rxc7 c4 38 Rd7 c3 39 Rxd5 c2 40 Rc5 and White has every chance of converting his advantage. Alternatively, 34...Bb3 35 Ree7 d4 is complicated, but pushing the central pawns may not be enough; for instance, 36 Rxg7+ Kf5 37 Rxh7 d3 38 Rad7 c4 39 g4+ Kf4 40 Kf2 with a mating net.

35 Rd7 d4 36 Rc1

Winning a pawn and thus ensuring the advantage.

36...Ra6 37 h4 Bf5 38 Rd5 Be6 39 Rdxc5 d3 40 R5c3 Kh5 41 g3 Ra2 42 Rxd3 Bh3 43 Rc7 (Diagram 32)

Unfortunately Black's counter-attack has led nowhere and the ending should now be won by White.

43...Kh6

If 43...Rg2+ 44 Kh1 Rxg3 45 Kh2 Bf5, then 46 Rc5! wins.

44 g4 Rg2+ 45 Kh1 Rf2 46 Rdd7 Bf1 47 Rxg7 Bd3 48 Rgd7 Rxf3 49 Kg2 1-0

49...Re3 50 Kf2 Re2+ 51 Kf3 Rc2 avoids an immediate loss, but after 52 Rxc2 Bxc2 53 Kf4 Bb1 (or 53...Bb3 54 Kf5) 54 h5 Bc2 55 Rf7, White wins the f-pawn and essentially the game.

Game 14
□ K.Kokolias ■ M.Turov
Kirykos 2005

1 e4 e5 2 Nf3 Nc6 3 Bc4 Nf6 4 d4 exd4 5 0-0 Bc5 (Diagram 33)

Diagram 33 (W)

Entering the Max Lange

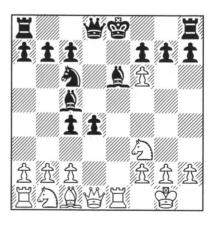

Diagram 34 (W)

The usual continuation

This is the starting point of a variation known as the Max Lange Attack.

6 e5 d5 7 exf6

This leads to the weird pawn structures associated with the Max Lange. Instead, 7 Bb5 would lead to a type of 'Modern Variation', but after 7...Ne4 8 Nxd4 0-0!, Black has a decent version and can look forward to obtaining a good game (cf. Games 12-13).

7...dxc4 8 Re1+

Here capturing on g7 looks tempting, but the main lines involve White keeping this option open for a while. Following 8 fxg7 Rg8 9 Bg5, the simplest way to solve Black's opening problems involves an instructive king walk: 9...Be7 10 Bxe7 Kxe7 11 Re1+ Kf6! 12 Nbd2 Kxg7 13 Nxc4 Kh8 and Black can look forward to the middle-game with confidence.

8...Be6 (Diagram 34) 9 Ng5

White seems to be generating a few threats on the kingside, which is just as well from his point of view, as Black seems to have the other flank under control.

9 fxg7!? is a dangerous surprise weapon which once caught me out. I suggest that Black meet this with 9...Rg8 10 Bg5 Be7 11 Bxe7 Qxe7! (in this precise position I consider capturing with the queen to be the most accurate; 11...Kxe7 12 Re4 d3?! 13 Nbd2 led to Black having a hard time in B.Taddei-G.Flear, French Team Ch. 2008) 12 Nxd4 Rd8! 13 c3 Nxd4 14 cxd4 Rxg7 15 Nc3, as in G.Neumann-S.Winawer, 2nd matchgame, Paris 1867, and now the solidifying 15...c6 is a safe way to obtain equal chances.

9...Qd5

9...Qxf6?? is the type of error that inexperienced players fall into: 10 Nxe6 fxe6 11 Qh5+ and Black loses his bishop on c5.

10 Nc3 Qf5 11 Nce4

A major alternative here is 11 g4, when Black has to play an anti-intuitive reply: 11...Qg6! (rather than the 'obvious' 11...Qxf6? which allows White a strong continuation: 12 Nd5 Qd8 13 Rxe6+ fxe6 14 Nxe6 Qd7 15 Ndxc7+ Kf7 16 Ng5+ Kg8 17 Qe2 and I don't think Black can save himself) 12 Nce4 (after the sharp 12 Nxe6 fxe6 13 Rxe6+ Kd7 14 f4 Black has a spectacular move to free himself: 14...Qxc2!!, when there is nothing better than 15 Qxc2 d3+ 16 Kg2 dxc2 17 Re4 gxf6 18 Rxc4 Be7 and it is White who is struggling to equalize) 12...Bb6 13 f4 0-0-0 14 f5 Bxf5 15 gxf5 Qxf5 was first seen in J.Blackburne-R.Teichmann, Nuremburg 1896. Several pawns and the vulnerable white king ensure that Black has adequate compensation for his piece.

11...0-0-0! (Diagram 35)

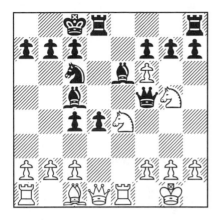

Diagram 35 (W)

Castling out of danger

Diagram 36 (W)

The white king is exposed

Another key move. Black needs to castle away from the heat.

12 g4

White must force the pace or Black's central preponderance will be decisive.

12...Qe5

But not 12...Qd5?? 13 fxg7 Rhg8 14 Nf6 Qd6 15 Nge4 Qe5 16 f4 d3+ 17 Kg2 Qd4 18 c3, M.Chigorin-A.Albin, Berlin 1897, when the black queen is trapped in the middle of the board.

13 Nf3?!

This turns out to be inappropriate now that White has weakened himself on the kingside. The critical move is 13 Nxe6 which is examined in the next game.

13...Qd5 14 fxg7 Bxg4!

A fine example of the importance of attacking chances rather than simply counting material.

15 gxh8Q Rxh8

White may have an extra rook (for two pawns!) but his pieces are not well placed.

16 h3 Bh5 17 Nf6 Qxf3 (Diagram 36) 18 Nxh5

In G.Moncamp-G.Flear, Marseille 2005, White decided to exchange off Black's major pieces, but was still unable to hold: 18 Qxf3 Bxf3 19 Re8+ Rxe8 20 Nxe8 d3 21 c3 Ne5 22 Bf4 Ng6 23 Bd2 Bc6 24 Nf6 Nh4 25 Rd1? (25 Be3 would make a fight of it) 25...Nf3+ 26 Kf1 Ba4 0-1.

18...Rg8+ 19 Ng3 Rxg3+!

This gives Black a strong attack, but is it enough for a win?

20 fxg3 Qxg3+ 21 Kf1 Qxh3+ 22 Kf2 Qh2+

The strongest continuation could be 22...d3+! 23 Be3 Ne5 24 Bxc5 Ng4+ 25 Qxg4+ Qxg4 26 Be3 Qf5+ 27 Kg1 dxc2 when Black's queen and five(!) pawns will probably prove to be too strong for White's rooks and bishop.

23 Kf1 Ne5 (Diagram 37)

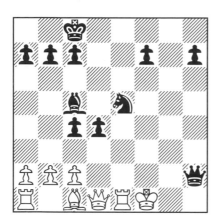

Diagram 37 (W)

Black has a strong attack

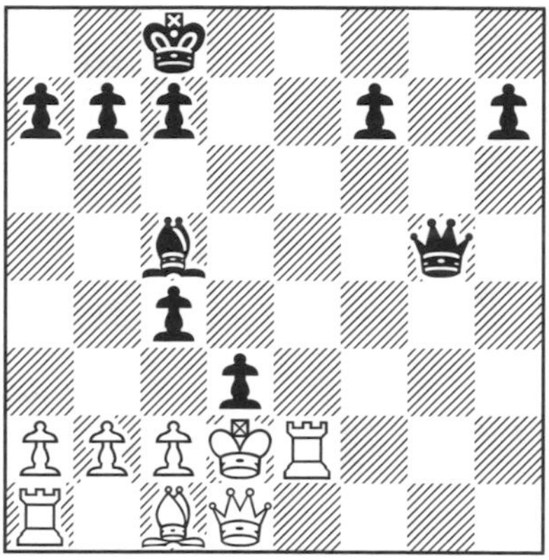

Diagram 38 (W)

How should White defend?

24 Rxe5?!

A panicky reaction. Better is 24 Qe2! when Black has no more than a draw: 24...Qh1+ (or 24...Qh3+ 25 Qg2 Qf5+ 26 Qf2 Qh3+ 27 Qg2) 25 Kf2 Qh2+ 26 Kf1 and so on.

24...Qh1+! 25 Ke2 d3+ 26 Kd2

26 cxd3? allows 26...Qg2+ 27 Ke1 Qf2 mate.

26...Qh2+ 27 Re2

27 Kc3? also leads to a quick mate following 27...Qxe5+ etc.

27...Qf4+ 28 Ke1 Qh4+ 29 Kd2 Qg5+ (Diagram 38) 30 Ke1??

Falling for a sucker punch! White could still survive with 30 Kc3!; e.g. 30...Qf6+ 31 Kd2 c3+ 32 bxc3 Qg5+ 33 Ke1 d2+ (33...Qh4+ 34 Kd2 Qf4+ is also drawn) 34 Rxd2 Qg1+ 35 Ke2, and there is no mate here as White has access to the d3-square!

30...d2+!

Sealing the escape square on d2.

31 Rxd2 Qg1+ 32 Ke2 Qf2 mate

Game 15
□ **L.Bergez** ■ **G.Flear**
Montauban 2000

1 e4 e5 2 Nf3 Nc6 3 Bc4 Bc5

Although this game began as a Giuoco Piano (see Chapter Three) it soon transposes to the Two Knights Defence.

4 0-0 Nf6 5 d4 exd4

It's also possible to capture with the bishop: 5...Bxd4, but winning a pawn this way doesn't ensure that Black has an easy time. For example, 6 Nxd4 Nxd4 7 f4 d6 8 fxe5 dxe5 9 Bg5 Be6 10 Na3 seems to give White enough compensation.

6 e5 d5 7 exf6 dxc4 8 Re1+ Be6 9 Ng5 Qd5 10 Nc3 Qf5 11 Nce4 0-0-0 12 g4 Qe5 13 Nxe6

The critical move.

13...fxe6 (Diagram 39) 14 fxg7

White also has 14 Bg5, which is an awkward move for the unprepared. The sharpest replies are 14...Bb6 and 14...h6, but 14...g6 is the safest; e.g. 15 f7 Be7 16 f4 Qg7 17 Bxe7 Nxe7 18 Ng5 d3, L.Raggini-G.Flear, St Affrique 1997, and now 19 Nxe6 Qxf7 20 Nxd8 Rxd8 is about equal.

14...Rhg8 15 Bh6

White maintains his g7-pawn and hopes that it will prove to be a thorn in Black's side.

15...d3 16 c3 Be7

Black's best move at this point isn't totally clear. Some books recommend 16...d2!? 17 Re2 Rd3, which is also very complex.

17 Qd2

After 17 Qf3 Qd5 we reach a position that was investigated in a Marshall-Capablanca match from a century ago. One of the games led to a quick draw as follows: 18 Qf7 Rde8 (or 18...Bh4 19 Rad1 Ne5 20 Qf4 Ng6 with equality) 19 Re3 Ne5 20 Qf4 Ng6, F.Marshall-J.Capablanca, 3rd matchgame, New York 1910, and after 21 Qf7 Ne5 22 Qf4 Ng6 etc the game was drawn by repetition.

17...Qd5 18 Qf4!? (Diagram 40) 18...Ne5?!

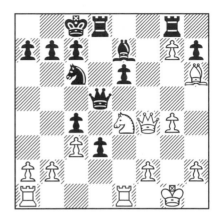

Diagram 39 (W)

The main line

Diagram 40 (B)

A complicated position

A mistake, but I'm in good company as Capablanca also erred in this manner! Black must really play 18...Bd6! here; e.g. 19 Nxd6+ cxd6 20 Qe4 Ne5 with a position which shouldn't be worse for him.

19 Nd2!

Covering f3 and hitting c4.

19...Bd6 20 Re4 Rd7 21 Qe3

White has consolidated his central forces and the pawn on g7 is starting to weigh on Black's mind!

21...Nf7!?

Sacrificing the a-pawn for some play. Capablanca decided to simplify into a worse ending here: 21...Bc5 22 Rxe5 Bxe3 23 Rxd5 Bxh6 24 Rxd7 Kxd7 25 Nxc4 Rxg7 26 h3 Bf4 (or if 26...Ke8, then 27 Rd1 b5 28 Ne5 d2 29 Kf1 Bf4 30 Nd3 Bg5 31 Nc5 and White is much better) 27 Rd1 h5 28 Rxd3+ Kc6 29 f3, but was still unable to scrape a draw, F.Marshall-J.Capablanca, 1st matchgame, New York 1910.

22 Qxa7 b5 23 Qa6+ Qb7 24 Qxb7+ Kxb7 25 Be3 Rxg7 26 a4! (Diagram 41)

Material is temporarily equal but now Black's structure comes under pressure.

26...c6 27 h3 Re7

Other moves don't save the day either: 27...Ng5 allows 28 Bxg5 Rxg5 29 Rxe6, while 27...e5 28 axb5 cxb5 29 Ra5 Kc6 is refuted by 30 Nxc4!, as 30...bxc4 31 Rxc4+

Kb7 32 Rb5+ Ka6 33 Rb6+ Ka5 34 b3 forces mate.

28 axb5 cxb5 29 Ra7+ Kc6 30 Rxe7 Bxe7 31 Rxe6+ Bd6 32 f4 Nd8 33 Rh6 (Diagram 42)

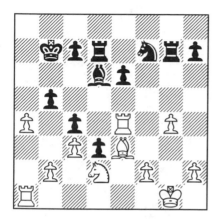

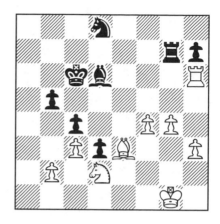

Diagram 41 (B)

Black comes under pressure

Diagram 42 (B)

White is winning

White's mobile kingside majority constitutes a decisive advantage.

33...Re7 34 Kf2 Ne6 35 Nf3 Kd7 36 f5 Nf8 37 Rf6 Re4 38 Ng5 Rxe3 39 Kxe3 Bf4+

The last throw of the dice.

40 Kf2

In fact 40 Kxf4 d2 41 Rd6+ Kxd6 42 Ne4+ should also win.

40...Ke7 1-0

With 40...Ke7 I had reached the time control, but I didn't wait for 41 Rf7+ Ke8 42 Rxf8+! etc.

 WARNING: Certain variations in certain openings need to be learnt thoroughly before playing them, otherwise one is courting disaster. The Max Lange Attack definitely comes into this category.

Game 16
□ **I.Rogers** ■ **M.Adams**
German League 1996

1 e4 e5 2 Nf3 Nc6 3 d4 exd4 4 Bc4 Nf6 5 0-0 Nxe4

The Classical Variation, which is definitely a sensible option for those who don't want to get involved in the complicated theory of the Max Lange Attack (Games 14-15).

6 Re1 d5 (Diagram 43)

Diagram 43 (W)	**Diagram 44 (W)**
The Classical Variation	White should regain his pawn

7 Bxd5

A temporary piece sacrifice to undermine Black's centre. Alternatives are unsatisfactory for White:

a) 7 Nc3 dxc3 8 Bxd5 Be6 9 Bxe4 Qxd1 10 Rxd1 cxb2 11 Bxb2 f6 and White will have to fight to regain his pawn.

b) 7 Nxd4 Nxd4 8 Qxd4 Be6 9 Bxd5 Qxd5 10 Qxe4 Qxe4 11 Rxe4 0-0-0 with a comfortable two-bishop edge for Black.

c) 7 Bb5 Bc5 8 Nxd4 0-0 with a type of Modern Variation where White is a clear pawn down.

7...Qxd5 8 Nc3

The point of White's previous move is that he now regains the piece with every chance of regaining his pawn as well.

8...Qa5

It's certainly possible to go the other way: 8...Qh5 9 Nxe4 Be6 10 Bg5 Bd6 11 Nxd6+ cxd6 12 Bf4 with a balanced game; for example, 12...Qd5 13 c3 Rc8 14 Nxd4 Nxd4 15 Qxd4 Qxd4 16 cxd4 Kd7 when a draw is the most likely result.

9 Nxe4 Be6 (Diagram 44) 10 Neg5

White can also play 10 Bd2, when Black has a choice:

a) 10...Bb4 11 Nxd4 Nxd4 12 c3 Be7 13 cxd4 Qd5 14 Bb4 Bxb4 15 Qa4+ Qc6 16 Qxb4 0-0-0 17 Rac1 Qb6 18 Qc3 Rxd4 19 Nc5 Rhd8 20 Nxe6 fxe6 21 Rxe6 is dead equal, I.Radulov-J.Smejkal, Raach 1969.

b) 10...Qf5 11 Bg5 h6 12 Bh4 Bc5 (aiming to maintain the extra pawn, but White may seek to destabilize Black's position with the sharp...) 13 b4 (...with complications if Black captures) 13...Bb6! (the sensible option; after 13...Bxb4 14 Nxd4 Nxd4 15 Qxd4 Bxe1 16 Qxg7, H.Messing-H.Stevic, Sibenik 2008, and other games suggest that Black may have to walk a tightrope to draw) 14 a4 a5! 15 b5 Nb4 16 Nxd4 Bxd4 17 Qxd4 0-0 18 Rac1 Rfe8 is equal, P.Gayson-A.Hynes, British League 2006.

10...0-0-0

Giving back the pawn to ensure free development. Despite castling long Black's king isn't any weaker than White's in the middlegame that follows.

11 Nxe6 fxe6 12 Rxe6 Bd6 (Diagram 45)

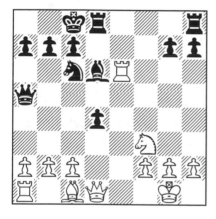
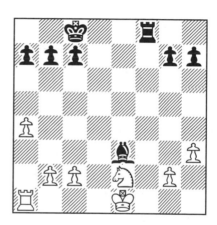

Diagram 45 (W)	Diagram 46 (B)
The position is roughly equal	Black is now slightly better

13 Qe2

13 Bg5 is a major alternative, against which Black has to decide if he is seeking more than half a point. Here are some sample lines: 13...Rde8 14 Qe2 (or 14 Qe1 Qxe1+ 15 Raxe1 Kd7 16 Rxe8 Rxe8 17 Rxe8 Kxe8 18 Kf1 Kd7 19 Bd2 h6 20 Ke2 Ke6 21 Kd3 Kd5 22 Nxd4 Nxd4 23 c4+ Ke6! 24 Kxd4 Be5+ with a drawish endgame, K.Hacat-M.Hughey, Edmonton 2000) 14...Kd7 15 Re4 Qf5 16 Re1 Rxe4 17 Qxe4

Rf8!? (trying for something more tense than the dead equality following 17...Qxe4 18 Rxe4 Re8) 18 Bd2 Bc5 19 Kf1 a5, R.Lahaye-M.Kazhgaleyev, Zwolle 2004, with sufficient tension for the stronger player to eke out a win.

13...Qh5 14 h3 Rhe8

14...Rde8 15 Bd2 Ne5! comes to the same thing.

15 Bd2 Ne5 16 Rxe8 Rxe8 17 Nxd4 Qxe2 18 Nxe2 Nc4

Here 18...Nf3+ also seems reasonable: 19 gxf3 Rxe2 20 Rd1 Bc5 21 b4 Bb6 22 c4 Bd4 23 Bg5 was lively but ultimately equal, M.Crepan-P.Potocnik, Slovenian Team Ch. 1994.

19 Be3 Nxe3

Capturing on b2, breaking up White's queenside, comes into consideration. For example, 19...Nxb2 20 Kf1 Nc4 21 Bd4 Be5 with a slight pull to Black due to his superior structure, P.Kirillov-A.Obukhov, Novosibirsk 2002.

20 fxe3 Bc5 21 Kf2 Rf8+ 22 Ke1 Bxe3 23 a4 (Diagram 46)

The type of position where the player with rook and bishop will try to create threats on more than one front, when the bishop should in theory be the superior minor piece.

23...Bc5 24 a5 a6 25 Ra4 Bf2+ 26 Kd2 Rd8+ 27 Kc3 Be1+

Adams is trying to hassle the white pieces before his opponent can get himself fully organized.

28 Kb3 Re8 29 Nf4 Re5 30 c3 Bg3 31 Nd3 Re3 32 Nc5 Bd6

White just needs one free move to bring his rook into the fray, so Adams continues to force the issue.

33 Ne4 Be7 34 Nd2 Re2

Winning material.

35 Re4!

The best defence. Pawn-down rook endings are often drawn if the weaker side has an active rook.

35...Rxd2 36 Rxe7 Rxg2 37 h4 h5 38 Ka3 Rg4 39 b4 b6

After 39...g5 40 hxg5 Rxg5 41 Rh7, there doesn't seem to be a sensible way for Black to activate his king.

40 axb6 cxb6 41 Ka4 g6 42 Re6 Kc7 43 Rf6 Rxh4 44 Rxg6 Rg4 45 Rh6 h4 46 Rh7+ Kc6 ½-½

After 47 Rh6+ it's too risky to advance up the board: 47...Kd5? 48 Rxb6 and Black is the only one in any danger!

Summary

In the principal 4 Ng5 variations White grabs a pawn and attempts to neutralize his opponent's attempts at activity. There is no consensual conclusion about this approach, it all comes down to a question of taste. If you like having the initiative and don't mind being a pawn down, then you'd be happy with Black; whereas if defending for a while isn't a problem for you, especially when there is the prospect of a long-term advantage (if you are successful!), then you could certainly try out the White side

In the Two Knights Defence with 4 d4 exd4 White does best to avoid 5 Ng5 as this may already be better for Black. Against the superior 5 0-0, Black has the choice between the highly tactical Max Lange Attack after 5...Bc5, or the solid Classical Variation with 5...Nxe4 which, however, often leads to drawish simplification.

The most popular variation nowadays is the Modern 5 e5, which can create a tense strategic struggle in the battle for central squares.

Chapter Three
Evans Gambit and Giuoco Piano

Introduction

These two openings arise after Black develops his bishop to the active-looking c5-square. In both cases White challenges the bishop and aims to gain time to construct his centre and prepare an attack.

In the Evans Gambit (Games 17-19) White does this directly with 4 b4, already baring his teeth and announcing to his opponent that there won't be a comfortable ride in the opening.

In the Giuoco Piano (Games 20-24) White instead plays c2-c3 and d2-d4, creating tension in the central arena before the players have had time to castle. We will examine Black's main options in the illustrative games that follow. My impression is that if Black is serious about challenging White's central aspirations, then he has to be willing to enter complications.

The other main option, 4 d3, leading to quieter play, was dealt with separately in Chapter One.

Evans Gambit

1 e4 e5 2 Nf3 Nc6 3 Bc4 Bc5 4 b4 (Diagram 1)

The Evans used to be considered as a swashbuckling attempt to attack at all costs. Nowadays this view has moderated, but few would argue with the premise that it is still a risky attempt to seize the initiative.

Strategy

White opens lines while gaining time against the c5-bishop and, as a result, is able to create some early threats with Black's king still in the centre. Naturally there is a price to pay for all this action: a pawn or two for a start, plus a compromised queenside, so if Black survives the early assault he may obtain the advantage.

Theoretical

Despite the sharp nature of this opening, the theory has not evolved that much in recent years due to a marked lack of interest by GMs. However, it is sufficiently dangerous to warrant some effort in learning a sensible antidote before allowing 4 b4. I make some suggestions in the following games.

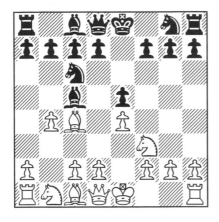

Diagram 1 (B)
Evans Gambit

Diagram 2 (B)
Evans Gambit Declined

Game 17
□ G.Kasparov ■ J.Piket
Amsterdam 1995

1 e4 e5 2 Nf3 Nc6 3 Bc4 Bc5 4 b4 Bb6

Some gambits are best declined, but not this one! By declining the Evans Black enables White to gain space on the queenside 'free of charge'.

5 a4 (Diagram 2) 5...a5

The alternative is 5...a6, when White has two tries:

a) 6 Nc3!? is sharpest, and after 6...Nf6 7 Nd5 Nxd5 8 exd5 Nd4 9 a5 Ba7, the shot 10 d6!? offers a pawn to bottle up Black's development. However, while White obtains practical compensation, this also offers Black chances; e.g. 10...cxd6 (or perhaps 10...Qf6!?) 11 c3 Ne6 12 0-0 0-0 13 d4 Qc7 14 Bd5 Rb8 15 Qd3 b5 16 axb6 Bxb6 17 Bd2 f5 was unclear in A.Morozevich-G.Kamsky, Moscow (blitz) 2008.

b) 6 c3 Nf6 7 d3 d6 8 0-0 is more positional and could also arise via 4 d3. Here White has chances for a pull due to his space preponderance. For example, after the sluggish 8...h6 9 Nbd2 0-0 10 Bb3 Ne7 11 Nc4 White gains a tempo. In Chapter

One we saw that one idea behind an early ...a7-a6 is that the bishop can drop back immediately to a7 avoiding such a loss of time. The game I.Glek-A.Yermolinsky, Wijk aan Zee 1997, continued with 11...Ba7 12 Be3 Be6 13 Bxa7 Rxa7 14 Re1 Ng6 15 d4 Bxc4 16 Bxc4 Ra8 17 Qc2 c6 and White had a small pull.

If Black instead decides to castle immediately he has to take into consideration the following pin: 8...0-0 9 Bg5 (a move tried on several occasions by Yudasin; 9 Nbd2 Ne7 10 Bb3 Ng6 11 Nc4 is a reasonable alternative) 9...h6 10 Bh4 g5 11 Bg3 (although 11 Nxg5?! would be tempting to attack-minded Evans players, Black can defend: 11...hxg5 12 Bxg5 Kg7 13 Qf3 Rh8 14 a5 Ba7 15 h4 Kg6! and then something like 16 Nd2 Bg4 17 Bxf6 Qd7 18 Qg3 Kxf6 clearly favours Black; compare this with Game 3, where a similar sacrifice on g5 was far more favourable for White) 11...Bg4 12 h3 Bh5 13 Nbd2 Kh8 with options and thus counter-chances on the kingside, L.Yudasin-A.Sherzer, Washington DC 2002.

6 b5 Nd4 7 Nxd4 Bxd4 8 c3 Bb6 9 d4 (Diagram 3)

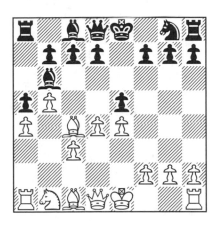

Diagram 3 (B)

Claiming the centre

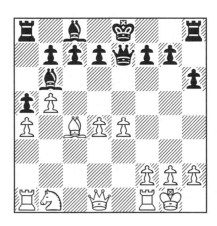

Diagram 4 (B)

Black needs to develop

White expands in the centre.

9...exd4

The pseudo-active 9...Qh4 has received some attention here: 10 0-0 Nf6 11 Nd2 d6 12 Nf3 Qh5 13 dxe5 dxe5!? (after 13...Nxe4 14 Qe1 d5 15 Bxd5 Black was a clear pawn down in S.Nadyrhanov-I.Komissarov, Smolensk 1997) 14 Ng5! (14 Ba3?! is inferior due to 14...Bg4) 14...Bg4 (14...Qxd1 15 Rxd1 Be6, L.Arnold-O.Sick, German League 1998, can be met by 16 Nxe6! fxe6 17 Re1 Rd8 18 Kf1 with an edge) 15 Qd2

(15 Bxf7+? falls short because of 15...Qxf7 16 Nxf7 Bxd1 17 Nxh8 Bb3) 15...0-0 16 h3 with a pull for White. The black queen is actually not that well placed and the threat of Ba3 is awkward. In my view 9...Qh4 is slightly dubious.

10 0-0 Ne7 11 Bg5

In a later game White tried 11 cxd4, but then Black was able to hit back in the centre and obtained a good position after 11...d5! 12 exd5 Nxd5 13 Ba3 Be6 14 Qh5? (not good; 14 Re1 is better, when 14...Qd7 followed by ...0-0-0 makes sense as Black's king would be safe with the queenside so blocked) 14...Nf4 15 Qf3 Bxc4 16 Qxf4 Qxd4, L.Riemersma-A.Mikhalevski, Amsterdam 1995.

11...h6 12 Bxe7

White could consider 12 Bh4, but Kasparov was intent on rapid development.

12...Qxe7 13 cxd4 (Diagram 4) 13...Qd6?!

This leads to fishing in troubled waters, a dangerous strategy when you are leaving most of your equipment at home! 13...0-0 14 Nc3 c6 is more natural, but then White could render Black's development difficult with 15 Rb1 Bc7 16 b6.

14 Nc3 Bxd4

After 14...Qxd4 Kasparov intended 15 Nd5! Qxc4 (alternatives are hardly improvements: 15...Qxd1 16 Rfxd1 and 15...0-0 16 Qxd4 Bxd4 17 Rad1 Be5 18 f4 Bd6 19 Kh1 leave Black with no good moves) 16 Rc1 Qa2 17 Rxc7! Bxc7 18 Nxc7+ Ke7 19 Nxa8 d6 20 Qc1 with a winning position, having already regained all his material.

15 Nd5!

I was present at the 'Kasparov University' summer camp in the late 1990's. GK himself gave a one hour lecture to each group, the theme in mine being that the 'quality' of pieces is more important than the 'quantity' and this game was one of his chosen examples.

 TIP: When assessing long-term sacrifices, consider the relative effectiveness of the pieces on the board, rather than just counting what's in the box.

15...Bxa1 16 Qxa1 0-0 17 e5 Qc5 18 Rc1 (Diagram 5)

Compare the effectiveness of White's forces to Black's!

18...c6 19 Ba2 Qa3 20 Nb6

Winning material, as Bxf7+ is threatened along with the rook.

20...d5 21 Nxa8 Kh8 22 Nb6 Be6 23 h3 Rd8 24 bxc6 bxc6 25 Rc3 Qb4 26 Rxc6 Rb8 27 Nxd5 Qxa4 28 Rc1 Qa3 29 Bc4 1-0

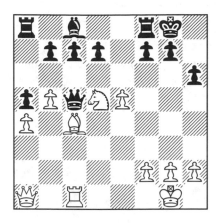

Diagram 5 (B)

Quality, not quantity

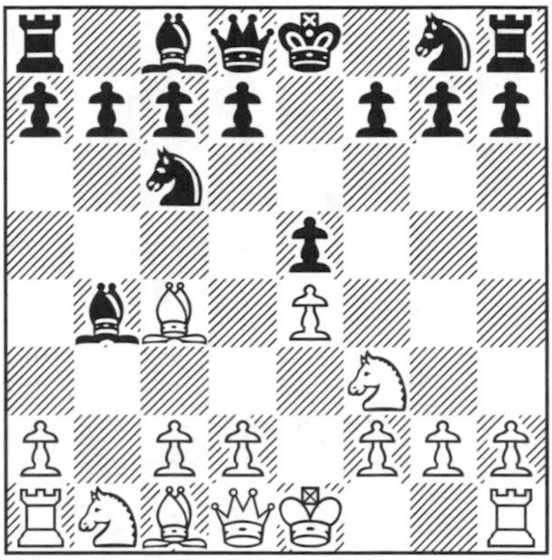

Diagram 6 (W)

Evans Gambit Accepted

Game 18
□ D.Leygue ■ G.Flear
Cap d'Agde 2006

1 e4 e5 2 Nf3 Nc6 3 Bc4 Bc5 4 b4 Bxb4 (Diagram 6)

I consider this to be the most principled reply.

For those who like going their own way, 4...d5!? is a little known move that gives Black a playable game; e.g. 5 exd5 Nxb4 6 0-0 Nf6 7 Nxe5 Nbxd5 8 d4 Be7 9 Bb3 0-0 10 c4 Nb6 11 Bb2, R.Felgaer-J.Pierrot, Argentine Ch., Buenos Aires 2000, and now I recommend 11...c5.

5 c3 Ba5 6 d4

6 0-0 is generally accepted as being too slow. Black then has a manoeuvre associated with Lasker, enabling him to obtain a comfortable game: 6...d6 7 d4 Bb6! 8 dxe5 dxe5 9 Qb3 (after 9 Qxd8+ Nxd8 10 Nxe5 Be6 White has regained his pawn, but this queenless middlegame offers Black the better prospects, as White's pawn structure is inferior and Black has no problems with development) 9...Qf6 10 Bg5 (forcing the pace to seek compensation) 10...Qg6 11 Bd5 Nge7 12 Bxe7 Kxe7 13 Bxc6 Qxc6 14 Nxe5 (finally regaining the pawn) 14...Qe6 15 Nc4 (15 Qa3+ gets nowhere due to 15...Qd6) 15...Rd8 16 Qa3+ Ke8, and although Black has been denied

castling rights, he stands well. His rooks are not inconvenienced by the king's position, while he can boast the bishop pair and so he should have full equality.

6...exd4 7 0-0

White continues in gambit style; i.e. developing rapidly in order to exploit the open lines. A pawn or two deficit is a secondary consideration. The alternative, 7 Qb3!?, is considered in the next game.

7...Nge7 (Diagram 7)

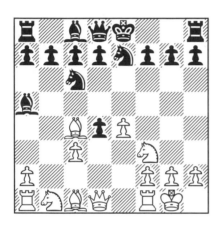

Diagram 7 (W)
Preparing ...d7-d5

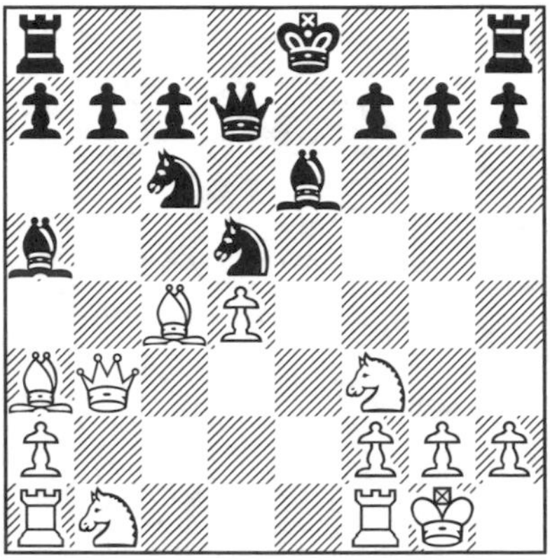

Diagram 8 (W)
Not worrying about b7

Preparing to play ...d7-d5 and not getting distracted by further greedy temptations.

8 cxd4

I actually think that 8 Ng5 is the strongest move here, against which, as in the Two Knights Defence, Black's best reply is 8...d5!. For example, 9 exd5 Ne5 10 Qxd4 (after 10 Bb3 0-0 11 Nxh7 Kxh7 12 Qh5+ Kg8 13 Qxe5 Nf5 14 Bd2 c5 15 dxc6 bxc6 Black had equalized in N.Short-M.Adams, Sarajevo 2000) 10...f6 11 Bb5+ (11 Bb3 Bb6 12 Qa4+ Bd7 13 Qe4 Bf5 14 Qa4+ Bd7 was drawn by repetition in F.Zeller-O.Boguslavsky, German League 2004) 11...c6 12 dxc6 bxc6 13 Be2 0-0 is unclear. At least with 8 Ng5 White isn't worse, whereas after 8 cxd4 I'm less sure.

8...d5 9 exd5 Nxd5 10 Ba3

I have also faced 10 Qb3, when Black must play 10...Be6! (maintaining the d5-strong point; the b7-pawn is less important) 11 Qxb7 Ndb4 12 Ne5, and now

12...Nxe5 13 Bxe6 Nec6 led to complications where Black was somewhat better, N.Doghri-G.Flear, Djerba 1998; but 12...Nxd4! would have best confirmed his superiority.

10...Be6!? 11 Qb3 Qd7!? (Diagram 8)

The solid 11...Bb4 is recommended by some, but it offers fewer winning chances for Black, so I still prefer my move. After 11...Bb4, best play could be 12 Bxb4 Ncxb4 13 a3 Nc6 14 Qxb7 Na5 15 Qb5+ (or 15 Qa6 Nxc4 16 Qc6+ Ke7 17 Qxc4 Re8, as suggested by influential analyst Marin) 15...c6 16 Qc5 Qb6 with equality.

12 Nbd2

Now 12 Qxb7?? is not recommended in view of 12...Rb8 13 Qa6 Rb6 winning material. Instead, 12 Ne5 may be strongest, when 12...Nxe5 13 Qxb7 Qc8 14 Bxd5 Qxb7 15 Bxb7 Rb8 16 Be4 is given as better for White by Marin, but Black has 16...f5! 17 Bc2 Nc4 18 Bc5 Bb6 with equal chances.

12...Bxd2

Black exchanges off some pieces to reduce the attacking potential of White's army.

 NOTE: It's often mentioned that the defender should aim to exchange pieces, whereas the attacking player should keep them on, but such broad generalities have many exceptions. What is left on the board is what matters.

13 Nxd2 Na5 14 Qg3 Nxc4 15 Nxc4

Here capturing the other knight's pawn is plausible, but definitely has its downside: 15 Qxg7? 0-0-0 16 Nxc4 Rhg8 17 Qxh7 Rxg2+! 18 Kxg2 Bh3+! with a winning attack.

15...f6

Defending g7, covering e5, and even preparing a potential escape square on f7 for the king. White has some play for the pawn, but Black's defences seem solid enough.

16 Qf3 0-0-0!

The best practical decision.

17 Rfc1 Kb8 18 Rab1 Nb6!

Protecting his majesty is Black's main priority for the moment.

19 Nxb6 cxb6! (Diagram 9)

I like this move. Capturing in this anti-intuitive way enables Black to form an impenetrable fortress around his king, after which he can turn his attention to other issues. For instance, if 20 Rb4 (defending the d-pawn) 20...Rc8 and Black is ready to seize the initiative.

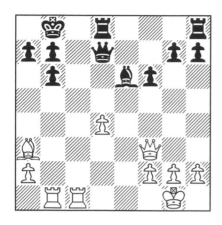

Diagram 9 (W)	**Diagram 10 (W)**
The black king is secure	Black has a winning attack

20 h3!?

Stopping ...Bg4 and giving some luft for his own king. The d-pawn is left *en prise*, but capturing it looks risky at first sight.

20...Qxd4!

Taking up the gauntlet! White's aim to complicate matters leads to a forcing line where Black comes out on top

21 Be7 Rd5 22 Qg3+ Qe5 23 Qxg7

In for a penny... but now Black obtains a winning attack.

23...Rg8 24 Qxf6 Qe4 (Diagram 10) 25 f3

I was hoping for 25 g4, when I had a nice finish in mind: 25...Rxg4+! 26 hxg4 Qxg4+ 27 Kf1 Rd1+! 28 Rxd1 Bc4+ 29 Ke1 Qe2 mate.

25...Qe2 26 Qf4+ Ka8 27 g4 Rd2 28 Qg3 Qe3+ 29 Kh1 Bd5 30 Rf1

Saving his king...

30...Qxe7 0-1

...but not the game.

Game 19
□ N.Short ■ P.H.Nielsen
Skanderborg 2003

1 e4 e5 2 Nf3 Nc6 3 Bc4 Bc5 4 b4 Bxb4 5 c3 Ba5 6 d4 exd4 7 Qb3!? (Diagram 11)

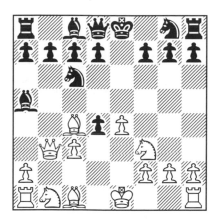

Diagram 11 (B)

A more dangerous line

Diagram 12 (B)

White is very active

Something of a Nigel Short speciality and, in my opinion, more dangerous than 7 0-0.

7...Qe7

Black has to choose between this and another queen move, 7...Qf6. Then N.Short-J.Piket, Zürich 2001, continued 8 0-0 Bb6 9 e5 Qg6 10 cxd4 Na5 11 Qa4 Nxc4 12 Qxc4 Ne7 13 Ba3 Qe6 14 d5!? (throwing more wood on the fire) 14...Qxd5 15 Qe2 Ng6 16 Nc3, and now Black should be fine after 16...Qe6 17 Qe4 f6!.

8 0-0 Bb6

Placing the bishop on a safer square and threatening ...Na5.

9 cxd4 Nxd4

Capturing this key central pawn looks best. Instead, 9...Na5 10 Qa4 Nxc4 11 Qxc4 comes into consideration as it eliminates one of White's dangerous bishops. However, White's centre remains in place and he thus obtains good practical chances: 11...d6 12 a4 c6 13 Nc3 Qd8 14 a5! (destabilizing Black's defences) 14...Bxa5 15 Bg5 f6 16 Bd2 Ne7 17 Rfe1 b5 18 Qb3 Bb6 19 e5! with a strong attack, E.Sutovsky-S.Smagin, Essen 2001.

10 Nxd4 Bxd4 11 Nc3 Nf6 12 Nb5 (Diagram 12) 12...d5

Probably best, as the alternatives 12...Bb6 13 Ba3 d6 14 e5! and 12...Be5 13 Ba3 c5 14 Rac1 Nxe4 15 Rce1 are not appetizing.

13 exd5 Bxa1 14 Ba3 Qe5 15 f4

Black may have an extra rook, but there are some dark storm clouds over his head.

15...Bd4+ 16 Kh1 Qe3 17 Nxd4

Capturing the rook is less wise: 17 Nxc7+ Kd8 18 Nxa8 Qxb3 19 Bxb3 and the knight is trapped in the corner.

17...Qxb3 18 Re1+ Kd8 19 Be7+

Gumming up Black's development.

19...Kd7 20 Nxb3 (Diagram 13)

Diagram 13 (B)

Black is not safe yet

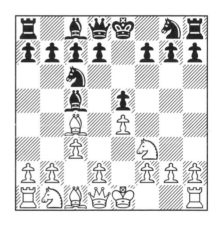

Diagram 14 (B)

The Giuoco Piano

White retains a strong initiative even without queens.

20...c6

Certainly not 20...b6?? 21 Bb5+ and wins.

21 d6 b6 22 Bxf7 c5

Or if 22...Nd5, then 23 Nd4 Nxf4 24 Nf3 with plenty of activity.

23 Nd2 Kc6 24 Nc4 Bf5 25 Ne5+ Kb7 26 a4

Later, Luke McShane suggested 26 Re3! with the idea of Rg3 and Rxg7, which seems to yield some winning chances.

26...h5 27 Bxf6 gxf6 28 Bd5+ Ka6 29 Bc4+ Kb7

But not 29...Ka5?? 30 Nc6+ Kxa4 31 Ra1 mate.

30 Bd5+ Ka6 31 Bc4+ Kb7 ½-½

Giuoco Piano

1 e4 e5 2 Nf3 Nc6 3 Bc4 Bc5 4 c3 (Diagram 14)

Strategy

White threatens to build a centre and Black needs to avoid playing too passively. In the main lines after 4...Nf6 5 d4 exd4 White can capture on d4 or, alternatively, play e4-e5. In both cases the game can become sharp right from the off and it's sometimes easy to forget the strategy. However, Black's most reputable lines involve him challenging in the central arena early on.

Theoretical

The Giuoco Piano (also know as the Italian Game) is one of the oldest openings around and the theory can at times go quite deep into the game. Therefore some book work will be necessary, but this is true of any variation where hand-to-hand fighting arises almost by force.

Game 20
□ A.Hauchard ■ L.Renaze
Cap d'Agde 2006

1 e4 e5 2 Nf3 Nc6 3 Bc4 Bc5 4 c3 Bb6 5 d4 Qe7 (Diagram 15)

With this move Black indicates that he aims to keep the centre solid, and by refusing to capture on d4, he denies the c3-square to a white knight.

6 Bg5!

White has fewer chances of obtaining any advantage if he just continues with routine development; e.g. 6 0-0 d6 7 h3 (stopping ...Bg4, but it could inspire his opponent to seek play against this potential weakness) 7...Nf6 8 Re1, and Black now has a couple of interesting lines with ...g7-g5 featuring in both:

a) 8...0-0 9 a4 a6 10 Bg5 h6 11 Bh4 Kh8 12 Nbd2 Rg8 13 Nf1 g5 14 Bg3 g4 with dynamic counterplay, B.Macieja-A.Chehlov, St Petersburg 1997.

b) 8...h6 9 a4 a6 10 Na3 g5! **(Diagram 16)** – one doesn't need to hit a bishop to play this move! Black seems to be doing fine here. 11 Bf1 (alternatives are probably worse: 11 Nxg5?! hxg5 12 Bxg5 is over-optimistic as after 12...Rg8 13 h4 exd4 14 Bd5 Bg4 15 Qd2 d3 Black was already winning, A.Reggio-S.Tarrasch, Monte Carlo 1903; or 11 dxe5 dxe5 12 Nh2 g4! 13 hxg4 Rg8 14 g5 hxg5 15 Be3 Bxe3 16 Rxe3 Rh8! 17 Bd5 Qf8 and the attack on the h-file was very strong, K.Honfi-M.Damjanovic, Sarajevo 1966) 11...g4 12 hxg4 Bxg4 13 Nc4 Bxd4?! (the more level-headed 13...Ba7! 14 Ne3 0-0-0 would be about equal) 14 cxd4 Nxd4 15 Be2 Nxe2+ 16 Qxe2 Rg8 was V.Spasov-D.Kontic, Niksic 1991. Black has some practical chances for his piece, but perhaps not enough after 17 Ra3!.

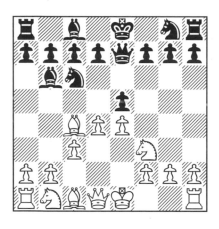

Diagram 15 (W)

Black strongpoints e5

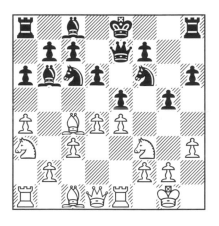

Diagram 16 (W)

Kingside counter-attack

6...Nf6 7 d5 Nd8 8 d6!

This pawn sacrifice keeps Black's development lagging badly on the queenside. Instead, 8 Nbd2 d6 9 Bd3 c6 10 Nc4 Bc7 11 Ne3 h6 12 Bh4 Rg8, as in G.Sax-V.Smyslov, Teesside 1975, gives Black an easier time. White has some space but Black has counterplay.

8...cxd6

The alternative is 8...Qxd6 9 Qxd6 cxd6 10 Bxf6 gxf6 **(Diagram 17)**.

Counting pawns we notice that Black has an extra one, but the gaping holes on d5 and f5 will leave him under pressure, as White sets about occupying these squares with his minor pieces: 11 Nh4 (11 Bd5 is imprecise because of 11...Nc6 12 Na3 f5! 13 Nc4 Bc7 14 Ng5 Ne7) 11...d5 (breathing space is more important than a virtually useless pawn) 12 Bxd5 d6 13 Na3 Be6 14 Rd1 Ke7 15 Nc4 Bc7 16 Ne3 and White retains a positional advantage, Z.Jovanovic-N.Mrkonjic, Osijek 2004.

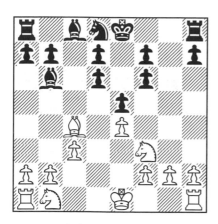

Diagram 17 (W)

Black has weak light squares

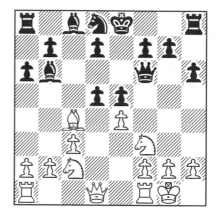

Diagram 18 (W)

Trying to free his position

9 0-0

After the immediate 9 Na3?!, Black could even contemplate grabbing the f-pawn: 9...Bxf2+!? 10 Kf1 (not 10 Kxf2?! Nxe4+) 10...Bb6 11 Nb5 d5! 12 Bxd5 Qc5 13 Qe2 Nxd5 14 exd5 0-0 with good chances, B.Kosmac-N.Jakubovic, Pula 1999.

9...h6

I suspect that 9...Ne6 may be superior, when 10 Bxf6 (or 10 Bh4 Nf4 which has been mentioned elsewhere as 'unclear') 10...Qxf6 11 Qxd6 Bc7 12 Qa3 offers chances for both sides.

10 Bxf6 Qxf6 11 Na3 a6 12 Nc2 d5 (Diagram 18)

It's unpleasant to be blocked in, so it's understandable that Renaze is willing to give back his additional pawn in order to liberate his light-squared bishop. If instead 12...Bc5, trying to hinder the white knight's route to the d5-square, then 13 b4 Ba7 14 Qd3 b5 15 Bd5 Rb8 16 a4 would lead to White retaining his relentless pressure. The extra pawn is of course worthless.

NOTE: It's not the quantity of pawns that count, it's their quality!

13 Qxd5 Nc6 14 Rad1 Bc7 15 Ne3 d6 16 Qd3

The knight is ready to hop to d5.

16...Ne7 17 Ne1!

Now the other knight joins in the manoeuvring game.

17...0-0 18 N1c2 Kh8 19 Nb4 (Diagram 19)

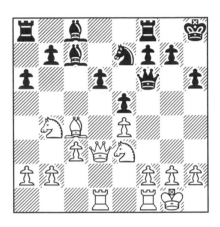

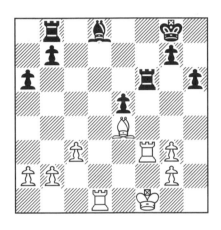

Diagram 19 (B)

The knights aim at d5

Diagram 20 (W)

White can win a pawn

Bearing down on d5! White has ensured the control of this outpost for some time.

19...Qg6 20 Nbd5 Nxd5 21 Nxd5 Bd8 22 f4 f5!

Attempting to free his position.

23 Qg3

Trading off Black's most useful piece. Another approach is 23 Qe3 Re8 24 Nb6, but then 24...exf4 25 Rxf4 d5! could complicate matters.

23...Qxg3 24 hxg3 Be6

If 24...Re8 25 fxe5 (25 exf5 Bxf5 26 Ne3?? fails to 26...Bb6) 25...Rxe5, then 26 g4!? maintains the initiative.

25 exf5 Bxd5

Seeking solace with opposite-coloured bishops. The following ending is better for White, but not necessarily winning.

26 Bxd5 Rxf5 27 Rf3

Avoiding 27 Bxb7?? Bb6+ when White is embarrassed.

27...Rb8 28 Be4 Rf6 29 Kf1 Kg8?!

29...Be7 30 fxe5 Re6 (not 30...dxe5? 31 Rd7) 31 exd6 Rxe4 32 dxe7 Rxe7 is somewhat better, although White still emerges with an extra pawn.

30 fxe5 dxe5 (Diagram 20) 31 Bxb7!

Winning a pawn.

31...Rxb7 32 Rxd8+ Kf7 33 b3 Ke6 34 Ra8 Rb6 35 Ke2 e4

Black's last chance is to generate some counterplay with the e-pawn, but White has everything under control.

36 Rxf6+ gxf6 37 Re8+ Kd5 38 Ke3 f5 39 c4+ Kd6 40 Kf4 Kd7 41 Rf8 Re6 42 Rxf5 e3 43 Rd5+ Kc6 44 Rd1 Kc5 45 Kf3 a5 46 Ke2 Rg6 47 Kxe3 Rxg3+ 48 Kf2 Rc3 49 Rd5+ Kb6 50 Rb5+ Ka6 51 Rh5 Rc2+ 52 Kf3 Rxa2 53 Rxh6+ Ka7 54 Rh5 Kb6 55 g4 a4 56 c5+ Kc6 57 bxa4 Rxa4 58 Re5 1-0

Game 21
□ N.Ninov ■ A.Rizouk
San Sebastian 2008

---

1 e4 e5 2 Nf3 Nc6 3 Bc4 Bc5 4 c3 Nf6 5 d4 exd4 (Diagram 21)

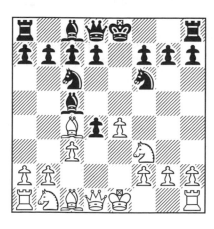

Diagram 21 (W)

Position after 5...exd4

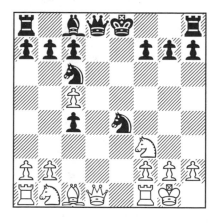

Diagram 22 (W)

Black is okay

6 e5

The main lines with 6 cxd4 Bb4+ are considered in the next three games. Whereas after 6 0-0 Black is able to equalize very quickly if he remembers the following few moves: 6...Nxe4! (not being afraid of the pin on the e-file) 7 cxd4 d5! (a timely counterpunch) 8 dxc5 (after 8 Bb5?! Bd6 Black has a clear extra pawn) 8...dxc4 **(Diagram 22)** 9 Qxd8+ (instead 9 Qe2 requires 9...Qd3! 10 Re1 f5 11 Nc3 0-0 12 Nxe4 fxe4 13 Qxe4 Bf5 14 Qh4 Rae8 with equality, D.Paulsen-V.Hort, Porz 1982) 9...Kxd8 10 Rd1+ Bd7 11 Be3 (now Black wriggles to harmonize his pieces) 11...Ke7 12 Na3 Be6 13 Rdc1 Rhd8 14 Nxc4 Rd5 with an edge to Black, B.Stein-O.Moen, Gausdal 1986.

6...d5 7 Bb5 Ne4 8 cxd4 (Diagram 23)

| **Diagram 23 (B)** | **Diagram 24 (W)** |
| Where should the bishop go? | Black must play actively |

8...Bb6!

Many players have opted for 8...Bb4+, but from bitter experience I find the resulting positions unpleasant to play with Black: 9 Bd2 Nxd2 (or 9...Bxd2+ 10 Nbxd2 Bd7 11 Bxc6 Bxc6 12 0-0 0-0 13 Rc1 a5 14 Re1 a4 15 Re3 and Black lacks a good plan, N.Ninov-G.Flear, Gien 2004) 10 Bxc6+ bxc6 11 Nbxd2 0-0 12 Rc1! (a Ninov speciality) 12...c5 13 dxc5 Bg4 14 0-0 Bxd2 15 Qxd2 Bxf3 16 gxf3 c6 17 f4 and Black was just a pawn down in N.Ninov-J.Zawadzka, Kalamaria 2006.

9 Be3

White often starts with 9 Nc3, and only after 9...0-0 does he play 10 Be3; for example, 10...Ne7 (more dynamic is 10...Bg4!? 11 Bxc6 bxc6 12 h3 Bh5 13 0-0 f5 14 Ne2 g5 15 Ng3 Bg6 with chances for both sides, N.Ninov-P.Schlosser, French Team Ch. 2008) 11 0-0 c6 12 Bd3 Nxc3 13 bxc3 Bf5 with solid equality, B.Macieja-L.Aronian, European Ch., Antalya 2004.

If White interposes 10 Bxc6 bxc6 before playing 11 Be3, Black has an enticing option in 11...f5!; e.g. 12 exf6 Qxf6 13 Nxe4 dxe4 14 Nd2 Ba6 15 Nxe4 Ba5+ 16 Nc3 Bxc3+ 17 bxc3 Qg6, when he obtained a strong attack on the light squares, B.Macieja-G.Vescovi, Bermuda 2004.

9...0-0 10 Bxc6 bxc6 (Diagram 24)

Black has to live with damaged pawns, so in order to compete he will need to find a way to stoke up counterplay, which will in turn involve getting his light-squared bishop working.

11 0-0 Bg4 12 Qc1

Unpinning while attacking a pawn.

12...f6

Alternatively, 12...f5!? 13 Nc3 f4 14 Bxf4 Bxf3 15 gxf3 Nxc3 16 bxc3 Rf5 17 Be3 Qh4 was complex in S.Cramton-V.Kosyrev, Internet (freestyle) 2005.

13 Qxc6 Bxf3 14 Qe6+ Kh8 15 gxf3 fxe5! (Diagram 25)

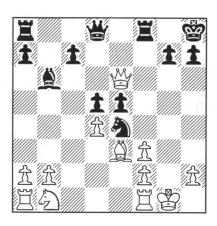
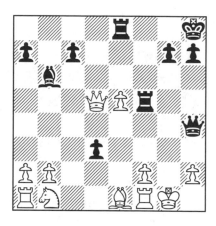

Diagram 25 (W)
Sacrificing for an attack

Diagram 26 (W)
White must defend carefully

Rizouk's big idea; Black burns his bridges seeking an attack.

16 fxe4 exd4 17 Bd2 Qh4 18 e5

Instead, 18 f3 holds onto certain squares but cedes others. Then a plausible line such as 18...Rae8 19 Qxd5 Qh3 20 Ba5 Re6! leaves the white king in dire straits, and the further 21 Rf2 c6 enables Black to win back his piece with interest.

18...d3 19 Be1

A sad retreat, but f2 needs defending.

19...Rae8 20 Qxd5 Rf5 (Diagram 26) 21 Qxd3

Here 21 Qc6!? comes into consideration but is ultimately suspicious: 21...Rfxe5 22 Nd2 R5e6 (note that at present 22...Rxe1? 23 Raxe1 Rxe1?? fails because of the back rank mate after 24 Qa8+) 23 Qf3 Bd4 24 Rb1 (24 Qxd3 now allows 24...Rxe1!) 24...Be5 25 h3 Rf6 and the attack is more than worth the piece; e.g. 26 Qxd3 (not 26 Qg4?? Rg6) 26...Qf4 27 Nf3 Qxf3 28 Qxf3 Rxf3 29 Kg2 Rd3 and Black is better.

21...Rg5+ 22 Kh1 Qg4

White now has little choice.

23 Qd5 Rgxe5 24 Qg2 Qxg2+ 25 Kxg2 Rxe1 26 Nc3 R1e5

Black has regained his piece but the exchange of queens has put paid to his attacking ambitions.

27 Rad1 h6 28 Rd3 R8e6 29 Rfd1 Rf5 30 R1d2 Kh7 ½-½

A creative effort by Black.

Game 22
☐ O.Nikolenko ■ D.Jakovenko
Moscow 2006

1 e4 e5 2 Nf3 Nc6 3 Bc4 Bc5 4 c3 Nf6 5 d4 exd4 6 cxd4 Bb4+ 7 Bd2 (Diagram 27) 7...Bxd2+

Instead, 7...Nxe4!? is my favourite way of handling this position; e.g. 8 Bxb4 Nxb4 9 Bxf7+ Kxf7 10 Qb3+ **(Diagram 28)**, when Black should be able to equalize, though obtaining winning chances involves some risk:

a) 10...Kf8 11 Qxb4+ Qe7 12 Qxe7+ Kxe7 13 0-0 Re8 14 Re1 Kf8 15 Na3 and now 15...c6! (15...Nf6 16 Nb5 Nd5 was slightly precarious for Black in V.Berlinsky-P.Motwani, Istanbul Olympiad 2000) 16 Ne5 d5 equalizes.

b) 10...d5!? (the ambitious choice) 11 Ne5+ Ke6 12 Qxb4 c5!? (12...Qf8 is comfortable for Black) 13 Qb5!? (a fairly new idea which caught me out recently) 13...a6 14 Qe2 cxd4 15 Nf3 Re8 16 0-0 with chances for both sides, E.Lie-M.Thinius, Gausdal 2003. Black's king needs to scurry away to safety and White will win back the d4-pawn.

8 Nbxd2 d5

This liberating move is considered to offer Black a reasonable game.

9 exd5 Nxd5 10 Qb3 Nce7

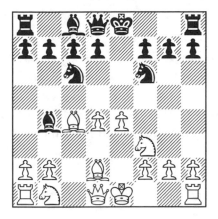

Diagram 27 (B)

This line is just equal

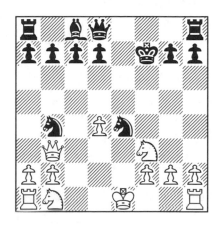

Diagram 28 (B)

White regains the piece

Although 10...Na5 is perfectly playable, it allows the repetition 11 Qa4+ Nc6 12 Qb3 and so on which may not suit everyone as Black. I personally don't like allowing this type of possibility in my own games.

White can of course try for more; e.g. 12 Bb5 (or 12 Ne5 0-0 13 Nxc6 Qe8+ 14 Kf1 Nb6, J.Cubas-S.Mareco, Mario Covas 2008) 12...Qe7+ 13 Ne5 Bd7 14 0-0 Nb6 15 Nxc6 bxc6 16 Qc2 cxb5 17 Rae1 Be6 18 d5 0-0 19 dxe6 fxe6 20 Qb3 Rad8, R.Zelcic-S.Mamedyarov, European Team Ch., Leon 2001, but in both cases Black has a comfortable game.

11 0-0 0-0 12 Rfe1 c6 (Diagram 29)

Black has a solid grip on the d5-square and his opponent's attacking chances, typical of IQP positions, are not a major worry.

13 Ne4

Here 13 a4 is often played. The motive is not to prevent ...b7-b5, which Black isn't intending for the time being, but to give White the options of Qb3-a3 (keeping the queens on) as well as a4-a5 (gaining space).

If, for example, White instead plays the natural-looking 13 Ne5, Black can respond with 13...Qb6 when the exchange of queens ensures comfortable equality, while

14 Qa3?! Qxd4 15 Nef3 Qf6 16 Ne4 Qf4 17 Nd6 Nf5 gave White insufficient compensation in D.Smerdon-D.Prasenjit, New Delhi 2007.

After the more critical 13 a4, Black has to decide how to react:

a) If now 13...Qb6, both 14 a5 and 14 Qa3 aren't straightforward for Black.

b) 13...a5 is perhaps simplest; e.g. 14 Ne5 Qc7 15 Ndf3 h6 16 Re2 Be6 17 Rae1 Rad8 18 Nd3 b6 with a rock-solid set-up, G.Arold-J.Gustafsson, Internet (blitz) 2004.

c) 13...Rb8!?, keeping the tension, is another try: 14 Ne4 (or 14 a5 f6!? 15 Ne4 Kh8 16 Qa3 Bg4 17 h3 Bh5 18 Nc5 Re8 19 Ne6 and despite the ugly hole on e6 Black was solid in C.Garcia Fernandez-O.Korneev, Madrid 2002) 14...Bf5 15 Qa3 h6 16 Rac1 a5 17 Ne5 Bxe4 18 Rxe4 Nf5, J.Nun-L.Keitlinghaus, Czech League 1994, and as in many IQP positions, White's pieces are slightly more active but Black has the better structure.

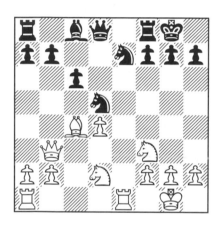

Diagram 29 (W)

Black has no worries

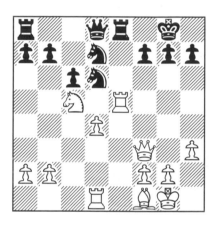

Diagram 30 (W)

Forcing further exchanges

13...Nb6

Now after 13...Qb6 White is able to sidestep the exchange of queens (as d4 isn't *en prise*); i.e. 14 Qa3 Bf5 15 Nc5 Qc7 16 Rac1 a5 17 Ne5 Rad8 18 Qf3 with an enduring initiative, R.Mamedov-A.Czernowski, Internet (blitz) 2004.

14 Bf1

A solid but somewhat slow way of reorganizing. However, the impatient 14 Bxf7+!? Rxf7 15 Neg5 Nbd5, R.Zelcic-B.Golubovic, Rijeka 2001, shouldn't be a problem for Black; while 14 Bd3 just encourages 14...Bf5! (an opportune moment to develop the bishop and stronger than 14...Ned5 15 Nc5 Rb8 16 Rac1 Nf4 17 Bb1

Qf6 18 Ne5 Qg5 19 Qf3 f6 20 Ned3 Nbd5 21 Nxf4 Nxf4 22 h4!, E.Van den Doel-I.Sokolov, Dutch Ch., Leeuwarden 2004, when Black's pseudo-active pieces were shown to be vulnerable) 15 Nc5 Bxd3 16 Qxd3 Rb8 17 Qa3 Nec8 18 Rad1 Nd6 19 Ne5 Qc7 20 Qg3 Rbd8 with equality, Nay Oo Kyaw Tun-A.Stefanova, Surabaya 2002.

14...Nf5 15 Rad1 Nd6 16 Nc5

Exchanging a pair of knights with 16 Nxd6 Qxd6 17 h3 Be6 suits Black fine, since if White fails to obtain anything concrete from his initiative, Black may start to think about how to exploit his superior structure.

16...Bg4

The bishop finally finds a way to develop.

17 h3 Bxf3 18 Qxf3 Re8 19 Re5 Nd7 (Diagram 30)

Forcing further exchanges.

20 Rxe8+ Qxe8 21 Qb3 Nb6 22 g3

The bishop will be redeployed to g2 to bear down on d5.

22...Qe7 23 Qa3

Threatening Nxb7!.

23...Qc7 24 Bg2 Rd8 25 b4 h6 26 Qb3

White has a positional threat of a well-timed advance d4-d5 (leading generally to a slight pull despite a symmetrical structure), but Black avoids this possibility.

26...Nb5 27 Qb2 Nc4 28 Qc1 Nb6 29 Qe3 Nc4 30 Qc1 Nb6 31 Qe3 Nc4 32 Qc1 Nb6 33 Qe3 Nc4 ½-½

Not very exciting, but a typical example of White's play being nullified if Black can obtain harmonious development.

Game 23
☐ N.Kurenkov ■ M.Turov
Moscow 2007

---

1 e4 e5 2 Nf3 Nc6 3 Bc4 Bc5 4 c3 Nf6 5 d4 exd4 6 cxd4 Bb4+ 7 Nc3 (Diagram 31) 7...Nxe4!

Here 7...d5 is inferior, as after 8 exd5 Nxd5 9 0-0 White has the advantage in all lines; e.g. 9...Bxc3 10 bxc3 0-0 11 Qd3 Nce7 12 Ba3 Re8 13 Ng5 Bf5 14 Qf3 and Black is under intolerable pressure, C.Garcia Fernandez-G.Yanez Acin, Lorca 2001.

8 0-0 Bxc3

Again Black has only one good move, since 8...Nxc3?! 9 bxc3 d5 (after 9...Bxc3?! 10 Ba3! White has a strong attack) 10 cxb4 dxc4 11 Re1+ Ne7 12 Qe2 Be6 13 Bg5 seems to favour White; e.g. 13...Qd5 14 Bxe7 Kxe7 15 Qc2 f6 16 Ng5! fxg5 17 Re5 Qxd4 18 Rae1 as pointed out by Bogoljubow.

9 d5!

This is known as the Møller Attack. Otherwise 9 bxc3 d5 leaves White short of compensation.

9...Bf6

The main line, in which Black retains his bishop.

10 Re1 Ne7 11 Rxe4 d6 (Diagram 32)

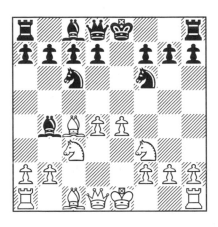

Diagram 31 (B)

The Møller Attack

Diagram 32 (W)

The main line

Many games have reached this position. For the pawn deficit White has the better development and more space and Black will have to defend precisely to keep his head above water. Objectively though I have to prefer Black.

Actually Black can also play 11...0-0 here (or on the previous move), since 12 d6 isn't as dangerous as previously thought: e.g. 12...cxd6 13 Bg5 (13 Qxd6 Nf5 14 Qd5 Ne7 15 Qd6 Nf5 is a draw by repetition) 13...d5 14 Bxd5 Nxd5 15 Qxd5 d6 16 Bxf6!? (otherwise 16 Rd4 is near equality) 16...Qxf6 17 Nd4 Rb8 18 Rae1 b6, as in J.Iruzubieta-G.Milos, Elgoibar 1993, leaves White slightly worse even after his best line 19 Nc6 Bb7 20 b4.

12 Bg5

The self-weakening tactical try 12 g4 isn't quite correct: 12...0-0 13 g5 Be5 14 Nxe5 Bf5!? (14...dxe5 15 Rxe5 Ng6 is also fine for Black) 15 Re1 dxe5 16 Rxe5 Qd7 17 Qf3 Ng6 18 Re1 Rfe8 and Black is for preference, C.Velasquez-C.Salas, Santiago 1997.

12...Bxg5 13 Nxg5 h6 14 Qe2

A practical necessity. Instead, 14 Nf3 0-0 just leaves Black a clear pawn up, while 14 Qh5 is also met by the cool-headed 14...0-0!.

14...hxg5 15 Re1

White's tripled-up major pieces ensure that he regains the piece, so Black now blocks the e-file to ease the pressure.

15...Be6! 16 dxe6

16 Re3!? is a recent nuance, but after 16...c6! 17 dxe6 f6 play transposes back to my recommended defence in the main line.

16...f6 (Diagram 33)

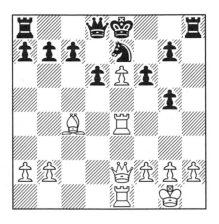

Diagram 33 (W)
Analysis favours Black here

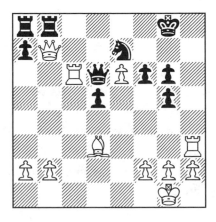

Diagram 34 (B)
White turns the tables

White must have mixed feelings about his passed pawn on e6. On the one hand it ties his opponent down to defence, but on the other it blocks the activity of his own pieces. Furthermore, White will always be a pawn down now and, with few prospects of launching any immediate attack, will need patience to probe away on all fronts, trying to provoke an error. Meanwhile Black is a long way from completing development and has yet to find a secure shelter for his king, so unravelling will require due care and attention.

It used to be thought that White could generally create enough play to justify his material deficit, but the most recent analyses suggest that with best play Black should come out on top.

17 Re3 g6?!

Probably not the best. Similar but preferable is 17...Kf8 18 Rh3!? (a typical plan to shake up the kingside) 18...Rxh3 19 gxh3 g6, when Black comes out more happily: 20 Qf3 Kg7 (20...f5? is bad due to 21 Qc3) 21 Qxb7 Qc8 22 Qf3 Rb8 23 b3 Qb7 24 Qd3 Rh8 with good play, A.Pyhala-L.Dobrovsky, Odessa 1989. Things seem easier for Black to handle now that a pair of rooks have been exchanged.

However, this is all just for the record. Instead, 17...c6! is best, as after 18 Rh3 Rxh3 19 gxh3 g6 White doesn't seem to be able to worry his opponent; e.g. 20 Qf3 (20 b4 Qb6 21 Qb2 0-0-0 22 b5 Rf8 is complicated, but Black is on top) 20...Qa5 21 Kf1 (21 Rd1 is also calmly met by 21...Qf5; while 21 Qxf6 Qxe1+ 22 Bf1 0-0-0, R.Bancod-S.Iuldachev, Jakarta 1997, is even worse) 21...Qf5 22 Qg4 0-0-0 and White runs out of steam, G.Sergeev-M.Novikov, Tula 2006.

18 Qf3

Forking the f6- and b7-pawns.

18...0-0

Black gets to castle but the pawn on e6 keeps his pieces tied up, so it's not evident that he is really any closer to co-ordinating his forces.

19 Qxb7 d5 20 Bd3 Qd6 21 Rc1 c6 22 Rh3!

The rook is quite actively placed here, which is one of the reasons it's often better for Black to eschew castling and leave his rook on the h-file.

22...Rfb8

The e-pawn is taboo: 22...Qxe6?? 23 Re3 etc.

23 Rxc6! (Diagram 34)

A strong blow that ensures some advantage for White.

23...Qxh2+

Otherwise 23...Rxb7 24 Rxd6 Rxb2 25 Rd7 Re8 26 Rxa7 is complex, but the outside passed a-pawn gives White an edge.

24 Kxh2 Rxb7 25 Rc2 Rb6 26 Re3 Rab8 27 b3

Material is now equal, and Black is still restricted by the passed e6-pawn.

27...f5?!

27...R8b7 would keep White's advantage down to a minimum.

28 Rc7 R8b7 29 Rd7 Kf8 30 Ba6!

A neat move that soon leads to a significant material gain.

30...Rxd7 31 exd7 Rd6 32 Bb5 d4

32...Kf7 33 Rc3 Ke6 34 Rc8 Rxd7 35 Bxd7+ Kxd7 was a lesser evil, but White should eventually be able to win here too.

33 Re6! Rd5 34 Rf6+ Kg7 35 Rf7+! Kxf7 36 Bc4 1-0

If Black insists on struggling on with 36...Nc6 then 37 Bxd5+ Ke7 38 Bxc6 d3 39 b4 d2 40 Ba4 and White comes out a piece to the good.

Game 24
☐ M.Vanderbeeken ■ G.Flear
Montpellier 2005

1 e4 e5 2 Nf3 Nc6 3 Bc4 Bc5 4 c3 Nf6 5 d4 exd4 6 cxd4 Bb4+ 7 Nc3 Nxe4 8 0-0 Bxc3 9 d5 Ne5 (Diagram 35)

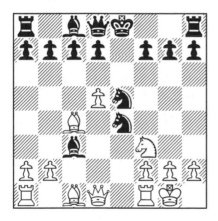 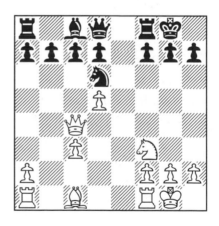

Diagram 35 (W)	Diagram 36 (W)
A safer approach for Black	White may not have enough

I like this move which avoids a great deal of theory. Kasparov apparently suggested this approach to Anand some years ago, before the Indian took on *Fritz 6* in a 'Man vs. Machine' match. It does seem to take the sting out of White's play and is simpler than 9...Bf6 (as in the previous game).

10 Qe2!?

Otherwise 10 bxc3 Nxc4 11 Qd4 and then 11...0-0! transposes back to the game. If Black gets greedy with 11...Ncd6, he will probably be mated very quickly; e.g. 12 Qxg7 Qf6 13 Qxf6 Nxf6 14 Re1+ Kf8 15 Bh6+ Kg8 16 Re5 Nde4 17 Nd2, J.Blauert-E.Schmittdiel, Königslutter 1988, and Black felt compelled to resign in view of 17...d6 18 Nxe4! dxe5 19 Nxf6 mate. Nice!

10...0-0 11 bxc3 Nxc4 12 Qxc4

Black also answers 12 Qxe4 with 12...Nd6.

12...Nd6 (Diagram 36)

It isn't totally clear that White really has enough for his pawn here. However, he would have following 12...Re8!? 13 Re1 Nd6 14 Rxe8+ Nxe8 15 Bg5, as with Black being too far behind in development White's initiative would persist. Exchanging a pair of rooks doesn't suit Black if his remaining rook will remain out of play for the duration.

13 Qd3

There are a couple of other moves, but they aren't dangerous for Black either: 13 Qf4 (or 13 Qd4 Nf5 14 Qd3 d6 15 Bg5, and now the untried 15...Qd7! could be best) 13...Re8 14 Re1 Rxe1+ 15 Nxe1 b5 16 Be3 Bb7 17 Rd1 Nc4 and Black took control, A.Zude-B.Spassky, German League 1990.

13...b6

In *Dangerous Weapons: 1 e4 e5* I mentioned 13...Qf6!? as possibly being better. Then White could try 14 Re1 b6 15 Bg5 Qf5 16 Qxf5 Nxf5 17 g4 h6 18 Bf4 Nd6 19 Bxd6 cxd6 20 Nd4, V.Anicic-B.Abramovic, Bar Sozina 2005, with an analogous position to the next note, where White was struggling to find full compensation.

14 Bg5!

Best, as it forces Black to make a concession; whereas 14 Ba3 doesn't test his defences: 14...Qf6 15 Qd4 (15 Nd4 Re8 16 Rfe1 Bb7 also enables Black to develop comfortably) 15...Qxd4 16 Nxd4 Bb7 17 Bxd6 cxd6 18 Nf5 (or if 18 c4 then 18...Rfc8 19 Rfc1 Ba6) 18...g6 19 Nxd6 Bxd5 20 Rfe1 Be6 and Black was somewhat better, *Fritz 6*-V.Anand, 3rd matchgame, Frankfurt 1999.

14...f6 15 Bf4 Bb7

15...Nf7 could be met by 16 d6!?.

16 Rfe1 Re8 17 c4

In my opinion the best chance for White is 17 Bxd6 cxd6 18 c4, locking up Black's bishop for a while, and the further 18...Ba6 19 Nd4 Qc7 20 Nf5 Re5 21 Rxe5 fxe5 22 Qg3 g6 23 Qg5 enabled White to equalize in T.Maas-Yin Hao, Rotterdam 1998.

17...Rxe1+ 18 Rxe1 Qf8 19 Bxd6 Qxd6 20 Nd4 g6 21 h4 Rf8 22 h5 Kg7 23 Qe3 (Diagram 37)

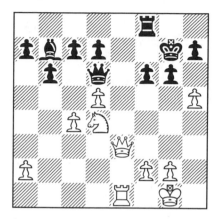

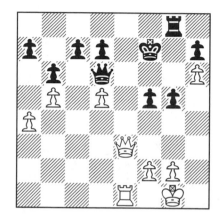

Diagram 37 (B)

Black still has the pawn

Diagram 38 (W)

Playing to win the h6-pawn

Although White has persistent pressure for the pawn, Black, who isn't in any real danger, has high hopes of unravelling and ultimately exploiting his material advantage.

 TIP: In positions where you have survived a gambit onslaught and would like to exploit your extra material, there can be great technical difficulties if your opponent still has the more active pieces, even if he has no direct threats. Often the best way to proceed is to adopt a 'slow but sure' approach; i.e. making sure that that you consolidate, improve your pieces, and nullify any potential avenues of attack before breaking out.

23...Ba6 24 h6+ Kf7 25 Nb5 Bxb5 26 cxb5

As White has control of the e-file, and Black a slightly vulnerable king, any attempts to break free are fraught with danger. So I decided to proceed with caution.

26...Rc8 27 a4 Qf8 28 Qb3 Qd6 29 Qe3 f5 30 Qd4 Qf6 31 Qc4 Qd6 32 Qd4 Rg8 33 Qe3 g5! (Diagram 38)

Finally showing my hand. The plan is simply to pick off the white h-pawn.

34 Qe2

Hebden's suggestion of 34 Qc3! could be best; for example, 34...Kg6 35 Rc1 Kxh6 36 Qxc7 Qxd5 37 Qxa7 Rg6, and now 38 a5 bxa5 39 Qxa5 yields good drawing chances for White, despite being a pawn down.

34...Kg6 35 Qd3 Rf8 36 g4

A last attempt to 'stay active', but now White's king becomes the one in most danger.

36...Kxh6 37 gxf5 Qf6 38 Qh3+ Kg7 39 Re3 Rf7 40 Rc3 Qe5 41 Qg3 Qxf5 42 Rxc7 Qxd5 43 Qc3+ Kg6 44 Rc8 Rf4 45 Qc2+ Kh6 46 Rc3 Rh4 47 f3 Rd4 0-1

Summary

After a little home study, Black should accept the Evans Gambit, when he can look forward to a good game. This is far preferable to declining the pawn, as then White gets a big position for free.

Most variations of the Giuoco Piano are perfectly fine for Black too, but only if one has a decent grounding in theory. In my opinion the most challenging line is 6 e5 (see Game 21), as the resulting positions are murky and the theory hasn't been fully investigated.

Chapter Four
Four Knights Game

Introduction

1 e4 e5 2 Nf3 Nc6 3 Nc3 Nf6 (Diagram 1)

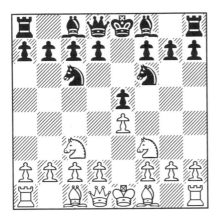

Diagram 1 (W)

The Four Knights Game

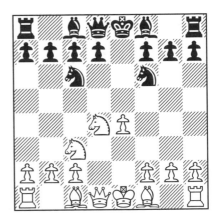

Diagram 2 (B)

The Scotch Four Knights

The diagram hints at why the opening was so-called! The Three Knights Game has an equally appropriate name and occurs at this point if Black tries various alternatives to 3...Nf6. However, these are rare and frankly inferior so I'll be concentrating on the natural development of the king's knight.

In the Four Knights the players bring out the cavalry before committing their other pieces. White has the privilege of going first so he has the choice of picking the type of game that arises with his fourth move.

The two main ideas are quite different in nature. The Scotch Four Knights (a hybrid system which can arise either via the Scotch Opening or the Four Knights move order) involves 4 d4 and leads to an open centre, whereas the slightly more popular Spanish Four Knights with...

4 Bb5

...tends to lead to a relatively closed centre after Black's main reply...

4...Bb4

...when the position remains symmetrical for the moment. A couple of other worthwhile tries by Black at the this point are 4...Nd4 and 4...Bd6 as in the final two games in this chapter.

Scotch Four Knights

1 e4 e5 2 Nf3 Nc6 3 Nc3 Nf6 4 d4 exd4 5 Nxd4 (Diagram 2)

The typical continuation is 5...Bb4 6 Nxc6 bxc6 7 Bd3 d5 8 exd5 cxd5 9 0-0 0-0 10 Bg5 (see Games 25 and 26).

Strategy

White presses with his slightly more active pieces. Black has to begin cautiously by supporting his centre and gradually activating and negating White's early initiative. In the later stages of the game Black's central preponderance may offer him chances for an advantage.

Theoretical

There have been many games in this line, but despite this, and the fact that the centre is fairly open, natural development and sensible piece deployment are more important than memory recall.

The two illustrative games below were both played in the same event by David Howell. The main problem he faced when preparing this line with Black was to find a way to obtain dynamic chances as well as a solid position. At the first attempt he fell for a tactical trick, but in Game 26 he produced some fireworks of his own.

Game 25
□ **W.So** ■ **D.Howell**
World Junior Championship, Yerevan 2007

---

1 e4 e5 2 Nf3 Nc6 3 Nc3 Nf6 4 d4

Setting the pace by seeking an open centre.

White also has two slightly offbeat ideas which tempt Black to commit himself: 4

a3 and 4 g3. Black can indeed play 4...d5 in both cases.

a) 4 a3 d5! 5 Bb5 (5 exd5 Nxd5 leads to the main line of the Scotch Four Knights *with reversed colours*, where the extra move a2-a3 makes little difference) 5...Nxe4 6 Nxe5 Qf6 and in my opinion White has nothing.

b) 4 g3 (the Glek System) 4...d5 5 exd5 Nxd5 6 Bg2 Nxc3 7 bxc3 Bd6 8 0-0 0-0 **(Diagram 3)** reaches a complex position; e.g. 9 Rb1 (or 9 d3 Bg4 10 h3 Bh5 11 Rb1 Rb8 12 g4 Bg6 13 Ng5 Be7 14 Ne4 f5!? with chances for both sides, J.Ehlvest-G.Kaidanov, US Open, Los Angeles 2003) 9...Rb8 10 d4 h6 11 Re1 Qf6 (or 11...Bg4 12 h3 Bxf3 13 Bxf3 Qf6 14 Be3 exd4 15 cxd4 Bb4 16 Rf1 Bc3 with mutual chances, S.Conquest-G.Flear, San Sebastian 2006) 12 Nd2 Bf5 13 Ne4 Qg6 14 Qd3 Rfe8 15 d5 Ne7 16 c4 b6 17 Qc3 Kh8 and Black was very solid in F.Amonatov-A.Chudinovskih, Moscow 2007.

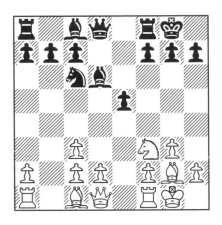

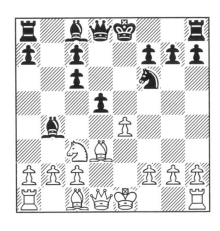

Diagram 3 (W)

The Glek System

Diagram 4 (W)

Competing in the centre

4...exd4 5 Nxd4

Instead, White sometimes employs the Belgrade Gambit with 5 Nd5!?. There is a suspicion this might be refuted with 5...Nxe4, but as that line is very complicated most practical players settle for 5...Be7; e.g. 6 Bf4 d6 7 Nxd4 0-0 8 Nb5 Nxd5 9 exd5 Ne5 with easy equality.

5...Bb4

Developing and pinning thus threatening the e4-pawn. One particularity here is that, unlike in other openings such as the Nimzo-Indian Defence, it's actually quite rare for Black to follow up with ...Bxc3+. In most cases White's play on the dark squares would be a more important factor than his broken pawns.

6 Nxc6 bxc6

Capturing towards the centre.

7 Bd3

White defends his e-pawn, but Black now competes for central influence.

7...d5! (Diagram 4) 8 exd5 cxd5

One way of avoiding the main line is with 8...Qe7+, but I don't think this quite equalizes; for example, 9 Qe2 Qxe2+ 10 Kxe2 cxd5 11 Nb5 Kd8 12 Rd1 with slight but enduring pressure.

9 0-0 0-0 10 Bg5 c6 (Diagram 5)

Solidifying the d5-square. Now White has active minor pieces and one less pawn island, so his structure is slightly easier to handle, but Black has a central pawn which may be a useful asset later.

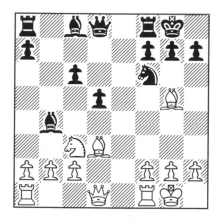

Diagram 5 (W)

White has fewer pawn islands

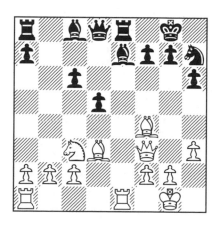

Diagram 6 (W)

White has a strong move

10...Be6 is also known, keeping the option of playing ...c7-c5 and expanding in the centre. This seems to hold true after 11 Qf3 Be7 12 h3 h6 13 Bh4 Rb8, when Black's forces are well mobilized and ...c7-c5 can be played in promising circumstances.

However, 11 Nb5! can be annoying: 11...c5 (11...Be7 12 Nd4 Bd7 13 Nf5 leaves White with a small pull due to the bishop pair) 12 a3 Ba5 13 b4 cxb4 (after 13...Bb6 14 c3! the knight will be able to sit on d4) 14 Qe1! h6 (14...bxa3 15 Bxf6 gxf6 16 Qe3, Y.Yakovich-T.Ernst, Gausdal 1991, favours White as Black's structure is too weak) 15 axb4 Bb6 16 Bh4 Re8 17 Qd2 a6 18 Nc3 with a edge for White, V.Malakhov-A.Grischuk, Moscow 1996.

11 Qf3

The most commonly played move, though White sometimes prefers to redeploy his knight immediately:

a) 11 Na4, when Black can react positively with 11...h6 12 Bh4 Re8 13 c4 Bd6 14 Rc1 Bf4! 15 Rc2 Bg4 16 f3 Be6 17 Bf2 dxc4 18 Bxc4 Nd5, as in S.Mikheev-V.Malaniuk, Tula 1999.

b) 11 Ne2, and now I quite like 11...h6 12 Bh4 Bd6 threatening ...Bxh2+. An instructive sequence would then be 13 Nd4 c5 14 Nf5 (14 Nb5!? followed by c2-c4 has been suggested as a possible improvement) 14...Bxf5! 15 Bxf5 Rb8 16 b3 Be5, when Black has very good pieces and some central control, while White's bishop pair has nothing to do. In fact Black is already better; for example, 17 Rb1 Qd6 18 Bg3 Bxg3 19 hxg3 Rfe8 20 Qf3 Re5 21 Rbe1 Rbe8 22 Rxe5 Qxe5 23 Bd3 h5, R.Tamai-V.Georgiev, Conegliano 2008, and White can only wait while Black tries to make something of his centre. Note how the solid knight plus influential pawns stifle any counterplay even in an open position.

11...Be7 12 Rfe1 Re8

There are a few other tries:

a) 12...Be6 13 Ne2 h6 is solid and reliable.

b) 12...Rb8!? is provocative: 13 Qe3 Bd6 14 Qxa7 Rxb2 with complications.

c) 12...h6? is downright bad because of 13 Bxh6 gxh6 14 Qe3, forking the e7-bishop and the h6-pawn, when White obtains a strong attack.

13 h3 h6 14 Bf4 Nh7? (Diagram 6)

This plan, which proves effective in the next game, doesn't work here with the f7-square so vulnerable.

 WARNING: Always be wary about moving a well-placed defensive piece.

Instead, equality could be achieved with the solid 14...Be6 15 Rad1 Nd7 16 Ne2 Bf6 17 Qg3 Bh4 18 Qf3 Bf6, B.Socko-T.Nyback, European Ch., Kusadasi 2006.

15 Bxh6! Ng5

An admission of failure. Unfortunately, White seems have too much of an attack after 15...gxh6 16 Bxh7+ Kxh7 17 Qxf7+ Kh8 18 Qg6 Bd7 19 Qxh6+ Kg8 20 Qg6+ Kf8 21 Re3!.

16 Bxg5 Bxg5 17 Rxe8+ Qxe8 18 Nxd5! (Diagram 7)

One tactical blow follows another!

18...Bd8

Or if 18...cxd5 simply 19 Qxd5 forks the rook and bishop.

19 Ne3 Rb8 20 b3 Qe5 21 Rd1 Bc7 22 Bc4

The game is essentially over already.

22...Be6 23 Bxe6 Qxe6 24 Qf5 Qe8 25 Rd4 g6 26 Qe4 Qf8 27 Qxc6 Bb6 28 Rd3 Rc8 29 Qf3 Bxe3 30 Qxe3 Rxc2 31 Qxa7 Qe8 32 Qe3 Qc8 33 Qe7 Qf5 34 Rd8+ Kg7 35 Qf8+ Kf6 36 Qd6+ Kg5 37 h4+ 1-0

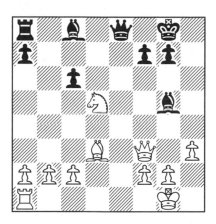

Diagram 7 (B)

Another tactical blow

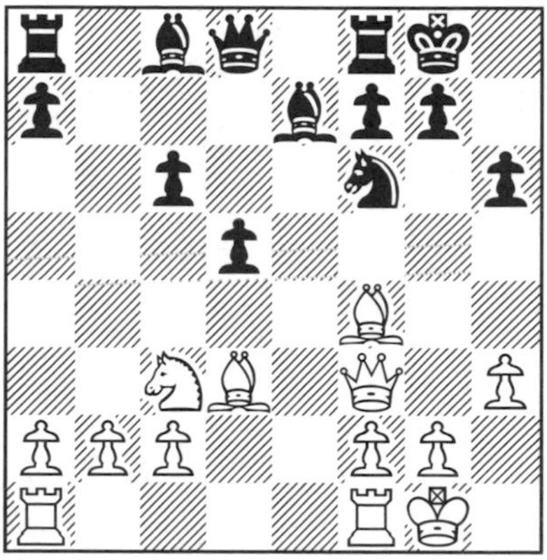

Diagram 8 (B)

Compare the previous game

Game 26
□ S.Ter Sahakyan ■ D.Howell
World Junior Championship, Yerevan 2007

1 e4 e5 2 Nf3 Nc6 3 Nc3 Nf6 4 d4 exd4 5 Nxd4 Bb4 6 Nxc6 bxc6 7 Bd3 d5 8 exd5 cxd5 9 0-0 0-0 10 Bg5 c6 11 Qf3 Be7 12 h3

Deviating from the 12 Rfe1 of the previous game.

12...h6 13 Bf4 (Diagram 8) 13...Nh7!

Trying for something more lively than the dry equality that follows in lines such as 13...Bd6 14 Rfe1 Rb8 15 b3 Rb4 16 Bxd6 Qxd6 17 Ne2, B.Rogulj-A.Brkic, Bezovac 2006.

14 Rfe1 Ng5 15 Qg3 Ne6 16 Bxh6?! (Diagram 9)

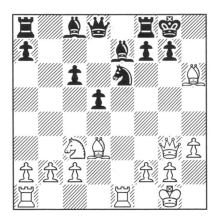 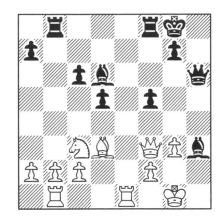

Diagram 9 (B)	**Diagram 10 (W)**
Not this time!	...f5-f4 is coming

White again takes the opportunity to capture on h6, but this time it is Howell's opponent who falls into the trap! Instead, 16 Be5 Re8 17 Rad1 Bd7 18 Bf5 Bf8 ensured dynamic equality and plenty of tension in D.Pavasovic-A.Beliavsky, Portoroz 1999. Indeed, after 19 Na4 Ng5 20 Bd3 Qa5 21 b3 Bd6, Black started to seize the initiative.

16...Bd6 17 Qg4?!

17 f4 was the lesser evil; e.g. 17...Qf6 18 Bg5 Nxg5 19 Qxg5 Qxf4 20 Qxf4 Bxf4, when this two bishop ending favours Black, but is certainly not as catastrophic as the game continuation.

17...Qf6 18 Bd2 Nf4 19 Qd1 Bxh3!

Now it is Black's turn to capture the h-pawn with a tactical shot!

20 Bxf4

20 gxh3? loses immediately to 20...Qg5+ 21 Qg4 Nxh3+.

20...Qxf4 21 g3

Or 21 gxh3 Qh2+ 22 Kf1 Qxh3+ 23 Ke2 Rae8+ and there is nowhere to hide.

21...Qh6

White's king is still rather shaky.

22 Qf3 Rab8 23 Rab1 f5! (Diagram 10)

A well-calculated thrust, the threat of ...f5-f4 being difficult to meet.

24 Nxd5

Amazing – as in Game 25, White again plays a combination with a temporary piece sacrifice on d5. However, Howell had seen further...

24...Bg4!

Not 24...cxd5? 25 Qxd5+ Kh8 26 Re6, whereupon White recovers his piece with interest.

25 Qg2 cxd5 26 Qxd5+ Kh8 27 Re6 Qh5

Now capturing on d6 allows ...Bf3 and mate!

28 Kg2 Qh3+ 29 Kg1 f4! 30 Rxd6 fxg3 31 Qg2 gxf2+ 32 Kf1 Rbe8 0-1

Black mates very quickly.

Spanish Four Knights

1 e4 e5 2 Nf3 Nc6 3 Nc3 Nf6 4 Bb5 (Diagram 11)

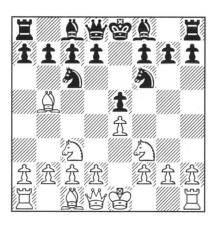

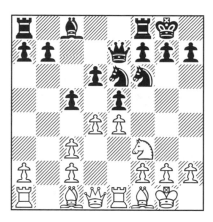

Diagram 11 (B)	**Diagram 12 (B)**
Spanish Four Knights	A typical continuation

This bishop development brings about the Spanish Four Knights. The main line continues:

4...Bb4

Black varies with 4...Nd4 in Game 29 and 4...Bd6!? in Game 30.

5 0-0 0-0 6 d3 d6 7 Bg5

Here Black usually decides to stop emulating his opponent with...

7...Bxc3 8 bxc3 Qe7

Or 8...Bd7 as in Game 28.

9 Re1 Nd8 10 d4 Ne6 11 Bc1 c5 12 Bf1 (Diagram 12)

A typical continuation, where the centre often remains closed in the early stages (see Game 27).

Strategy

In the main line with 4...Bb4 Black will seek a convenient moment to deviate from mirroring his opponent's moves. White's lead in development enables him to create some pressure with 7 Bg5, as the pin along the h4-d8 diagonal can be a nuisance. In return, Black aims to find a way to negate the effects of the pin while keeping his whole position solid. This generally involves ceding the bishop pair but holding onto the e5-strongpoint.

After 4...Nd4 the position can become more lively, especially if White takes up the gauntlet and snatches the offered e-pawn.

Theoretical

There are some sharp lines with 4...Nd4, but following 4...Bb4 positional understanding is a more important quality than learning long sequences. So overall, the Spanish Four Knights is less theoretical than most openings.

Game 27
□ **P.Svidler** ■ **A.Karpov**
Cap d'Agde (rapid) 2003

---

1 e4 e5 2 Nf3 Nf6 3 Nc3 Nc6 4 Bb5 Bb4

The main line of the Spanish Four Knights; this move is almost twice as common as the second most popular option 4...Nd4.

5 0-0 0-0 (Diagram 13) 6 d3

One of the annoying aspects of this variation from Black's point of view is that White can play for a draw by 6 Bxc6 dxc6 7 Nxe5 Re8 8 Nd3 Bxc3 9 dxc3 Nxe4 10 Bf4 Bf5 with a lifeless position.

Another problem with copying moves is that White has slightly more options. So there are practical reasons for Black to seek alternatives as early as move four.

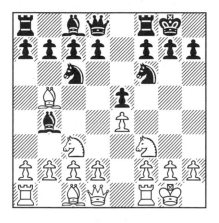

Diagram 13 (W)

Mirror image chess

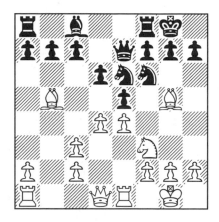

Diagram 14 (W)

The Metger Unpin

6...Bxc3

Breaking the symmetry slightly earlier than usual (6...d6 7 Bg5 Bxc3 etc is more common), though it usually transposes.

It's generally considered dubious to continue to copy White, but maybe it is playable: 6...d6 7 Bg5 Bg4!? (instead of the normal 7...Bxc3) 8 Nd5 Nd4 (strange, but it has been played a few times) 9 Nxb4 Nxb5 10 Nd5 Nd4 11 Qd2! and now Black does (at least in principle) finally have to find some moves for himself!

Here 11...Nxf3+ is necessary (but not 11...Bxf3? 12 Bxf6 gxf6 13 Qh6), when 12 gxf3 Bxf3 13 Bxf6 gxf6 14 Qe3 c6! (14...Bh5 15 Qh6 Bg6 16 f4 c6 17 fxe5 fxe5 18 Nf6+ Kh8 19 h4 gave White a strong attack in R.Ponomariov-S.Azarov, European Junior Ch. 1995) 15 Qxf3 cxd5, S.Daniliuk-D.Lybin, Russia 1993, leaves White with only a small pull.

I should perhaps mention that somebody with a sense of humour played 11...Qd7? 12 Bxf6 Bxf3 against Capablanca in a simultaneous display. The Cuban duly won with 13 Ne7+ Kh8 14 Bxg7+ Kxg7 15 Qg5+ Kh8 16 Qf6 mate.

7 bxc3 d6 8 Bg5 Qe7 9 Re1 Nd8

Black's manoeuvre (the knight will come to e6 hitting the bishop on g5) is known as the Metger Unpin and is Black's principal defence. However, as we'll see, it doesn't release all the pressure.

10 d4 Ne6 (Diagram 14) 11 Bc1

11 Bh4 is considered inferior as Black has a clear-cut plan to generate counter-attacking chances: 11...Nf4 12 Nd2 Kh8! 13 Bf1 h6 14 f3 g5 15 Bg3 Rg8, G.Kamsky-J.Timman, Tilburg 1991.

11...c5

Pinski suggests 11...Rd8 12 Bf1 c6 "with equality". However, despite the fact that Black thus avoids creating a potential weakness on d5, this is a superficial assessment. After 13 Nh4 (or similarly 13 g3 Qc7 14 Nh4) 13...g6 14 g3 Ne8 15 Bg2 N8g7 16 Be3 Bd7 17 Qd2 Be8 18 f3, as in O.Nikolenko-V.Malaniuk, Budapest 1990, White has several tempting ideas, Nunn's preference being Qf2 (indirectly defending the knight) followed by f3-f4.

12 Bf1

A mysterious-looking retreat! In fact White places his bishop on a flexible square, from where it can go to g2 or h3, while still surveying the a6-f1 diagonal. Naturally, there are alternatives:

First of all, just in case you hadn't noticed, 12 dxe5?! dxe5 13 Nxe5?? drops a piece to 13...Nc7, so by withdrawing the bishop from a loose square, White renews this threat.

Another plan involves placing, and then cementing, the bishop on d5 with 12 Bc4 Rd8 13 Bd5 Nf8 14 dxe5 dxe5 15 c4, as in M.Chandler-V.Salov, Reykjavik 1991. It looks as if White has made good progress, but Salov demonstrates that Black can live with this: 15...Ng6 16 h3 Rb8 17 a4 b6 18 Nh2 Be6 19 Qf3 Ne8 20 Ng4 Nd6 (the knight proves to be rather well placed here) 21 Ne3 Qh4 22 Nf5 Bxf5! 23 exf5 Ne7 24 g4 Nxd5 25 cxd5 f6 and in this blocked position the knight is the superior piece (the bishop can't do very much!) and Black went on to win.

12...Rd8

After 12...Qc7 13 d5 Nd8 14 Nh4 Ne8 15 g3 Qe7 16 Nf5 Bxf5 17 exf5, as in T.V.Petrosian-A.Lilienthal, USSR Ch., Moscow 1949, White won a classic game by opening the position for his bishops.

13 g3 (Diagram 15)

I consider Black's position more difficult to play, probably because White is so flexible and thus ready for anything.

 WARNING: Don't be too dogmatic about the relative value of bishops and knights. Pawn structures evolve and consequently so does the potential of the minor pieces.

13...Rb8

Here Black's best option isn't that evident:

a) 13...cxd4 14 cxd4 b6 15 Bb2 Bb7 has been tried a few times. It seems odd to open up lines willingly when the opponent has the bishop pair, but Black's pieces have also improved their potential and 16 Bd3 Rac8! doesn't look that clear.

b) 13...Qc7 14 d5 Nf8 is somewhat passive as Black lacks space; e.g. 15 Nh4 Re8 (after 15...Ng6, Pinski gives 16 Bg5 Nxh4 17 Bxh4 Qe7 18 f4 Re8 19 f5 followed by the general advance of the kingside pawns) 16 Bg5 N6d7 17 Qh5 Nb6 18 a4 Bd7 19 a5 Nc8 20 Nf5 Bxf5 21 exf5 Ne7 22 Bb5 Rec8 23 Qg4 with a strong attack, S.Iuldachev-R.Kholmov, Kazakhstan 1994.

c) 13...Nf8 14 Nh4 (now if 14 d5 Ng6 White has fewer options) 14...Bg4 15 f3 Bd7 is recommended by Pinski as unclear. The game continuation, with the additional moves ...Rb8 and a2-a4, favours White very slightly as Black cannot really play ...b7-b5. In similar fashion White could consider 16 a4 here, followed by the same manoeuvre as Svidler with continuing pressure.

14 a4 Nf8 15 Nh4 Bg4 16 f3 Bd7 17 Ng2!? (Diagram 16)

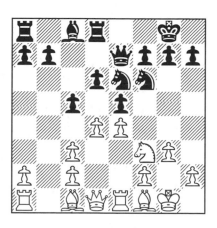

Diagram 15 (B)

White's game is easier

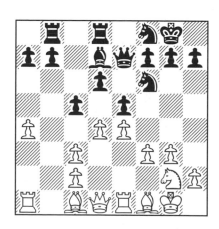

Diagram 16 (B)

The knight heads for e3

The knight will be well posted on e3.

17...Qe8?!

Undoubtedly an error, even if the idea is tempting. The precise 17...h6!, followed by ...Qe8 (when he finds the time!), should grant Black reasonable prospects.

18 Bg5!

Unpleasant.

18...Qe6?

18...Qe7 19 Ne3 Be6 would be less bad, but White would still have the better chances and could even consider 20 f4.

19 Ne3 h6 20 Bc4

This obliges Black to make a serious concession.

20...Qh3 21 Bxf6 gxf6

Black's structure is a shambles and Svidler doesn't hesitate to probe where it hurts.

22 f4! cxd4 23 f5! (Diagram 17)

A tactical point to finish the game off quickly: the black queen is trapped.

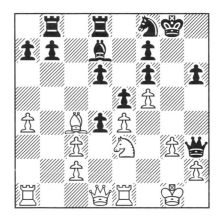

Diagram 17 (B)

The black queen is trapped

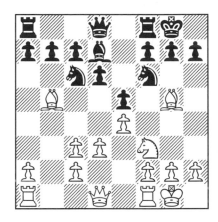

Diagram 18 (W)

Black develops naturally

23...dxe3 24 Bf1 Bxf5 25 Bxh3 Bxh3 26 Qh5 Be6 27 Qxh6 d5 28 Rxe3 dxe4 29 Qxf6 Nh7 30 Qh6 Rbc8 31 Rxe4 Rxc3 32 Rxe5 Rc6 33 Rg5+ 1-0

Game 28
□ **A.Khamatgaleev** ■ **M.Sorokin**
Calcutta 2001

1 e4 e5 2 Nf3 Nc6 3 Nc3 Nf6 4 Bb5 Bb4 5 0-0 0-0 6 d3 d6 7 Bg5 Bxc3 8 bxc3 Bd7

(Diagram 18)

I prefer this idea to the main line as Black develops naturally and White's strategy is less straightforward.

8...h6 9 Bh4 Bd7 is similar; e.g. 10 Re1 (10 Rb1 would return to the main line) 10...Ne7! (exploiting the fact that the bishop on b5 is *en prise*) 11 Bxd7 Nxd7 12 d4 Qe8 13 Nd2 Ng6 14 Bg3 Qe6 15 Nf1 Rad8 16 Qf3 Rfe8 17 h3 Qc4 and Black was better in A.Skripchenko-G.Flear, Djerba 1998. The bishop on g3 is a spectator and White's weakened queenside is coming under scrutiny.

9 Rb1 h6 10 Bh4 Qe7!?

Most attention has been reserved for 10...a6 11 Ba4 (11 Bxc6 Bxc6 12 Re1 Re8 13 Nd2 b5 14 Nf1 d5 offers nothing for White, B.Spassky-L.Portisch, Bugojno 1986) 11...Rb8 12 Bb3 (in order to maintain the tension; Black has no problems after the slower 12 h3 Ne7! 13 Bxd7 Nxd7 14 Qd2 Qe8, M.Ferguson-G.Flear, Hastings 1995/96; while the forcing 12 d4!? Nxd4 13 Nxd4 Bxa4 14 Nf5 Bb5 15 Rxb5 axb5 16 f4 offered White enough compensation for a draw, but no more than that, A.Rizouk-G.Flear, Hastings 2001/02) 12...Qe7 13 Re1 (or similarly 13 Qc1 Na5 14 Re1 Nxb3 15 cxb3 Qe6 16 d4, S.Smagin-A.Yusupov, Essen 2001, and now 16...Nh5! with equality) 13...Na5 14 d4 Rbd8 15 Qc1 Nxb3 16 axb3 Bg4 17 Nd2 g5 18 Bg3 Nh5 19 Nc4 Nf4, J.Nunn-J.Smejkal, German League 1992, is still the key game. Black has reasonable play at this point, though he eventually lost.

11 Qd2 Kh8 12 Rfe1 Rad8 13 d4 b6 (Diagram 19)

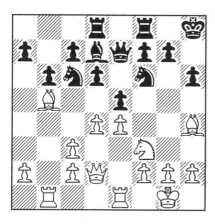

Diagram 19 (W)

Covering his weaknesses

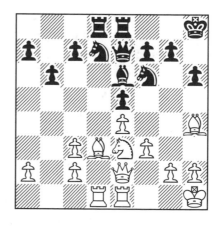

Diagram 20 (W)

Black remains very solid

Black intends to cover any potential weaknesses before aiming for ...Rg8 and ...g7-g5 with play down the g-file.

14 Qe2

Closing the centre always gives White more space, but his broken queenside means he can't do a great deal with it; for example, 14 d5 Nb8 15 Bd3 Bg4 16 Qe3 Rg8!? and I would be happy with Black.

14...Nb8 15 Bd3 Rde8

15...Rg8!? is perhaps slightly more precise, since if White can be provoked to capture on e5 then the other rook will be better placed on d8.

16 Rbd1 Rg8

Black has calmly manoeuvred and is ready for kingside action.

17 dxe5 dxe5 18 Nd2 Bg4

Provoking f2-f3 in order to limit White's options. 18...g5 is plausible, but after 19 Bg3 Black can't continue with ...Nh5, so he decides to be patient instead.

19 f3 Be6 20 Nc4 Nbd7 21 Kh1 Rd8

Cautious. Again 21...g5!? is tempting, but then Black would have had to judge 22 Bg3 Nh5 23 Bxe5+ Nxe5 24 Nxe5. Nevertheless, this looks playable, as after 24...Nf4 25 Qe3 Bh3! 26 Nxf7+ Qxf7 27 gxh3 Nxh3, White's extra pawn is hardly a major concern, and Black has a nice grip on the dark squares.

22 Ne3 Rge8 (Diagram 20) 23 c4!?

An anti-positional move, blocking in his own bishop, but White has a tactical idea in mind. 23 Bc4 was suggested by Tsesarsky, but then Black could consider 23...Qa3 24 Rd2 Nc5, aiming for counterplay on the queenside at the risk of allowing broken kingside pawns.

23...c6 24 Nd5!

The point, but Black is ready.

24...cxd5 25 cxd5 Bxd5 26 exd5 g5

There are no knights to hop into f5, so Sorokin felt that this was the moment to hit back.

27 Qd2?

Simply 27 Bg3 Nxd5 28 Qe4 N5f6 29 Qf5 would ensure that White has compensation for the pawn. The two bishops are rather dangerous with h2-h4 coming.

27...Nc5

If 27...gxh4 then 28 Qxh6+ Kg8 29 Qg5+ draws.

28 Bb5 Rxd5 29 Qe3?

The final mistake as 29 Qc1 was essential.

29...Red8! (Diagram 21)

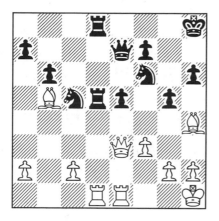

Diagram 21 (W)

White loses a piece

Diagram 22 (W)

Rubinstein's Defence

With both d1 and h4 *en prise* White now loses a piece.

30 Rxd5 Nxd5 31 Qc1 gxh4 32 Qxh6+ Kg8 33 Bc4 Rd6 34 Qh5 Nf4 35 Qg4+ Kf8 36 Qc8+ Rd8 37 Qg4 Qf6 38 g3 hxg3 39 hxg3 Ng6 40 Qh5 Kg7 41 Kg2 0-1

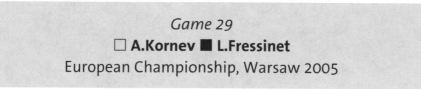

Game 29
□ **A.Kornev** ■ **L.Fressinet**
European Championship, Warsaw 2005

1 e4 e5 2 Nf3 Nc6 3 Nc3 Nf6 4 Bb5 Nd4 (Diagram 22)

Rubinstein's Defence.

5 Ba4

The variation 5 Nxd4 exd4 6 e5 dxc3 7 exf6 can be a problem for those seeking an interesting game as Black (and ultimately chances to take the whole point). After 7...Qxf6 (7...cxd2+?! is too risky: 8 Bxd2 Qxf6 9 0-0 Be7 10 Bc3 Qg5 11 Re1! Qxb5 12 Qg4! with a strong if not decisive attack, W.Shipman-Weber, New York Open 1985) 8 dxc3 Qe5+ 9 Qe2 the early simplification is frankly boring. This is the main downside of 4...Nd4.

115

On the other hand, 5 Nxe5 both lacks bite and allows Black good chances with 5...Qe7; e.g. 6 f4 Nxb5 7 Nxb5 d6 8 Nf3 Qxe4+ 9 Kf2 Qc4 10 a4 Be6 11 Re1 Kd7!?, M.Yeo-M.Hebden, British League 2002.

5...Bc5

Black shows his willingness to sacrifice a pawn for rapid development. This is a far more spirited approach than 5...Nxf3+ 6 Qxf3 which leaves White with a safe pull.

Another gambit line for Black involves 5...c6!? 6 Nxe5 d5! (preferable to the forcing 6...d6 7 Nf3 Bg4 8 d3, as this seems to be better for White; e.g. 8...Nd7 9 Be3 Nxf3+ 10 gxf3 Bh5 11 d4 Qf6 12 Rg1 Qxf3 13 Qd3 Bg6 14 d5 Ne5 15 Qf1 Be7 16 Rg3 Qh5 17 f4, P.Acs-J.Pinter, Hungarian Team Ch. 2001) 7 d3 Bd6 8 Nf3 (or 8 f4 Bc5 9 exd5 0-0 10 Ne4 Nxe4 11 dxe4 Qh4+ 12 g3 Qh3 with dynamic play) 8...Bg4 9 Be3 dxe4 10 Nxe4 Nxe4 11 Bxd4 Qa5+ 12 c3 Ng5 13 Be3 Bxf3 14 gxf3 Qf5 and Black had good compensation, K.Shanava-I.Khenkin, European Ch., Dresden 2007.

6 Nxe5 0-0

Black just gets on with his development, the philosophy being that the pawn minus won't matter unless White is able to develop fully and consolidate.

7 Nd3 Bb6 (Diagram 23)

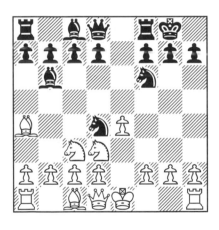

Diagram 23 (W)

Black just develops

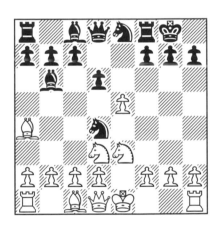

Diagram 24 (B)

An important crossroads

8 e5

Pushing back Black's knight. This move has largely taken over as White's favourite here.

Instead, the simple 8 0-0 d5 9 Nxd5 Nxd5 (or maybe 9...Nxe4!?) 10 exd5 Qxd5 doesn't worry Black who has plenty of open play for his pawn, whereas White's development is lethargic and not showing any signs of waking up!

After 8 Nf4, Black should be aiming to hit back with ...d7-d5. For example, 8...d5!? (it seems 8...c6 9 d3 d5 also yields enough compensation: 10 0-0 Bg4 11 Qd2 dxe4 12 dxe4 Re8 13 Kh1 g5 14 f3 gxf4 15 fxg4 Bc7 16 Qd3 Ne6, C.Bauer-L.Fressinet, French Ch., Chartres 2005) 9 Nfxd5 Nxd5 10 Nxd5 Qh4 11 Ne3 f5 12 exf5 Bxf5 13 0-0 Rf6 14 Nxf5 Rxf5 15 Bd7 Nf3+ 16 gxf3 Rh5 17 h3 Qg3+ 18 Kh1 Rxh3+ 19 Bxh3 Qxh3+ led to a draw in D.Navara-A.Shirov, Prague 2004.

8...Ne8

White must be careful not to drop too far behind in development, particularly as the queenside will take time to unravel.

9 Nd5

The main choice, since it is now largely recognized that 9 0-0 d6 10 exd6 is well met by 10...Nf6! (a more dynamic option than 10...Nxd6 11 Nd5 c6 12 Ne3 Qh4 13 c3, when White wriggled out and later exploited his extra pawn, F.Jenni-J.Gustafsson, Lippstadt 2003). For example, 11 d7 (after 11 dxc7 Qd6! Black's attack starts to take on serious proportions) 11...Bxd7 12 Bxd7 Qxd7 13 Ne1 Rae8 14 Nf3 Ng4 15 h3 f5! (critical; Black sacrifices a piece for the attack) 16 d3 Qd6 17 hxg4 Nxf3+ 18 Qxf3 fxg4 19 Qd5+ Qxd5 20 Nxd5 Bxf2+ 21 Kh1? (21 Rxf2 Re1+ 22 Kh2 Rxf2 23 Be3 Rxg2+ 24 Kxg2 Rxa1 needs testing, but still gives an advantage to Black according to Nunn) 21...Re5 22 Nf4 Bg3 23 Bd2 Ref5 24 Rae1 g5 and Black won in M.Rüfenacht-M.Shchebenyuk, correspondence 1986.

9...d6 10 Ne3 (Diagram 24) 10...c5!?

10...c6 is an alternative that could be worth investigating. V.Anand-V.Ivanchuk, Monte Carlo (blindfold rapid) 1995, continued 11 c3 Nf5 12 0-0 Bc7 13 f4 f6 14 Bc2 Qe7 15 exf6 Nxf6 with sufficient activity for the pawn.

However, I don't trust the old main line with 10...dxe5?! 11 Nxe5 Qg5 12 N5c4 f5, as 13 h4! seems to put it under a cloud: 13...Qf6 (White was also on top after 13...Qg6 14 Ne5 Qf6 15 f4 Nc6 16 d4 Nxd4 17 Nd5 Qd6 18 Be3, A.Motylev-A.Shirov, Moscow 2001; and also after 13...Qe7 14 c3 f4 15 Nxb6 fxe3 16 dxe3 Nf3+ 17 gxf3 axb6 18 Bc2, G.Ginsburg-T.Halasz, Austrian Team Ch. 2006) 14 f4 Nd6 15 c3 Nxc4 (15...Nc6 is objectively better, but still insufficient for equality after 16 Nxb6 axb6 17 d4) 16 Nxc4 Qg6 and Black was fishing in troubled waters but had insufficient compensation following 17 Kf1 Be6 18 Ne5 Qg3 19 cxd4 in A.Motylev-A.Shirov, FIDE World Ch., Moscow 2001.

TIP: In gambits, sometimes the disparity between a position offering 'sufficient play' and an analogous one yielding 'not enough compensation' hinges on a subtlety. Often the only way to understand these judgements fully is by comparing several lines and complete games to see the consequences of a seemingly minor, but in fact important difference.

11 c3 Nf5 12 Bb3 dxe5

12...Qh4 is a decent alternative; for example, 13 Qf3 Nxe3 14 dxe3 Bc7 15 e4 dxe5 16 Nxc5 b6 17 Bd5 Rb8 18 Nd3 Nf6 19 Qg3 Qxg3 20 hxg3 Nxd5 21 exd5 Rd8 and Black had adequate counter-chances for the pawn in T.Sammalvuo-J.Norri, Finnish Ch., Helsinki 1996.

13 Nxe5 Nxe3 14 fxe3

Otherwise 14 dxe3 Qg5 15 Nd7 Bxd7 16 Qxd7 Qxg2 17 Bd5 is about equal.

14...Qg5 15 d4

The forcing line 15 Nxf7 Rxf7 16 Bxf7+ Kxf7 17 0-0+ looks convenient for White at first sight, but on further reflection one realizes that the two minor pieces are going to be more effective than White's rook and pawns.

15...Qxg2 16 Rf1 Nd6 17 Qf3 Qxf3 18 Rxf3 (Diagram 25)

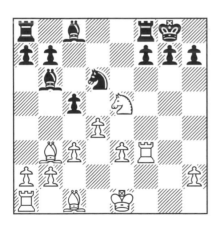

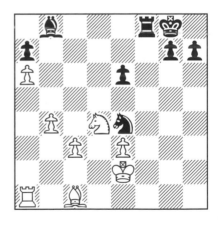

Diagram 25 (B)
Material is now equal

Diagram 26 (B)
White is leading the race

Material is now equal, but White's pressure against f7 is slightly annoying. This explains White's choice on move fourteen...

18...Be6!?

...and Black's on move eighteen! This nullifies the pressure along the diagonal, albeit at the cost of an inferior pawn structure.

19 Bxe6 fxe6 20 Ke2 Rxf3 21 Nxf3 Rf8 22 a4 Ne4?!

22...a6 is more solid.

23 a5 Bc7 24 a6!

Softening up Black's queenside.

24...b5 25 dxc5 Nxc5 26 Nd4!?

A double-edged decision, angling for an exchange of pawns: b5 for h2.

26...Bxh2 27 b4 Ne4 28 Nxb5 Bb8 29 Nd4! (Diagram 26)

White aims to accelerate his queenside play. On the slower 29 c4, then perhaps 29...h5! and the race is on.

29...Nxc3+ 30 Kd3 Nd5 31 Nc6 Bd6 32 b5 Nb4+ 33 Nxb4 Bxb4 34 b6!

The a6-pawn, soon to be supported by the white king, becomes the key element in the position.

34...axb6 35 Kc4 Ba5 36 Kb5 Ra8 37 Bb2 g5 38 Rc1 Bd2 39 Rc7 1-0

There is no hope after 39...Bxe3 40 Rg7+ Kf8 41 Rxh7.

> *Game 30*
> ## ☐ K.Spraggett ■ L.Bruzon Bautista
> ### Buenos Aires 2005

1 e4 e5 2 Nf3 Nc6 3 Bb5 Nf6 4 Nc3

Note the move order. This illustrates why the line is sometimes called the Spanish Four Knights, as the position can arise from both openings.

4...Bd6!? (Diagram 27)

Not the prettiest move in the world but an effective one. Black defends the e5-pawn while carrying on with development.

> **NOTE: Aesthetic and effective are not the same thing!**

5 d3

This is the most trustworthy move (bearing in mind that 5 0-0 0-0 6 d3 is similar).

Alternatives are less challenging if Black reacts appropriately:

a) The wild attempt 5 g4?! can be met by 5...Bc5!, which isn't exactly a loss of a tempo because the position has changed: White's additional move g2-g4 has weakened his structure, and after 6 g5 Ng4 7 Rf1 h6! Black has good play.

b) 5 d4 Nxd4 6 Nxd4 exd4 7 Qxd4 Qe7 is also easy for Black, with ...Be5 in the air.

c) 5 Bxc6 dxc6 6 d4 aims to obtain a kingside majority as in the Spanish Exchange. Black has to be a little careful but should be able to equalize: 6...Bg4 (or 6...exd4 7 Qxd4 0-0 8 Bg5 c5 9 Qd3 h6 10 Bh4 g5 11 Bg3 with a quick draw in M.Zaitsev-A.Kosten, German League 2008) 7 dxe5 Bxf3 8 Qxf3 Bxe5 9 Bf4 Bxf4 10 Qxf4 0-0 11 0-0 Re8 12 Rfe1 Qe7 13 a3 Rad8 14 Rad1 Nd5 was solid enough in I.Nataf-Z.Almasi, European Club Cup, Kemer 2007.

Diagram 27 (W)

Strange but effective

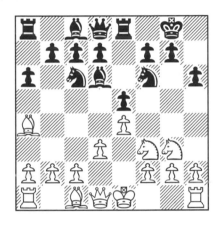

Diagram 28 (W)

Clearing f8 for the bishop

5...a6

5...0-0 allows the pin with 6 Bg5 when, after chasing White's other bishop by 6...a6 7 Ba4 b5 8 Bb3, Black has nothing better than a loss of time with 8...Be7.

6 Ba4

6 Bxc6 dxc6 would yield an innocuous version of the Spanish Exchange.

6...h6 7 Ne2 0-0

The queenside can wait – as I learnt to my cost: 7...b5 8 Bb3 Bb7 was strongly met by 9 Ng3 Ne7 10 Nh4! and I was struggling in M.Nepeina Leconte-G.Flear, French Team Ch. 2009.

8 Ng3 Re8 (Diagram 28) 9 a3

A sign that White wants to keep his light-squared bishop on the a2-g8 diagonal.

Instead, after 9 c3 Bf8 Black would soon be able to play ...d7-d5, a plan known in both the Spanish and Quiet Italian. Here, however, Black saves a tempo as he is able to achieve ...d7-d5 in one go without making a pit stop on d6.

9...b5 10 Bb3 Bf8 11 0-0 d6

A prudent choice, but the more enterprising 11...d5! yields clear equality; e.g. 12 exd5 Nxd5 13 Re1 Bb7 14 Ne4 and now either 14...Nf6 or 14...Nd4, though not 14...Qd7?? due to 15 Bxh6 gxh6 16 Bxd5 etc.

12 Bd2 Be6 13 Bxe6 Rxe6 14 c4!?

White places his pawns on light squares after the exchange of bishops, but Black finds an interesting way to react positively.

14...bxc4 15 dxc4 Nd4 16 Ba5

16 Be3 would allow the annoying 16...c5.

16...Nxf3+ 17 Qxf3

Black's bishop on f8 won't be able to have much influence as yet, but everything else is in order in his camp.

17...Qb8 18 Rab1 Qb7 19 Rfe1 c6 20 Qe2 g6

Gradually improving his position. White isn't going anywhere.

21 Red1 Rb8 22 Nf1 d5! (Diagram 29)

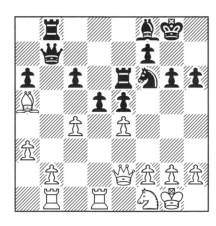

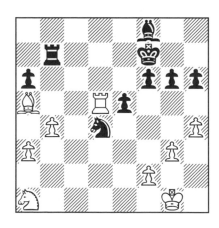

Diagram 29 (W)

The liberating move

Diagram 30 (W)

White's pieces aren't working

Being able to play this liberating move is a sign that Black has everything under control.

23 exd5 cxd5 24 cxd5 Nxd5

Black has an edge as he has a greater presence in the centre. Note that the e-pawn helps support a possible outpost on f4 or d4.

25 Qe4

25 Bd2 Qb3 also leaves Black more active.

25...Nf4 26 Qxb7 Rxb7 27 Rd8 Kg7 28 Nd2 Rc6

The rook will shortly be heading for c2.

29 g3 Ne6 30 Rd5 f6 31 b4 Kf7 32 Nb3 Rc2 33 h4

On 33 Rd2 Black has a choice between 33...Nd4 34 Rxc2 Nxc2 or 33...Rxd2 34 Nxd2 Nd4.

33...Ra2 34 Ra1 Rxa1+ 35 Nxa1 Nd4 (Diagram 30)

White's pieces just aren't working, particularly the knight on a1!

36 Bd8 Rb8 37 Ba5 Rc8 38 Rd7+ Ke6 39 Rc7 Rxc7 40 Bxc7 Nb5 0-1

Picking off the a-pawn, and the b-pawn will probably soon drop as well.

Summary

From White's point of view the various Four Knights systems are employed mainly with positional considerations in mind. After 4 Bb5 Black can, if he desires, seek a more complex game with 4...Nd4, but this requires White to be in a sporting mood. Manoeuvring is more the order of the day after 4...Bb4, where White's extra tempo tends to give him a nagging edge.

Chapter Five
Scotch Game

Introduction

1 e4 e5 2 Nf3 Nc6 3 d4 exd4 4 Nxd4 (Diagram 1)

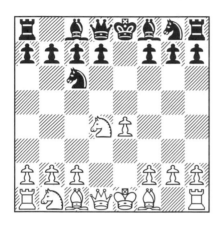

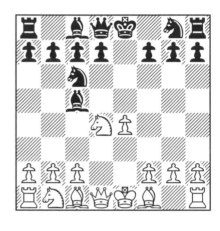

Diagram 1 (B)

The Scotch Game

Diagram 2 (W)

The classical 4...Bc5

The Scotch Game involves White opening the centre with 3 d4 and then recapturing with the knight. The gambit variations involving 4 c3 and 4 Bc4 are considered in the next chapter.

After 4 Nxd4 Black's most common fourth move is 4...Bc5, attacking the knight, when White must immediately answer the threat. The most popular way has been 5 Be3 (Games 32 and 33), maintaining the tension for now, whereupon Black reacts with the active-looking 5...Qf6, essentially hoping to gain time for development.

In recent years many White players have employed a radically different strategy introduced by 5 Nxc6, as we'll see in Game 31.

In the diagram position, 4...Nf6, hitting the e4-pawn, comes a close second in the popularity stakes. If White responds with 5 Nc3 we transpose to the Scotch Four Knights covered in the previous chapter. However, 5 Nxc6 bxc6 6 e5 (the Mieses Variation) is the most enterprising option and is the subject of Games 34 and 35.

Strategy

One glance at the central pawns and it is evident that White can hope for certain advantages. The e-pawn is on the fourth rank, controls f5 and d5, and doesn't get in the way of either of White's bishops.

Black, on the other hand, will require time to get both bishops activated, without one of them being hampered by the d-pawn, and even then it's unlikely that he will obtain space parity in the centre.

So in order to counter the negative aspects of the structure, Black usually aims either for quick development with 4...Bc5, or to obtain a concession by hitting the e-pawn with 4...Nf6.

Theoretical

Reasonably so. Until twenty years ago the Scotch was a quiet backwater, but once Kasparov showed an interest the theory moved on by leaps and bounds. Nowadays many lines are treacherous for the unprepared and Black needs to learn at least some theory not to end up with a passive game.

Black plays 4...Bc5

Game 31
□ G.Kasparov ■ N.Short
11th matchgame, World Championship, London 1993

1 e4 e5 2 Nf3 Nc6 3 d4 exd4 4 Nxd4 Bc5 (Diagram 2) 5 Nxc6

It's only in the last twenty years or so that this move has shown any popularity at all, but now it is all the rage.

Otherwise, along with 5 Be3 (seen in the next two games), White has also tried:

a) 5 Nb3 Bb6 6 a4 a6 7 Nc3 d6 (the seemingly active 7...Qf6 tends to open Pandora's box, as crazy lines such as 8 Qe2 Nge7 9 Nd5 Nxd5 10 exd5+ Ne7 11 a5 Ba7 12 h4 d6 13 Ra4 are both complicated and dangerous for Black) 8 Nd5 Ba7 9 Be3 (other ideas are not particularly testing: 9 Qf3 Be6 10 Qg3?! can be met by 10...Bxd5! 11 exd5 Nb4 12 Qxg7 Qf6 13 Qxf6 Nxf6 with the initiative, I.Salonen-

I.Skrjabin, Espoo 2006; while 9 Be2 Nf6 10 0-0 Nxd5 11 exd5 Ne5 12 Bf4 Ng6 13 Bg3 0-0 14 Qd2 Bd7 15 Rfe1 Qf6 gave Black a solid position, M.Adams-V.Kotronias, Halkidiki 1993) 9...Bxe3 10 Nxe3 (White settles for a space advantage) 10...Nf6 11 Bd3 0-0 12 0-0 Re8 13 f3 Be6 14 c4 **(Diagram 3)**.

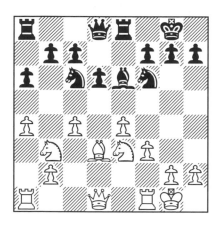

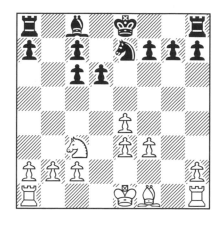

Diagram 3 (B)	Diagram 4 (W)
If not on the light squares...	White has a slight pull

Black is now denied any chance of achieving the liberating ...d6-d5 break, but he is able to counter White's greater space by generating play on the dark squares: 14...a5 15 Rf2 Nd7 16 f4 f6 17 Rd2 Qb8! 18 Kh1 Qa7 and Black was fine in S.Rublevsky-A.Naiditsch, Dortmund 2004.

b) 5 Nf5?! is rare and probably best met by 5...d5!, when the complications after 6 Nxg7+ Kf8 7 Nh5 Qh4 8 Ng3 Nf6 9 Be2 dxe4 seem to favour Black.

5...Qf6 6 Qd2

It may look innocuous but 6 Qf3 is one of the hottest options in the whole Open Games family! The resulting queenless middlegame seems easier to play for White. Indeed, although the theory is still developing, Black hasn't yet found a sure-fire equalizing method. For example, 6...Qxf3 7 gxf3 bxc6 8 Be3! (8 Nd2 d5 9 Rg1 Ne7 10 Nb3 Bd6 11 c4 dxe4 12 fxe4, as in G.Jones-T.Michalczak, Porto San Giorgio 2007, is comfortably met by 12...Ng6 13 h3 Be5 with equality) 8...Bxe3 (after 8...Bb6!? 9 c4 and only then 9...Bxe3, it seems that the additional move c2-c4 is quite useful; e.g. 10 fxe3 Rb8 11 b3 d6 12 Rg1 Ne7 13 Nc3 0-0 14 0-0-0 Be6 15 f4 f5 16 c5! Rbd8 17 Bh3 with a pull for White, Ni Hua-D.Jakovenko, Ergun 2006) 9 fxe3 Ne7 (here 9...Rb8 is ineffective due to 10 Bc4!) 10 Nc3 d6 **(Diagram 4)** 11 Rg1! (if 11

0-0-0 then 11...g5!? is an interesting plan, competing for space and dark squares; e.g. 12 Rg1 h6 13 f4 Ng6 14 e5 dxe5 15 Bg2 Bd7 16 Ne4 Ke7 with chances for both sides, J.Tomczak-M.Bartel, Wroclaw 2009) 11...0-0 12 f4 f5 13 Bc4+ Kh8 14 e5 dxe5 15 0-0-0 Ng6 (or 15...exf4 16 exf4 Rb8 17 Rde1 Ng8 18 Na4 and White is better, D.Howell-J.Werle, London 2009) 16 Ne2 gives White some initiative. The game E.Najer-V.Akopian, Russian Team Ch. 2007, continued 16...a5 17 a4 exf4 18 exf4 Ba6 19 Bxa6 Rxa6 20 Rd7 Raa8 21 Rxc7 Rfe8 22 Rg2 Re4 and Black was on his way to holding the draw, though it wasn't that comfortable along the way.

6...dxc6

Opening the c8-h3 diagonal and keeping the structure compact. Black will aim for piece pressure in the centre to negate the fact that White's kingside majority may be an important issue later in the game.

Capturing with the other pawn, 6...bxc6 – towards the centre! – has its points. Black avoids giving White the majority, retains his pawn presence in the centre, and sometimes the open b-file may be useful. For example, 7 Nc3 (or 7 Bd3 Ne7 8 0-0 Ng6!? 9 Kh1 Ne5 10 Be2 Qh4 11 Qf4 Qxf4 12 Bxf4 d6 13 Nc3 0-0 14 Na4 Ng6! and Black was fine, M.Devereaux-G.Flear, British League 2003) 7...Ne7 8 Na4 Bb6 (if White captures, then ...a7xb6 gives Black a rock-solid structure) 9 Bd3 0-0 10 0-0 d6 11 Kh1 Qg6 12 Qe2 Re8 13 Bd2 f5 (seeking counterplay) 14 e5!? was S.Rublevsky-A.Beliavsky, World Chess Cup, Hyderabad 2002, and now Postny suggests 14...Bd7 with a complex position.

The third way, 6...Qxc6, used to be considered inferior due to 7 Bd3 Nf6 8 0-0 0-0 9 b4!, but this is still playable for Black: 9...Bd4 10 c3 Bb6 11 c4 Bd4 12 Nc3 b5 13 Nd5 Nxd5, and now either 14 exd5 (V.Afromeev-M.Novikov, Tula 2006) or 14 cxd5 (L.Kernazhitsky-G.Khliastikov, Kiev 2004) yields only a nominal space advantage for White.

7 Nc3 Be6 8 Na4! (Diagram 5)

First played in this game, Kasparov's move is still considered to be the most challenging.

The older 8 Bd3 allows Black to castle long, 8...0-0-0, after which he has relatively comfortable development. Following 9 Qf4 Qxf4 10 Bxf4, White has the superior majority and the possibility that he may emerge into a good ending, but in practice Black is active enough: 10...Ne7 11 Bd2 (or 11 Bg3 Ng6 12 f4 Rhe8 13 Ne2 Bg4 14 h3 Bh5 15 f5 Bxe2 16 Kxe2 Ne5 with equality, S.Smagin-P.Van der Sterren, Prague 1992) 11...Bd4 12 f4 c5 13 0-0-0 Nc6 14 a3 f6 15 Nd5 f5 16 Ne3 fxe4 17 Bxe4 g6 and Black is fine, S.Dvoirys-E.Romanov, Cheliabinsk 2007.

8...Rd8

Gaining a tempo, but giving up on castling long.

9 Bd3

Now if 9 Qf4?!, Wells gives 9...Bxf2+ 10 Kxf2 Qd4+ 11 Be3 Qxa4 with the advantage, while 9...Qd4! looks even stronger.

9...Bd4

9...Bd6 is reckoned to be a concession as it cedes the a7-g1 diagonal. However, after 10 Qe3 b6 White must further delay his development by pushing his central pawns in order to demonstrate any advantage: 11 f4! (better than 11 0-0 Nh6 12 Qg5 Qe5 13 Qxe5 Bxe5 14 Bg5 f6 15 Bxh6 gxh6, which wasn't clear in V.Moiseev-A.Arakeljan, Donskoj 2005) 11...Bb4+ 12 c3 Be7 13 Be2 Qh4+ 14 g3 Qh3 15 f5 Bd7 16 Qf3 and Black's pieces are rather tangled, T.Lampen-J.Norri, Finnish Ch., Helsinki 2000.

10 0-0 (Diagram 6)

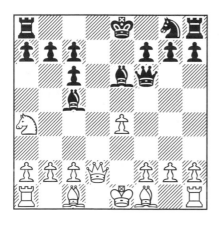

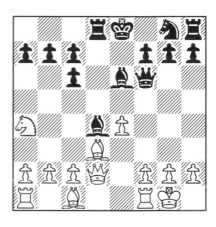

Diagram 5 (B)

Challenging the bishop

Diagram 6 (B)

Black should play actively

10 c3 virtually forces Black to play tactically with 10...Bxf2+, but several games have then demonstrated a clear route to equality; e.g. 11 Qxf2 Rxd3 12 Qxf6 Nxf6 13 Nc5 Rd8 14 Nxb7 Rb8 15 Nc5 Rb5! 16 b4 Nxe4 17 a4 Rxc5! 18 bxc5 Bc4, as in G.Mastrokoukos-S.Skembris, Athens 1996.

10...Ne7

This is now generally considered inferior.

10...a6 is another frequently-played move which doesn't equalize; e.g. 11 Qa5 Qe5 12 Qxe5 Bxe5 13 Be3 Nf6 14 f4 Bd4 15 Bxd4 Rxd4 16 Nc5 Bc8 with an edge for White due to his superior majority and general control, V.Tseshkovsky-A.Stambulian, Krasnodar 2004.

So it turns out that it is better to play actively, to which end I quite like 10...Qh4!?; for example, 11 Qf4 Qh5 12 Qg3 Ne7 13 Be3 Bf6! as in Zs.Polgar-Xie Jun, 3rd matchgame, Women's World Ch., Jaen 1996.

Another way is to hit back with 10...b5!, at least attempting to do something about the annoying knight! Then we have a divergence:

a) 11 c3 bxa4 12 cxd4 Qxd4 13 Qg5, when Black has many options, but 13...a3! is considered best; e.g. 14 Be3 Qf6 15 Qxf6 Nxf6 16 Bc2 axb2 17 Rab1 Rb8 18 Bxa7 Rb7 19 Bd4 Bxa2 20 Rxb2 Rxb2 21 Bxb2 0-0 and a draw looks to be the most likely result, as indeed occurred in A.Danin-K.Bryzgalin, Sepukhov 2002.

b) 11 Nc3 Ne7 12 a4 b4! (rather than 12...a6 13 axb5 axb5 14 Kh1 0-0 15 f4 Qh4 16 Ne2 Bb6 17 f5, when White had the initiative in V.Ivanchuk-F.Amonatov, Odessa rapid 2007) 13 Ne2 c5 with equality, J.Nunn-G.Flear, Isle of Man 1994.

11 c3 b5

More combative than 11...Bb6 12 Nxb6 axb6 13 Qe2, which would ensure White of a pleasant edge with his bishops and kingside majority.

12 cxd4 Qxd4 13 Qc2 Qxa4

13...Qxd3?! 14 Qxd3 Rxd3 15 Nc5 Rd8 16 Bf4 Rc8 17 a4 leaves White clearly better, J.Smeets-M.Sebag, Hengelo 2002.

14 Qxa4 bxa4 (Diagram 7)

Black has a rotten structure but is at least ahead in development, giving him some practical chances.

15 Bc2 Bc4 16 Re1

Another promising option is 16 Rd1 Rxd1+ 17 Bxd1 Bb5 18 Bf4 f5 19 exf5 Nxf5 20 Bxc7 Kf7, M.Crosa Coll-M.De Souza, Rio de Janeiro 2002, again with some advantage to White due to his bishops and better pawns.

16...Bb5 17 Be3 Nc8 18 Bc5

White was later successful with 18 b3!, opening up the position for his bishops; e.g. 18...axb3 19 Bxb3 Rd3 20 Rec1 Nb6 21 Bc2 Ra3 22 Bb3 f6 23 Rc3 Ra6 24 f4 and Black was struggling, J.Lautier-M.Turner, French Team Ch. 2000.

18...Nb6 19 Rad1 Rxd1 20 Rxd1 a6 21 f4 Nd7 22 Ba3

Wells later suggested 22 Bd4 f6 23 e5 to obtain a passed pawn before Black gets organized.

22...h5!

Black can't castle, but this doesn't mean his king is badly placed – just his rook, so Short sets about solving the problem.

23 Kf2 Rh6 24 e5 c5 25 Bf5 Rb6 26 Rd2 g6 27 Bc2 Re6 28 Kg3 Nb6! (Diagram 8)

Time to activate.

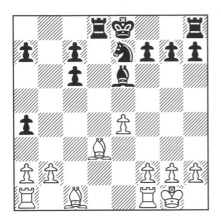

Diagram 7 (W)
Black has a rotten structure

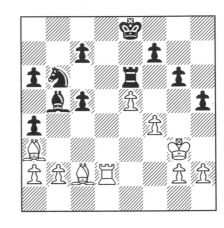

Diagram 8 (W)
Activating his pieces

29 Bxc5 Nc4 30 Rd5 Nxb2 31 f5 Bc6 32 Rd2?

Here the desperado 32 Rd8+! Kxd8 33 fxe6 was correct; e.g. 33...Ke8 34 exf7+ Kxf7 35 e6+ Kxe6 36 Bxg6 and White still has winning chances.

32...gxf5 33 Kf4 Nc4 34 Re2 f6! 35 Bxf5 Rxe5 36 Bd3 Bd5 37 Bd4?!

37 Bxc4 Bxc4 38 Rxe5+ fxe5+ 39 Kxe5 Bxa2 40 g3 would have been more prudent, with a draw as White could then blockade the dark squares.

37...Rxe2 38 Bxe2 Ke7 39 Bxh5 Bxg2 40 Bd1 a3 41 h4 Bd5 42 h5 Ne5 43 h6 Bxa2 44 Bc5+ Kf7 45 Bc2 (Diagram 9) 45...Bc4?!

Now Short may even have been able to obtain some winning chances: 45...Ng6+ 46 Ke3 Be6 47 Bxa3 f5 with advantage for Black.

46 h7 Kg7 47 Bf8+ Kh8 48 Be7 Bd3 49 Bxf6+ Kxh7 50 Bxe5 Bxc2 ½-½

> *Game 32*
> ☐ **V.Baklan** ■ **V.Golod**
> German League 2006

1 e4 e5 2 Nf3 Nc6 3 d4 exd4 4 Nxd4 Bc5 5 Be3

White aims to maintain his hold on d4.

5...Qf6 6 c3

The weird, though not bad, 6 Nb5!? Bxe3 7 fxe3 Qh4+ 8 g3 Qd8 gives White some development time at the cost of a devalued structure. After 9 Qg4 I suggest 9...Kf8! (rather than create weaknesses with 9...g6; losing castling rights is a lesser concession); e.g. 10 Qf4 d6 11 N1c3 Ne5 12 h3 Bd7 13 Nd4 Ng6 14 Qf2 Qf6 and Black is well dug in, S.Kristjansson-H.Stefansson, Icelandic Ch., Reykjavik 2005.

6...Nge7 (Diagram 10) 7 Bc4

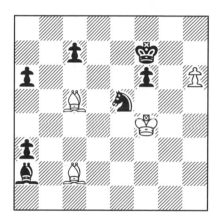

Diagram 9 (B)

Now Black has chances

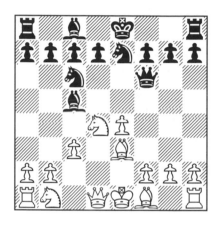

Diagram 10 (W)

A standard position

Instead of this natural bishop development, a quiet plan that I used to consider quite robust involves 7 g3, intending to play Bg2 and 0-0 with a comfortable life. However, the recently introduced 7...h5! (a dynamic rejoinder) is an appropriate antidote: 8 h3 h4 9 g4 Ng6, when White is invited to play more sharply than originally intended: 10 Qd2 Nce5 11 Be2 Bxd4 12 cxd4 (12 Qxd4 Nf4 is equal) 12...Nf3+ 13 Bxf3 Qxf3 14 Rh2 Qxe4 15 f4 0-0 (or perhaps 15...f5! 16 Nc3 Qf3 and Postny prefers Black) 16 f5 Re8 with a double-edged struggle, T.Radjabov-A.Beliavsky, European Ch., Warsaw 2005.

7...b6!?

Defending one bishop and preparing to develop the other. The most popular moves, 7...Ne5 and 7...0-0, are examined in the next game.

8 0-0

8 Qd2!? has also been played a few times, a recent example being 8...Qg6!? (8...Bb7 9

b4 Bxd4 10 cxd4 Qg6 11 f3 0-0-0 12 d5 Ne5 13 Bb3 f5 14 Nc3 fxe4 15 Nxe4 Nf5 16 Bf4 Rde8 17 0-0-0, R.Lau-G.Flear, Brussels rapid 1992, always felt somewhat worse, as White's bishop pair and space preponderance were difficult to cope with) 9 0-0!? Ne5 10 Be2 Qxe4 11 b4 Bd6 12 f3 Qg6 13 Nb5, when White had sufficient compensation for the pawn, Y.Dembo-S.Haslinger, European Union Ch., Liverpool 2008.

8...0-0 9 Qd2 Qg6 10 f3 (Diagram 11)

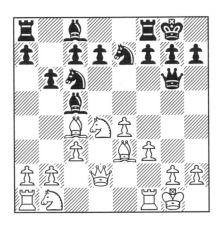

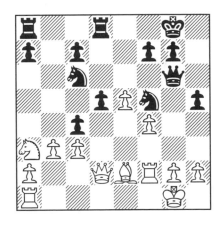

Diagram 11 (B)

White plays solidly

Diagram 12 (B)

Opening lines for the bishop

Baklan employs a solid approach, hoping to maintain his space superiority.

10...Rd8!

Aiming for ...d5, whereas J.Tomczak-R.Lubczynski, Polish Ch., Opole 2007, saw another way of achieving this freeing break: 10...Ne5 11 Be2 d5 12 f4 N5c6 13 f5 (a common theme in this line: the pawns advance to push Black's pieces out of the way) 13...Qf6 14 Kh1 dxe4 15 Bg5 e3! 16 Qxe3 (16 Bxf6 exd2 17 Bxg7!? might have been better) 16...Bxd4 17 cxd4 Nxf5 18 Qd2 Qxd4 19 Qc2 Qd6 20 Bf4 Qg6 and Black had survived, while keeping his material advantage.

11 Bd3 Ne5 12 Be2 d5 13 f4 N5c6

Compared to the previous note, Black has the extra move ...Rd8 here, so White naturally doesn't want to allow the opening of the d-file.

14 e5 Bf5?!

It feels slightly suspicious to give up the bishop so easily, and I feel that Black should try 14...Nf5 15 Bd3 Ncxd4 16 cxd4 Be7 instead. In any event Black needs to maintain his hold on the f5-square.

15 Nxf5 Nxf5 16 Bxc5 bxc5 17 Na3 c4 18 Rf2 h5

Just in case White decides to play for g2-g4.

19 b3! (Diagram 12)

Line opening is in White's interest, as he has the only remaining bishop.

19...cxb3 20 axb3 Nce7 21 Nc2 a5 22 Nd4 c5 23 Nxf5 Nxf5 24 Bf3

With bishop versus knight and fewer pawn islands, it's not surprising that White has the better chances here.

24...Rab8

24...Ne7 can be met by the surprising 25 c4!, and if 25...dxc4 26 Qc1 Rab8 27 Qxc4, Black's queenside pawns are very weak.

25 Bxd5 Kh7 26 c4!

Maintaining the outpost on d5.

26...Nd4 27 Re1 Kh8

White also dominates matters after 27...Nxb3 28 Qa2; e.g. 28...f5 29 Rb2 Nd4 30 Rxb8 Rxb8 31 Qxa5.

28 Qxa5 Nxb3 29 Qc7 Rf8 30 f5 (Diagram 13)

The pawns advance and Black is clearly in trouble.

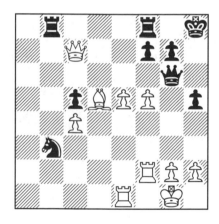

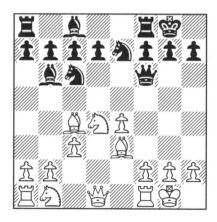

Diagram 13 (B)

Black is clearly in trouble

Diagram 14 (W)

The solid option for Black

30...Qg5 31 f6 gxf6 32 Rxf6 Rbc8 33 Qd6 Nd4 34 Ref1 Rcd8 35 Qb6 Rb8 36 Rh6+

Exchanging queens is the most straightforward way to win.

36...Kg7 37 Qf6+ Qxf6 38 Rhxf6 Rbe8 39 Rxf7+ Rxf7 40 Rxf7+ Kg6 41 Rc7 Rxe5 42 Rxc5 Kg5 43 Rc8 Re1+ 44 Kf2 Re2+ 45 Kf1 Rb2 46 Re8!

White slowly unravels. There is no hurry; the essential thing is to avoid any tricks.

46...h4 47 Re5+ Kf6 48 Re4 Nf5 49 Re2 Rb1+ 50 Kf2 Rc1 51 Re1 Rc3 52 Re4 Kg5 53 Ke1 h3 54 g3 Ra3 55 Re2 Ne3 56 Be6 Kf6 57 Bxh3 Nxc4 58 Kf2 Ne5 59 Kg2 Rc3

Black would be able to draw if he could exchange rooks and sacrifice his knight for the g-pawn, but he isn't given the opportunity.

60 Rf2+ Kg7 61 Be6 Nd3 62 Rf7+ Kg6 63 Rf1 Rc2+ 64 Kg1 Rc5 65 h4 Re5 66 Bc4 Nc5 67 Kg2 Kg7 68 Rf7+ Kh8 69 Kf3 Re1 70 Rf8+ Kg7 71 Rg8+ Kf6 72 g4 Rc1 73 g5+ Kf5 74 Rf8+ Kg6 75 Rf4 Nd7 76 Bd3+ Kh5 77 Be2 Kg6 78 Rd4 Ne5+ 79 Kf4 Nf7 80 Bd3+ Kg7 81 Rd7 Kf8 82 g6 Nh6 83 Kg5 Ng8 84 Rf7+ Ke8 85 Bb5+ Kd8 86 Rf8+ Ke7 87 Re8+ Kd6 88 Rxg8 Rc5+ 89 Kf6 Rxb5 90 g7 1-0

Game 33
□ **E.Najer** ■ **A.Naiditsch**
European Club Cup, Kallithea 2008

---

1 e4 e5 2 Nf3 Nc6 3 d4 exd4 4 Nxd4 Bc5 5 Be3 Qf6 6 c3 Nge7 7 Bc4 Ne5

Statistically, the main defence for Black. The second-placed option is 7...0-0 8 0-0 Bb6 **(Diagram 14)**, which has the benefit of being quite solid, albeit slightly lacking in dynamism.

Here White has a wide choice:

a) 9 f4 d6 10 Nc2 Be6 11 Bd3 Rad8 12 Bxb6 axb6 13 Nba3 Qh6 14 Nb5 Rc8 15 f5 Bd7 16 c4 Ne5 17 Nc3 Kh8 18 Be2 Ng8 and Black remained solid despite his comparative lack of space, R.Ponomariov-L.Ostrowsky, Swidnica (rapid) 1998.

b) 9 Kh1 d6 (9...Rd8!? is interesting) 10 Nb5 Be6 11 Bxe6 fxe6 12 Bxb6 cxb6 13 Nd2 (13 Qxd6 is well met by 13...Rad8 14 Qg3 Qxf2!) 13...Rad8 14 Qg4 Ng6 15 g3 Nge5 16 Qe2 a6 with equality, Zhang Pengxiang-N.Short, UK-China match, Liverpool 2007.

c) 9 Nc2 d6 10 Bxb6 axb6 11 f4 Be6 12 Bd3! (further exchanges would ease Black's life) 12...Rxa2 13 Rxa2 Bxa2 14 Nd2 Be6 15 Ne3 Qh6 16 g4! with compensation as the pawns are very restrictive, D.Petrosian-A.Khudiakov, Alushta 2008.

d) 9 Na3 d6 10 Ndb5!? (this puts pressure on the c7-square so Black must come out of his shell; instead 10 Nac2 Bd7 was hardly threatening and Black was comfortable in M.Galyas-H.Vonthron, Budapest 1995) 10...a6 11 Nxd6 Bxe3 (11...Rd8? fails to the neat tactical shot 12 e5! Qg6 13 Bxb6 cxb6 14 Qe2, as in J.Van der Wiel-A.David, Mondorf 1991) 12 Nxc8 Bc5 13 Nxe7+ Qxe7 14 b4 Bd6 15 Qc2 Rae8 and Black had good play for the pawn, A.Zapata-W.Arencibia Rodriguez, Merida 1992.

8 Be2 Qg6 9 0-0 d6 (Diagram 15)

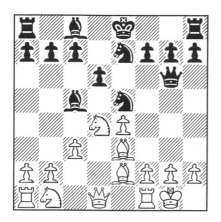

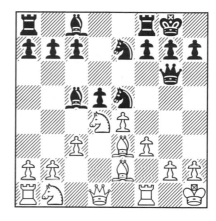

Diagram 15 (W)
Another crossroads

Diagram 16 (W)
A timely pawn break

White now has three important moves.

10 f3

The direct 10 f4 has been shorn of its terrors: 10...Qxe4 11 Bf2 Bxd4 12 cxd4 N5g6 13 Nc3 Qxf4 14 Nb5 0-0 15 Nxc7 Rb8 16 d5 (objectively best is 16 Nb5 Nf5 17 Nxa7 with equality, B.Gelfand-A.Beliavsky, Paris rapid 1991) 16...b6 17 Nb5 Qg5! and Black has the edge, A.Lastin-A.Aleksandrov, Minsk 2000.

I once lost a bad game to 10 Kh1, but Black's defensive methods are now better understood: 10...Qxe4 (after 10...0-0 11 f4 Qxe4 12 Nd2 Qxe3 13 Nc2 Ng4 14 Nxe3 Nxe3 15 Qa4 Nxf1 16 Rxf1, E.Berg-P.Acs, European Junior Ch. 1996, material is approximately balanced, but experience suggests that the side with the queen must be preferred) 11 Nd2 Qg6 12 Nb5 (12 Bh5 Qd3 13 Be2 Qg6 14 Bh5 is a drawing attempt, but Black can avoid this with 12...Bg4! 13 Bxg6 Bxd1 14 Bxf7+ Kxf7 15 Raxd1 Bxd4 16 Bxd4 N7c6, when the position is equal, but not drawn! S.Ganguly-A.Khalifman, FIDE World Ch., Moscow 2001) 12...0-0 13 Nxc7 Rb8 14 Bh5 Qf5 15 f4 N5c6 16 Nc4 and now 16...b5! seems to equalize, S.Rublevsky-I.Khenkin, Russian Team Ch. 2008.

10...0-0 11 Kh1 d5 (Diagram 16)

 TIP: When deciding whether or not to make a central pawn break, it's useful to ask whether this move benefits your pieces more than your opponent's. Another question to bear in mind is how would you otherwise organize your play if you don't resort to this plan.

12 f4!?

The better known 12 Nd2 is actually less challenging as Black has time to complete his development unhindered: 12...dxe4 13 fxe4 (13 Nxe4 doesn't isolate the e-pawn, but yields nothing: 13...Bb6 14 Bf2 Nf5 with equality, L.Milov-A.David, Bastia rapid 2005) 13...Bg4 14 Bf4 Bxe2 15 Qxe2 Bd6 16 Nb5 (this looks the natural way to try to hand out some punishment, but it fails to ruffle Black's feathers; if instead 16 Rad1 Rae8 17 Bxe5 Bxe5 18 Qb5 Bxd4 19 cxd4 Qb6 the position seems equal, S.Rublevsky-Kir.Georgiev, European Club Cup, St Vincent 2005) 16...N7c6 17 Nxd6 Qxd6 18 Nc4 Qe6 19 Ne3 Ng6 and Black is fine, V.Baklan-A.Delchev, Balaguer 2006.

12 Nf5?! is too wild. After 12...Nxf5 13 Bxc5 (if 13 exf5 Qd6) 13...dxe4 14 fxe4 Nh4 15 Rg1 Re8 16 Nd2 Bg4, as in E.Schmittdiel-B.Latzke, Württemberg 2007, Black has the superior structure and his knight pair have no reason to envy White's bishops.

12...Qxe4 13 b4

13 Bg1 Nc4 14 Bf3 Qg6 15 Qe2 c6 16 a4 was agreed drawn in S.Movsisian-Z.Hracek, Czech League 2001 – prematurely in my opinion, as Black is surely better. For example, after 16...Qh6! 17 b3 (if 17 Nd2 Nxd2 18 Qxd2 Bd6; while 17 Nf5?? is refuted by 17...Nxf5 18 Bxc5 Ng3+) 17...Bxd4 18 Bxd4 Nf5 19 Bf2 Ncd6 it doesn't feel like White has adequate compensation to me. All in all I prefer Black.

13...Bb6

13...Qxe3 14 bxc5 b6 15 cxb6 Nc4 16 bxc7 Ng6 17 Bxc4 dxc4 18 Nd2 was messy in F.Amonatov-A.Aleksandrov, Zvenigorod 2008, but White managed to maintain some advantage and eventually win.

As both that and the game continuation are a little shaky, 13...Bxd4 may be best here – see the next note.

14 Bg1 (Diagram 17) 14...Bh3!?

Tempting, but probably not quite sound; though it's better than 14...Nc4?? 15 Bxc4 dxc4 16 Re1, when Black loses a piece with virtually nothing to show for it.

Knaak analyses 14...Bxd4 and suggests that it is the best move (so perhaps Black should have played this one move earlier?). Then 15 Bxd4 (after 15 cxd4 Nd7 16 Bd3 Qe6 17 Qc2 White wins his pawn back and shouldn't be worse) 15...N5c6 (now if 15...Nd7 16 Bd3 Qe6 17 Re1 Qd6 18 Na3 c6 19 f5!? then White has sufficient compensation with space, development and the bishop pair on his side) 16 Bd3 Qe6 17 f5 Qh6 18 f6 Ng6 is totally unclear according to Knaak.

15 Rf2 Bxd4 16 cxd4

Following 16 Qxd4 Ng4 17 Qxe4 Nxf2+ 18 Bxf2 dxe4 19 gxh3 Nd5 Black must be fine, White's structure and development being so poor.

16...Ng4 17 Rf3

Better than 17 Bxg4? Bxg4 18 Qxg4 Qxd4, or 17 Bf3 Nxf2+ 18 Bxf2 Qxf4 19 gxh3 c6, both of which clearly favour Black.

17...Bxg2+ 18 Kxg2 Nf5 (Diagram 18) 19 Qd2?

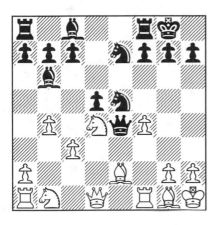

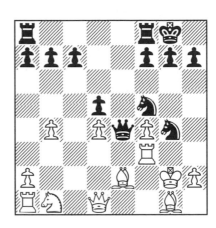

Diagram 17 (B)

How should Black continue?

Diagram 18 (W)

And how should White defend?

Natural, but bad. White should have played the cool 19 Kh1! and then:

a) 19...Nh4? fails to 20 Nc3.

b) 19...Nge3 (the intended move?) also seems inadequate after 20 Qd3 Nc2 (20...Nxd4 falls short after 21 Qxe4 dxe4 22 Rxe3 Nc2 23 Rc3 Nxa1 24 Rc1!) 21 Nc3 Qxd3 22 Bxd3 Nh4 (or 22...Nxa1 23 Bxf5) 23 Rh3 and so on.

c) 19...Rfe8 was perhaps the only way to grovel, although 20 Bd3 Qe6 21 Nc3 consolidates, when Black's two pawns for the piece are not going to be enough.

19...Nh4+ 20 Kg3 Qg6!

Now the attack continues unabated.

21 Kxh4 Nf6 22 Re3

22 Rg3?? gets mated after 22...Qh6+ as White needs g3 for his king. If he tries 22

Rf1, he would go down to 23...Qh6+ 23 Kg3 Ne4+ forking.

22...Qxg1 23 Bf3 Rae8

The big problem for White, apart from his vulnerable king, is his inability to develop his queenside.

24 Re5 Ne4 25 Bxe4 Rxe5 26 dxe5 dxe4 (Diagram 19)

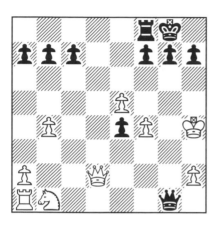

Diagram 19 (W)

Black is winning

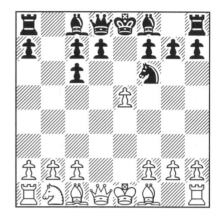

Diagram 20 (B)

The Mieses Variation

27 a4

27 Qb2 would enable White finally to move his queen's knight, but too late as 27...Rd8 28 Nc3 (or 28 Na3 Qe3 29 Rf1 Rd3) 28...Qe3 29 Rf1 Rd2 is crushing.

27...e3 28 Qe2 Re8 0-1

Black plays 4...Nf6

Game 34
□ N.McDonald ■ M.Hebden
Southend 2007

1 e4 e5 2 Nf3 Nc6 3 d4 exd4 4 Nxd4 Nf6 5 Nxc6

The other option, 5 Nc3, transposes to the Scotch Four Knights (see Chapter Four).

5...bxc6 6 e5 (Diagram 20)

The thematic move. It's as if White is trying to punish Black for having dared develop his knight so early!

6...Qe7

Pinning.

7 Qe2

Unpinning! Now Black really must move his knight. One of the main features of this, the Mieses Variation, is the fact that both sides have blocked in their king's bishop, so development tends to be clumsy and somewhat unnatural.

7...Nd5 8 c4 Ba6

The alternative, 8...Nb6, is examined in the next game.

9 b3 (Diagram 21)

Diagram 21 (B)

A critical juncture

Diagram 22 (W)

Black seeks the initiative

9...0-0-0!?

If I had this position as Black, this wouldn't be my choice, as I consider 9...g5 to be superior.

However, first of all I should mention 9...g6, after which White has 10 f4! (now with the e-pawn secured Black has to be careful not to run out of space) 10...Bg7 (10...Qb4+ 11 Bd2 Qb6 12 Nc3 Bb4 13 Qd3 Nxc3 14 Bxc3 Qa5 15 Bxb4 Qxb4+ 16 Qd2 Qxd2+ 17 Kxd2 c5 was close to equality, though 18 h4 still offered White a pull in J.Hector-T.Ernst, Swedish Ch., Lidköping 1999) 11 Qf2 Nf6 (11...Nb6 is met by 12 Ba3) 12 Be2! (now if 12 Ba3 Black has 12...Ng4! 13 Qe2 Qe6) 12...Ne4 13 Qe3 f5 14 Ba3 d6 15 Nd2 was messy, but White came out on top in A.Goloshchapov-A.Moiseenko, Ordzhonikidze 2000.

So going back to 9...g5!, we understand that this eccentric-looking move is directed against f2-f4, which is now less appetizing for White. Instead, 10 g3 is normal, when 10...Bg7 11 Bb2 0-0-0 12 Bg2 Rde8 13 0-0 Bxe5 14 Qxe5 Qxe5 15 Bxe5 Rxe5 16 cxd5 Bxf1 17 Kxf1 cxd5 is the critical tabiya and has been tested in numerous encounters (including A.Areshchenko-M.Hebden, Gibraltar 2008). The chances in this ending, with rook and two pawns versus knight and bishop, seem to be more or less equal.

10 g3 f6

Black's three main options are equally popular, with 10...g5 (similar to 9...g5 in the previous note) scoring slightly higher than the others.

The third line is 10...Re8 11 Bb2 f6 12 Bg2 (Black has spent so much time to attack the e-pawn, White decides he can let it go without so much as a blink!) 12...fxe5 13 Nd2 (if 13 0-0 h5!? 14 Qd2 Nf6 gives Black counterplay against the king) 13...h5 14 0-0-0 Qb4 15 Ne4 Qa5 16 Kb1 Ba3 17 Qd2, when White obtained plenty of compensation in S.Rublevsky-V.Mikhalevski, European Club Cup, Vilnius 1995, even after simplification with 17...Qxd2 18 Rxd2 Bxb2 19 Kxb2 Nb6 20 Rc1 Kb8 21 a4! etc.

11 e6?!

11 Bg2 fxe5 12 0-0 is more to the point; for example, 12...Nf6 13 Bb2 Re8 14 Re1 h5 (14...Bb7 15 Nd2 Qf7 16 a3, M.Müller-H.Wegner, German League 1992, gives Black the harder position to play, as his king is the more vulnerable of the two monarchs and his pieces more difficult to co-ordinate) 15 Qd2 Qb4 (15...Qc5 16 Nc3 h4 17 Na4 Qb4 18 Qxb4 Bxb4 19 Rxe5 gave White a pull in Y.Dembo-S.Husari, Budapest 2003) 16 Rxe5 Rxe5 17 Bxe5 Qxd2 18 Nxd2 Bb4 19 Nf3 Re8 20 Bxf6 gxf6 21 Bh3 and White won the endgame in G.Jones-M.Hebden, British League 2007, as Black's damaged structure turned out to be more significant than the bishop pair.

11...f5! (Diagram 22)

Black seeks the initiative, not a pawn-counting contest!

After the inferior 11...dxe6 12 Bg2 Nb4 13 0-0 Bb7 14 Nc3 Black has an extra pawn, but his development is backward and the queenside is not easy to handle; e.g. 14...c5 15 Bxb7+ Kxb7 16 Be3 Qe8 17 Na4 Qc6 18 a3 Na6?! (too passive; 18...Nd3 19 f4 e5 would still have been unclear) 19 Nc3 Bd6 20 b4! and White's attack was under way, D.Marciano-G.Moncamp, Cannes 2000.

12 Bh3 Qf6

Gaining time for development.

13 Bb2 Bb4+ 14 Kf1 Qh6! 15 exd7+ Kb8 16 Kg2

Or 16 Bxf5 Rhf8 17 Qd3 Bc5. In any event White's undeveloped forces now have difficulty in defending against all the threats.

16...Rxd7 17 a3 Bc5 18 Re1

18 Qc2 runs into 18...Nf4+! 19 gxf4 Qg6+ 20 Kf3 Qh5+ 21 Kg2 Rd6 22 Bxf5 Rf8 with a winning attack.

18...Re7 19 Qd2 f4! (Diagram 23)

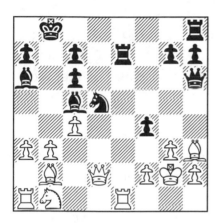

Diagram 23 (W)

Black has a vicious attack

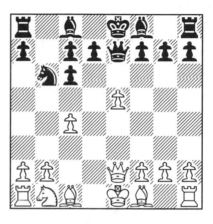

Diagram 24 (W)

Black plays 8...Nb6

20 Bg4?

20 Rxe7 Bxe7 21 Bg4 would hold everything together, but I suspect that, rather than recapture on e7, Hebden would have continued 20...f3+! 21 Kxf3 Qxh3 with a vicious attack; e.g. 22 Bxg7 Rg8 23 cxd5 Bxe7 etc.

Otherwise 20 cxd5? is bad, since 20...f3+ 21 Kxf3 Qxh3 would then be even stronger.

20...Rxe1 21 Qxe1 fxg3 22 hxg3 Rf8 23 Bf3

White succeeds in covering the f2-square, but Black's active pieces can create other threats...

23...Bc8! 24 g4 Rxf3

24...Nf4+ 25 Kg1 Bxf2+! would also have won.

25 Kxf3 Qh3+

Or here 25...Qf4+ 26 Kg2 Qxg4+ 27 Kh2 Nf4 mates quickly.

26 Ke4 Bxg4 27 Nd2 Bf5+ 28 Ke5 Ne7 0-1

All roads lead to mate! For instance, 28...Bd6+ 29 Kd4 Qd3 mate.

Game 35
□ **V.Tseshkovsky** ■ **I.Kovalenko**
Russian Team Championship 2008

1 e4 e5 2 Nf3 Nc6 3 d4 exd4 4 Nxd4 Nf6 5 Nxc6 bxc6 6 e5 Qe7 7 Qe2 Nd5 8 c4 Nb6 (Diagram 24)

In the previous game Black played 8...Ba6, but the bishop sometimes turns out to be badly placed on that square. So here Black drops his knight back instead, deciding that he would prefer to place his light-squared bishop elsewhere.

9 Nc3 Qe6 10 Qe4

White obtained nothing after 10 b3 a5 11 Qe3 Bb4 12 Bd2 a4 13 Rc1 axb3 14 axb3 0-0 15 Bd3 Ra5 in A.Motylev-M.Sosnicki, Polanica Zdroj 1999.

10...g6 11 f4!?

Alternatively, White could develop his bishop first: 11 Bd3 Bg7 12 f4 0-0 13 0-0 Ba6 14 b3, but after 14...d5! (the key liberating idea) 15 cxd5 cxd5 16 Qe2 Bxd3 17 Qxd3 c5 18 Ba3 Rfc8 Black had no problems, D.Pavasovic-J.Pinter, Croatian Team Ch. 2005.

11...Bb7

After 11...Bg7, White can get a pull with 12 c5 Nd5 13 Bc4.

The clearest way seems to be the immediate 11...d5!; for example, 12 exd6 (no better is 12 cxd5 cxd5 13 Qc2 a6 14 Be2 Be7 15 0-0 0-0 16 a4 Rb8 17 a5 Nd7 18 Qd1 d4!, R.Zelcic-H.Stevic, Croatian Ch., Split 2008) 12...cxd6 13 Be3 Bg7 14 0-0-0 Bxc3 15 Qxe6+ Bxe6 16 bxc3 0-0-0 17 Bd4 Rhg8 with full equality, S.Movsesian-Z.Almasi, German League 2002.

12 a4!

Probing and provoking a weakness.

12...a5

Again 12...d5!? comes into consideration.

13 Bd3 0-0-0 14 0-0 Bc5+ 15 Kh1 (Diagram 25)

A typical scenario in this line. Black has developed quickly, but his minor pieces and queenside pawns are in a traffic jam and he will need time to reorganize.

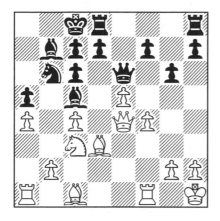

Diagram 25 (B)

A typical scenario

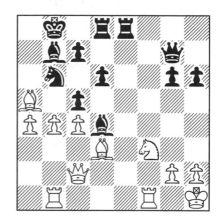

Diagram 26 (B)

Starting a pawn storm

15...d6 16 Qe2 Bd4 17 Ne4 c5 18 Rb1

'Slow but sure' summarizes White's approach here.

18...Rhe8

Snatching the a-pawn would lead to Black getting tangled up again; e.g. 18...Nxa4?! 19 Ra1 Bc6 20 Ng5 Qe8 21 Nf3 and White has the initiative.

19 b3 Kb8

No doubt Black wanted to avoid 19...dxe5 20 f5! gxf5 21 Ng5! (the obvious 21 Nxc5? Bxc5! 22 Bxf5 Qxf5 23 Rxf5 Be4 gives Black too much wood for the queen) 21...Qe7 22 Bxf5+ etc.

20 Ng5 Qe7 21 e6!?

A 'bottling up' pawn sacrifice to slow down any Black counterplay.

 NOTE: Chess time can't always be as easily measured as material, but is often more important.

21...fxe6 22 Bd2

In any case White can win the a-pawn at leisure, so he won't have a material deficit for long.

22...h6?!

This weakens Black's structure. I prefer 22...Qd7!, intending to meet 23 Bxa5 (or 23 Rbe1) with 23...e5.

23 Nf3 e5 24 fxe5 Bxe5 25 Bxa5 Qg7 26 Qc2

Now Black's problem is that he hasn't much to bite on.

26...Bd4 27 b4! (Diagram 26)

Tseshkovsky gets his queenside rolling. 26...g5 would have been met in the same way.

27...Ka7 28 b5

The plan now is to sweep away Black's defences with a4-a5.

28...d5 29 Nxd4 Qxd4 30 Bc3 Qg4 31 h3 Qd7 32 a5 Nxc4 33 b6+

The attack plays itself, as they say.

33...cxb6 34 axb6+ Kb8 35 Bf6 Ne3 36 Qxc5 Nxf1 37 Rxf1 Qc6 38 Qd4

There is no sense in exchanging queens: Black's king is very weak, whereas White's is as safe as houses.

38...Rd7 39 Bxg6 1-0 (Diagram 27)

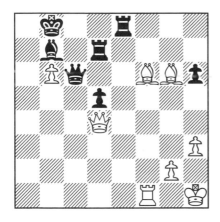

Diagram 27 (B)

Black resigned

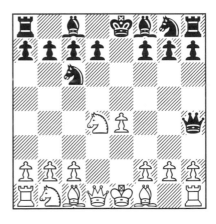

Diagram 28 (W)

The Steinitz Variation

Black resigned as 39...Re2 can be met decisively in several ways, one of them being 40 Bh5! Re4 41 Be5+ Rxe5 (or 41...Kc8 42 Rf8+ Rd8 43 Bg4+ Rxg4 44 Qxg4+ Qd7 45 Rxd8+ Kxd8 46 Bf6+ etc) 42 Qxe5+ Qd6 43 Rf8+ Bc8 44 Qe8 Qc6 45 Bg4 and wins.

Black plays 4...Qh4

Game 36
□ Z.Azmaiparashvili ■ J.Hector
San Sebastian 1991

1 e4 e5 2 Nf3 Nc6 3 d4 exd4 4 Nxd4 Qh4!? (Diagram 28)

The Steinitz Variation, in which Black's queen courageously volunteers for the front! This line has seen some interest because 'grabbing a pawn and holding the fort' is one way of obtaining a complex game with winning chances.

5 Nb5

White can also play 5 Nc3, when 5...Bb4 6 Be2 Qxe4 7 Nb5 transposes to the game (and was in fact the course taken) while avoiding other possibilities for Black, such as in the next note.

5...Bb4+

Black doesn't necessarily have to go pawn-grabbing, despite the reputation of his fourth move! For example, 5...Bc5!? 6 Qf3 Nd4 7 Nxd4 Bxd4 8 c3 Bb6 9 Nd2 d6 was seen in M.Sibarevic-M.Chiburdanidze, Banja Luka 1985, when 10 Bb5+ (or 10 Nc4 Nf6 11 Nxb6 axb6 12 Bd3 0-0 13 0-0 Re8 and Black has enough play – Gutman) 10...c6 11 Be2 Nf6 12 Nc4 Bc7 13 Qf4 Qxf4 14 Bxf4 Be6 15 Nxd6+ Bxd6 16 Bxd6 Nxe4 17 Bf4 leaves White with only a nominal edge.

6 N1c3

Or 6 Bd2 Qxe4+ (Black could still hold back with 6...Bc5!?) 7 Be2 (Diagram 29) 7...Kd8 (7...Qxg2? is foolhardy, as after 8 Bf3 Bxd2+ 9 Nxd2 Qh3, as in J.Gallagher-J.L.Costa, Bern 1991, White could have played 10 Nxc7+! Kd8 11 Nxa8 Nf6 12 Nc4 Re8+ 13 Ne3, when Black wouldn't get anything like enough for his rook) 8 0-0 Bxd2 9 Nxd2 (or 9 Qxd2 a6 10 N1c3 Qh4 11 Na3 Qd4 12 Bd3 Nge7 13 Nc4 b5 14 Ne3 d6 15 Rad1 Be6 16 Qc1 with practical compensation) 9...Qf4 10 g3 Qh6 11 Nc4 Nge7 12 Qd3 a6 13 Nd4 Nxd4 14 Qxd4 Nc6 15 Qc3 Re8, as in J.Mieses-M.Chigorin, Hastings 1895, though after 16 Rfe1 White still has clear pressure for the pawn, a view endorsed by Lev Gutman, the leading specialist in this line.

TIP: A rule of thumb is that in the opening a pawn is worth about three tempi for development.

6...Qxe4+

Black should probably take his courage in his hands and capture the pawn! The alternative 6...Ba5 7 Bd2 a6 8 Na3 b5 (if 8...Bxc3 9 Bxc3 Qxe4+ 10 Be2! Nf6 11 Bxf6 gxf6 12 0-0 Gutman prefers White) 9 g3 Qe7 10 Bg2 is more comfortable for White who intends 0-0, Re1 and Nd5.

7 Be2 Bxc3+ 8 bxc3!

8 Nxc3 maintains the pawn structure but is a shade slow, so much so that Black can even get greedy: 8...Qxg2!? 9 Bf3 Qg6 10 Nd5 Kd8, and although White must have some compensation given Black's awkwardly-placed king, Black holds firm.

8...Kd8 9 0-0 (Diagram 30) 9...Nf6 10 Be3 Re8 11 Re1 Qd5

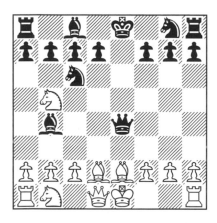

Diagram 29 (B)

The c7-pawn needs defending

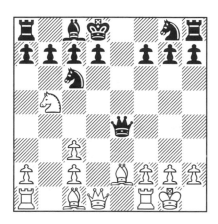

Diagram 30 (B)

White has great compensation

After 11...d6, the continuation 12 Rb1 Bd7?! 13 c4 Ne5 14 c5! Bc6 15 Bf1 Qg6 16 Nd4 Bd5 17 Bf4 Nfd7 18 Bg3 dxc5 19 Nb5 Be4 20 Qd2 led to White obtaining a strong attack in G.Vescovi-A.Rodriguez Vila, Sao Paulo 2005. Gutman, however, considers 12...Re7! to be best when after each of 13 c4 Bg4; 13 Bf3 Qh4 14 Nxa7 Rxa7!; and 13 Nd4 Nxd4 14 cxd4 Bg4, he quite likes Black. His analysis requires further tests but this could be the key line in the whole of the Steinitz variation.

12 Qc1!

Declining the exchange of queens with a neat manoeuvre.

12...Qf5 13 Qa3 d6 14 Rad1 Re7 15 c4

White's initiative endures and Black can only hope that the shield in front of his king will hold.

15...Be6 16 Bf3 Rd7 17 Bxc6 bxc6 18 Nd4 Qh5 19 Bg5! (Diagram 31)

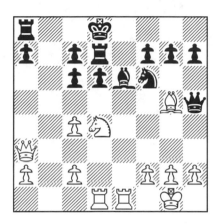

Diagram 31 (B)

White has a crushing position

Now White has a crushing position, whereas 19 Nxc6? Ke8 20 Nd4 Re7 would allow the black king to escape the worst.

19...c5

On 19...Qxg5 White has 20 Rxe6! Qc5 21 Qa6 and wins.

20 Bxf6+ gxf6 21 Nc6+ Ke8 22 Qb2 Qh4 23 Qb7 Rad8 24 Rd3 1-0

The rook is heading for g3; e.g. 24...Qxc4 25 Rg3 Kf8 26 Nxd8 Rxd8 27 Qxc7 Rd7 28 Qb8+ Ke7 29 Rg8 and mate comes soon. A model display by White and a good example of the dangers that Black exposes himself to in this line.

Summary

The Scotch is one of White's best options and leads to a number of rich and complex variations. Many of these have the advantage of being less worked out than other Open Games, so there is more opportunity for individual interpretation.

For Black, I don't trust 4...Qh4, but both 4...Bc5 and 4...Nf6 introduce reliable systems.

Chapter Six
Central Gambits

Introduction

In the chess world the 'Romantic era' was a period when chess was all about attacking like crazy whatever the consequences. At that time 1 e4 was by far the most common first move and 1...e5 the main reply, so the leading masters were particularly concerned about the consequences of sharp tactical play in the Open Games.

A number of openings come to mind when we think about this type of chess: the King's Gambit and the Evans Gambit to cite a couple. There are also several involving an early d2-d4, where White again forcefully opens lines and, when followed up with the sacrifice of a pawn or two, generates an initiative.

The idea of an aggressive d2-d4 will not be new to those who have already examined the Two Knights Defence in Chapter Two. However, there are certain move orders that can have independent significance and these will be highlighted in this chapter.

My recommendation for Black, in general, is not to be too greedy, as White then gets the type of position he is seeking. Furthermore, defending against an early attack can be a trying experience!

More specifically, against the Danish and Göring Gambits reacting with an early ...d7-d5 to liberate one's position is appropriate, while against the Urusov and Scotch Gambits simply transposing to the Two Knights Defence is the most prudent approach.

Strategy

White wants to pressurize Black from the start. Open lines, a lead in development and the chance to play for tricks, tactics and an attack are what motivate him.

In return, Black can snatch material and hold out, but the better defences usually involve him giving back most, if not all, of the booty in order to catch up in development and thus nullify White's attacking ambitions.

Theoretical

Yes, these gambits can be theoretical, but if you play my recommended lines there won't be that much to learn from Black's point of view, though some knowledge of the Two Knights Defence will be useful.

Danish Gambit

1 e4 e5 2 d4 exd4 3 c3 (Diagram 1)

Diagram 1 (B)	**Diagram 2 (W)**
Danish Gambit	Black is three pawns up

Accepting the gambit, 3...dxc3, is often met by 4 Bc4 (as in Game 37) – White is already two pawns down and he doesn't even recapture on c3! Black has to decide how much material to snatch and then how to avoid any damage from White's more active pieces. For example, one line goes 4...cxb2 5 Bxb2, but I consider this to be rather dangerous for Black.

My recommendation is to decline the gambit with 3...d5, when the usual sequence 4 exd5 Qxd5 5 cxd4 Nc6 6 Nf3 transposes to the Göring Gambit.

Some players are known as having an 'attacking style'. These days this usually means attacking in a measured way, when the opportunity arises and from a strategically superior game. A century ago, however, the aim of attacking right from the start was a more normal frame of mind, and it would often succeed as both opening knowledge and defensive technique were relatively poor.

The Central Gambits, including the Danish, had their heyday in that epoch, but are rarely seen in tournaments today as the antidotes are now well known.

Nevertheless, despite any assumption that these lines are 'archaic', who wouldn't dream of playing a game such as the following...

Game 37
☐ H.E.Atkins ■ H.Jacobs
London 1915

1 e4 e5 2 d4 exd4 3 c3 dxc3 4 Bc4 Nf6 5 Nf3

5 Nxc3 Nc6 6 Nf3 is more normal these days, transposing to the Göring Gambit.

5...Nxe4

It seems that Black has an appetite!

6 0-0 Nd6 (Diagram 2)

Black is three pawns up and attacking the bishop, but White has a big lead in development. Would you prefer having White or Black?

7 Nxc3!?

Offering the bishop incites further stimulation for Black's greed! In the modern epoch, many players would have preferred 7 Bd3 with some practical chances for the pawns.

7...Nxc4 8 Re1+ Be7 9 Nd5 Nc6 10 Bg5 f6 11 Rc1

11 Bf4 is possible, but Atkins doesn't seem that fond of retreating bishops!

11...b5 12 Rxc4

Fair enough, who needs that rook anyway?

12...bxc4 13 Ne5 (Diagram 3)

Throwing more wood on the fire!

13...fxg5??

Cracking under the pressure. 13...fxe5 was correct, as 14 Nxe7 Nxe7 15 Rxe5 0-0! would leave the attacking side short of compensation; e.g. 16 Bxe7 Qe8 17 Qd5+ Qf7 or 16 Rxe7 d5 17 Qd4 Rf7 and White remains material down. A tricky and somewhat precarious defence that wouldn't have been easy to find over the board.

14 Qh5+ g6 15 Nf6+!

A star move that wins; whereas 15 Nxg6 hxg6 16 Qxh8+ Kf7 only leads to perpetual check.

15...Bxf6 16 Nxg6+ Qe7

A sure sign that things have gone wrong!

17 Rxe7+ Bxe7

Atkins now finishes off in the most elegant way.

18 Ne5+ Kd8 19 Nf7+ Ke8 20 Nd6+ Kd8 21 Qe8+ Rxe8 22 Nf7 mate (Diagram 4)

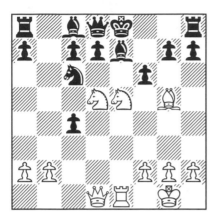

Diagram 3 (B)	**Diagram 4 (B)**
More wood on the fire	Quality, not quantity!

As I've mentioned before, it's the *quality* of your pieces that count, not the *quantity* – that is, according to Kasparov and Atkins!

Göring Gambit

1 e4 e5 2 Nf3 Nc6 3 d4 exd4 4 c3 (Diagram 5)

After 4...dxc3, White continues with 5 Nxc3 or 5 Bc4 (see Game 38). The principles are essentially the same as in the Danish Gambit.

In Bryson-Flear (Game 39) I examine my recommended defence 4...d5, declining the generous offer of a pawn.

Game 38
□ **I.Nataf** ■ **G.Horvath**
Paris 1995

1 e4 e5 2 Nf3 Nc6 3 d4 exd4 4 c3 dxc3 5 Bc4

The other main line is 5 Nxc3 Bb4 6 Bc4 d6 **(Diagram 6)** (otherwise 6...Nf6 returns to the game) and then:

a) 7 Qb3! Qe7 8 0-0 Bxc3 9 Qxc3 Nf6 10 Re1 Ne5 11 Bb5+ c6 12 Nxe5 cxb5 13 Nc6 (or perhaps 13 Nf3 0-0 14 Bg5) 13...Qc7 14 Nd4 with sufficient compensation, according to Emms.

Diagram 5 (B)
Göring Gambit

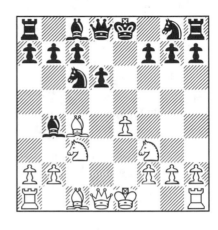

Diagram 6 (W)
White plays 5 Nxc3

b) 7 0-0 is less precise: 7...Bxc3 8 bxc3 Nf6 9 e5 Nxe5 10 Nxe5 dxe5 11 Qb3 (after 11 Qxd8+ Kxd8 12 Bxf7 Ke7 13 Bb3 Be6 Black is more than comfortable) 11...Qe7 12 Ba3 c5 13 Bb5+ Kf8 14 f4 e4 15 f5 b6 16 Bc6 Rb8 17 Qa4 was A.Blees-H.Hoeksma, Groningen 1997, but after 17...a6! 18 Rad1 Bb7 19 Bxb7 Qxb7 20 Bc1 h6 it's hard to believe that White would have enough.

5...Nf6 6 Nxc3 Bb4 7 e5

7 0-0 Bxc3 8 bxc3 d6 would transpose to line 'b' in the previous note.

7...d5! (Diagram 7)

The appropriate reaction, yet again, when faced with e4-e5. Alternatives would cede time and territory to White.

 WARNING: Gambits are dangerous if you neglect development and allow your opponent to dominate the central arena.

8 exf6 dxc4 9 Qxd8+

9 Qe2+ Be6 10 fxg7 Rg8 11 Bg5 can be well met by 11...Nd4!, E.Varnusz-G.Kluger, Hungarian Ch., Budapest 1961.

9...Nxd8 10 fxg7 Rg8 11 Bh6 Ne6 12 0-0-0 Bxc3 13 bxc3 Nxg7 (Diagram 8)

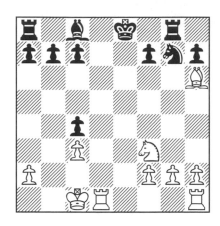

Diagram 7 (W)	**Diagram 8 (W)**
The standard reaction	A critical moment

Much better than 13...Nc5? 14 Ng5 Nd3+ 15 Rxd3 cxd3 16 Nxh7 Ke7 17 Re1+ Be6 18 f4 f5 19 g4, when White was already winning in D.Levy-N.Karaklajic, Cienfuegos 1972.

14 Nd4?

14 Rhe1+ is critical:

a) 14...Be6?! 15 g4 Rd8 (15...Ke7 16 Nh4 Ne8 17 h3 Nd6 18 f4 offers an initiative for White according to Müller & Voigt) 16 Nd4 c5?! (or if 16...Rd5 17 f4) 17 Nf5! spells trouble for Black, D.Sermek-Z.Gyimesi, Kecskemet 1992.

b) 14...Ne6! (my preference) 15 Bf4 f6!? (or possibly 15...Kf8 16 Bh6+ Ke7 17 Nh4, as in V.Bakhrakh-Z.Gyimesi, Budapest 1994, when 17...b6! looks fine for Black) 16 Bxc7 Kf7 17 Bg3 b5 18 Rd5 a6 with full equality.

14...Bd7 15 Rhe1+ Ne6 16 Nf5

White has no threats, so there is time for...

16...Rxg2

White now thrashes about seeking some tricks.

17 Ng7+ Kd8 18 Nxe6+ fxe6 19 f4!?

Better is 19 Rxe6 Rg6 (rather than 19...Rxf2?? 20 Bg5+ Kc8 21 Re8+! and Black goes red!) 20 Rxg6 hxg6 when Black has an extra pawn, but the presence of opposite-coloured bishops would give White decent drawing chances.

19...b6!

Making an escape route for the king.

20 Rxe6 Rxa2 (Diagram 9)

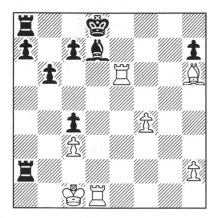

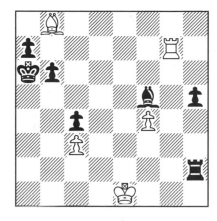

Diagram 9 (W)	**Diagram 10 (B)**
The passed a-pawn is strong	But it's the h-pawn that wins

21 Rd4!?

21 Rf6 came into consideration, as after 21...Ra1+ 22 Kd2 Rxd1+ 23 Kxd1 Black can't untangle without making a concession or two; e.g. 23...Ke7 (or 23...Kc8 24 Rf7 Bg4+ 25 Kc1 Kb7 26 Rxh7 Rd8) 24 Bg5 Ke8 25 Bh6 Rc8 and Black still has plenty of work to do.

21...Kc8 22 Re7 Bf5 23 Rd5 Rc2+ 24 Kd1 Rxh2

24...Bd3!? is another winning attempt, though 25 Rdd7 Kb7 26 Rxc7+ Ka6 27 Rxc4 Rxh2 28 Rd4 is still very complicated.

25 Bg7

Keeping the bishops is a practical option, especially as the double-rook ending after 25 Rxf5 Rxh6 26 Rff7 Rc6 27 Rxh7 Kb7 should see Black taking the whole point.

25...Rh5!?

Slightly laborious, but after 25...Bg4+ 26 Kc1 Kb7 27 f5 White has counterplay.

26 Be5 Kb7 27 Rxc7+ Ka6 28 Ke1

If 28 Rxc4, then 28...Be6 and Black wins the exchange; e.g. 29 Ra4+ Kb7 30 Rdd4 Bb3+ or 30 Rb5 Bd7.

28...Rg8 29 Bg7 Re8+ 30 Be5 Re6 31 Rd2 Rh1+ 32 Kf2 Rh2+ 33 Ke1 Reh6 34 Rxh2

Rxh2 35 Rg7 h5 36 Bb8 (Diagram 10)

Winning back one pawn, but now the black h-pawn is rolling.

36...h4 37 Rxa7+ Kb5 38 Rf7 Bd3 39 f5 Re2+ 40 Kd1 h3 41 f6

Or if 41 Rf6 Rg2 42 Rh6 Bxf5 43 Rh5, then 43...Ka4! 44 Rxf5 h2 is the simplest win.

41...h2 42 Bxh2 Rxh2 43 Rf8 Rf2 44 Ke1 Rf3 45 Kd2 Ka4 46 f7 Kb5 0-1

Game 39
□ D.Bryson ■ G.Flear
British Championship, Edinburgh 1985

1 e4 e5 2 Nf3

Against the Danish 2 d4 exd4 3 c3, Black should still play the same way with 3...d5!, when 4 exd5 Qxd5 5 cxd4 Nc6 6 Nf3 transposes below. The game Herzog-Flear (see the note to White's 15th move) did follow this route.

2...Nc6 3 d4 exd4 4 c3 d5! (Diagram 11)

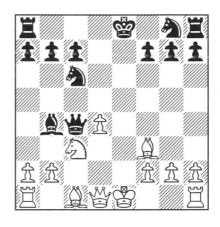

Diagram 11 (W)	**Diagram 12 (W)**
The simplest solution	Capablanca's idea

This straightforward solution stops White having his fun. Black doesn't bother chasing pawns; he prefers to catch up in development and equalize comfortably.

5 exd5 Qxd5 6 cxd4 Bg4 7 Nc3 Bb4 8 Be2

8 a3?! is inferior, as Black has 8...Bxf3! 9 axb4 Qe6+ 10 Be2 Bxe2 11 Nxe2 Nf6 12 0-0 0-0 13 b5 Nb4, obtaining at least equality due to his superior pawn structure, M.Voigt-M.Chandler, German League 2002.

8...Bxf3!

The point behind ceding the bishop without being pushed becomes clear after Black's next move.

If Black, instead, just continues developing rapidly and White is allowed to castle in peace, the position becomes quite complex. Black's active-looking pieces don't always gel quite as well as White's, something to remember if you are tempted by the ambitious 8...0-0-0. Here are some sample lines: 9 0-0 Qa5 (9...Bxc3 10 bxc3 Nf6 11 Be3 Rhe8 12 c4 yields a clear advantage for White due to his mobile pawns and bishop pair) 10 Be3 (better than 10 Ng5?! Bxe2 11 Qxe2 Nxd4 12 Qc4 Nh6 13 Be3 b5! which clearly favoured Black in G.Drakakis-E.Koutsogiannis, Nikea 2006) 10...Nf6 and there is the danger that Black's pieces lack targets while White makes progress; e.g. 11 Na4 (or 11 h3 Bh5 12 Na4 Qd5 13 a3 Ba5 14 Rc1 Qd6 15 Nc5 Bb6 16 Qa4, W.Kaufman-Y.Masserey, Swiss Team Ch. 1996) 11...Rhe8 12 h3 Bh5 13 a3 Bd6 14 Rc1 (14 g4!? Nxg4 15 hxg4 Bxg4 16 d5 looks good for White, though it's a courageous attempt!) 14...Qf5, D.Bryson-I.Sietaj, Novi Sad Olympiad 1990, and then perhaps 15 Nc5 with a pull.

Essentially 8...0-0-0 is more risky, but not necessarily inferior.

 TIP: When you are building a repertoire and there are several alternatives to choose from, pick the one that you feel the most comfortable with, even if top GMs prefer another.

9 Bxf3 Qc4! (Diagram 12)

Capablanca's idea, preventing White from castling. Indeed, his best is now to seek the exchange of queens which leads to an equal game. Of course 9...Qxd4?? 10 Bxc6+ would be naïve.

10 Be3?!

Played in the spirit of the gambit, but it isn't really correct. Nor is 10 d5 Nd4! particularly good either.

Instead, 10 Qb3 Qxb3 11 axb3!? is a rare idea, when Black can capture on d4 with fascinating complications, but 11...Nge7 is simple and good; e.g. 12 0-0 a6 13 Ra4 Bd6 14 Ne4 0-0-0 with equality, J.Stocek-G.Timoscenko, Czech League 2000.

However, 10 Bxc6+ is the main move here. Then Black can avoid broken pawns by recapturing with the queen, but this allows White to castle with good prospects due to his lead in development. So Black usually plays 10...bxc6! and now:

a) 11 Qb3 Qxb3 12 axb3 Ne7 (12...a5!? might also be good) 13 Ra6 Kd7! 14 0-0 Rhb8 15 Ne4 Bd6 16 Nxd6 cxd6 17 Ra3 Rb7 with an edge to Black, J.Moreno Ruiz-V.Gallego Jimenez, Madrid 1992. Black's play down the b-file makes 11 Qb3 look dubious.

b) 11 Qe2+ Qxe2+ 12 Kxe2 0-0-0 (Marin recommends an alternative plan: 12...Ne7 13 Be3 Kd7!? 14 Rac1 Rab8 15 Kd3 Bxc3 16 bxc3 Rb2 17 Rc2 Rhb8, as in V.Bondarenko-E.Najer, Moscow 1996) 13 Be3 Ne7 **(Diagram 13)** and Black has more or less equalized. Müller and Voigt claim a slight pull with the plan of placing the white king on c4 with 14 Kd3! (certainly a better chance than 14 Rhd1 Rhe8 15 a3 Ba5 16 Kf3 Bb6 17 Na4 Nf5 where Black is at least equal, A.Miles-J.Nunn, Islington 1970), but after 14...c5! (probably best, and equalizes in my opinion; whereas 14...Nf5!? 15 Kc4 Ba5 offers chances for both sides, but there is the danger that Black's bishop will get locked out of play, while White also has the more active king – even so, a draw is still the most likely result) 15 Kc4 cxd4 (or 15...Bxc3 16 bxc3 cxd4 17 Bxd4 Nc6) 16 Bxd4 Nc6 17 Rad1 Rxd4+ 18 Rxd4 Bxc3 19 Kxc3 Nxd4 20 Kxd4 Re8 is totally sterile.

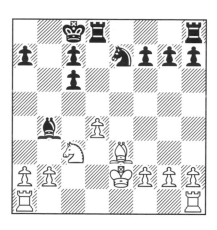

Diagram 13 (W)

The position is roughly equal

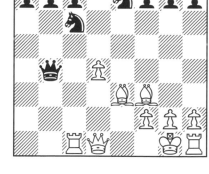

Diagram 14 (W)

Improving on Capablanca

10...Bxc3+

There is no reason not to take this pawn.

11 bxc3 Qxc3+ 12 Kf1 Qc4+ 13 Kg1 Nge7 14 Rc1

Carrying on regardless, another pawn is offered...

14...Qxa2

...and taken with thanks.

15 Ra1

In A.Herzog-G.Flear, Graz 1984, White tried 15 d5, but following 15...Ne5 16 Be4 f5 17 Rc2 Qb3 18 d6 Rd8! Black had a big advantage.

15...Qc4 16 Rc1

This was the end of the game in F.Marshall-J.Capablanca, Lake Hopatcong 1926, with the players accepting a draw by repetition. However, Black has better than settling for half the spoils!

16...Qa2 17 Ra1 Qc4 18 Rc1 Qb4! (Diagram 14)

An improvement in my opinion.

19 Rb1 Qd6 20 Rxb7 0-0

Black completes his development and has an extra pawn. Naturally, with White's bishop pair and the broken black queenside there will be some compensation, but I still believe that Black is better.

21 g3 Nd5 22 Kg2 Rab8?

Intent on exchanges; whereas 22...Na5! 23 Rb1 (or if 23 Rb5, then 23...Nc3 24 Qd3 Nxb5 25 Qxb5 Qb6) 23...Nc4 would have maintained an edge.

23 Rxb8 Nxe3+

I was pleased to eliminate one of the bishops.

24 fxe3 Rxb8 25 Qa1! g6!?

The negative view here is that I was panicking about the back rank, but a more positive one is that I decided to challenge for the initiative.

Instead, 25...Ne7!? 26 Rb1 (26 Qxa7 Rb2+ inconveniences White's king) 26...Rb6 27 Rc1! would be about equal (rather than 27 Qxa7? Rxb1 28 Qa8+ Nc8 29 Qxc8+ Qf8).

26 Rc1

Winning the pawn back with a satisfactory position.

26...Ne7 27 Qxa7 Rb2+ 28 Kg1 (Diagram 15)

Now both sides have chances.

28...Qb4! 29 Rd1

29 Qxc7?? loses to 29...Qd2 etc.

29...Qc3 30 Qa8+ Kg7 31 Qe4 Nf5 32 Qd3 Qb4!?

32...Rb3 wins a pawn, but then 33 Qxc3 Rxc3 34 e4 Rxf3 35 exf5 Rxf5 36 Rc1 leads to a drawn rook endgame.

33 Bd5 h5 34 e4 Nh6 35 Qf3?!

The more careful 35 Rc1 followed by Qc3 should be about equal.

35...c6!

An interesting attempt to gain the advantage.

36 Bxc6 Qc4 37 Bd7 Qc2 38 h3 Qh2+ 39 Kf1 f5! 40 exf5 Qxh3+ 41 Ke1 (Diagram 16) 41...gxf5?

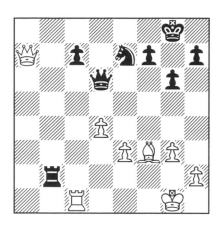

Diagram 15 (B)

Both sides have chances

Diagram 16 (B)

Here I missed a win

Missing my chance! Here 41...Qh2! wins; e.g. 42 f6+ Kh7 43 Kf1 Ng4! and Black mates very quickly.

42 Rd2 Rb1+ 43 Rd1 Rxd1+ 44 Kxd1 h4 45 Bxf5!

Giving his piece up to eliminate Black's remaining pawns.

45...Nxf5 46 Qb7+ Kf6 47 Qb6+ Kg5 48 gxh4+ Kf4

Black still hopes to create a mating net but this proves to be impossible.

49 Qf6 Qd3+ 50 Kc1 Ke4 51 Qe6+ Kf3 52 Qc6+ Ke3 53 Qc2 Qa3+ 54 Qb2 Qa5 55 Qb3+ Kf4 56 Qb8+ Kg4 57 Qc8 Kxh4 58 d5 Qa1+ 59 Kc2 Qa4+ 60 Kb2 Qb4+ 61 Kc2 Qe4+ 62 Kb2 Ne3 63 Qh8+ Kg4 64 d6

Black really will have to capture the d-pawn soon.

64...Qb4+ 65 Kc1 Qxd6 66 Qg7+ Kf3 67 Qc3 Ke4 68 Qb4+! ½-½

As 68...Qxb4 gives rise to an elegant stalemate.

Scotch Gambit

1 e4 e5 2 Nf3 Nc6 3 d4 exd4 4 Bc4 (Diagram 17)

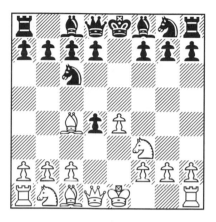

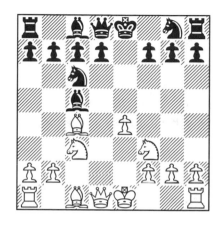

Diagram 17 (B)

The Scotch Gambit

Diagram 18 (B)

Black accepts the gambit

Although this position defines the Scotch Gambit, White's move order is frequently used simply as a transpositional tool.

4...Bc5!?

At this point 4...Nf6, transposing to the Two Knights Defence, is generally recognized as the strongest move here.

5 c3

5 0-0 Nf6 also enters the Two Knights Defence, this time into the Max Lange Attack.

5...dxc3

Here 5...Nf6!, transposing to the Giuoco Piano, is best.

6 Nxc3 (Diagram 18)

This position could conceivably also have arisen via a Danish or Göring Gambit! Alternatively, White was successful with 6 Bxf7+!? Kxf7 7 Qd5+ Kf8 8 Qxc5+ in Game 40.

6...d6

6...Nf6 7 e5 is slightly awkward; e.g. 7...Ng4 8 Bxf7+ Kxf7 9 Qd5+ and White is somewhat better.

7 Bg5

Less precise is 7 0-0 Nf6 8 Bg5 Bg4! which experience suggests is promising only for Black.

7...Nge7 8 0-0

Now it's time to castle. Instead White could try 8 Nd5?! leading to some notorious complications after the provocative 8...f6 9 Bxf6 gxf6 10 Nxf6+ Kf8 11 Qc1 Ng8 12 Nh5 Bb4+! 13 Kf1 Qe7 14 Qf4+ Ke8 15 Bxg8 Rxg8 16 Nf6+ Kf8 17 Ng5 Rxg5 18 Nxh7+ Kg8 19 Nxg5 Qg7, but the last word, as given by Müller and Voigt in 2003, seems to be that Black has the advantage.

8...h6 9 Bh4 0-0 10 Nd5 (Diagram 19)

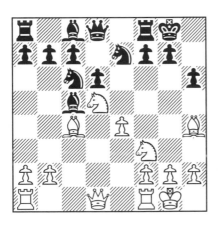

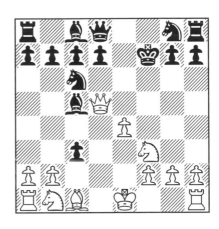

Diagram 19 (B)

White has attacking chances

Diagram 20 (B)

Check to the king

White has adequate compensation for the pawn and a complicated struggle lies ahead; for example, 10...Qd7 (or 10...Be6 11 b4 Bxb4 12 Qb3 Bc5 13 Nxe7+ Nxe7 14 Bxe6 fxe6 15 Qxe6+ Rf7, M.Cornette-A.Koulitchenko, Pau 2000) 11 b4 Nxd5 12 bxc5 Nf4 13 cxd6 Na5 14 Rc1 Nxc4 15 Rxc4 Qxd6 16 Qc2 Bg4 17 Bg3, D.Houpt-J.Del Carril, correspondence 1998.

Game 40
☐ E.Sveshnikov ■ V.Kupreichik
Hastings 1984/85

1 e4 e5 2 Nf3 Nc6 3 d4 exd4 4 Bc4 Bc5 5 c3 dxc3

Rather than transpose to the Giuoco Piano or the Two Knights with ...Nf6, Black decides to snatch the offered pawn.

6 Bxf7+

Taking advantage of the exposed position of the c5-bishop in order to regain the pawn. The alternative is 6 Nxc3, continuing to make a gambit of it – see the introductory notes above.

6...Kxf7 7 Qd5+ (Diagram 20) 7...Kf8

Actually Black can keep the pawn by playing 7...Ke8 8 Qxc5 cxb2 9 Bxb2, but then White has a great bishop and plenty of compensation; e.g. 9...Nf6 10 0-0 d6 11 Qc4 Qe7 12 Nc3 Bg4 13 Nd5 Qf7? 14 Ng5 Qg6 15 f4 with a crushing position, L.Radics-T.Gal, Nyiregyhaza 1999.

8 Qxc5+ d6

8...Qe7 9 Qxe7+ Ngxe7 10 Nxc3 a6 11 0-0 d6 12 h3 h6 13 Be3 Kf7 was slightly more comfortable for White in T.Ravi-K.Sasikiran, Indian Ch., Nagpur 1999.

9 Qc4!?

Sveshnikov likes this move, although the natural 9 Qxc3 Qf6 10 Bg5 Qxc3+ 11 Nxc3 would again be slightly better for White who leads in development.

9...Bg4 10 Nxc3 Bxf3 11 gxf3 Qf6 12 f4 Qf7 13 Qb5!

Black has the greater problems co-ordinating his forces in the middlegame.

13...Nd4 14 Qd3 Ne6 15 f5 Nc5 16 Qc2 Qc4 17 Be3 (Diagram 21)

Black's activity turns out to be of limited value as only two of his pieces are in play – the rest are not offering much support!

17...Nf6?!

The petulant 17...Nd3+ at least disrupts White for a while, thus gaining time for some development; e.g. 18 Kd2 Nb4 19 Qb1 Nf6 20 a3 Nc6 21 b3 Qa6 22 Qd3, or perhaps 22 Kc2!? Re8 23 Kb2, with a small pull for White in each case.

18 0-0-0 Re8 19 f3

Stifling any counterplay.

19...Ncd7 20 Rd4

Increasing the pressure by building up his forces, while Black still hasn't resolved the problem of his misplaced king.

20...Qc6 21 Kb1 Re7 22 Qe2 Ne5 23 Bg5 Qc5 24 Rhd1 Nc6 25 Rc4 Qe5 26 Nd5 Rf7

White has more than one way to break through but Sveshnikov's choice is elegant...

27 Bf4 Qe8 (Diagram 22) 28 Nxc7! Rxc7 29 Bxd6+ Re7 30 e5 Nd7 31 f4!

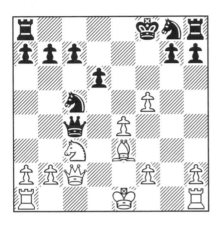

Diagram 21 (B)
Black needs to develop

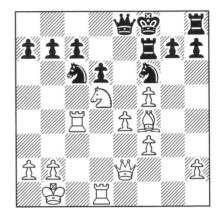

Diagram 22 (W)
White to play and win

Black is too tangled to put up any resistance.

31...h5 32 Qd3 Rh6

The rook finally comes into play but it's too late to make a difference.

33 Bxe7+ Kxe7 34 Qa3+ Kf7 35 e6+ Rxe6 36 fxe6+ Qxe6 37 Qd3 Nf6 38 f5 Qe5 39 Rc2 Kg8 40 Re2 Qc5 41 a3 Kh7 42 Rg2 Ne5 43 Qc2 Qe3 44 Rdg1 Neg4 1-0

Resigning before White plays 45 Rg3 and 46 h3.

Urusov Gambit

1 e4 e5 2 Bc4 Nf6 3 d4 exd4 4 Nf3 (Diagram 23)

Here the wisest option is 4...Nc6! reverting to the now familiar Two Knights Defence.

Instead...

4...Nxe4!?

...is the Urusov Gambit Accepted, when a typical continuation is...

5 Qxd4 Nf6 6 Bg5 Be7 7 Nc3 Nc6 8 Qh4 (Diagram 24)

Diagram 23 (B)
Urusov Gambit

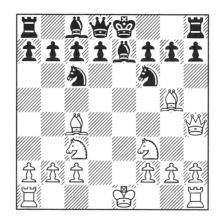

Diagram 24 (B)
White has tremendous activity

...and White has tremendous activity for the pawn; e.g. 8...d6 9 0-0-0 0-0 10 Bd3!
h6 11 Bxh6! gxh6 12 Qxh6 Be6 13 Ng5 with a decisive attack already,
M.Tavakolian-U.Gebhardt, German League 2008.

Don't even think about going down that road. Play the Two Knights!

Summary

White employs various move orders and gambit lines in an attempt to throw Black
off his guard. From the other side, Black can counter some of these systems with a
quick ...d7-d5 (as in Game 39), and the rest by a willingness to switch to the Two
Knights or Giuoco Piano with ...Nf6.

Chapter Seven
King's Gambit

- Introduction
- King's Gambit Accepted
- King's Gambit Declined

Introduction

1 e4 e5 2 f4 (Diagram 1)

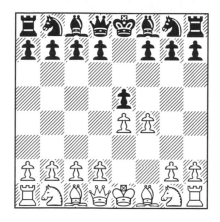

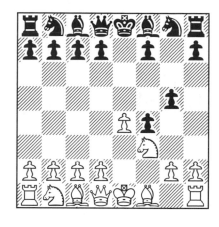

| **Diagram 1 (B)** | **Diagram 2 (W)** |
| The King's Gambit | Playing to keep the pawn |

An opening with a long history, the King's Gambit was closely associated with the romantic (i.e. mate or bust!) era of the 19th century. These days few strong grandmasters play it that often, as it is not considered to be one of the most challenging weapons at White's disposal.

Objectively it seems there are several ways for Black to achieve a satisfactory game, and in some cases White is the one who has to be the most careful.

Strategy

White immediately challenges Black's central bastion and hopes that the opening of the f-file will lead to pressure for him. The downside is not just the sacrifice of a pawn, but the self-weakening of White's kingside.

Black can take the pawn and hold onto it, thus denying White play along the f-file, but then White develops more rapidly and often obtains attacking chances.

A more modern approach is either to decline the gambit, or capture on f4 and then find a timely way to return the pawn whilst obtaining positional concessions from White.

Theoretical

Old theory is still theory so, yes, to a certain extent, but there haven't been that many developments in recent years.

King's Gambit Accepted

Game 41
□ J.Brenninkmeijer ■ G.Ligterink
King's Gambit tournament, Groningen 2002

1 e4 e5 2 f4 exf4 3 Nf3

The Bishop's Gambit, 3 Bc4, can be tricky if you are unprepared. However, Black has several reasonable replies, such as 3...Nf6 (3...Nc6!?, intending 4 Nf3 g5 or 4 d4 Nf6, is also interesting) 4 Nc3 Bb4 (an ambitious try, inviting complications; otherwise 4...c6 is solid and reliable; e.g. 5 Bb3 d5 6 exd5 cxd5 7 d4 Bd6 8 Nf3 0-0 9 0-0 Be6 10 Ne5 Nc6 11 Bxf4 Rc8 with equality, N.Short-A.Karpov, Buenos Aires 2000) 5 e5 d5 6 Bb5+ c6 7 exf6 cxb5 8 Qe2+ Be6 9 Qxb5+ Nc6 10 Nf3 Qxf6 11 Qxb7 Rc8 12 Nxd5 Qf5 13 Nc7+, L.Paulsen-I.Kolisch, 11th matchgame, London 1861, and now I quite like 13...Kd8!.

3...g5 (Diagram 2)

This is perhaps the critical test of the whole of the King's Knight's Gambit.

4 h4

After 4 Bc4 Bg7! Black doesn't have any problems consolidating his pawn front (see the note to White's fifth move in Game 43). Material hunting with 4...g4, on the other hand, can be met by 5 0-0! – a coffee-house approach known as the Muzio Gambit. After 5...gxf3 6 Qxf3 Qf6 7 e5 Qxe5 8 Bxf7+!? Kxf7 9 d4 Qxd4+ 10 Be3, as in A.Shirov-J.Lapinski, Daugavpils 1990, White has a big lead in development for the sacrificed material. Hardcore materialists might be surprised to learn that White has an enormous score in this line, as it is very difficult for Black to defend in practice.

4...g4 5 Ne5

With h2-h4 inserted instead of a 'developing' move, sacrificing a piece with 5 Bc4 isn't sound. So White usually plays 5 Ne5 here, which is known as the Kieseritzky Gambit.

5...Nf6 6 Bc4 (Diagram 3)

Continuing with his direct approach.

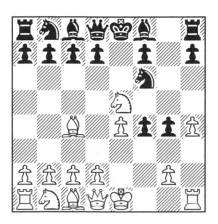

Diagram 3 (B)	**Diagram 4 (W)**
Attacking the weak f7-square	White has excellent compensation

6...d5 7 exd5 Bd6 8 d4

8 0-0 Bxe5 9 Re1 (the Rice Gambit) 9...Qe7 10 c3 was the height of fashion at the turn of the 19th and 20th centuries, but has been abandoned as it looks downright dubious after 10...Nh5 11 d4 Nd7 12 Bb5 Kd8 13 Bxd7 Bxd7 14 Rxe5 Qxh4 15 Rxh5 Qxh5 16 Bxf4 Re8 17 Nd2 Qxd5 and so on.

8...Nh5 9 0-0

Better than the ugly 9 Nc3?! Qe7 10 Kf2, as 10...Bxe5 11 Re1 Nd7 12 Bb5 Qxh4+ 13 Kg1 0-0 14 dxe5 g3 is clearly better for Black, J.Murey-M.Hebden, Paris 1988.

9...Qxh4 10 Qe1

White forces the exchange of queens to avoid coming under attack.

10...Qxe1 11 Rxe1 0-0 (Diagram 4)

With his central control and active pieces, plus the inflexible and vulnerable black kingside, White has excellent positional compensation for the pawn.

12 Bb3

There is perhaps more than one way for White to gain an advantage here, as 12 Nc3 also seems promising; e.g. 12...Bf5 (or 12...Nd7 13 Nxg4 Nb6 14 Be2 Re8 15 Ne5

Bxe5 16 dxe5 Rxe5 17 Bd2 Bd7 18 Bf3 Rae8 with an edge due to the bishop pair, L.Riemersma-P.Van der Sterren, Dutch Ch., Eindhoven 1993) 13 Nb5 Nd7 14 Nxd6 cxd6 15 Nxd7 Bxd7 16 Bd3 f5 17 Bd2 a5 18 a4 b6 19 b3 Rae8 20 Rxe8 Rxe8 21 b4 and again White's bishops offer him a pull, E.Berg-H.Stefansson, Reykjavik 2000.

12...Bf5 13 Nc3 Nd7 14 Nc4 Rae8 15 Rf1!

White maintains his central bind and now turns his attention to Black's kingside.

15...Ng3 16 Bxf4! Nxf1 17 Nxd6 cxd6 18 Rxf1

The exchange sacrifice is only temporary as White will quickly regain the material.

18...Kg7 19 Bxd6 Kg6 20 Bxf8 Nxf8 (Diagram 5)

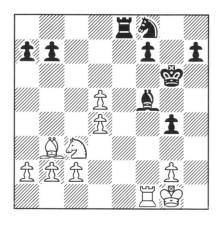

Diagram 5 (W)	Diagram 6 (B)
Now White is a pawn up	Black loses more material

21 d6

The d-pawn advances, creating threats and increasing the influence of the bishop.

21...Ne6 22 Nb5 Rd8 23 d5 Nc5 24 c4 a6?

Black could put up greater resistance with 24...Bd3 25 Rf4 a6 26 Nd4 h5, although White's majority is still superior even after the loss of the d6-pawn.

25 Nd4 Bd3 26 Bc2! Bxc2 27 Nxc2 Rxd6 28 Ne3 h5 29 b4!

The queenside rolls forward.

29...Nd3 30 c5 Rf6 31 Rd1 Nf2

After 31...Nxb4 32 a3 Na2 33 d6 Black saves his knight but loses the game.

32 Rd4 g3 33 Nf1 1-0 (Diagram 6)

Black is going to lose material and there is the problem of stopping the d-pawn.

Game 42
□ A.Fedorov ■ A.Shirov
Polanica Zdroj 2000

1 e4 e5 2 f4 exf4 3 Nf3 g5 4 h4 g4 5 Ne5 d6!

The most straightforward defence. Black sacrifices his g-pawn, but in return obtains quite rapid development.

6 Nxg4 Nf6 (Diagram 7)

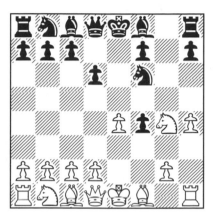

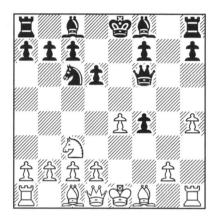

Diagram 7 (W)
Black scores better here

Diagram 8 (W)
The critical variation

 NOTE: White actually has a negative score from this position, which is why many believe that 3...g5 represents Black's best defence.

7 Nf2?!

This retreat could be considered as a loss of time, especially as the knight is placed on such an uninspiring square. One could go on to argue that if White is bending some basic principles, he needs to come up with some good reasons to justify himself! But the statistics don't lie: White's prospects from this position are not great. Indeed, he only scores a paltry 35% with this move.

Instead, 7 Nxf6+ Qxf6 8 Nc3 almost achieves parity (statistically, that is), and after 8...Nc6 **(Diagram 8)** White has several options:

a) 9 d3 Be6 10 Qd2 Bh6 and Black stands quite happily.

b) 9 d4 Qxd4 10 Bxf4 Qxd1+ 11 Rxd1 Be6 with no problems for Black.

c) 9 Bb5 is more tricky, but if Black plays 9...Kd8!? he should be fine; e.g. 10 Bxc6 (or 10 Be2 Rg8 11 Bf3 Nd4 12 Ne2 Nxf3+ 13 gxf3 Bd7, S.Van Eijk-S.Grover, Essent 2008) 10...bxc6 11 d3 Rg8 12 Qf3 Bh6 13 Qf2 Rb8 14 Ne2 Rxb2 15 Bxb2 Qxb2 16 0-0 Qxc2 17 Nxf4 Qxf2+ 18 Rxf2 Bg7 with equality, A.Fier-R.Leitao, Guaralhos 2006.

d) 9 Nd5 Qg6 is sharpest of all, and then:

d1) 10 Nxc7+?? is not recommended: 10...Kd8 11 Nxa8 Qg3+ 12 Ke2 Nd4 mate.

d2) 10 Qf3 is best countered by 10...Nd4! 11 Qd3 Ne6 12 Qf3 Bh6!? (12...Nd4 repeats, but you may prefer to play a longer game...) 13 d3 c6 14 Nxf4 Nxf4 15 Bxf4 Bg4 16 Qf2 Bxf4 17 Qxf4 0-0-0 which yields equal chances.

d3) 10 d3 Qg3+ 11 Kd2 looks bizarre, but probably leads to perpetual check with best play, such as the plausible 11...Nb4 (or 11...Ne7) 12 Nxc7+ Kd8 13 Nxa8 Qe3+ 14 Kc3 Qc5+ 15 Kd2 Qe3+ etc. If Black needs to win at all costs then 11...Be6 12 c3 0-0-0 is perhaps the best try, but after 13 Kc2 White's king is safe and thus he may be slightly better.

7...Rg8

If instead 7...Nc6 8 d4 Bh6, White is able to develop his king's bishop without leaving the g-pawn *en prise*, though even then Black shouldn't be worse; e.g. 9 Be2 Qe7 10 Nc3 Bd7 11 Bf3 (11 Nd5!? Nxd5 12 exd5 Nb4 13 c4 Bf5, A.Fedorov-J.Timman, FIDE World Ch., Las Vegas 1999, is analogous to the main game except that Shirov managed to obtain an additional and *highly useful* move ...Rg8 – see below) 11...0-0-0 12 a3?! (missing the point; preferable is 12 Ne2 d5 13 e5 Ne4 14 Nd3 f6 with an unclear position, while 14 Nxf4 Qb4+ 15 c3 Nxc3 16 N2d3 is more or less balanced according to Shirov) 12...Nxe4! 13 Nd5 Qe8 14 0-0 f5 and Black was better in N.Short-A.Shirov, Madrid 1997.

8 d4 Bh6 9 Nc3 Nc6! (Diagram 9)

The most precise move, and scoring as much as 71% for Black!

Fedorov has also faced 9...Qe7 10 Nd3 Bg4 (10...Nxe4!? is not as catastrophic for Black as claimed in some sources, but 11 Nd5 Qd8 12 Qe2 f5 13 Nf2! still offers White an edge) 11 Be2 Bxe2 12 Qxe2 Nc6 13 e5 dxe5 14 dxe5 Ng4 (Bangiev analysed 14...Nd4 15 exf6 Qxe2+ 16 Nxe2 Nxc2+ 17 Kf2! Nxa1 18 Bxf4 Bxf4 19 Ndxf4 Nc2 20 Rc1 Nb4 21 Rxc7, which seems to offer White plenty of compensation) 15 Nd5 Qd7 16 Nf6+ Nxf6 17 exf6+ Kf8 18 0-0 left White somewhat better in A.Fedorov-G.Timoshenko, Rumanian Team Ch. 1998.

10 Nd5

Shirov suggests 10 Nd3 in his notes, but then 10...Bg4 11 Be2 Bxe2 12 Nxe2 Nxe4 looks good for Black.

However, White does have a playable alternative in 10 Bb5!; e.g. 10...Rxg2 11 Bxf4! (11 d5?! a6 12 Bf1 Rxf2 13 Kxf2 Ne5 yields excellent compensation for Black, M.Crosa-R.Hungaski, Sao Paulo 2005) 11...Ng4! (11...Bxf4 12 Qf3 Rxf2 13 Qxf2 Nh5 14 Rg1 Kf8 15 Be2 turned out better for White in V.Ramon-F.Izeta Txabarri, Benasque 1990) 12 Bxh6 Nxf2 13 Qf3 Nxh1 14 0-0-0 Rg6 15 Rf1 with unclear complications.

10...Nxd5 11 exd5 Qe7+

I presume that Fedorov had something up his sleeve to improve on 11...Ne7 12 Qe2 Kf8! 13 g4 Nxd5 14 g5 Bf5! 15 Bd2 Qd7 16 0-0-0 Re8 17 Qf3 Qa4, A.Fedorov-S.Pedersen, Aars 1999, where Black was fine.

12 Be2 Nb4 13 c4 Bf5! (Diagram 10)

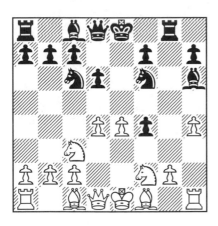

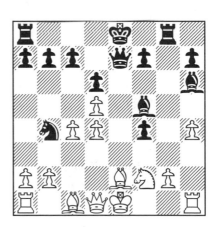

Diagram 9 (W)

Black plays precisely

Diagram 10 (W)

A very strong sacrifice

Sacrificing a piece in this manner seems to be very effective here, whereas after 13...Rxg2 14 Kf1 Rxf2+ 15 Kxf2 Qe4 16 Rg1 Kf8 17 a3 Nc2 18 Bf3 Qf5 19 Bg4 White seems to be alright.

14 Qa4+

14 0-0 0-0-0 15 Bg4 Qd7 is also clearly better for Black according to Shirov.

14...Kf8 15 Qxb4 Re8 16 Qd2 Rxg2 17 Kf1 Rg3

The winner felt that 17...Be4!? 18 Rh3 would let White fight on, though even here 18...f5! looks very strong for Black.

18 Qd1 Be4 19 Rh2 f5

White's extra material is irrelevant as he can never develop his queenside – Black's attack is simply too strong.

20 Nxe4

If 20 Bd2, then 20...Qg7! shatters any illusions.

20...fxe4 21 Bg4

21 Bh5 Qg7 22 Rh1 is refuted by 22...e3! 23 Qd3 f3! (Shirov).

21...e3! 22 Bf3 Qg7 23 Rh1 Rg2! 0-1 (Diagram 11)

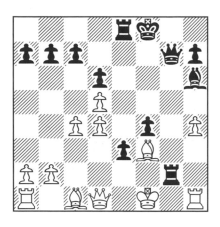

Diagram 11 (W)
White resigned

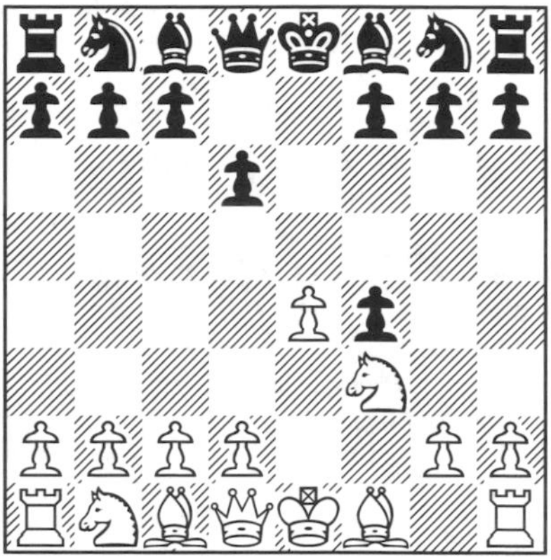

Diagram 12 (W)
Fischer's Defence

Game 43
□ **A.Fedorov** ■ **Z.Gyimesi**
Croatian Team Championship 2001

1 e4 e5 2 f4 exf4 3 Nf3 d6 (Diagram 12)

Fischer's Defence, the idea of which is to play ...g7-g5 next move, while avoiding the Kieseritzky – though, as we have seen, Black has nothing to fear there.

4 d4

4 Bc4 is answered by 4...h6!, again preparing ...g7-g5. But not 4...g5? immediately, because of 5 h4! g4 6 Ng5 and White is clearly better.

4...g5 5 h4!

 NOTE: Experience has taught the world that White needs to break up the kingside pawn phalanx before Black has a chance to reinforce it with ...Bg7 and ...h7-h6.

So the slower 5 Bc4 is no longer played very often, due to 5...Bg7 and then:

a) 6 h4 h6! (holding the structure firm at this point makes it hard for White to justify the pawn deficit) 7 c3 Nc6 (in the 19th century people would just grab a piece whatever discomfort it entailed; e.g. 7...g4 8 Qb3 gxf3 9 Bxf7+ Kf8 10 Bh5 Qe7 11 Bxf3 Nf6 12 Bxf4 Nc6 13 0-0 Qf7 14 Qa3 Kg8 15 Nd2 Bd7 16 Rf2 and White had two pawns plus long-term pressure for the piece, W.Hanstein-T.Von Heydebrand, Berlin 1839) 8 Qb3 Qe7 9 0-0 g4!? (disruptive) 10 Nh2 f3 11 Nxg4 Bxg4 12 Qxb7 Nxd4! 13 Qxa8+ Kd7 14 Rf2 Nf6 15 Qxa7 Nxe4 and Black had a very strong attack, A.Rodriguez Vila-D.Schneider, Osasco 2004.

b) 6 0-0 Nc6 7 c3 h6 **(Diagram 13)**

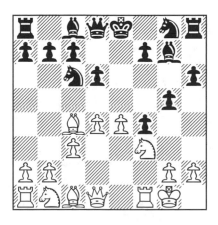
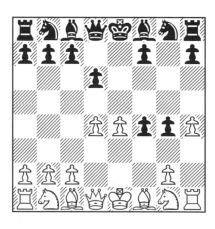

Diagram 13 (W)
A typical Hanstein Gambit

Diagram 14 (B)
The main line Fischer

A typical position from the Hanstein Gambit, but it's not considered to be very promising for White; e.g. 8 b4 (or 8 g3 Bh3 9 gxf4 Qd7! 10 Kh1 0-0-0 11 fxg5 hxg5 12 Bxg5 Nf6 13 Nbd2 Bxf1 14 Qxf1 Rdg8 15 Nh4 d5 favoured Black in A.Zajaryni-K.Khruschiov, Kishinev 2001) 8...Nf6 9 b5 Ne7 10 e5 Nfd5 11 Qb3 Be6 12 Nbd2 0-0 13 Ne4 a6 14 bxa6 bxa6 15 Rb1 Rb8 and Black again was on top, F.Zeller-K.Volke, Swiss Team Ch. 2006.

The modern day philosophy of ensuring decent development (rather than the 19th century way of just snatching material) has rendered the Hanstein Gambit obsolete.

5...g4 6 Ng1 (Diagram 14)

6 Ng5? is another old sacrifice that has been relegated to the scrapheap, as after 6...f6! White has insufficient play for the piece; e.g. 7 Nh3 gxh3 8 Qh5+ Kd7 9 Bxf4 Qe8, O.Salmensuu-M.Welin, Stockholm 1998.

6...f5!?

There are many possibilities at this point, and this is the one that scores highest at 60% for Black! Nevertheless, I'm not sure that it is the best:

a) 6...f3 used to be popular, but Gallagher's move 7 Bg5! has proved difficult to counter: 7...Be7 8 Qd2 f6 9 Bh6 f2+ 10 Kxf2 f5 11 Nc3 Nf6 12 Bd3 c5 (12...fxe4 13 Nxe4 Nxe4+ 14 Bxe4 d5 15 Bd3 Bxh4+ 16 g3 Bf6 17 Re1+ Kf7 18 c3 is also more comfortable for White) 13 exf5 Rg8 14 Re1 favours White, J.Hector-H.Jonkman, Wijk aan Zee 2003.

b) 6...Bh6 (once the main line, but now challenged by other moves as it doesn't seem to equalize) 7 Nc3 c6 8 Nge2 Qf6 9 g3 fxg3 (after 9...f3 10 Nf4 Qe7 11 Bd3, White's central control turns out to be more important than Black's extra and protected passed pawn; e.g. 11...Bg7 12 Be3 h5 13 Qd2 Nd7 14 0-0-0 Nf8 15 Rhe1 Bd7 16 e5 with a strong attack, J.Gallagher-S.Jackson, British Ch., Blackpool 1988) 10 Nxg3 Bxc1 11 Rxc1 Qh6 12 Bd3 Qe3+ 13 Nce2 Ne7 14 Qd2 Qxd2+ 15 Kxd2 d5 16 Rce1 with excellent play for White, N.Short-V.Akopian, Madrid 1997.

c) 6...Qf6 (one of my pet lines) 7 Nc3 Ne7 8 Nge2 Bh6 (if 8...f3 9 Nf4 Bh6 10 g3 and the rock-solid control of f4 tends to mean that Black's protected passed pawn cannot be exploited) 9 Qd2 Nbc6 10 Nb5 (or 10 Nd5 Nxd5 11 exd5 Ne7 12 Nxf4 0-0 13 Qf2 Bxf4 14 Qxf4 Qxf4 15 Bxf4 Nxd5 16 Bh6 Re8+ 17 Kd2 Bf5 and Black is better, J.Shaw-G.Flear, Perth 1992) 10...Kd8 11 d5 (Gallagher notes that 11 e5!? Qf5! 12 exd6 Nd5 13 dxc7+ Kd7 is dangerous for White) 11...Ne5 12 Nxf4 a6 13 Nd4 g3 with chances for both sides, J.Gallagher-G.Flear, Lenk 1992.

7 Nc3 Nf6 8 Bxf4

Better than 8 Qe2 Bh6 9 exf5+ Kf7, which led to a strong attack for Black in V.Shevchenko-A.Raetsky, Russia 1992.

8...fxe4 9 d5! (Diagram 15)

Much better than 9 Qd2, which allows 9...d5! stabilizing the centre; e.g. 10 Be5 c6 11 Nge2 Be6 12 Nf4 Bf7 13 Nd1 Nbd7 14 Ne3 Nxe5 15 dxe5 Qc7! and White had already been badly outplayed in J.Hector-P.Leko, Copenhagen 1995.

9...Bg7

9...Nh5!? has been considered to be too slow, but I'm not that sure. 10 Bg5 Be7 11 Bb5+ Kf7 12 Nge2 a6 13 0-0+ Kg8 14 Ba4 Bxg5 15 hxg5 Nd7 16 Nf4 Nxf4 17 Qxg4 yielded a crushing attack in A.Fedorov-I.Ibragimov, Katrineholm 1999, but only the weak move 11...Kf7? upset the apple-cart. Instead, after 11...c6!, the continuation 12 dxc6 bxc6 13 Bxe7 Qxe7 14 Bxc6+ Nxc6 15 Qd5, proposed by Sandstrom, can be met by 15...Bb7 16 Qxh5+ Qf7 which isn't clear at all.

10 Bc4 Nbd7

Following 10...0-0 11 Nge2 Nh5 12 Be3 Qe8 13 Qd2 a6 14 Bb3 Nd7 15 0-0-0, White obtained decent compensation in H.Eberl-I.Hristov, correspondence 2002.

11 h5! 0-0 12 h6 Ne8 13 Nge2

Better than 13 Qxg4 Nb6 14 Qg3 Rxf4! when the complications favour Black.

13...Bxc3+

13...Be5 would be met by 14 Be3 with Qd2, 0-0-0 and Nd4 in mind. In the meantime, Black will find it hard to free his somewhat cramped position.

14 bxc3 Ne5 15 Bb3 Ng6 16 Qd2 a5? (Diagram 16)

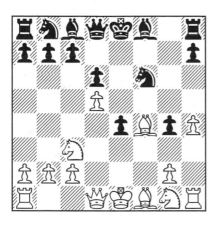
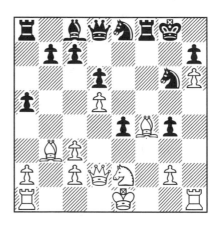

Diagram 15 (B)	**Diagram 16 (W)**
White prevents ...d6-d5	A fatal error

Almost certainly a fatal error. Instead, eliminating the bishop was necessary: 16...Nxf4 17 Nxf4 e3! (stronger than 17...Qg5 18 Ne6 Qxd2+ 19 Kxd2 Rf6 20 Raf1 and White has excellent compensation) 18 Qxe3 Qg5 with a messy position. White should perhaps continue 19 0-0!? Qxh6 20 Qg3, when the result remains in doubt.

17 Bg5 e3

On 17...Qd7, Fedorov intended 18 a4 followed by Nd4 and 0-0-0 with good play.

18 Qxe3 Nf6 19 0-0 Qe8

The point behind 17...e3 was to win this tempo to unpin, but White still has great pressure.

20 Qd4! Nh5

If 20...Qxe2, then 21 Rae1 pushes the black queen out of the way, and following 21...Qa6 22 Rxf6, the plausible 22...Qa7 (pinning) is met by 23 Rxg6+! as 23...hxg6 24 Qxa7 Rxa7 25 Re7 Rf7 26 Re8+ wins material and the game for White.

21 Ng3 Rxf1+ 22 Rxf1 Ne5 23 Nxh5 Qxh5 (Diagram 17)

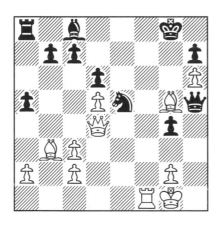

Diagram 17 (W)

White has a forced mate

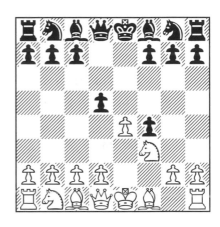

Diagram 18 (W)

The Modern Defence

24 Qxe5! 1-0

Mate follows after 24...dxe5 25 d6+ Be6 26 Bxe6+ Kh8 27 Bf6.

Game 44
☐ **V.Zvjaginsev** ■ **A.Kunte**
World Chess Cup, Khanty-Mansiysk 2007

1 e4 e5 2 f4 exf4 3 Nf3 d5 (Diagram 18)

The so-called Modern Defence. Black captures the gambit pawn, but then reacts immediately by offering one of his own in order to open the centre and liberate his pieces.

4 exd5 Nf6

The normal move. The pawn structure is particularly asymmetric as White has two extra pawns on the queenside, whereas Black has a 4-2 majority on the kingside. An unbalanced middlegame struggle is in prospect.

The alternative 4...Bd6 was played unsuccessfully in a famous game (see below), and probably due to this fact has been considered inferior in certain quarters.

 WARNING: Be wary of judgements in old pre-computer books, especially when strong players continue to do the opposite to what the author suggests!

However, White's percentage is only marginally better than in the main line and strong players continue to venture 4...Bd6, so it is probably perfectly playable:

a) 5 Bb5+ is possible, when Black should react with 5...c6, further opening lines and freeing his minor pieces; e.g. 6 dxc6 Nxc6 7 d4 Nge7 8 0-0 0-0 9 c4 Bg4 10 Nc3 Nf5!? was J.M.Flouzat-G.Flear, St Affrique 2001, where Black was successful after 11 Bxc6 bxc6 12 Ne2 g5 13 Qd3 Re8 14 h3 Bxf3 15 Qxf3 with 15...Nxd4!, destroying White's centre. This variation could equally arise from the Nimzowitsch Counter-Gambit: 2...d5 3 exd5 c6!? 4 dxc6 (4 Nc3!) 4...Nxc6 5 Bb5 exf4 6 Nf3 Bd6 and so on.

b) 5 Nc3 was B.Spassky-D.Bronstein, USSR Ch., Leningrad 1960, which we shall now follow: 5...Ne7 6 d4 0-0 7 Bd3 Nd7?! (a little sluggish; in more recent times the plan of 7...Ng6 followed by ...c7-c6 has been shown to be acceptable) 8 0-0 h6? (this turns out to be too slow; instead, two possible defences have been suggested: 8...Nf6 9 Ne5 Nfxd5 10 Nxd5 Nxd5 11 Bxf4 Nxf4 12 Rxf4 Qg5! with equality, and 8...Ng6!? 9 Ne4 Nf6 10 Nxd6 Qxd6 11 c4 Bg4 – the former one holds up to scrutiny, but the latter one can be met by 12 Qb3 when I prefer White) 9 Ne4! Nxd5 10 c4 Ne3 11 Bxe3 fxe3 12 c5 Be7 13 Bc2! (Spassky aims for an attack) 13...Re8 14 Qd3 e2? (an attempt at distracting White's pieces from visions of mate; the superior 14...Nf8! would offer Black much needed solidity) 15 Nd6!? (the patient 15 Rf2! would create difficulties for Black without any risk) 15...Nf8? **(Diagram 19)** (it is too late for this now; correct was 15...Bxd6! 16 Qh7+ Kf8 17 cxd6 which looks danger-ous, but Black can survive: 17...exf1Q+ 18 Rxf1 cxd6 19 Qh8+ Ke7 20 Re1+ Ne5 21 Qxg7 Rg8! 22 Qxh6 Qb6! 23 Kh1 Be6 24 dxe5 d5 with equality!) 16 Nxf7! (crunch!) 16...exf1Q+ 17 Rxf1 Bf5 (what else? – both 17...Kxf7 18 Ne5+ Kg8 19 Qh7+! Nxh7 20 Bb3+ Kh8 21 Ng6 mate, and 17...Qd5 18 Bb3! Qxf7! 19 Bxf7+ Kxf7 20 Qc4+ Kg6 21

Qg8! are hopeless) 18 Qxf5 Qd7 19 Qf4 Bf6 20 N3e5 Qe7 (if 20...Bxe5 21 Nxe5 Qe7 22 Qe4 is crushing) 21 Bb3 Bxe5 22 Nxe5+ Kh7 23 Qe4+ 1-0. Perhaps the most famous King's Gambit of the last fifty years.

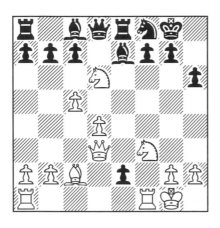

Diagram 19 (W)

Spassky to play and win

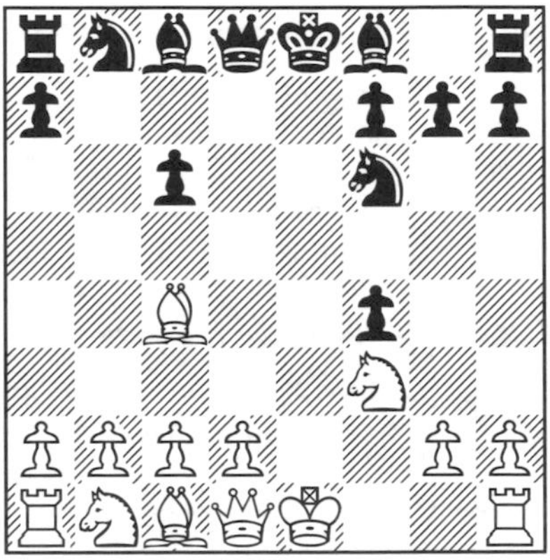

Diagram 20 (B)

Position after 6...bxc6 7 Bc4

5 Bb5+ c6

This is more reliable than 5...Bd7 which has dropped out of use; e.g. 6 Bc4 Qe7+ 7 Be2 Nxd5 8 c4 Nb6 9 0-0 Nc6 10 d4 g5 11 Nc3 and White had plenty of compensation for his pawn in S.Bücker-G.Flear, Bünde 1985.

6 dxc6 Nxc6

The alternative 6...bxc6 accepts broken pawns, but in return gains a tempo, while the pawn on c6 will help restrain White's majority. After 7 Bc4 **(Diagram 20)** Black has to make a decision.

a) 7...Bd6 8 Qe2+ (this check, leading to an early queen swap, is usually recommended; the straightforward 8 0-0 0-0 9 d4 Bg4 10 Bb3 Nbd7 11 Nbd2 Nb6 was fine for Black in M.Erdogdu-D.Campora, Istanbul Olympiad 2000) 8...Qe7 9 Qxe7+ Kxe7 10 0-0 Re8 (more precise than 10...Be6 11 Re1 Nbd7 12 d4 Rhe8 13 Bxe6 fxe6 14 Nbd2 h6 15 Nc4 g5 16 h4 when White had some pressure, E.Bhend-G.Barcza, Zürich 1959) 11 Re1+ Kf8 12 Rxe8+ Nxe8 13 d4 Bf5 14 Bb3 Nd7 and Black's position seems to be solid enough, B.Svensson-O.Kinnmark, Swedish Ch., Boras 1979.

b) 7...Nd5 first is preferred in the theoretical works; e.g. 8 0-0 Bd6 9 Nc3 Be6 10 Ne4 Be7 11 Bb3 0-0 12 d4 a5 13 c4 Nb6 14 Bxf4 a4 with equal chances, D.Campora-C.Bielicki, Argentine Ch., Buenos Aires 1986.

7 d4 Qa5+ 8 Nc3 Bb4 9 0-0 0-0 10 Bd3

After 10 Bxc6 Black has the intermediate 10...Bxc3!, when 11 bxc3 bxc6 12 Bxf4 Qxc3 13 Qd2 Qxd2 14 Nxd2 Nd5 15 Bd6 Rd8 gave him full equality in E.Moser-M.Godena, Calvia Olympiad 2004.

10...Bd6 11 Bd2 Qh5 12 Ne2 g5 (Diagram 21)

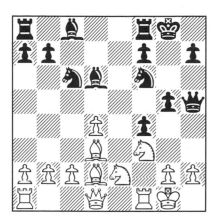

Diagram 21 (W)

Black gets going first

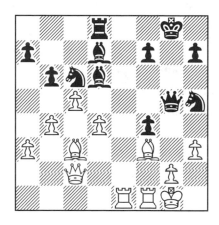

Diagram 22 (B)

Now it's White's turn

Black clearly hopes to make something of his kingside preponderance.

13 h3 Bd7 14 c4 Rfe8 15 a3 Rad8 16 b4

In turn White activates his own majority.

16...b6 17 Qc2 Rxe2!?

A dramatic and unexpected exchange sacrifice. Otherwise 17...g4 18 hxg4 Bxg4 also looks interesting.

18 Bxe2 g4 19 Bc3!

Consolidating, at the cost of returning material, is definitely best. The obvious move would be to capture on g4, but then the attack after 19 hxg4 Nxg4 20 Qb2 Re8 21 Bd3 Re6 would be difficult, if not impossible, to parry.

19...gxf3 20 Bxf3 Qg5

Two pieces for rook and pawn are often more than a fair trade, but here White retains a powerful centre, while Black's attacking chances have dissipated.

21 Rae1 Nh5

Not really effective, but White is probably better whatever; for instance,

21...Bxh3?? drops the knight on c6, or if 21...Rc8!? 22 c5 White's bishop pair and pawn front are very strong assets.

22 c5 (Diagram 22) 22...bxc5 23 dxc5 Bf8?!

23...Bc7 is better, though White would still have pressure after 24 Qb2.

24 Bxh5

Winning the f-pawn and opening up play for his rooks.

24...Qxh5 25 Rxf4 Be6 26 Qf2

Not bad, but even better is 26 Rxe6! fxe6 27 Qe4 Qd5 28 Rg4+ Kf7 29 Qxh7+ with a stronger attack than in the game.

26...Ne7 27 Rxe6

A little tardy. White's hesitation enables the black knight to help bolster the defences.

27...fxe6 28 Rg4+ Ng6 29 Qf6 Re8 30 c6

30 Qh8+ Kf7 31 Qf6+ Kg8 only repeats moves.

30...Qh6! 31 c7 Qg7 32 Qxe6+!

If 32 h4 then 32...Qxf6 33 Bxf6 Kf7 34 Bd8 Ne7 and Black seems to hold by the skin of his teeth.

32...Rxe6 33 Bxg7 Rc6 34 Be5 Kf7 35 Bg3 (Diagram 23)

Three pawns, one of them on the seventh, offers White great compensation for the piece.

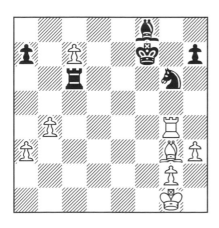

Diagram 23 (B)

White has great compensation

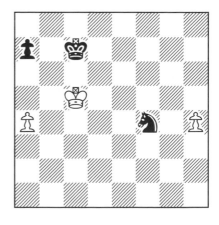

Diagram 24 (B)

White holds the draw

35...Bg7 36 b5

White should have played 36 Re4! which, apart from anything else, cuts off the black king from the c-pawn; e.g. 36...Ne7 37 b5 Rc3 38 Kh2 Nc8 (rather than 38...Nd5?! 39 Ra4) 39 a4 Ne7 40 a5 Nd5 41 Re2! Bf6 (if 41...Nxc7 42 b6 axb6 43 axb6 Na6 44 Ra2 Nc5 45 Ra7+ Kg6 46 Rxg7+ etc) 42 Ra2! and Black's position is precarious.

36...Rc1+ 37 Kh2 h5 38 Ra4

Black now holds by a miracle, but 38 Re4 is no longer dangerous due to 38...h4 39 Bd6 Bf8 40 Bxf8 Kxf8 and ...Rxc7.

38...h4 39 Bd6 Ke6 40 Ra6 Kd7

Suddenly Black's king is able to help out and, with the essentials under control, it's his turn to try to win!

41 Rc6 Rxc6 42 bxc6+ Kc8 43 g3 Ne5 44 a4 Nf7 45 Bf4 Bh6 46 Bxh6 Nxh6 47 gxh4 Nf5 48 h5 Kxc7 49 Kg2 Kxc6 50 Kf3 Kd6 51 Kf4 Ke6 52 Ke4 Ng3+ 53 Kd4 Nxh5 54 Kc5 Kd7 55 Kb5 Kc7 56 h4 Nf4 57 Kc5 (Diagram 24)

Black's knight cannot help out on both wings at the same time, so the game is drawn.

57...Kb7 58 Kb5 Nh5 59 Kc5 Nf6 60 Kb5 a6+ 61 Kc5 Kc7 62 a5 Ne4+ 63 Kd5 Ng3 64 Kc5 Nh5 ½-½

King's Gambit Declined

Game 45
□ A.Mista ■ S.Azarov
European Championship, Plovdiv 2008

1 e4 e5 2 f4 Bc5 (Diagram 25)

Black doesn't want to get involved in any sharp gambit play and prefers a natural developing move.

> **NOTE: Declining any gambit is a practical approach for Black if he can obtain a satisfactory position without much risk.**

Another way to aim to deny White his fun is with 2...d5, countering immediately in the centre. After 3 exd5, apart from 3...exf4 (accepting the gambit after all), Black has two noteworthy counter-gambit options:

a) 3...e4 (the Falkbeer Counter-Gambit) 4 d3 Nf6 5 dxe4 Nxe4 6 Nf3! (after 6 Be3 the critical line is 6...Bd6 7 Nf3 0-0 8 Bc4 Nd7) 6...Bc5 7 Qe2 **(Diagram 26)** 7...Bf5 8 Nc3 Qe7 9 Be3 Nxc3 10 Bxc5 Nxe2 11 Bxe7 Nxf4 12 Ba3, as in D.Bronstein-M.Tal, USSR Team Ch. 1968. Naturally there are many other possibilities, but this is a slightly dangerous line for Black in my opinion. For instance, here 12...Nxd5 13 0-0-0 Be6 has been recommended as best, but then 14 Bc4 c6 15 Rhe1 Nd7 16 Ng5 seems good for White.

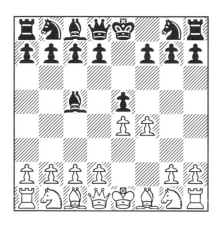

Diagram 25 (W)

The King's Gambit Declined

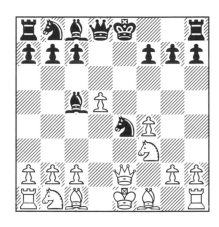

Diagram 26 (B)

A typical Falkbeer

b) 3...c6 (the Nimzowitsch Counter-Gambit) 4 Nc3 exf4 (only now, once the centre has been shaken up) 5 Nf3 Bd6 6 d4 Ne7 7 dxc6 Nbxc6 is similar to some lines arising from 3...d5 (compare Game 44). After the plausible 8 Bc4 0-0 9 0-0 Bg4 10 Ne4 Bc7 11 c3 Ng6 12 Nf2 Bh5 13 Qd3, as in M.Olesen-H.Gretarsson, Gausdal 1995, Black has active minor pieces but White's centre holds firm. Practice has seen White score heavily here, suggesting that his position is easier to play.

 TIP: If you intend to decline the King's Gambit, I wouldn't recommend 2...d5.

3 Nf3 d6 4 Nc3

The sharpest approach is 4 c3 **(Diagram 27)**, aiming to gain a tempo while building a pawn front with d2-d4. Black has to be on his guard not to allow White to achieve his aims unopposed:

Diagram 27 (B)

White plays 4 c3

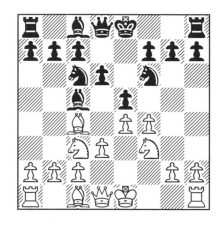

Diagram 28 (B)

The standard KGD set-up

a) 4...Nf6 5 d4 exd4 6 cxd4 Bb4+ 7 Bd2 Bxd2+ 8 Nbxd2 Qe7 9 Bd3 Nxe4 10 Nxe4 d5 11 0-0 dxe4 12 Bxe4 0-0 13 Qd3 h6 14 Ne5 Nd7 with equality in P.Charbonneau-L.Christiansen, Richmond, Canada 2002, is one way.

b) 4...Bg4!? is rarer but could be worth investigating; e.g. 5 fxe5 dxe5 6 Qa4+ Bd7! 7 Qc2 Qf6! (highly praised by Martin de Zeeuw in *New in Chess*) 8 Bc4 Bg4 9 Rf1 Bxf3 10 Rxf3 Qh4 11 Kd1 (11 g3 Qxh2 12 Bxf7+ Ke7 is unclear) 11...Nf6 with interesting play and balanced chances, B.Stanley-S.Bass, correspondence 2002.

c) 4...Bb6 5 d4 (5 Na3 is slower, but doesn't stop Black reacting actively: 5...Nf6 6 d3 can be countered by 6...Ng4 7 d4 f5, and 6 Nc4 by 6...exf4 7 d3 Be6 8 Nxb6 axb6 9 Bxf4 Bxa2!) 5...exd4 6 cxd4 Bg4 7 Be3 (7 Nc3 allows 7...Bxf3!) 7...Nf6 8 Nc3 (8 h3 Bxf3 9 Qxf3 is best met with 9...d5) and now:

c1) 8...Nc6 is mistimed due to Marin's 9 h3! as his analysis shows: 9...Bxf3 10 gxf3 Nh5 (now if 10...d5 11 Qd2! dxe4 12 fxe4 Bxd4 13 0-0-0 offers White a good initiative) 11 Rg1 Qh4+ 12 Bf2 Qxf4 13 Nd5 Ba5+ 14 b4 Nxb4 15 Qa4+ Nc6+ 16 Qxa5 Nxa5 17 Nxf4 Nxf4 18 Rxg7, and even Black's best move 18...d5 doesn't equalize.

c2) 8...Nxe4! (more reliable) 9 Nxe4 Qe7 10 Qd3 (10 Qc2 f5 11 h3 Bxf3 12 gxf3 d5 is given as equal by Marin) 10...Bf5 11 Qb5+ Bd7 12 Qd3 Bf5 equalizes easily but only by allowing a draw!

4...Nf6

4...Nc6!? is considered by some books to be less precise, as White can then pin with 5 Bb5, but after 5...Bg4 6 d3 Nge7 Black has no particular problems.

5 Bc4 Nc6 6 d3 (Diagram 28) 6...a6

My feeling is that 6...Bg4! is the strongest move here, developing a piece and not committing the king.

A recent game of mine has perhaps coloured my judgement, but I don't really like 6...0-0 that much, as this falls in (a little too easily) with White's plans: 7 f5 Na5 8 Bg5 with an annoying pin. Now any Black counterplay on the queenside doesn't quite seem to balance this out; e.g. 8...c6 9 a3 Nxc4 (9...b5 10 Ba2 Nb7 11 g4 b4, W.Becker-S.Lejlic, Berlin 1997, is another way of prising open some lines on the queenside) 10 dxc4 a6 11 Qd3 b5 12 0-0-0 bxc4 13 Qxc4 Qa5, R.Eames-G.Flear, British League 2009, with a double-edged struggle where I still prefer White slightly.

Instead, after the superior 6...Bg4!, play could proceed as follows:

a) 7 h3 Bxf3 8 Qxf3 exf4! (8...Nd4 9 Qg3 leads to murky complications) 9 Bxf4 (or 9 Bb5 0-0 10 Bxc6 bxc6 11 Bxf4 d5 12 0-0-0 Rb8 and Black has adequate counterchances) 9...Nd4 10 Qd1 (10 Qg3 is well met by 10...Nh5) 10...c6 11 Na4 (or if 11 Qd2 I like 11...d5!) 11...b5 12 Nxc5 dxc5 13 Bb3, P.Kostenko-A.Bezgodov, Tula 1999, and now 13...c4! was the move to equalize.

b) 7 Na4 **(Diagram 29)** when Black has a couple of worthwhile tries:

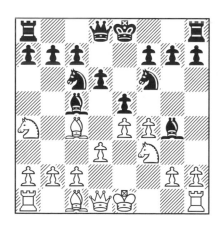

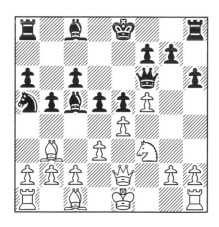

Diagram 29 (B)
Position after 6...Bg4 7 Na4

Diagram 30 (W)
Black tries to open lines

b1) 7...Nd4!? 8 Nxc5 dxc5 9 fxe5 (perhaps 9 c3!? as Spielmann tried on another occasion) 9...Nd7 (better than 9...Nxe4?! 10 0-0!) 10 Bf4 Qe7 11 c3! (11 0-0?! is too routine: 11...0-0-0 12 Qd2 Bxf3 13 gxf3 g5!? 14 Bg3 h5 15 c3 h4 and Black is even slightly better, R.Spielmann-I.Rabinovich, Moscow 1925) 11...Nxf3+ 12 gxf3 Bh5 13 Qe2 Nxe5 14 Bxe5 Qxe5 15 Qe3 with a pull for White, R.Wade-L.Schmid, Heidelberg 1949.

b2) 7...0-0! (almost certainly best) 8 Nxc5 (if 8 f5 Na5 9 Nxc5 dxc5 10 h3 Bxf3 11 gxf3 Nxc4 12 dxc4 Qxd1+ 13 Kxd1 Rad8+ 14 Ke2 Nh5! 15 Rg1 f6 is comfortable for Black – Marin) 8...dxc5 9 0-0 (9 h3? Bxf3 10 Qxf3 b5! 11 Bb3 Nd4 12 Qf2 c4 favoured Black in A.Ledger-M.Marin, Barcelona 2005) 9...Qd6 10 f5 Nd4 11 a4 a6 12 c3 b5 13 cxd4 Bxf3 14 Qxf3 bxc4 15 dxe5 Qxe5 with balanced chances, A.Fedorov-M.Marin, Rumanian Team Ch. 2000.

7 Nd5

7 Rf1!? is an interesting try, but 7...Be6 8 Bxe6 (alternatively 8 Nd5 Bxd5 9 exd5 Nd4 10 fxe5 dxe5 11 Bg5 h6 12 Bxf6 Qxf6 13 Nxd4 Qh4+ is equal) 8...fxe6 9 fxe5 dxe5 is fine for Black, since the doubled pawns cannot be put under pressure.

7...h6

No better is 7...Nxd5 8 Bxd5 0-0 9 f5 Nd4 10 c3 Nxf3+ 11 Qxf3 c6 12 Bb3 b5 13 h4 Kh8 14 g4 Ra7 15 Bg5 f6 16 Bd2, Al.Sokolov-V.Karpatchev, Nizhnij Novgorod 1998, which was pleasant for White due to his kingside pressure.

8 f5 Na5 9 Qe2

9 b4!? is quite interesting; e.g. 9...Nxd5 10 bxc5 Nf6 11 Bb3 dxc5 12 Nxe5 Nxb3 13 axb3 Qd4 (a better choice was 13...Bxf5! 14 Bb2 Be6 15 0-0, although White still has good compensation according to Conquest) 14 Bf4 Nxe4 15 dxe4 Qxe4+ 16 Qe2 Qxe2+ 17 Kxe2 Bxf5 18 Kd2! with some advantage to White, S.Conquest-J.Smejkal, German League 1996.

9...b5 10 Nxf6+ Qxf6 11 Bd5

Provoking ...c7-c6 to limit the scope of Black's light-squared bishop.

11...c6 12 Bb3 d5 (Diagram 30)

Proposing to sacrifice a pawn for open lines. In general White's advance f4-f5 fits in better with a closed position, so he correctly ignores the offer.

13 Be3

Not 13 exd5? (on general principles, but if you need to be shown something more specific, then...) 13...Nxb3 14 axb3 cxd5 15 Nxe5 0-0 and Black's development advantage will be too important.

13...d4

Closing the position means that he will have to try and expand with ...c5-c4 to counter-balance White's eventual g4-g5. Instead, keeping the tension with

13...Bd6!? came into consideration.

14 Bd2 Bb6 15 g4 Qe7 16 Qg2 Bb7 17 Qg3 Nxb3

Black has waited long enough!

18 axb3 Bc7 19 Rg1 f6 20 h4 c5 21 g5 (Diagram 31)

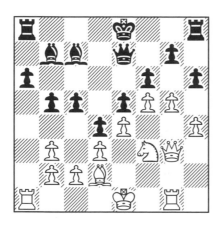 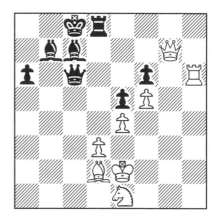

Diagram 31 (B)

The thematic breakthrough

Diagram 32 (B)

Black has a neat tactic

The thematic kingside advance is achieved, so now the black king has to run away from the centre at last.

> NOTE: Evidently this type of push can be more dangerous if Black has already castled kingside, hence there is merit in having a certain reluctance to commit the king early.

21...hxg5 22 hxg5 0-0-0 23 Ke2 Qd6 24 Rh1 c4!

Finally Black is ready to counter on the other flank.

25 Rxh8 Rxh8 26 gxf6 gxf6 27 Qg7 Rd8 28 bxc4 bxc4 29 Rh1 c3!

Seeking more open lines before White can press against the weak spot on f6.

30 bxc3 dxc3 31 Bxc3 Qc5 32 Bd2 Qxc2 33 Ne1

White holds his central fortress and gains time to put pressure on f6. The position is rapidly becoming critical.

33...Qc6 34 Rh6!? (Diagram 32)

Here 34 Rh8 would be about equal; instead Black has to make a decision.

34...Qb5?

Missing a neat tactic: 34...Rxd3! 35 Nxd3 (not 35 Kxd3? Qxe4+ 36 Kc3 Ba5+ and the attack is too strong) 35...Qxe4+ 36 Kd1 Qxd3 37 Qf8+ Bd8 38 Qc5+ Kb8 39 Rh8 Qf1+ and with the possibility of giving a long series of checks, Black shouldn't be worse.

35 Rh7 Qd7 36 Qg6 Qd6 37 Qf7 Rd7 38 Rh8+ Rd8 39 Rh7 Rd7 40 Qg8+ Rd8 41 Qc4

A good square, from which the white queen both defends and probes at the same time.

41...Kb8 42 Rf7 Rh8

Seeking weaknesses, but White is in control.

43 Nf3 Bb6?

43...Bd8 would be more tenacious.

44 Bb4 Qd8 45 Qe6

The f6-pawn falls, so Black must now launch a desperate counter-attack.

45...Rg8 46 Be7?

46 Qxf6! would have been easier.

46...Rg2+ 47 Ke1 Ba5+ 48 Kf1 Qxd3+! 49 Kxg2 Qe2+ 50 Kg3 Be1+ 51 Kg4! (Diagram 33)

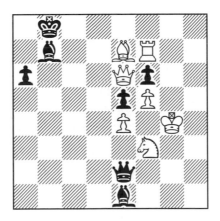

Diagram 33 (B)
The white king escapes

Stronger than 51 Nxe1 Qxe1+ 52 Kg4 Qe2+ with a draw.

51...Qxe4+ 52 Kh5 Qxf3+ 53 Kg6 Qg2+ 54 Kh7 Bf2 55 Bxf6 Ka7 56 Bxe5 Qh1+ 57 Kg8 a5 58 f6 Qe4 59 Rd7 Qg2+ 60 Rg7 Qf3 61 f7 Bc5 62 Bd6 Bxd6 63 Qxd6 Bd5 64 Qc7+ Ka6 65 Rg6+ Kb5 66 Rb6+ Ka4 67 Qc2+ 1-0

After 67...Bxb3 68 Qxb3+ White exchanges all the pieces and promotes his pawn.

Summary

The King's Gambit is one of those openings that can strike fear into the player on the receiving end if he isn't well prepared.

There are, however, several adequate antidotes, such as 2...Bc5 (Game 45) for positional players, and 2...exf4 3 Nf3 g5 (especially Game 42) for those who don't mind a scrap.

Chapter Eight
Vienna Game

Introduction

1 e4 e5 2 Nc3 (Diagram 1)

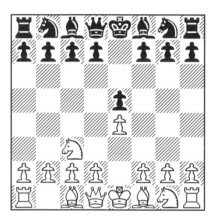

Diagram 1 (B)	**Diagram 2 (B)**
The Vienna Game	White plays 3 f4

The Vienna is defined by White developing his queen's knight with 2 Nc3, but the general nature of the opening will only be decided over the next few moves. Some lines can be particularly sharp, such as 1 e4 e5 2 Nc3 Nc6 3 f4 exf4 4 Nf3 g5; whereas in total contrast, the quiet 1 e4 e5 2 Nc3 Nf6 3 Bc4 Nc6 4 d3 Na5 involves virtually no tactics in the early stages.

There are also a number of transpositional possibilities; for example into the Four Knights or Scotch Four Knights if White plays an early Ng1-f3.

Strategy

The most popular reply is 2...Nf6, when White has three completely different plans of action:

a) 3 f4 is typical of the King's Gambit, but here Black can counter successfully with 3...d5!, as 4 fxe5 Nxe4 (the main line) is generally recognized as not advantageous for White.

b) 3 Bc4 Nf6 4 d3 often aims for harmonious development in a similar way to the

Quiet Italian. However, as White hasn't committed his king's knight he has the option of playing it to e2, or even playing an early f2-f4, again as in a King's Gambit.

c) 3 g3, with the clear intention of fianchettoing the king's bishop, is a fairly recent strategy. Black needs to decide whether just to develop in classical style or react actively in the centre or on the kingside.

After 2...Nc6, White can also opt for a quieter game reminiscent of other variations with 3 Bc4, 3 g3, or 3 Nf3 (heading for the Four Knights), but the critical option is 3 f4!? (the Vienna Gambit) when play indeed resembles the King's Gambit, and Black's first decision is the same: accept or decline!

Theoretical

The bolder lines with an early f2-f4 can be quite sharp and therefore are quite theoretical; whereas the quieter lines involving Bc4, d2-d3 and Nge2, or those based on g2-g3, don't require much memory work.

Black plays 2...Nf6

Game 46
□ K.Van der Weide ■ R.Pruijssers
Haarlem 2007

1 e4 e5 2 Nc3 Nf6 3 f4 (Diagram 2) 3...d5! 4 fxe5

Black is already very comfortable after 4 exd5 Nxd5.

4...Nxe4 5 Nf3

5 Qf3 is occasionally seen, but isn't dangerous if Black reacts with 5...Nc6!. For example, 6 Bb5 (after 6 Nxe4 simply 6...Nd4 is pleasant, if not already advantageous for Black; e.g. 7 Qc3 dxe4 8 Ne2 Nc6 9 Ng3 Qd5 10 Bc4 Qxe5 11 0-0 Bc5+ 12 Kh1 0-0 13 Qxe5 Nxe5 14 Nxe4 and it was White who was fighting for equality in A.Tzermiadianos-A.Mastrovasilis, Greek Ch., Athens 2002) 6...Nxc3 **(Diagram 3)**, and now whichever pawn White recaptures with, Black plays the same simplifying manoeuvre to equalize:

a) 7 bxc3 Qh4+ 8 g3 Qe4+ 9 Qxe4 dxe4 10 Bxc6+ bxc6 11 Ne2 Be7 (or possibly 11...Ba6!?) 12 Nd4 (if 12 Rf1 0-0 13 Rf4 f6 14 exf6 Bxf6, the bishops should offer Black an advantage) 12...Bd7 13 Rf1 0-0 14 Rf4 c5 15 Nb3 Rae8 16 Rxe4 Bf5 17 Re2 Bxc2 and Black wasn't worse, B.Kazic-D.Poljakov, Yugoslav Ch., Novi Sad 1945.

b) 7 dxc3 Qh4+ (or 7...a6 8 Bxc6+ bxc6 9 Qg3?! Bf5 10 Qf2 Qd7 11 Nf3 Be7 12 Be3 0-0 and Black had no problems, G.Antal-T.Roussel Roozman, Budapest 2008) 8 g3 Qe4+ 9 Qxe4 dxe4 10 Bf4 h6 11 Ne2 g5 12 Be3 Bg7 13 Nd4 Bd7 14 e6 fxe6 15 Nxc6 a6 16 Bc4 Bxc6 17 Bxe6 Rd8 18 0-0 Bd5 19 Bf5 0-0 with equality, H.Nakamura-A.Yermolinsky, US Ch., Stillwater 2007.

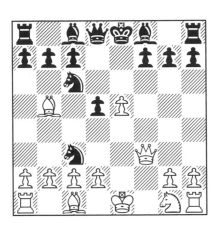

Diagram 3 (W)

Position after 6...Bxc3

Diagram 4 (W)

White has no advantage

5...Be7

The main move here, but I have a penchant for 5...Bc5!?, with which I've had good results. White can allow the check on f2 or 'gain' a tempo with d2-d4:

a) 6 Qe2 Bf2+ 7 Kd1 Nxc3+ 8 dxc3 Bb6 (8...Bh4!? has been recommended but no one seems to have played it) 9 Bg5 Qd7 and now both sides need to reorganize their pieces; e.g. 10 Qd2 (or 10 Kd2 h6 11 Bh4 Qa4 12 Qb5+ Qxb5 13 Bxb5+ c6 14 Bd3 0-0 15 Nd4 Nd7 16 e6 Ne5 and I prefer Black, A.Boog-M.Godena, Geneva 1993) 10...0-0 11 Bd3 c5 12 c4 dxc4 13 Bxc4 Nc6 14 h3 Qxd2+ 15 Kxd2 Re8 16 Rae1 Be6 with at least equality, P.Lehtivaara-G.Flear, Lenk 1992.

b) 6 d4 Bb4 (White has won his tempo but is now faced with a pin) 7 Bd2 Bg4 **(Diagram 4)** (another pin to keep White busy!).

I don't think White can obtain any advantage here; for example:

b1) 8 Nxe4 dxe4 9 Bxb4 exf3 10 Qd2 (or 10 gxf3 Qh4+ 11 Ke2 Nc6, J.Sorensen-G.Flear, Hastings 1988/89) 10...Nc6 11 Bc3 Qd5 12 h3 Be6 13 gxf3 0-0-0, L.Ljubojevic-V.Ciocaltea, Skopje Olympiad 1972.

b2) 8 Be2 c5!? (or 8...Nc6 with equality, as I've had in some rapid games) 9 a3 Bxc3 10 bxc3 Nc6 11 0-0 0-0 12 Be1 f5!?, M.Pena Dieguez-J.Fernandez Garcia, Seville 2004.

b3) 8 Bd3 Bxf3 9 Qxf3 Qh4+ 10 g3 Nxd2 11 Kxd2, J.Hector-S.Petersen, Copenhagen 2007, and now 11...Qxd4! is best.

There is more than one way for Black to get a good game in this line, with 5...Bc5!? being my favourite. However, 5...Nc6?! is wrong, as this just encourages 6 Bb5.

6 Qe2 (Diagram 5)

After 6 d4 0-0 (or 6...Bb4!?, transposing to the previous note) 7 Bd3 f5 8 exf6, Black has 8...Bxf6! when he shouldn't be worse (the difference with 8...Nxf6 is that White's pieces then become more active; e.g. 9 0-0 Nc6 10 Bg5 Bg4 11 Qd2 Bh5 12 Rae1, R.Réti-R.Michell, Marienbad 1925). After 8...Bxf6! 9 0-0 Nc6 10 Ne2 (simplification is drawish: 10 Nxe4 dxe4 11 Bxe4 Nxd4 12 Ng5 Bf5! 13 c3 Bxg5 14 Bxg5 Qxg5 15 Qxd4 Bxe4 16 Qxe4 with equality, R.Spielmann-R.Réti, Vienna 1924) 10...Nb4, exchanging off White's light-squared bishop, leads to at least equality: 11 Bb5 Bd7 12 Bxd7 Qxd7 13 c3 Nc6 14 Nf4 Ne7 (or 14...Rad8!) 15 Qb3 c6 16 Nd2?! (16 Nd3 Rae8 17 Be3 Ng6 18 Rae1 is safer) 16...Nd6 17 Nh5 Bg5 18 Nf3 Bxc1 19 Raxc1 Ng6 and Black had chances for the initiative, A.Konstantinopolovsky-V.Rauzer, Kiev 1940.

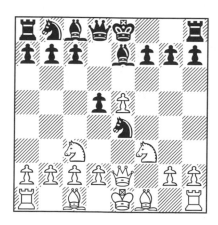

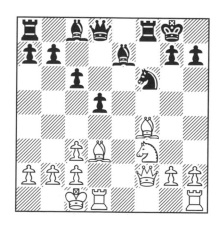

Diagram 5 (B)

Position after 6 Qe2

Diagram 6 (B)

White has greater harmony

6...Nxc3

A case can be made for avoiding this capture and maintaining the tension. Here are a couple of examples:

a) 6...f5 7 d3 Nc5 8 Be3 Ne6 9 d4 0-0 10 Qd2 c6 11 g3 b5 12 Ne2 Nd7 13 Nf4 Nb6 14 b3 a5 15 Bd3 a4 16 0-0, where White has extra space but otherwise the position isn't that clear, D.Andreikin-E.Romanov, Russian Junior Ch. 2008.

b) 6...Ng5 7 d4 c6 8 Be3 0-0 9 0-0-0 Na6 10 h4 Nxf3 11 gxf3 f6 12 f4 fxe5 13 fxe5 Nc7 14 h5 and White has the better chances as he has the safer king, M.Adams-Xu Jun, Cap d'Agde 1994.

My feeling is that 6...Nxc3 is simplest and probably best.

7 dxc3 0-0

Natural enough, but 7...c5 is the most precise; e.g. 8 Bf4 Nc6 9 0-0-0 Be6 10 h4 (10 c4 d4 11 h4 h6 12 a3 Qa5 13 Qf2 0-0-0 14 Bd3 Qa4 15 Nd2 Na5 16 Kb1 b5!? was double-edged in J.Hector-V.Inkiov, Copenhagen 1990) 10...h6 11 g3 Qd7 12 Bg2 0-0-0 13 h5 Na5 14 b3 Nc6 15 Qf2 Qc7 16 Kb1 Kb8 with equality, M.Adams-V.Anand, 4th matchgame, Linares 1994. Castling long proved to be a good idea for Anand here – hence my preference for 7...c5, delaying committing Black's king.

8 Bf4 Nd7?!

This looks slightly odd, but in a couple of moves Black's idea will become clear. Nevertheless, Black should again play 8...c5, intending to place the knight on the more active c6-square; e.g. 9 0-0-0 Qa5 10 a3 (10 Kb1!?) 10...Be6 11 Bg5 Nc6 12 Bxe7 Nxe7 13 Ng5 Qb6 14 Qh5 h6 15 Nxe6 Qxe6 and I was happy with my lot in J.Hector-G.Flear, Nancy 1988.

9 0-0-0 c6 10 Qf2 f6?!

My feeling is that this plan is correct when White castles kingside, but is less convincing with White going long as it just seems to render Black's king more vulnerable. Here 10...Qa5 11 Kb1 Nc5 might still give Black a satisfactory game.

11 exf6 Nxf6 12 Bd3 (Diagram 6)

White has the more harmonious development and is ready to put pressure on Black's king.

12...Qa5 13 Rhe1!

Gaining a tempo for development is better than the routine 13 Kb1 Ne4 14 Qe3 Bf5, when Black wouldn't have any particular problems.

13...Bc5 14 Qh4 Qxa2 15 Be5 Ne4?

Losing immediately, though in any case the defence isn't easy with White's pieces being far more effective on the front that counts; e.g. 15...h6 16 Bxf6 Rxf6 17 Re8+

Rf8 (or if 17...Bf8, simply 18 Rde1) 18 Rxf8+ Bxf8 19 Qh5 with a very strong attack.

16 Rxe4! dxe4 17 Qxe4 (Diagram 7)

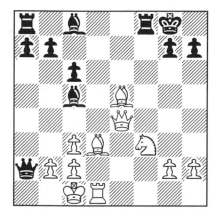

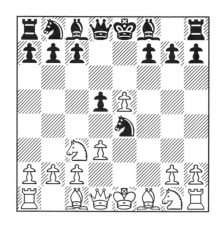

Diagram 7 (B)	**Diagram 8 (B)**
Black is lost	White plays 5 d3

White's threats are decisive.

17...Bf5 18 Bc4+ Rf7

If 18...Kh8, then 19 Bxg7+! Kxg7 20 Qe5+ followed by 21 Bxa2 wins easily.

19 Bxa2 1-0

After 19...Bxe4 20 Bxf7+ Kxf7 21 Ng5+ Kg6 22 Nxe4 Be3+ 23 Kb1 Re8 24 Re1 White emerges with an extra piece.

Game 47
□ D.Otero ■ Y.Gonzalez Vidal
Cuban Championship, Santa Clara 2005

1 e4 e5 2 Nc3 Nf6 3 f4 d5 4 fxe5 Nxe4 5 d3 (Diagram 8) 5...Nxc3

Black has two other moves here, but these have been more or less played out – the first to a win for White, the second to a draw.

a) 5...Qh4+? 6 g3 Nxg3 7 Nf3 Qh5 8 Nxd5 Nxh1 9 Nxc7+ Kd8 10 Nxa8 and Black is definitely worse; e.g. 10...Be7 11 Bg2 Bh4+ 12 Kf1 Nc6 13 d4 Bg4 14 Be3 Kc8 15

Bxh1! Rd8 16 Qe2 Nxd4 17 Qc4+ Nc6 18 Nxh4 Qxh4 19 Bg2 Kb8 20 Nc7 Kxc7 21 h3 Qg3 22 Bf2 1-0 C.Kiffmeyer-J.Dannehr, German Junior Ch. 1970.

b) 5...Bb4 6 dxe4 and only then 6...Qh4+ is acceptable if Black doesn't mind a quick draw: 7 Ke2 Bxc3 8 bxc3 Bg4+ 9 Nf3 dxe4 10 Qd4 Bh5 11 Kd2 **(Diagram 9)** (11 Ke3 Bxf3 12 gxf3 Qe1+ 13 Kf4 Qh4+ is a draw; or if 12 Bb5+ c6 13 gxf3 Qh6+ 14 Ke2 Qh3 15 Rd1, then 15...exf3+ is given a '!' by Vukovic but even 15...0-0!? is possible) 11...Qg4! (11...Bxf3? is bad this time: 12 gxf3 Nc6 13 Qxe4 Qf2+ 14 Kd1 0-0-0+ 15 Bd3 with a big advantage to White, Z.Rahman-K.Chatterjee, Calcutta 1994) 12 h3 Qf4+ 13 Ke1 Qg3+ 14 Qf2 Qxf2+ 15 Kxf2 exf3 16 gxf3 Nd7 17 Bd3 (after 17 f4 Bg6 18 Bd3 Nc5 the inferior enemy structure should favour Black) 17...Bg6 18 Ba3 Nb6 19 c4 0-0-0 with equality, J.Malo Guillen-J.Eslon, Cordoba 1995.

Diagram 9 (B)

Equal with best play

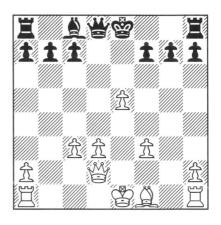

Diagram 10 (B)

Black should hit back

6 bxc3 Nc6 7 Nf3 d4 8 Be2

I have faced 8 cxd4 on a few occasions, but consider it to be less dangerous than the text move: 8...Bb4+! (rather than 8...Nxd4 9 c3 Nxf3+ 10 Qxf3 which gives White high hopes of generating an initiative due to his centre) 9 Bd2 Bxd2+ 10 Qxd2 Nxd4 11 c3 Nxf3+ 12 gxf3 **(Diagram 10)** 12...f6! (this was recommended to me by Gary Lane when we were playing a tournament in Malta together; the more popular 12...Qh4+ 13 Qf2 Qf4 14 Qg3 Qe3+ 15 Be2 Bf5 16 f4 doesn't look so easy as White's central pawn phalanx can go from strength to strength, hence I think it is better to hit back at the centre immediately) 13 f4 fxe5 14 fxe5 0-0 15 0-0-0 and now Black has several ways to achieve at least equality – the main thing is not to allow White to get his central pawns rolling; e.g. 15...Qd5 (15...Be6 16 d4 Qh4 wasn't easy for White to handle either, J.Grech-G.Flear, Malta 1989) 16 d4 Bg4 17 Bg2 Bf3 18 Bxf3 Rxf3 19 Rhe1 Qc4 20 Kb2 Raf8 21 Re2 Rxc3! and Black won in C.Mariette-C.Flear, French Team Ch. 1991.

8...Bc5

8...dxc3 9 0-0 (not 9 d4?! Bg4 10 Be3 Be7 11 0-0 Nb4, which already favoured Black in D.Isaacson-B.Spassky, Tel Aviv Olympiad 1964) 9...Bc5+ transposes to the main line, though it does avoid White's idea in the next note.

9 0-0

9 c4!? is less well known and not at all bad; for example, 9...0-0 10 0-0 Bg4 11 Rb1 Rb8 12 Bf4 Qe7 13 Qe1 wasn't clear in M.Walek-P.Buchinek, Czech Ch., Luhacovice 1993.

9...dxc3+ 10 Kh1 0-0 11 Qe1 Nd4 12 Bd1 (Diagram 11)

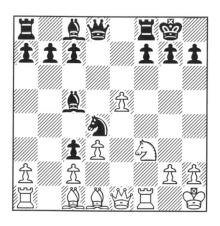 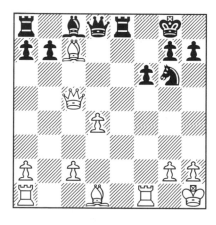

Diagram 11 (B)

What now for Black?

Diagram 12 (B)

The bishops give White an edge

Black's main problem after this move is deciding on his plan of action, as he has many options, including a few that go astray!

Instead, 12 Qxc3 is also possible, but after 12...b6 (defending the bishop on c5), White has to be wary of the threat to his bishop on e2 as well as a skewer with ...Nxf3 and ...Bd4. For example, 13 Qd2 f6! (M.Traldi-D.Ippolito, Philadelphia 2000) 14 exf6 Nxe2 15 Qxe2 Qxf6 with a small edge to Black.

12...Re8

12...Nxf3 13 Bxf3 Re8 is not recommended, as after 14 Qg3 the threats of Bg5 and Bh6 offer White dangerous attacking chances.

However, 12...f6 again comes into consideration; e.g. 13 Qxc3 (or 13 Bf4 Bb6 14 Rb1 Qd5 15 exf6 Rxf6, M.Pavlov-B.Vogt, Trencianske Teplice 1974, when Vogt analyses 16 Nxd4 Bxd4 17 Qe8+ Rf8 18 Bf3 as giving chances for both sides) 13...Bb6! (preferable to 13...b6, which is now well met by 14 Ba3 fxe5 15 Bxc5 bxc5 16 Qxc5 Qd6 17 Qxd6 cxd6 18 c3 with an edge, O.Ekebjaerg-A.Idema, correspondence 1983) 14 Ba3 is approximately equal according to Glazkov & Tseitlin, though I prefer Black's position following 14...Rf7.

13 Qxc3 Nxf3

After 13...Bb6 White would be wise to sidestep the potential skewer with 14 Rb1!, when matters are far from clear.

14 Qxc5 Nxe5 15 Bf4 f6?

The source of Black's future difficulties. Instead, 15...Qf6! could have been played, as 16 Bh5 Qf5 17 Bxe5 Qxh5 18 Qxc7 looks about equal. Another possibility is 15...Qe7 16 Qxe7 Rxe7 17 Re1 f6 18 d4 Nc6 19 Rxe7 Nxe7 20 Bxc7 Be6 and Black has no problems.

16 d4 Ng6 17 Bxc7 (Diagram 12)

There is no reason not to capture on c7. Now White's bishop pair should offer him some advantage.

17...Qe7 18 Bf3

Avoiding the exchange of queens with 18 Qc3 might allow Black to seize the initiative with 18...Be6 19 Qg3 Bc4 20 Rg1 Qf7.

18...Qxc5 19 dxc5

The doubled pawns are not weak – in fact they play the role of fixing the opposing structure.

19...Ne7 20 Rfe1 Kf7 21 Rab1 Nc6 22 Bd5+ Be6

White now wins a pawn and obtains serious winning chances.

23 Rxe6 Rxe6 24 Rxb7 Rae8 25 Bd6+ Kg6 26 Bxe6 Rxe6 27 h3 Re1+ 28 Kh2 Re2 29 Bf8

The most precise as this wrecks Black's kingside.

29...h5 30 Rxg7+ Kf5 31 Rh7 Rxc2 32 Rxh5+ Kg6 33 Rd5 Kf7 34 Bh6 Rxa2 (Diagram 13) 35 h4?

A second passed pawn starts to advance, but White should really harmonize his forces first, so 35 Rd6 Ne5 36 Bf4 looks a better try.

NOTE: Passed pawns must be pushed, but only when the pieces are good and ready.

35...Ne7 36 Rd2

If 36 Rd7 Ke8 37 Rd2, Black would again obtain excellent drawing chances; e.g. 37...Ra4 38 g3 Nf5 39 Re2+ Kf7 40 Bc1 Rc4 41 Ba3 Rc3.

36...Ra4 37 g3 Nf5 38 Bf4 Rc4

38...Nxh4!? looks equally playable.

39 Rd7+ Kg6 40 Bd6 Nxd6 41 cxd6 Rd4

With Black's pieces well placed and his a-pawn as a decoy, the draw is assured.

42 Kh3 f5 43 Rd8 a5 44 h5+ Kg7 45 Ra8 Rxd6 46 Kh4 Rd4+ ½-½

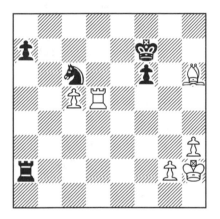

Diagram 13 (W)

White has winning chances

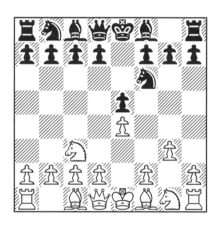

Diagram 14 (B)

White plays 3 g3

Game 48
□ P.Leko ■ V.Kramnik
6th matchgame (rapid), Budapest 2001

1 e4 e5 2 Nc3 Nf6 3 g3 (Diagram 14)

Although top GMs don't play offbeat Open Games very often, this 'fianchetto Vienna' makes for a decent surprise weapon.

3...d5

The simplest solution. Black opens the centre and aims for good piece play.

 NOTE: In many Open Games, if White resorts to slow or flank play, then ...d7-d5 is more often than not the way to counter.

Classical-style development with 3...Nc6 4 Bg2 Bc5 5 Nge2 d6 **(Diagram 15)** is plausible.

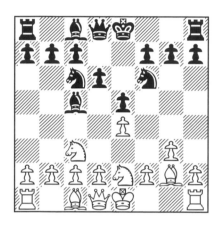

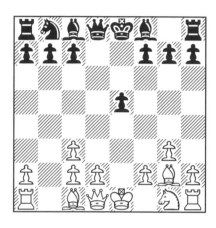

Diagram 15 (W)

Classical development

Diagram 16 (B)

Position after 6 bxc3

White has quite some choice as to how to develop and it's hard to draw many definite conclusions, but he almost certainly does best not to castle too quickly:

a) 6 0-0 h5!? 7 d3 (or 7 h3 h4 8 g4 Nxg4 9 hxg4 Bxg4 10 Kh2 Qd7 11 f3 h3 12 Bh1 Be6 with practical chances for the piece, P.Natacheev-V.Varavin, Kazan 2008) 7...h4 8 Bg5 hxg3 9 Nxg3 Nd4 10 Nh5 Ne6 11 Nxg7+ Nxg7 12 Nd5 Nxd5 13 Bxd8 Nf4 14 Bg5 Nge6 15 Bxf4 Nxf4 16 Kh1 Be6 and Black had a fantastic attack in J.Augustin-J.Nunn, European Team Ch., Moscow 1977.

b) 6 d3 a6 7 h3 (a cat and mouse approach) 7...Be6 8 0-0 h6 (after 8...Qd7!? 9 Kh2 h5 10 Nd5 0-0-0 11 b4 Ba7 12 Be3 Bxd5 13 exd5 Nd4 14 Nxd4 Bxd4 15 Rb1 White had more trumps up his sleeve, A.Morozevich-Z.Almasi, Istanbul Olympiad 2000) 9 Nd5 Qd7 10 Kh2 Bxd5 11 exd5 Ne7 12 c4 Nf5 13 Nc3 0-0 14 Ne4 Nxe4 15 dxe4 Ne7 with equality, A.Dragojlovich-Y.Gozzoli, La Fère 2007.

However, I'm not that keen on Black's set-up if White just plays the direct...

c) 6 Na4! (62% for White), obtaining the bishop pair; for example, 6...Be6 (6...0-0 7 0-0 Bb6 is solid, but the soon-to-be bishop pair and flexible pawns should still favour White) 7 d3 Qd7 8 h3 Bb6 9 Nxb6 axb6 10 c4!? as in J.Mieses-J.Blackburne, Leipzig 1894, and I prefer White as Black is short of counterplay.

Although a number of players stronger than me seem to like this method of development, so that my point of view may not hold that much water, don't expect me to play like this as Black! I don't like giving up the bishop pair too lightly at the best of times and here I don't see much going for Black in return.

4 exd5 Nxd5 5 Bg2 Nxc3 6 bxc3 (Diagram 16) 6...Bd6

Developing the bishop to where it defends the e-pawn.

Another idea is 6...Be7!? 7 Nf3 Nc6 8 0-0 0-0 9 Re1 Bf6 (so Black loses a tempo to defend the e5-pawn, but now keeps a closer eye on the d4-square) 10 d3 (10 Rb1 Rb8 11 d3 Bg4 12 h3 Be6 13 c4 Qd7 14 Kh2 Rfe8 15 Bb2 Bf5 16 Nd2 Nd4 was dynamic for Black, A.Soltis-L.Ljubojevic, New York Open 1985) 10...Be6 11 Nd2 Qd7 12 Ba3 Rfe8 13 Qb1 Rab8 14 Ne4 Be7 15 Bxe7 Qxe7 16 Qb5 Bd7 as in C.Marcellin-G.Flear, Montpellier 2002, which was quickly drawn due to a repetition.

The bishop can also be placed on c5; for example, 6...Nc6 7 Ne2 Bc5 (this position could be reached with 6...Bc5 7 Ne2 Nc6) 8 0-0 0-0, when L.McShane-A.Shirov, Drammen 2004, continued 9 Rb1 (9 d3 can be met by 9...Bg4 10 h3 Bh5 11 Rb1 Bb6) 9...Bb6 10 c4 e4! (tactical ingenuity from Shirov; 10...Bg4 11 h3 Bh5 is more conventional and not bad either) 11 Nf4 (11 Bxe4?! is unsatisfactory due to 11...Bg4; e.g. 12 Kh1 Re8 or 12 Kg2 Qd7) 11...Re8 12 Rb5 Ne5 13 Rd5 Qe7 14 Re1 c6? (here 14...f5 would be better for Black who has the more harmonious pieces) 15 Rxe5 Qxe5 16 Rxe4 Qxe4 17 Bxe4 Rxe4 18 d3 Re8 19 Bb2 and White had survived!

7 Nf3 0-0 8 0-0 Nd7

8...Nc6 is another possibility, transposing to the Glek System of the Four Knights: 2 Nf3 Nc6 3 Nc3 Nf6 4 g3!? with 4...d5 5 exd5 Nxd5 6 Bg2 Nxc3 7 bxc3 Bd6 8 0-0 0-0 – see the notes to White's 4th move in Game 25.

9 d4 h6 10 Re1 exd4 11 cxd4 Nb6 (Diagram 17)

Challenging for the c4-square. Instead, 11...Re8 12 Rxe8+ Qxe8 13 c4 c5 14 Bb2 Nb6 15 Rc1 Be6 16 d5 Bg4 17 h3 favoured White slightly, D.Lima-J.Rubinetti, Sao Paulo 1993.

12 Ne5

Alternatively 12 Qd3 Qf6 (but not 12...Be6?! due to 13 Rxe6! fxe6 14 Bxh6! with a strong attack; e.g. 14...gxh6? 15 Qg6+ Kh8 16 Qxh6+ Kg8 17 Bh3! and wins – Finkel) 13 c4 Bf5 14 Qb3 Be6 and now 15 d5!? Qxa1 16 Bb2 Qxe1+ 17 Nxe1 Bf5 was unclear in A.Finkel-J.M.Degraeve, European Club Cup, Rethymnon 2003. Instead, 15 Ne5! gives White a small pull according to Lukacs as White can hold onto his central pawn front – which is perhaps true, though Black is very solid. For example,

15...c6 16 Bf4 Rfe8 17 a4 (as given by him) could be met by 17...Bxe5! 18 Bxe5 Qd8 and the centre comes under some pressure: 19 a5 Nxc4 20 Qxb7 Bd5 looks equal, and 19 Rac1 f6 20 Bf4 Qxd4 is unclear.

12...c6 13 c3

A tame move. More appropriate is 13 a4 a5 14 Qd3 Be6 15 Ba3 with equality.

13...Be6

If, as here, Black is able to hold onto the c4- and d5-squares, then he has good chances of consolidating his superior structure.

14 Qh5 Re8 15 Bf4 Nd5 16 Bd2 Nf6 17 Qd1 Bd5 18 Qc2?

Better is 18 Rb1! Qc7! 19 c4 Bxg2 20 Kxg2 c5! (rather than 20...Bxe5 21 Rxe5 Rxe5 22 Bf4 which isn't clear) 21 Qf3 b6 22 Bc3 cxd4 23 Bxd4 Rac8 with only a small pull for Black.

18...Bxg2 19 Kxg2 Bxe5 20 dxe5 Qd5+ 21 f3 Rxe5 22 c4 Qe6 23 Rxe5 Qxe5 24 Re1 Qc5 25 Be3 Qa3 26 Bc1 Qf8? (Diagram 18)

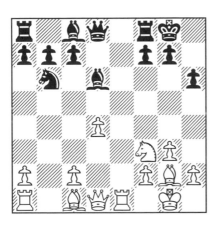

Diagram 17 (W)

Fighting for the light squares

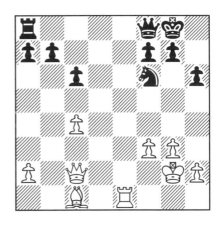

Diagram 18 (W)

Black goes astray

An oversight. Instead, 26...Qb4! 27 Bd2 Qd6 28 Bf4 Qd7 would leave White with very little to show for his pawn deficit.

27 Qb2!

Forking two pawns (Qxb7 and Bxh6 are threatened).

27...Re8 28 Rxe8 Qxe8 29 Bxh6 gxh6 30 Qxf6 Qe2+ 31 Kg1 Qxc4 32 Qxh6 Qd4+

Or 32...Qxa2 33 Qg5+ with perpetual check.

33 Kg2 c5 34 Qg5+ Kf8 35 Qg4 Qd2+ 36 Kf1 Qd1+ 37 Kf2 Qd2+ 38 Kf1 Qxa2 39 Qc8+ Kg7 40 Qxc5 Qa1+ ½-½

After 40...Qxh2 White again has perpetual check: 41 Qd4+ Kh7 42 Qe4+ Kg8 43 Qg4+ Kh8 44 Qd4+ etc.

1 e4 e5 2 Bc4 Nf6 3 Nc3 (Diagram 19)

Naturally, in the context of this chapter, 2 Nc3 Nf6 3 Bc4 would be the normal move order.

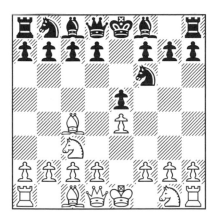

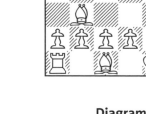

Diagram 19 (B)	**Diagram 20 (W)**
White plays 3 Bc4	The Frankenstein-Dracula

3...Nc6

The most natural move, simply continuing development.

However, if Black is in the mood for complications he can opt for 3...Nxe4!?, steering the game towards the so-called Frankenstein-Dracula variation! The name reflects that the whole line is weird and scary! The horror story continues as follows: 4 Qh5 (4 Nxe4 d5 and 4 Bxf7+ Kxf7 5 Nxe4 d5 offer White nothing) 4...Nd6 5 Bb3 (instead 5 Qxe5+ Qe7 6 Qxe7+ Bxe7 7 Bb3 Nf5 8 Nf3 c6 9 d4 d5 10 Ne2 0-0 11

0-0 Nh4 leads to boring equality, I.Rogers-A.Shirov, Spanish Team Ch. 1998) 5...Nc6 (if he is having second thoughts Black can cop out with 5...Be7; e.g. 6 Nf3 Nc6 7 Nxe5 g6 8 Nxc6 dxc6 9 Qf3 0-0 or 8 Qe2 Nd4 9 Qd3 Nxb3 10 axb3 Nf5 11 0-0 d6 12 Nf3 c6 13 b4 0-0 14 b5 d5 15 bxc6 bxc6 16 Re1 a5 again with equality, V.Anand-V.Ivanchuk, Roquebrune rapid 1992) 6 Nb5!? g6 7 Qf3 f5 8 Qd5 Qe7 (avoiding mate but giving away the queen's rook) 9 Nxc7+ Kd8 10 Nxa8 b6 **(Diagram 20)**.

Black is a rook down in the opening, but it is precisely this position many who play 3...Nxe4 are seeking. Black has a lead in development, a strong central pawn mass, the knight on a8 is condemned, and there are plenty of fascinating variations – all for a mere rook! Computers are confused by such bizarre positions with a material imbalance, so correspondence players in particular adore the intricacy and possibilities for original thinking in the F-D variation.

a) 11 Nxb6 grabs a pawn with the trapped – and soon to be lost anyway – knight, but is regarded as inferior; for example, 11...axb6 12 Qf3 Bb7 13 Qh3 Nd4 14 d3 f4! 15 Bd2 h5 16 0-0-0 g5 17 f3 N6f5!, when Black has ideas of playing ...Qg7 and ...g5-g4. Black probably has good compensation and maybe even the advantage, V.Panbukchian-N.Ninov, Albena 1988.

b) 11 d3 Bb7 12 h4 f4 13 Qf3 Nd4 14 Qg4 Bh6 (14...Bxa8 is supposed to be a shade too slow as White then has time to castle; e.g. 15 Bd2 Bh6 16 0-0-0 N6f5 17 Kb1!? or 17 c3 Nxb3+ 18 axb3 Qe6 19 Re1 Re8 20 Nf3 d6 21 Ng5 and White was better in R.Amrein-P.Hardicsay, Budapest 1998, though Black later escaped with a draw) 15 Bd2 e4 16 0-0-0 e3 17 fxe3 Nxb3+ 18 axb3 fxe3 19 Be1 e2+ 20 Rd2 Bxd2+ 21 Kxd2 Re8 22 Qg5 Bxg2 23 Rh2 Bxa8 24 Nxe2, when the material balance had been restored, R.Liiva-J.Norri, Finnish Team Ch. 1996.

A spine-tingling line that can be fun, but only for courageous souls!

4 d3 Na5

Chasing the bishop in this way is also my preference, but there are two other principle lines. The first is 4...Bc5 5 f4 d6 6 Nf3, transposing to the King's Gambit Declined (see Game 45). The second option involves 4...Bb4 **(Diagram 21)** and then:

a) 5 Bg5 h6 6 Bxf6 Bxc3+ 7 bxc3 Qxf6 8 Ne2 d6 9 0-0 g5 (9...Be6 10 Bb3 0-0 11 d4 Bxb3 12 axb3 a6 13 Qd3 Rfe8, V.Tomescu-I.Efimov, Reggio Emilia 2000/01, is solid albeit lacking ambition) 10 d4 Ne7 11 Qd2 (11 f3 h5 12 g3?! is slightly premature, as after 12...h4 13 g4 Ng6 14 Rb1 Kf8 15 Qd2 Kg7 16 Qe3 b6 Black has no problems on the evidence of H.Jonkman-A.Bezgodov, Pardubice 1996) 11...Ng6 12 Rad1 Nf4 13 g3 Nh3+ 14 Kg2 Qg6 15 f3 0-0 16 Qe3 b6 17 Kh1 Kh8 18 Rd2 Bb7 19 dxe5 dxe5 20 Bd5 with a small plus for White, Mi.Tseitlin-I.Naumkin, Moscow 1998.

b) 5 Nge2 d5 6 exd5 Nxd5 7 0-0 Be6 8 Bxd5 Bxd5 9 f4 0-0 10 f5 f6 11 Ng3 Re8 12

Nce4 Bf8 13 Qg4 Kh8 14 Be3 gave White the slightly freer development in K.Müller-L.Schandorff, German League 2006, but Black is solid and can hope that an eventual opening of the position will favour the bishops.

5 Nge2

5 Qf3 is another White try, against which I think that it is prudent to keep the bishop on e7; for example, 5...c6 6 Nge2 d6 7 h3 Be7 8 0-0 0-0 9 Ng3 Ne8 10 a3 Nxc4 (note that only now, when the bishop is finally ready to drop back, does Pavasovic chop it off) 11 dxc4 g6 12 Bh6 Ng7 13 Qd3 Be6 14 Rad1 Qa5 15 Kh1 Rad8 and Black has everything in order, M.Srbrenic-D.Pavasovic, Bled 2008.

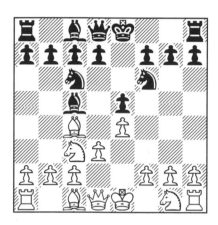

Diagram 21 (W)

Black plays 4...Bb4

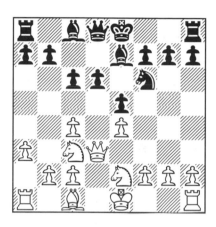

Diagram 22 (W)

A standard 5...c6 position

5...Nxc4

I prefer 5...c6! here, which is a useful waiting move and induces White to move his a-pawn before exchanging minor pieces: 6 a3 (I am less sure that the often recommended 6 a4 is such a good idea as it weakens the dark squares: 6...Nxc4 7 dxc4 Bc5 8 0-0 d6 9 Qd3 Be6 10 b3 a5 11 h3 Qb6 12 Kh1 0-0-0 with decent chances for Black, L.Trent-A.Ashton, British League 2005; while 6 0-0 can even be met by 6...b5!? 7 Bb3 b4 8 Nb1 d5 and Black was making a decent fight for the centre, N.Short-A.Onischuk, Groningen 1996) 6...Nxc4 7 dxc4 d6 8 Qd3 Be7 **(Diagram 22)** 9 Bg5 (9 0-0 Be6 10 Bg5 h6 11 Bxf6 Bxf6 12 Rad1 Qe7 gives White nothing either, R.Hess-D.Ippolito, Mashantucket 2005) 9...h6 10 Bxf6 (10 Bh4 Be6 11 f4 can be met by a Sicilian-style counter-sacrifice 11...g5!? 12 fxg5 Ng4 with dynamic counterplay, B.Ivanovic-V.Kovacevic, Bugojno 1984) 10...Bxf6 11 Rd1 Be6 12 b3 0-0 13 a4

Be7 14 0-0 f5 15 f4 Qa5 and the opening up of the game favoured the owner of the bishops (i.e. Black) in P.Dobrolowski-M.Grabarczyk, Krakow 1999.

6 dxc4 Bc5

 WARNING: Any plan involving an early ...c7-c6 and ...Be7 now would leave Black a tempo down on the previous note.

7 f3

After 7 0-0, simplest is 7...d6 8 Qd3 Be6 9 b3 0-0 10 Na4 Nd7 11 Ng3 a5 with equality, A.Shabalov-A.Ivanov, New York Open 1994. Instead, when faced with this position, Karpov played the 'semi-mistaken' 8...c6 9 b3 Be6 (essentially playing the same position a tempo down) 10 Na4 Nd7 11 Nxc5 Nxc5 12 Qe3 b6 13 f4 f6 14 Ba3 Nb7, N.Short-A.Karpov, Tilburg 1990, when 15 f5 would have kept a slight pull for White according to Karpov.

7...d6 8 Qd3 Be6 9 b3 Nd7 10 Be3 (Diagram 23)

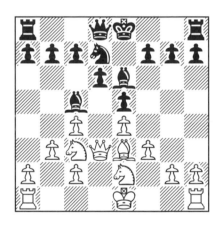 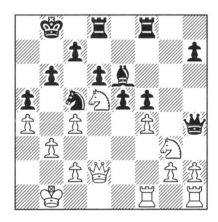

Diagram 23 (B)	Diagram 24 (W)
The game is balanced	Now Black is slightly better

10...a5

Adams is known as quite a cautious player with Black. Here, for instance, he waits for White to show his hand before committing his king.

After 10...0-0, White could try the daring 11 g4!?; e.g. 11...Qh4+ 12 Ng3 h5 13 0-0-0 (13 gxh5 is met by 13...f5!) 13...hxg4 14 fxg4 Bxg4 15 Rdg1 Bxe3+ 16 Qxe3 Kh7 17 Kb2 g6 18 Nb5 Qh6 19 Qf2 f5? (19...Qf4! wouldn't be so clear, though White's kingside possibilities are still dangerous) 20 Nxc7 and White had obtained favourable complications in S.Mamedyarov-N.Gurieli, Dubai 2004.

11 a4 Qh4+ 12 Ng3 g6 13 0-0-0 0-0-0

Unlike in the previous note, there is no danger of Black facing an opposite-wings attack now.

14 Kb1 Kb8 15 Rdf1 f5! 16 f4

In order to counter the black f-pawn's advance, but from here on, although White keeps his solidity, Black has the more flexible structure.

16...Rhe8 17 exf5 gxf5 18 Bxc5 Nxc5 19 Qd2 b6 20 Nd5 Rf8 (Diagram 24)

Black has emerged with the slightly more comfortable position.

21 Rf3 Rde8 22 Rhf1 Qh6 23 Nc3 Bc8

Adams is in no hurry and just continues to improve his pieces.

24 h3 Bb7 25 R3f2 Qg6 26 Nge2 h5 27 g3 Rf7 28 Qe3 Qh6 29 Qc1 Qh7 30 Qe3 Bc6 31 Kc1 h4!

Shaking up the white kingside.

32 gxh4 Bd7 33 Rg1 Qxh4 34 Rfg2 Qh8 35 Kb1 Rh7 36 Rg3 Bc6 37 Qf2 Rf8 38 Qe3 Rh4 39 Ka2 Ne6

White is finally obliged to release the tension.

40 fxe5 dxe5 41 Rg6 f4?

After all that hard work Adams gives his opponent a chance! The superior 41...Rxh3 would leave White with a miserable position.

42 Nxf4! exf4 43 Qxe6 Qxc3 44 Qxc6 Qxc2+ 45 Ka3 Rxh3 46 Qb5 (Diagram 25)

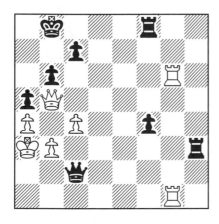

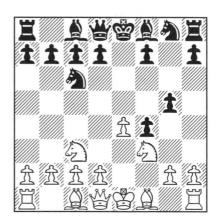

Diagram 25 (B)

White is likely to draw

Diagram 26 (W)

The Vienna Gambit

Black is a clear pawn up, but with only major pieces on the board White has decent drawing chances.

46...Qf2 47 c5!

Smashing up Black's structure.

47...Qxc5+ 48 Qxc5 bxc5 49 Rc6 Rh5

After 49...f3 50 Rxc5 f2 51 Rf1 Rg3 52 Rc2 Rg2 53 Kb2 Kc8 54 Rd2, Black wouldn't be able to make progress.

50 Rg7 Rc8

Nor does 50...f3 lead to anything, due to 51 Rcxc7 f2 52 Rb7+ with a draw.

51 Rf7 Kb7 52 Rcf6

The rest is merely a case of Adams trying to come to terms with the fact that he has thrown away half a point.

52...c4 53 Rxf4 cxb3 54 R7f5 Rch8 55 Kxb3 c6 56 Rxh5 Rxh5 57 Rf3 Kb6 58 Rg3 Rh4 59 Rf3 Rb4+ 60 Ka3 Rd4 61 Kb3 Kc5 62 Rh3 Rd5 63 Rg3 Re5 64 Rh3 Kd4 65 Rh4+ Kd5 66 Rh3 Kc5 67 Rg3 Re4 68 Rg5+ Kb6 69 Rg3 Rb4+ 70 Ka3 Rd4 71 Kb3 Kc5 72 Rh3 Rd5 73 Rc3+ Kd6 74 Rh3 Re5 75 Rg3 Rd5 76 Rh3 Rf5 77 Rd3+ Ke5 78 Rc3 Kd6 79 Rd3+ Rd5 80 Rh3 Rd4 81 Rh5 Rd5 ½-½

Vienna Gambit

Game 50
□ A.Kogan ■ Z.Gyimesi
Budapest 1996

1 e4 e5 2 Nc3 Nc6 3 f4!? exf4

Accepting the pawn and trying to keep it is the acid test of this variation. Otherwise, 3...Bc5 4 Nf3 d6 transposes to the King's Gambit Declined (see Game 45).

4 Nf3 g5 (Diagram 26) 5 h4

The Hamppe-Allgaier Gambit, by which White breaks up the black pawn phalanx at the cost of a piece. White has two other options:

a) 5 Bc4 Bg7! 6 d4 d6, a form of the Hanstein Gambit (from the King's Gambit, see

Game 43), isn't particularly dangerous for Black.

b) 5 d4 (the Pierce Gambit) 5...g4! (piece-grabbing seems to be best here; 5...Bg7 6 d5 Ne5 7 d6! has proven to be better for White, as did 5...d6 6 d5 Ne5 7 Bb5+! Bd7 8 Bxd7+ Nxd7 9 Qd4 f6 10 h4 g4 11 Ng5 in J.Arnason-M.Adams, Manila Olympiad 1992) 6 Bc4 gxf3 **(Diagram 27)** and now White has three serious ways to seek compensation for his piece:

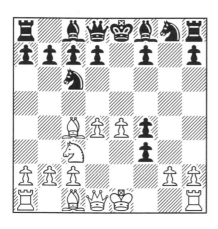 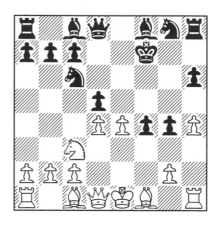

Diagram 27 (W)

The Pierce Gambit

Diagram 28 (W)

The main line Hamppe

b1) After 7 Bxf4, Glazkov and Tseitlin give 7...Qf6! 8 Nd5 Qxd4 9 Qxd4 Nxd4 10 Nxc7+ Kd8 11 Nxa8 fxg2 12 Rg1 Nxc2+ with advantage to Black.

b2) 7 Qxf3 d5 8 Nxd5 (8 Bxd5 Nxd4 9 Bxf7+ Kxf7 10 Qh5+ Kg7 11 0-0 came to nothing after 11...Nf6 12 Qg5+ Kf7 13 Bxf4 Rg8, A.Shabalov-A.Sherzer, Philadelphia 1994) 8...Nxd4 9 Qxf4 Bd6 10 Qf2 Nc6 11 Bf4 Ne5 was A.Mortazavi-A.Miles, London Lloyds Bank 1994, and now 12 Bxe5 Bxe5 13 Nb6 Qe7 14 Nxa8 Qb4+ 15 Qd2 Qxc4 16 0-0-0 Bd6 would have been unclear.

b3) 7 0-0 should be met by 7...Nxd4! 8 Bxf4 (if 8 Qxd4 Qg5! 9 Rf2 Bc5 10 Bxf4 Qxg2+ 11 Rxg2 Bxd4+ 12 Rf2 d6 is good for Black, A.Zaearnyi-R.Breahna, Bucharest 1996) 8...Bc5! 9 Kh1 (9 Bxf7+ Kxf7 10 Be3 Ke8 11 Bxd4 Bxd4+ 12 Qxd4 Qf6 13 Qd3 Ne7 14 Rxf3 Qe5 also favours Black, R.Polaczek-T.Karolyi, Prague 1988) 9...d6 10 Be3 Be6 11 Bxd4 fxg2+ 12 Kxg2 Bxc4 13 Bxh8 Bxf1+ 14 Qxf1 Qd7 and Black went on to win in Mi.Tseitlin-D.Marciano, Bucharest 1993.

I would conclude that Mortazavi-Miles (as in 'b2') is White's best chance to revive this wild gambit.

5...g4 6 Ng5 h6

A more convincing way of winning the piece than 6...f6?! 7 Qxg4 h5 8 Qf5 Nce7 9 Qxf4 fxg5 10 Qxg5 d5 11 Be2 with good play for White, I.Rees-J.Rudd, Monmouth 2001.

7 Nxf7 Kxf7 8 d4

The alternative is 8 Bc4+ d5 9 Bxd5+ Kg7 10 d4, when Black has tried various moves, but 10...Bd6! is my favourite. This provokes White to advance his e-pawn thus ceding the d4-square to Black. For example, 11 Bxc6 bxc6 12 e5 Bb4 13 Bxf4 Be6 14 Qd3 Ne7 15 0-0-0 Bxc3 16 Qxc3 Nd5 and White resigned in G.Welling-V.Mikhalevski, Gibraltar 2001, as he has nothing for his piece.

8...d5 (Diagram 28)

Black offers up a pawn in order to liberate his pieces. In the game Gyimesi actually played 8...Nf6, after which 9 Bxf4 Bb4 10 Be2 d5 11 0-0 Bxc3+ 12 bxc3 transposed below.

9 Bxf4

Simply capturing the f-pawn is White's most dangerous response. The point that both players need to grasp is that once White completes development Black's draughty king is in danger of over-exposure. Taking the d5-pawn is less troublesome for Black:

a) 9 exd5 Qe7+ 10 Be2 f3 11 gxf3 (J.Corzo-J.Capablanca, 6th matchgame, Havana 1901) is well met by 11...g3!, since if 12 dxc6 then 12...g2 13 Rg1 Qxh4+ 14 Kd2 Qxd4+ 15 Bd3 Bc5 wins. In the 8th game Corzo tried to improve with 10 Kf2, but this proved no better after 10...g3+ 11 Kg1 Nxd4 12 Qxd4 Qc5 13 Ne2 Qb6. At this point 14 b4 Bxb4 15 Be3 has been suggested, but 15...Bc5! 16 Qxf4+ Nf6 17 Bxc5 Qxc5+ 18 Qd4 Qxd4+ 19 Nxd4 Nxd5 20 Bc4 c6 yields a clear advantage for Black.

b) 9 Nxd5 f3 10 gxf3 Nge7 11 Bc4 Nxd5 12 Bxd5+ Kg7 leads to a messy game, but Black isn't in serious danger after the exchange of knights.

9...Bb4

9...dxe4 could be worth examining; e.g. 10 Bc4+ Kg6 11 d5 (Rome vs. Bologna, correspondence 1898) and now 11...Na5!?.

10 Be2 d5 11 0-0 Bxc3 12 bxc3 Kg7 13 c4!

An idea of theoretician Dr V.Trumberg at the end of the 19th century. White has interesting play for the piece, though it's not clear that it is enough.

13...Nxe4!

After 13...dxe4 14 d5 Ne7 15 Be5 Rf8 16 Qd4 White has strong pressure, I.Glazkov-V.Soloviev, Moscow 1975.

14 cxd5 Qxh4! 15 dxc6 g3?? (Diagram 29)

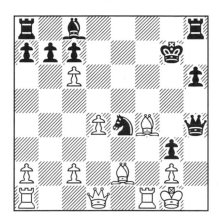

Diagram 29 (W)

A decisive... blunder!

At first sight this looks decisive – how is White to defend against mate? – but in fact it loses. Whereas Konikowski's move 15...Re8! would be promising for Black; e.g. 16 cxb7 Bxb7 17 Be5+ Rxe5! 18 dxe5 Rd8 and wins, or 16 Bxg4 Bxg4 17 Qd3 bxc6 18 Bxc7 c5! with good chances to consolidate.

16 Be5+ Kg6

If 16...Kh7 17 Rf7+ Kg8 18 Rg7+ Kf8 19 Qf1+ wins, while 16...Kg8 17 Bc4+ Kh7 18 Rf7+ forces mate.

17 Bh5+!

The point, as originally analysed by Trumberg. Black has no choice but to exchange queens, so that after taking the rook White emerges with a won position.

17...Qxh5 18 Qxh5+ Kxh5 19 Bxh8 bxc6 20 Rf8 Bb7 21 Rxa8 Bxa8 22 c4 c5 23 d5 Nd6 24 Rc1 c6 25 Be5 Nf7 26 d6!

A decisive combination, bringing the game to a swift conclusion.

26...Nxe5 27 Re1 Nf7 28 d7 Bb7 29 Re7 Nd8 30 Re8 Nf7 31 Rf8 1-0

Very complicated indeed all that – one wrong move and Black was lost – but objectively he should be fine.

 WARNING: Even if a book tells you that a line is good, it won't be in practice unless you have learnt the moves and understand them properly.

One reason for playing 2...Nc6 would be to have learnt this theory (and more!) and be ready to navigate the dangers. Another is to duck out with 3...Bc5 and try to steer play into the calmer waters of a King's Gambit Declined.

Summary

The various systems in this chapter are all connected, if only loosely, by the fact that White starts with 2 Nc3. In response Black has two main options, 2...Nf6 and 2...Nc6, and in both cases can expect to obtain a reasonable game. Furthermore, he has a fair say in what type of position will arise.

Although the Vienna is quite rare (3.5% of Open Games) some basic preparation should enable Black to avoid any danger of being unfavourably surprised or move-ordered.

Chapter Nine
Other White Systems

Introduction

In this chapter we examine three diverse systems that complete our study of Open Games where White varies from the Spanish. The remaining chapters will deal Black's ways of avoiding it after 1 e4 e5 2 Nf3.

Bishop's Opening

1 e4 e5 2 Bc4 (Diagram 1)

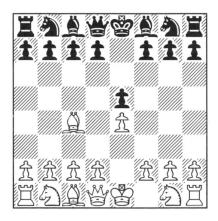   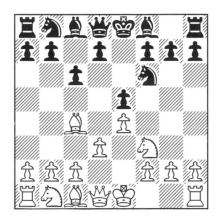

Diagram 1 (B)	**Diagram 2 (B)**
The Bishop's Opening	Black has a choice of plans

The Bishop's Opening is particularly popular as this is often the route chosen by White players to steer the game towards Chapter One. This indeed comes about if he follows up with d2-d3 and Black brings his knights out to f6 and c6 in short order.

One of the characteristics of this particular move order is that it avoids Petroff's Defence, 2 Nf3 Nf6 (see Chapter Twelve), against which it is notoriously difficult for White to get an advantage from the opening. So, for easy non-theoretical development in the Open Games, avoiding the Spanish and Petroff along the way, many are happy to employ 2 Bc4.

Here is a summary of the most typical continuations, many of which transpose to earlier chapters.

2...Nf6 3 d3

Alternatively:

a) 3 Nc3 transposes to a type of Vienna Game (see Chapter Eight, Game 49).

b) 3 d4 exd4 4 Nf3!? is the Urusov Gambit examined briefly at the end of Chapter Six (page 164). As noted there, Black's best response is 4...Nc6! transposing to the Two Knights Defence.

c) 3 Nf3?! Nxe4 4 Nc3 is the Boden-Kieseritzky Gambit, which can also arise via Petroff's Defence (2 Nf3 Nf6 3 Bc4?! etc). It is regarded as inferior, since 4...Nc6 reaches a line of the Two Knights Defence known to be comfortably equal for Black (see the introduction to Chapter Two). Furthermore, Black might even keep the pawn with 4...Nxc3 5 dxc3 f6!, when he has good chances for the advantage; e.g. 6 Nh4 (or 6 0-0 d6 7 Nh4 g6 8 f4 Qe7! 9 f5 Qg7) 6...g6 7 f4 c6! 8 f5 d5 9 fxg6 dxc4 10 Qh5 Kd7 11 g7 Bxg7 12 Qg4+ Kd6! 13 Qxg7 Qf8 14 Qg3 Be6, K.Engstrom-K.Moberg, Borlange 1992.

3...c6

The most common move here is 3...Nc6, when 4 Nc3 is the Vienna Game (see Game 49 again), while 4 Nf3 is a Quiet Italian (see Chapter One).

4 Nf3 (Diagram 2)

Now there are two typical plans for Black. The first involves 4...d5 5 Bb3 Bd6 (defending the e-pawn after gaining time in the centre) 6 Nc3 dxe4 7 Ng5 0-0, as seen in Game 51, where Black obtains free development at the cost of granting White access to the e4-square. The second idea, featuring 4...Be7 5 0-0 d6 (defending e5 solidly, but giving up on ...d7-d5), leads to manoeuvring very much in the fashion of Chapter One.

Game 51
□ **L.Bruzon Bautista** ■ **L.Dominguez**
Havana 2005

---

1 e4 e5 2 Bc4 Nf6 3 d3 c6

More vigorous is 3...d5 4 exd5 Nxd5, which leads to a slightly daring line of the 'Quiet Italian' after 5 Nf3 Nc6 6 0-0. However, I don't really trust Black's position (see 4...d5 in the notes to Game 5).

4 Nf3 d5

Pushing the d-pawn to d5 isn't the only way for Black to handle his defence. For instance, 4...Be7 is possible, intending to play in a more restrained manner. Indeed, in the following examples Black is able to obtain a perfectly satisfactory game: 5 0-0 (actually threatening the e-pawn, whereas 5 Nxe5?? Qa5+ would have been more than embarrassing) 5...d6 **(Diagram 3)** and now:

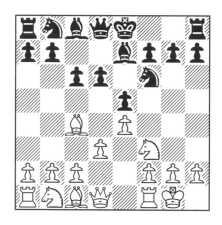

Diagram 3 (W)

Black plays ...d7-d6

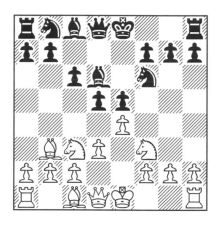

Diagram 4 (B)

Black plays ...d7-d5

a) 6 Bb3 0-0 7 c3 Nbd7 8 Re1 plays in a 'Quiet Italian' style, but Black has different manoeuvring possibilities due to the position of his queen's knight; e.g. 8...Nc5 9 Bc2 Bg4 10 h3 Bh5 11 Nbd2 Ne6 12 Nf1 Nd7 13 Ng3 Bxf3 14 Qxf3 g6 15 Be3 Bg5 16 Rad1 Bxe3 17 Qxe3, B.Gelfand-A.Yusupov, Munich 1994, and Black could count on equality with 17...Qb6.

b) 6 Re1 0-0 7 Nbd2 Nbd7 8 a3 Qc7 (Black has a type of Philidor set-up, rather than the usual closed Italian or Spanish where the queen's knight would be on c6) 9 Ba2 b5 10 Nf1 a5!? 11 Ng3 Nc5 12 c3 Be6 and again Black has full equality, V.Anand-I.Sokolov, London (rapid) 1995.

5 Bb3 Bd6

Here 5...dxe4? is premature because of 6 Ng5.

However, 5...Bb4+ requires some discussion. By developing the bishop with check

Black aims to deny the b1-knight the desirable c3-square, and after 6 c3 he has no problem to equalize; e.g. 6...Bd6 7 Bg5 dxe4 8 dxe4 h6 9 Bh4 Qe7 10 Nbd2 Nbd7 11 Nc4 Bc7 with equality, V.Rogowski-A.Sulypa, Alushta 2000.

White does better with 6 Bd2!, obtaining rapid development. For example, 6...Bxd2+ 7 Nbxd2 Qc7 8 0-0 0-0 9 Re1 Bg4 (after 9...Re8 10 d4 exd4 11 exd5 Rxe1+ 12 Qxe1 cxd5 13 Nxd4, White has a pleasant edge in something like a good version of a French Tarrasch) 10 h3 Bxf3 11 Qxf3 dxe4 12 Nxe4 Nxe4 13 Rxe4 Nd7 14 d4 exd4 15 Re7 Qd6 16 Rae1 with advantage, B.Vogt-O.Romanishin, Riga 1981.

6 Nc3 (Diagram 4) 6...dxe4

Closing the centre while gaining space with 6...d4 7 Ne2 c5 leads to a totally different type of game, and one in which Black has achieved over 50% in practice. Play could continued 8 c3 (8 Ng3 Nc6 9 a3 h6 10 Nh4 g6 11 h3 Bd7 12 Bd2 Qe7 13 Qc1 Ng8 14 Nf3 0-0-0 offers chances for both sides, A.Domont-A.Raetsky, Saas Almagell 2005) 8...Nc6 9 0-0 h6 10 Ng3 g6 (Black prevents White's minor pieces from coming to f5 or g5) 11 cxd4 cxd4 12 a3 Qe7 13 Bd2 Bd7 14 Bc4 Kf8 15 h3 Kg7 16 Nh2 Rac8 with equality, J.Sorensen-I.Sokolov, Copenhagen 1991.

7 Ng5

Despite appearing rather dry, the simple 7 Nxe4 Nxe4 8 dxe4 **(Diagram 5)** has – perhaps surprisingly – achieved quite a high percentage for White. His lead in development gives him a slight pull, even with the symmetrical structure and lack of pawn breaks. So Black has to be vigilant here:

Diagram 5 (B)

Not so easy equality

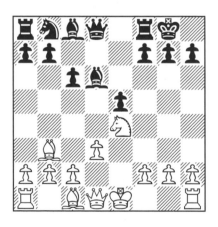

Diagram 6 (B)

Position after 9 Nxe4

a) 8...Qe7? looks natural and safe enough, but it gets Black into trouble straight away, due to 9 Ng5! 0-0 10 Nxh7!! Kxh7 11 Qh5+ Kg8 12 Bg5 Qc7 13 Rd1 Nd7 14 Rd3 Nc5 15 Rg3 and White's attack was too strong in N.Mitkov-C.Gabriel, Pula 2000.

b) 8...0-0 doesn't necessarily ease Black's defence as 9 Bg5 wins an important tempo, and after the further 9...Qc7 10 Qd2 Bg4 11 0-0-0 Be7 12 Bxe7 Qxe7 13 Qd6! Qxd6 14 Rxd6, White had pressure in V.Zhelnin-P.Tishin, Tula 2000.

c) 8...Bg4 pinning could be best; e.g. 9 h3 Bh5 10 Bg5 (or 10 0-0 Na6 11 c3 ½-½ N.Mitkov-O.Jovanic, Ljubljana 2003 – the draw may indicate that Mitkov didn't like his position very much) 10...f6 11 Be3 Na6 12 Qe2 Qe7 13 0-0-0 Nc5 14 Bxc5 Bxc5 15 g4 Bf7 16 Bxf7+ Qxf7 17 Kb1, when Black has to be careful but is close to equality, I.Rogers-V.Tseshkovsky, Vrsac 1987.

Sometimes White takes back with the pawn thus retaining all the minor pieces: 7 dxe4 Na6 8 Bg5 (or 8 Be3 Qe7 9 Nd2 0-0 10 h3 Nc5 11 Qf3 Ne6!? 12 Ne2, T.Stepovaia Dianchenko-A.Maric, Belgrade 2000, and now 12...Bc5 is comfortable for Black) 8...h6 9 Bh4 g5 10 Bg3 Qe7 11 Qe2 Nc5 12 0-0-0 Bg4 13 h3 Bh5 14 Qe3 Nfd7 15 Rd2 0-0-0 16 Rhd1 Bc7 17 Bc4 Bb6 18 Qe2 f6 with equality, O.Sikorova-M.Velcheva, European Women's Ch., Varna 2002.

7...0-0 8 Ncxe4 Nxe4 9 Nxe4 (Diagram 6) 9...Bf5

9...Bb4+?! is less precise; e.g. 10 c3 Be7 11 0-0 Bf5 12 Qh5 Bxe4 13 dxe4 Nd7 14 Rd1 Qc7 15 Bh6 Nc5 16 Qg4 Bf6 17 Be3 Nxb3 18 axb3 Rfd8 19 Rxd8+ Qxd8 20 h3 a6 21 Rd1 and White had a small but enduring edge, R.Fontaine-J.M.Degraeve, Paris 2003.

10 Qf3

Capturing the bishop on d6 doesn't seem to give White anything: 10 0-0 Na6 11 Nxd6 Qxd6 12 Qf3 Be6 13 Bxe6 (after 13 Qg3?! Bxb3 14 axb3 Nb4 it was White who had to be careful to equalize, V.Anand-V.Kramnik, Frankfurt rapid 1998) 13...Qxe6 14 Re1 Rfe8 15 a3 Nc7 16 Qg3 Qg6 with equality, N.Mitkov-A.Huzman, European Club Cup, Albufeira 1999.

10...Bxe4 11 dxe4

If White recaptures with the queen then ...Nc5 will come with tempo.

11...Nd7 12 c3

Similar is 12 0-0 Nc5 13 Bc4 b5 14 Be2 Qe7 15 c3 a5 16 Be3 a4 17 Rad1 Rfd8 18 g3 Ne6 with near equality as in Z.Efimenko-V.Golod, Montreal 2005. White has the bishop pair but Black has constructed a solid barricade.

12...a5 13 0-0 Nc5

Later Dominguez & Ibarra proposed 13...Qf6!? 14 Rd1 a4 15 Bc2 Rfd8 16 Be3 Qxf3 17 gxf3 Be7 18 f4 b5 as level, although this line hangs by a thread and could do with checking.

14 Bc2 b5 (Diagram 7)

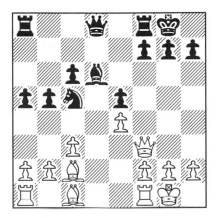

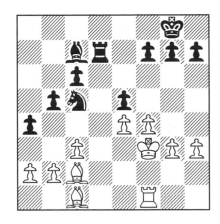

Diagram 7 (W)

Black gains space

Diagram 8 (B)

White has a slight pull

Black gains space on the queenside and has an influential knight, thus reducing the significance of the bishop pair. Nevertheless, if the game eventually opens up then White's bishops could be a key factor.

15 Be3

White soon gave up trying to win after 15 Rd1 Qe7 16 Be3 Rfd8 17 Qg4 a4 18 Bg5 f6 19 Be3 Kh8 20 Rd2 and a draw was agreed in M.Godena-A.Motylev, European Ch., Istanbul 2003.

15...Qc7 16 Qe2

In his notes Dominguez suggests 16 Qf5 Ne6 (or if 16...a4, then 17 Rfd1 Ne6 18 b4 axb3 19 Bxb3) 17 a4 Bc5 18 Bd2 Rad8 19 Rad1, keeping a slight pull for White. Certainly the queen is more active here and any ideas of ...g7-g6 could prove weakening.

16...a4 17 Rad1 Ne6 18 g3

We have the same structure as in Efimenko-Golod (see the note to move 12). As in that game, it proves hard for White to demonstrate anything concrete.

18...Bc5 19 Bc1 Rad8 20 Kg2 Rxd1 21 Rxd1 Rd8 22 Rf1

Further exchanges would ease the defence, so Bruzon instead decides to play for f2-f4.

22...Bd6 23 Qg4 Qd7 24 h3 Nc5 25 Qxd7 Rxd7 26 f4 Bc7?!

This manoeuvre turns out to be slightly clumsy. Instead 26...f6 27 Rd1 Kf7 28 Be3 Be7 would be more natural and gives White less to nibble at.

27 Kf3 (Diagram 8)

White hopes to make something of his active-looking kingside advances, but of course Black remains very solid.

27...Kf8 28 Be3 Bb6 29 Ke2

29 b4!? axb3 30 axb3 might be slightly more dangerous.

29...Ke7 30 h4

Or perhaps 30 fxe5!? as Black is somewhat tangled up.

30...Rd8 31 f5

In the game we soon see that having more space isn't really enough, so White would perhaps do better to maintain the tension or else open the position at once (as he could have done last move).

31...f6 32 g4 h6 33 Rh1 Rh8

Now g4-g5 proves difficult to achieve under favourable circumstances.

34 Rh3 Nd7 35 Bd2 Bc5 36 c4 Kd6

Hurrying to bolster the queenside.

37 cxb5 cxb5 38 b3 axb3 39 Bxb3

The bishop now has some freedom, but in return Black obtains access to c4, when progress becomes an unrealistic aim for White.

39...Nb6 40 Rd3+ Kc6 41 Rg3 Nc4 42 Bc1 Bd4 43 Rg2 Kc5 44 Kd3 Rd8 45 Kc2 Rh8 46 Kd3 Rd8 47 Kc2 Rh8 ½-½

Ponziani's Opening

1 e4 e5 2 Nf3 Nc6 3 c3 (Diagram 9)

White's third move defines Ponziani's Opening and shows his intention to build a pawn centre with d2-d4 on the next move. However, this is a somewhat optimistic plan when White doesn't have a lead in development and it proves relatively ineffective if Black hits back immediately; i.e. at the e4-pawn.

Diagram 9 (B)	**Diagram 10 (W)**
Ponziani's Opening	A typical 3...d5 position

Game 52
□ **J.Hector** ■ **A.Khalifman**
London 1991

---

1 e4 e5 2 Nf3 Nc6 3 c3 Nf6

The most practical response in my opinion.

The sharp gambit-style reaction 3...f5 is met by 4 d4, when I prefer White in the complications that follow.

Black's best scoring move is actually 3...d5, pre-empting White's intended central action, but unless you are willing to learn it really well (remember the Ponziani is rare, occurring about 1% of the time) it could be risky. White has two main replies, in both cases pinning Black's queen's knight:

a) 4 Bb5 dxe4 5 Nxe5 Qd5 (5...Qg5 is also critical but extremely complicated) 6 Qa4 Ne7 7 f4! (inferior is 7 Nxc6 Nxc6 8 0-0 Bd6; e.g. 9 Re1 0-0 as Black has a clear development advantage even if White snatches the e-pawn, while 9 d3 exd3 10 c4 Qh5 11 Bxc6+ Ke7 12 g3 bxc6 13 c5 Qxc5 14 Nc3 Be6 favoured Black in N.Batsiashvili-P.Skatchkov, Yerevan 2004) 7...Bd7! (preferable to 7...exf3 8 Nxf3 a6 9 Be2 Bd7 10 0-0 Ng6 11 Qd1 Be7 12 d4 Bf6 13 Nbd2 0-0 14 Bc4 Qh5 15 Ne4 Be7 which is more comfortable for White, A.Lukin-V.Malaniuk St Petersburg 1995) 8

Starting Out: Open Games

Nxd7 Kxd7 9 Bc4 Qf5 10 d4 exd3 11 0-0 Rd8 12 b4?! (more circumspect is 12 Bxd3 Qc5+ 13 Kh1 Kc8 with equality) 12...Nd5 13 Qb3 Kc8 14 a4 a5 and as White's attack didn't work, Black was better in A.Olsson-J.Hector, Swedish Ch., Umea 2003.

b) 4 Qa4 Bd7!? (after 4...f6 5 Bb5 Ne7 we have actually transposed to the Spanish: 2 Nf3 Nc6 3 Bb5 Nge7 4 c3 d5 5 Qa4 f6 – this is quite a rare move order but it did occur in G.Laketic-M.Sorokin, Cheliabinsk 1991, continuing 6 exd5 Qxd5 7 0-0 Bd7 8 d4 exd4 9 cxd4 Ne5 10 Nc3!? Nxf3+ 11 gxf3 Qf5 12 d5 Ng6 with messy complications) 5 exd5 Nd4 6 Qd1 Nxf3+ 7 Qxf3 Nf6 8 Bc4 e4 **(Diagram 10)** yields a gambit line where the overall results have been in Black's favour.

 NOTE: The main idea behind Black's ambitious play is to seize the initiative with rapid development. He hopes to exploit the fact that the move c2-c3 can leave White with an ugly structure and problems developing the queenside.

For example: 9 Qe2 Bd6 10 d4 0-0 (or, with an alternative plan, 10...h6 11 h3 0-0 12 Bb3 b5 13 g4 Nh7 14 h4 f5 15 gxf5 Bxf5, J.Maiwald-O.Romanishin, Lippstadt 2004) 11 Bg5 (after 11 h3 Re8 12 Be3 a6 13 Nd2 Rb8 14 Bb3 b5 15 0-0 h6 16 f3 Qe7, as in R.Zelcic-V.Malaniuk, Montecatini Terme 1995, the extra pawn is more or less compensated by Black's general activity, even if he isn't doing anything dramatic) 11...h6 12 Bh4 g5 13 Bg3 Bxg3 14 hxg3 Kg7 15 Na3 Bg4 16 Qf1 Nxd5 17 Nc2 c6 with balanced chances, A.Alexikov-G.Timoshenko, Ukrainian Team Ch. 2007.

4 d4 (Diagram 11)

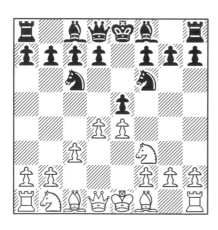 

Diagram 11 (B)
The 3...Nf6 main line

Diagram 12 (W)
White has more space

224

4...Nxe4

The most reliable. 4...exd4!? is more risky (this can also arise from central gambits such as the Göring: 2 Nf3 Nc6 3 d4 exd4 4 c3 Nf6!? etc), as following 5 e5 Ne4 6 Qe2 Black has to be very precise: 6...f5 7 exf6 d5 8 Nbd2 Qxf6 9 Nxe4 dxe4 10 Qxe4+ Qe6 (with a playable game but this line probably favours White very slightly) 11 Bd3 dxc3 12 0-0 Qxe4 13 Bxe4 Bd7 14 Bxc6 (or 14 bxc3 0-0-0! 15 Ng5 Re8) 14...Bxc6 15 Re1+ Kd8! 16 Ne5 Be8 17 bxc3 Kc8, D.Chevallier-G.Flear, French Team Ch. 1989.

5 d5

After 5 dxe5 d5 6 Bb5 Bc5 7 0-0 0-0 Black should be fine in a position akin to the Modern Variation of the Two Knights Defence in Chapter Two. If White tries to make something of c2-c3 with 8 b4, then 8...Bb6 9 a4 a5 10 bxa5 Nxa5 11 Ba3 Bc5 obtains comfortable equality, L.Ljubojevic-M.Filip, Nice Olympiad 1974.

5...Ne7 6 Nxe5 Ng6

Black has lost some time with his knight, but now White has to make a decision.

7 Nxg6?!

I think this natural move is unwise and that White should simply seek a quiet game here with 7 Qd4 Qe7 8 Qxe4 Qxe5 **(Diagram 12)**. The early exchange of queens won't exactly set the board on fire, but White has more space and little risk in playing like this. For example:

a) 9 Bd3 Bc5!? (trying to stay reasonably active) 10 0-0 0-0 11 Nd2 d6 12 Nc4 Qxe4 13 Bxe4 Re8 14 Bxg6 (if 14 Bd3 a5, followed by ...b7-b6 and ...Bb7, pressurizes the d-pawn) 14...hxg6 15 b4 b5 16 bxc5 bxc4 17 cxd6 cxd6 18 Bf4 Bf5 with equality, L.Ljubojevic-V.Anand, Monte Carlo (blindfold rapid) 1995.

b) 9 Qxe5+ Nxe5 and then:

b1) 10 Nd2 Be7 11 Nc4 Nxc4 12 Bxc4 d6 13 Be3 Bf6 14 0-0 (perhaps 14 Kd2) 14...Bd7 equalized in S.Zeidler-G.Flear, British League 2007. Although it may not seem that likely here, I even obtained winning chances in this game: 15 Bd4?! Bxd4 16 cxd4 0-0-0 17 Bd3 Rde8 18 Rac1 Re7 19 f3 Rhe8 20 Kf2 g6 21 Rc2 a6 22 Rfc1 Bb5 and Black had a slight pull.

b2) 10 Bf4 Bd6 (less dynamic, though perfectly sound is 10...d6 11 Be2 Be7 12 0-0 Bd7 13 Nd2 0-0-0 14 Rac1 h6 with equality, N.Carton-G.Flear, British Ch., Eastbourne 1990) 11 Bg3 0-0 12 Nd2 f5 13 f3 b6 14 0-0-0 Bb7 15 Nc4 Nxc4 16 Bxc4 f4 17 Bf2 Rae8 and Black was again fully equal, R.Kleeschaetzky-R.Slobodjan, German Ch., Altenkirchen 2001.

Alternatively, 7 Qe2 Qe7 8 Qxe4 Qxe5 transposes; but White should steer clear of the artificial development evident in K.Shirazi-G.Flear, Montpellier 2001: 7 Nd3 Bd6 8 g3 Qe7 9 Be2 0-0 10 0-0 f5 11 Bh5 b6 12 Re1 Qf7 13 Nf4 Bb7 where Black had the upper hand.

7...hxg6 (Diagram 13)

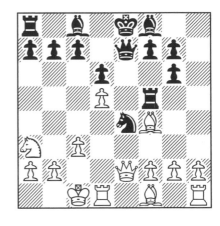

Diagram 13 (W)	Diagram 14 (W)
The rook enters the game...	...and takes a leading role

The opening of the h-file (thus effectively developing Black's rook) gives the second player some dynamic options.

8 Qe2

White's d- and h-pawns are exposed and if he isn't careful he may lose one of them very quickly...

a) 8 Be3 Qe7 9 Qe2 (if 9 Nd2 Ng3!, or similarly 9 Be2 Ng3! as I had in E.Chaplin-G.Flear, Argèles rapid 2008) 9...Rh5 10 g3 (10 c4 Qe5 11 a3 avoids losing a pawn, but Black is still more than comfortable) 10...Rxd5 11 Bg2 Re5 12 0-0 d5 13 c4 Nxg3 14 hxg3 d4 and Black was clearly better, C.Baker-G.Flear, English counties match 1992.

b) 8 Bd3 Nf6 9 Qf3 Qe7+ 10 Be3 Qe5 11 Nd2 d6 12 c4 Rxh2 13 Rxh2 Qxh2 14 Bd4 Bg4 15 Qe3+ Kd7 and again Black was on top, T.Upton-G.Flear, Isle of Man 2002.

8...Qe7 9 Bf4 d6

Instead, 9...c6?! is rather slow: 10 g4 cxd5 11 Nd2 Nc5 12 0-0-0 Qxe2 13 Bxe2 gave White a useful lead in development in J.Hector-M.Krasenkow, Ostend 1990, while Black's extra pawn (d5) is not going to survive for long.

On the other hand, 9...Rh5!? (a daring way of hunting down the d-pawn) seems to be a worthwhile alternative: 10 g4 (after 10 f3 Nc5 11 Qxe7+ Bxe7 12 Na3 Rxd5 13 Nb5 Ne6 Black stands well; while if White is intent on counting pawns with 12 Bxc7 d6 13 c4 b6 he could well end up with a piece less!) 10...Rxd5 11 Bg2 Nc5! 12 Qxe7+ Bxe7 13 Bxd5 Nd3+ 14 Kd2 Nxf4 15 c4 d6 16 Nc3 c6 17 Bf3 g5 and Black had sufficient positional compensation for the exchange, P.Brochet-G.Miralles, French Team Ch. 2002.

10 Na3 Rh5!

More consequent than 10...Nf6; e.g. 11 0-0-0 Qxe2 12 Bxe2 Bg4 13 f3 Bd7 14 Nb5 Kd8 15 g4, when White had a significant space advantage, A.Delchev-J.Plachetka, Metz 2002.

11 0-0-0

After 11 Nb5, precise replies are called for: 11...Kd8!? (11...Rxd5 12 Nxc7+ Qxc7 13 Qxe4+ Qe7 should favour White slightly) 12 c4 Rf5! (playing actively; whereas 12...Bd7 13 Nd4 gives White a certain control of events and the black king could prove to be awkwardly placed; note that there is no tactical solution with 13...g5? as 14 Qxh5 Ng3+ 15 Ne6+! Bxe6 16 Qxg5 wins for White) 13 g3 (or 13 Be3 Nxf2!) 13...g5! and Black is winning the battle for the initiative.

11...Rf5! (Diagram 14)

Again the energetic rook!

12 Qe3

Not 12 Be3? Nxf2! winning a pawn.

12...Nf6 13 Bb5+

The position is actually rather unclear, White's space and safer king balanced out by Black's solidity and potential for hitting back; e.g.

a) 13 Nb5 Qxe3+ 14 Bxe3 Kd8 15 Nd4 Re5 16 Bf4 Ne4!, P.Soderberg-L.Simoes dos Reis, correspondence 1999.

b) 13 Bc4 Qxe3+ 14 Bxe3 a6 15 Rhe1 Be7 16 Bd4 b5 17 Bb3 Bb7 18 Nc2 Kf8 is equal according to Marin. White has more space but Black is not particularly constrained and has counterplay against d5. 18...Kd7!? 19 c4 Rh8 also comes into consideration.

13...Kd8 14 Qf3?

This proves to be a mistake. Better is 14 Rhe1 Qxe3+ (snatching the d-pawn is risky now: 14...Rxd5 15 Rxd5 Nxd5 16 Qd2 Be6 17 Bg5 and Black comes under pressure) 15 Bxe3 a6 16 Bc4 b5 17 Bb3 Bb7, when neither side would be particularly unhappy with their lot.

14...Qe4!

Black does well to trade queens, enabling him to complete development without worrying about any direct attack on his king. Furthermore, White is no longer able to defend his f-pawn correctly.

15 Qxe4 Nxe4 16 Be3 Nxf2 17 Bxf2 Rxf2 18 Rhf1 Rxf1 19 Rxf1 f5 (Diagram 15)

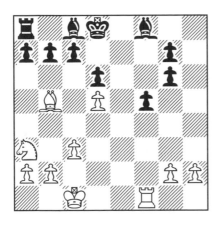 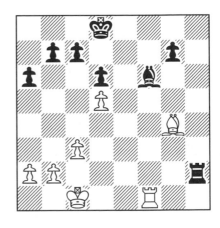

Diagram 15 (W)

Black is a pawn up

Diagram 16 (W)

White wants to trade rooks

White still has a clear lead in development but he cannot do much against his opponent's shell-like structure. Black's extra pawn soon becomes the main issue.

20 Rf3 a6 21 Bd3 Ke7!? 22 g4 fxg4

One of the points behind Black's previous move.

23 Rf1 Bf5 24 Kd2

Here 24 Bxf5 gxf5 25 Rxf5 looks obvious, but after 25...g6 26 Rf2 (and not 26 Rf4?? Bh6) 26...Bh6+ 27 Kc2 Rf8 Black catches up in development and is ready to start exploiting his extra pawn.

24...Kd7 25 Nc4 Be7 26 Ne3

The idea is to devalue Black's majority, but...

26...Rh8!

...demonstrates that White's kingside can also be attacked.

27 Nxf5

Rather than 27 Rf2? Bg5 with a deadly pin.

27...Rxh2+ 28 Kc1 gxf5 29 Bxf5+ Kd8 30 Bxg4 Bf6 (Diagram 16)

Despite the opposite-coloured bishops, which often make endgames rather drawish, Black has some chances with his extra pawn and active pieces.

31 Rf3 Rg2 32 Be6 Rh2 33 Rh3! Rxh3

After 33...Rg2 34 Rh8+ Ke7 35 Bc8 White even regains the pawn.

34 Bxh3 b6 35 Bf1 a5 36 Kc2 Ke7 37 b3 Be5 38 c4 Kf6 39 Kd3 Kf5 40 Ke3 g5 41 Bd3+ Kg4 42 Kf2 Kf4 43 Bg6 Bd4+ 44 Kg2 b5

Black is unable to create a second passed pawn.

45 Be8 b4 46 Ba4 ½-½

Centre Game

1 e4 e5 2 d4 exd4 3 Qxd4 (Diagram 17)

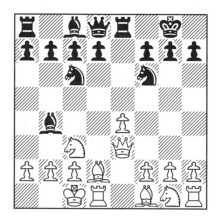

Diagram 17 (B)	**Diagram 18 (W)**
The Centre Game	The 4...Nf6 main line

Of course we learn very early in our chess careers that bringing the queen out before the other pieces is generally unwise, since the opponent will gain time by attacking such a valuable asset. However, it should be remembered that there are exceptions to every rule in chess!

In this case White opens the centre and hopes to be better able to exploit the open lines and his slight space advantage, even if this means losing some time with his queen. The Centre Game is one of those openings that is hard to believe but shouldn't be underestimated. Andrew Greet recently aimed to revive this rare sideline (less than 1% of Open Games) in *Dangerous Weapons: 1 e4 e5*, so it may become more popular in future.

Game 53
□ Z.Vukovic ■ G.Todorovic
Yugoslav Team Championship 1995

1 e4 e5

Another early queen sortie, 2 Qh5, looks like a beginner's move, but GM Hikaru Nakamura played this in his experimental period! Then 2...Nc6 3 Bc4 (with a threat!) 3...g6 4 Qf3 Nf6 5 d3 Bg7 6 Ne2 d6 7 h3 looks reasonable enough for Black, though there is the danger that White might be able to obtain some play on the kingside. So perhaps 5...Nd4! 6 Qd1 d5! should be played, taking the initiative in the centre, which (as White has lost three tempi with his queen!) looks the best way to punish this offbeat and nameless opening.

2 d4 exd4 3 Qxd4 Nc6 4 Qe3

4 Qa4 is reminiscent of a popular line of the Scandinavian in reverse, but it isn't effective as Black can just play natural moves and equalize; e.g. 4...Nf6 5 Bg5 Be7 6 Nc3 0-0 7 0-0-0 d6 8 Bb5 Bd7 followed by ...a7-a6, N.Resika-P.Lukacs, Budapest 2000.

4...g6

Black doesn't fianchetto his king's bishop very often in the Open Games, but with White's queen and bishop 'the wrong way round' to worry Black on the kingside, this move can be justified.

The better known main line is also satisfactory, though more complicated to handle in practice: 4...Nf6 5 Nc3 Bb4 6 Bd2 0-0 7 0-0-0 Re8 **(Diagram 18)**. In this line Black castles quickly and bears down on the e-file to exploit the (unfortunate) position of the white queen.

a) After 8 Bc4, Black might aim for a solid position with 8...d6 and ...Be6, but it should be remembered that the central pawn structure (akin to the Scotch Game) favours White slightly if he can consolidate. So a more vigorous reaction has its points; e.g. 8...Na5 9 Be2 d5!? 10 Nxd5 Nxd5 11 Qd4 Nc6 12 Qxd5 Bxd2+ 13 Qxd2 (or if 13 Rxd2 Qe7 14 Nf3 Bg4) 13...Qxd2+ 14 Rxd2 Rxe4 15 Nf3 Bg4 with equality, L.Mikhaletz-P.Blatny, Czech League 2001.

b) 8 Qg3 is most often seen, when 8...Rxe4! wins a pawn (as 9 Nxe4? Nxe4 forks the queen and bishop), but things are not that clear; e.g. 9 a3 Bd6 (winning a tempo to get the rook out of harm's way) 10 f4 Re8 11 Bd3 Bf8 (or 11...Bc5 12 Nf3 d5 13 Rde1 with compensation, A.Shabalov-A.Ivanov, US Ch., Key West 1994) 12 Nf3 d6 13 f5 (keeping Black tied down; Black now needs to react quickly to avoid coming under attack) 13...d5 14 Rhe1 Rxe1 15 Rxe1 d4 16 Nb5 a6 17 Nxc7 and White re-established material equality in I.Nepomniachtchi-P.Harikrishna, Moscow 2007, but Black had equal chances with play against the stranded knight on c7.

5 Bd2 Bg7 6 Nc3 Nf6

Black doesn't need to be afraid of e4-e5 – see the next note.

7 0-0-0

After 7 e5, Black gains a tempo with 7...Ng4 **(Diagram 19)**, when White has to decide where to place his queen:

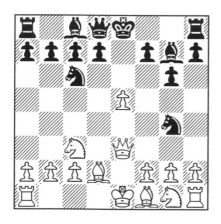 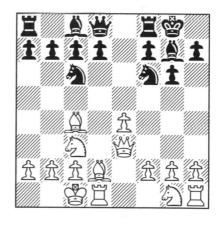

Diagram 19 (W)	**Diagram 20 (B)**
The queen must move	A potentially strong bishop

a) 8 Qe4 d6! (Black shouldn't be afraid to switch to gambit-mode; instead 8...Ngxe5 9 f4 d5 10 Qxd5 leaves White slightly better) 9 exd6+ Be6 10 Ba6 (or 10 dxc7 Qxc7 11 Be2 Rd8) 10...Nd4 11 Bxb7 f5 12 Qd3 Rb8 with compensation according to Marin (who stops here); e.g. 13 Nb5 (or 13 Nge2 c5) 13...Rxb7 14 Nxd4 Qxd6 15 Bc3 0-0 (15...Ne5 16 Qh3 Bd5 is equally good) 16 Ngf3 Bd5 17 0-0 Be4 18 Qc4+ Bd5 19 Qd3, repeating the position.

b) 8 Qe2 d6! (again the right recipe; I don't trust 8...Ngxe5 9 f4 Nd4 10 Qe4 d5 11 Qxd4 Nf3+ 12 Nxf3 Bxd4 13 Nxd4 c5 14 Nf3 d4 15 0-0-0 with three pieces for the queen, A.Smith-J.Littlewood, Guernsey 1989) 9 exd6+ Be6 and so on.

c) 8 Qg3 h5 (8...Ngxe5 is met by 9 f4, though 8...d6!? could still be considered) 9 Nf3 d6 (after 9...Ngxe5 10 Nxe5 Bxe5 11 Bf4 Bxf4 12 Qxf4 Qe7+ 13 Be2 Qe5 14 Qd2, White has some compensation) 10 Bg5 f6?! (I prefer 10...Bxe5!? 11 Nxe5 Qxg5 12 Nd5 0-0 13 f4 Qd8 14 Nxg4 Bxg4 15 Qc3 Re8+ 16 Kf2 Re6, which is unclear) 11 exf6 Bxf6 12 h4 Qe7+ 13 Be2 Bxg5 14 Nxg5 Bf5 15 Nd5 Qg7 with an edge for White, S.Solovjov-A.Smirnov, St Petersburg 2007.

So 8 Qg3 is critical, though Black has at least two improvements on Smirnov's play.

In contrast 7 Be2 is too tame; e.g. 7...0-0 8 0-0-0 Re8! with equality according to Marin. This type of position, but with the knight offside on a5, can be seen in the main game.

7...0-0 8 Bc4 (Diagram 20) 8...Na5

Best played immediately, that is before the bishop settles in on c4!

8...Re8 is the main alternative, and then:

a) 9 f3 Na5 10 Bd3 d5! looks good; e.g. 11 Qg5 h6 12 Qh4 d4 13 Nb5 a6 (or 13...Nc6 14 Bxh6 Nh7!) 14 Na3 c5 15 Bxh6? Nh7! 16 Qf4 g5 17 Qd2 Bxh6 and Black was a piece up, S.Sanchez Castillo-M.Weeks, Reykjavik 2006.

b) 9 Nf3 Na5 (Black could play more solidly with 9...d6 10 h3 Be6, which is effective even if it is less principled: 11 Bxe6 Rxe6 12 Rhe1 d5 13 Qf4 Nxe4 14 Nxe4 Rxe4 15 Rxe4 dxe4 16 Qxe4 Qe8 17 Re1 Qd7 with near equality, or perhaps 12...Qe8!? to keep the tension instead of 12...d5) 10 Bd3 d5 11 Nxd5 Nxd5 12 Qc5 (otherwise 12 Qg5 Qxg5 13 Nxg5 Nf6 14 Bxa5 h6 15 Nf3 b6 was equal in L.Mikhaletz-S.Ovsejevitsch, Ukrainian Ch. 2001) 12...Nf6 (not 12...Qf6?!, when Greet points out that 13 e5! is strong) 13 Qxa5 Nxe4 (or after 13...b6 14 Qa3 Bb7 15 Bc3 Black has insufficient compensation) 14 Bxe4 Rxe4 15 Bc3! with some advantage to White.

9 Be2

If 9 Bd3!? then 9...d5 hits the nail on the head: 10 exd5 (here 10 Nxd5 Nxd5 11 Qc5 fails to impress because of 11...Qf6 12 Qa3 Nf4) 10...Nxd5 11 Qc5 Nxc3 12 Bxc3 b6 with equality.

9...Re8 (Diagram 21) 10 Qg5

Moving the queen off the e-file while attacking the loose knight on a5 looks logical, but Andrew Greet questions whether pushing the black knight back to where it needs to go is actually best.

Instead, he suggests 10 Qf4 d6 (perhaps 10...d5!? 11 Be3 c6 is worth a look) 11 g4 Nc6 12 g5! (if 12 h4 Ne5 13 g5 then 13...Nh5! isn't that clear, K.Litz-T.Lagemann, Internet 2001) 12...Nd7 13 h4 with a dangerous attack. Greet is right to prefer

White here; for instance, after 13...Be5 the continuation 14 Qe3 Bd4 15 Qg3 Nc5 16 f3 Be5 17 Qg2 is strong as h4-h5 is coming.

All this illustrates some potential difficulties for Black if he plays too sluggishly; he needs to react more energetically in the centre before White's attack gets a good head of steam. Having studied this line I think that Black can improve with 11...b6!; e.g. 12 g5 (or 12 f3 Be6) 12...Nxe4! 13 Nxe4 Rxe4 14 Qxe4 Bb7 (the point) 15 Qf4 Bxh1 16 Nf3 Bxf3 17 Bxf3 Rb8, which looks quite playable for Black and best assessed as 'unclear', since White has some compensation for the pawn.

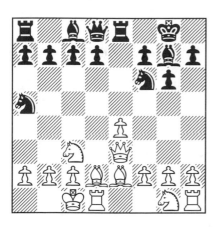

Diagram 21 (W)

Eyeing the white queen

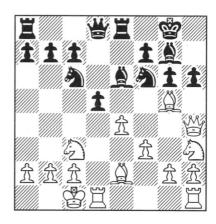

Diagram 22 (W)

White has nothing here

 TIP: If your opponent is preparing an attack on a flank, it will only be dangerous if he has the time and plenty of central control. So don't give him an easy ride: hit back in the centre and quickly!

10...Nc6 11 f3 d6 12 Qh4 Be6

Or 12...a6 13 Nh3 b5 with counterplay, as mentioned by Marin.

13 Nh3 d5 14 Bg5?!

Better is 14 Ng5! d4 15 Nxe6 Rxe6 16 Be1 Rd6 17 Nb5 Rd7, keeping things rather unclear.

14...h6 (Diagram 22) 15 exd5?

Already the losing move; although after the superior 15 Bxh6 Nxe4 16 Bg5 Nxc3! (more ambitious than 16...Nxg5 17 Nxg5 Bxc3 18 bxc3 Qf6 19 Kb2 Qg7, when chances are approximately equal) 17 Bxd8 Nxe2+ 18 Kb1 Raxd8 19 Ng5 Bc8 Black is still probably better, as his three pieces are likely to be more effective than White's queen.

15...hxg5 16 Nxg5 Bxd5 17 Bc4

This may look tricky and trappy, but Black holds firm and – putting it quite simply – a piece is a piece! Even if White ever achieves a check on h7, the black king always has f8.

17...Ne7! 18 g4

On 18 Nge4, Black can even play 18...Nf5 19 Nxf6+ Qxf6 20 Qxf6 Bxc4! (the queen is trapped) 21 Ne4 (or 21 Qg5 Bh6) 21...Kf8 and will emerge with his extra piece in the bag.

18...Qd6 19 Kb1 c6 20 Rhe1 Qf4 21 Bd3 Nf5 22 Bxf5 gxf5 23 Nxd5 cxd5 24 Rg1 Re2 25 c3 fxg4 26 Nxf7 Kxf7 27 fxg4 Rh8 0-1

Summary

Black has several ways to combat the Bishop's Opening. After 3...Nc6 play usually transposes to either the Quiet Italian or Vienna Game, which economizes one's need for preparation. The plan featured in Game 51 (with 3...c6, 4...d5 and 5...Bd6) certainly isn't bad, but could be described as slightly passive. Instead, a number of strong players are attracted to the flexible set-up 3...c6, 4...Be7 and 5...d6, with the option of ...Nd7-c5 (see the note to Black's fourth move in Game 51). This approach could offer Black more opportunities to outplay a weaker opponent in the middlegame.

In the Ponziani, unless Black is well prepared for the complications of 3...d5, I recommend that he take a prudent approach with 3...Nf6, after which he can look forward to a fairly safe equality from the opening.

The Centre Game is by no means lacking in bite and needs to be treated with respect. Nevertheless, White's early queen moves cost him time and Black should be able to obtain adequate play, the best practical choice being 4...g6, as Black's development is then very natural.

Chapter Ten
Black Avoids 2...Nc6 – Introduction

Introduction

After **1 e4 e5 2 Nf3 (Diagram 1)**,

Diagram 1 (B)	**Diagram 2 (W)**
If not 2...Nc6, then what?	The Elephant Gambit

Black usually responds with 2...Nc6 (83% of the time), but some players prefer to avoid the Spanish and, if they can, steer the game into different channels.

The most common of these are Petroff's Defence 2...Nf6 (11%) covered in Chapter Twelve, and Philidor's Defence 2...d6 (5%) in Chapter Eleven. Both of these openings have the reputation of being solid, but a shade passive, especially in the main lines. The Petroff, in particular, has been fairly popular at 2600+ level, where it is used as a drawing weapon, as White has few chances to get more than the shade of an edge out of the opening.

Another more offbeat idea, though in the same solid positional vein, is 2...Qe7. This can resemble a slightly odd Philidor after 3 Nc3 c6 4 d4 d6 5 Be2 Nf6 6 0-0, when, as Black's queen is not actually that well placed, the most popular move is the tempo-wasting 6...Qc7. Naturally, such a unpromising system hasn't gained much popularity.

Some players enjoy their gambits so much they even like to play them with Black at the earliest possible moment. Even if they know that their system is dodgy, they rely on their opponent not knowing the theory to get lively play. An extremely rare one is 2...Bc5 3 Nxe5 Nc6, when White, at the very least, can obtain a solid advantage following Khalifman's suggested 4 Nf3 Qe7 5 Nc3 Nf6 6 d4 Nxe4 7 Nxe4 Qxe4+ 8 Be3, thanks to his superior development.

The better known of these gambits are the Elephant (2...d5) and the Latvian (2...f5) and I'll be concentrating on these here. One thing worth noting is that, overall, the Latvian Gambit (which accounts for less than 1% of Open Games) and the Elephant (less than 0.5%) score almost as well in practice as more respectable openings. At a lower level they may still have some mileage, but in general I don't think it's a good idea to play dubious openings hoping somehow to trick your opponent. You are more likely to lose a dreadful game than obtain attacking chances, especially against anyone who knows any theory. Nevertheless, there are some gamblers out there who don't agree and they will play in casinos even if the odds are stacked against them!

I shall just give one game with each and in both cases demonstrate a promising system for White – but first of all a strong warning:

WARNING: The strongest continuations against the Elephant and Latvian are widely known and these openings are borderline refuted.

Elephant Gambit

Game 54
□ **M.Parligras** ■ **A.Gunnarsson**
Calvia Olympiad 2004

1 e4 e5 2 Nf3 d5 (Diagram 2)

The Elephant Gambit can be thought of as a wild attempt by Black to seize the initiative, even at the cost of a pawn. Despite one's disbelief, the immediate opening of lines for his bishops does make some sense, so White has to play carefully to benefit from any objective advantage.

3 exd5 Bd6

There are two alternatives here:

a) 3...e4 is the main one; e.g. 4 Qe2 Nf6 (or 4...f5 5 d3 Nf6 6 dxe4 fxe4 7 Nc3 Bb4 8 Qb5+ c6 9 Qxb4 exf3 10 Bg5 cxd5 11 0-0-0 Nc6, M.Tal-A.Lutikov, USSR Team Ch. 1964, and now 12 Qh4 Be6 13 Ne4 should be well on the way to winning) 5 d3 Qxd5 (both 5...Bb4+ 6 c3 0-0 7 dxe4 Be7 8 Qc2! and 5...Be7 6 dxe4 0-0 7 Nc3 Re8 8 Bd2 Bb4 9 0-0-0 Bxc3 10 Bxc3 Nxe4 11 Qe3! are clearly better for White – Khalifman) 6 Nfd2! (6 dxe4 Qxe4 7 Nc3 Bb4 8 Bd2 Qxe2+ 9 Bxe2 0-0 doesn't give White very much, A.Kovchan-P.Skatchkov St Petersburg 2003) 6...Nc6 7 Nc3 Qa5 8 Nb3 (stronger than 8 Ndxe4 Be6) 8...Qb4 9 Bd2 Be6 10 Nxe4 Qa4 (or if 10...Qb5 11 Nxf6+ gxf6 12 Bc3 Rg8, T.Navinsek-P.Skatchkov, Zadar 2004, then 13 g3 is good) 11 Nc3 Qa6 12 d4 Qxe2+ 13 Nxe2 Ne4 14 c3 0-0-0 15 Be3 f5 16 0-0-0 and White is a clear pawn up, K.Rukhaia-P.Skatchkov, Yerevan 2004.

b) 3...Qxd5 4 Nc3 Qa5 is the only other worthwhile try, when Black has a somewhat shaky Scandinavian (and if he is heading for this type of position then meeting 1 e4 with 1...d5 would be more sensible!); e.g. 5 Bc4 Nc6 6 0-0 Bd6 7 d3 Nge7?! (but if 7...Nf6 8 Bd2 with a big edge) 8 Ng5! Nd8 9 Bd2 c6?? (a blunder, whereas after 9...0-0 10 Nce4 Qb6, Black should at least survive the opening) 10 Nb5 winning material, O.Salmensuu-J.Vetemaa, Jarvenpaa 1999.

4 d4

White also seeks open lines to facilitate rapid development.

4...e4 5 Ne5 (Diagram 3)

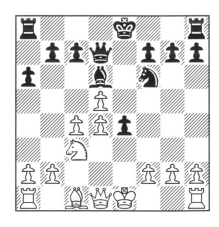

Diagram 3 (B)

The main line

Diagram 4 (B)

White is just a pawn up

5...Nf6

After 5...Ne7, Khalifman suggests 6 Bb5+ (or if 6 c4 c5!?, White could obtain an advantage with 7 dxc6 Bxe5 8 cxb7 Bxb7 9 dxe5 Qa5+ 10 Nc3 Qxe5 11 Qg4! as recommended by Pliester) 6...c6 7 dxc6 bxc6 8 Be2 Bxe5 9 dxe5 Qa5+ 10 Nd2 Be6 11 0-0 Qxe5 (or 11...0-0 12 Nxe4 Qxe5 13 Bd3, I.Asaritis-W.Muir, correspondence 1962) 12 Nc4 Bxc4 13 Bxc4 with a clear advantage as the two bishops should dominate the knight pair in this open position.

6 Bb5+

There is more than one way to skin an elephant. After 6 c4 c5 7 dxc6 Nxc6 8 Nxc6 bxc6 9 Nc3 Qc7 10 h3 0-0 11 Be2 Rb8 12 Qc2 Re8 13 Be3 Bf5 Black has free development, but this shouldn't be enough compensation since White has no real weaknesses, H.Mas-P.Corbin, Yerevan Olympiad 1996.

6...Bd7

Here 6...c6 7 dxc6 bxc6 8 Be2 Bxe5 9 dxe5 Qa5+ 10 Nd2 is unplayable for Black, as 10...Qxe5 11 Nc4 is close to catastrophic.

7 Nxd7 Nbxd7 8 c4

Holding onto the extra pawn, while also badly cramping Black. Alternatively, 8 Bg5 0-0 9 Bxd7 Qxd7 10 Bxf6 gxf6 11 c4 Kh8 12 Nc3 Rae8 13 Qe2 is another decent try for an advantage, Z.Byambaa-E.Kromhout, Bled Olympiad 2002.

8...a6 9 Bxd7+ Qxd7 10 Nc3 (Diagram 4)

If I had to summarize the state of play here, I would suggest that White simply has an extra pawn. The unbalanced structure at least enables Black to hope for some counter-chances, but it looks rather vague from where I am sitting.

10...0-0 11 0-0 Rae8

The immediate 11...b5 is best met by Pliester's 12 Bg5.

12 h3 b5 13 b3 Qf5 14 Be3 g5

Desperately seeking some counterplay.

15 f3!

White is ready to break out.

15...Bf4 16 Qd2 exf3 17 Bxf4 b4!?

17...Qxf4 18 Qxf4 gxf4 19 Rxf3 Ne4 20 cxb5! Nxc3 21 Rxc3 axb5 22 Rxc7 leaves White with a couple of extra pawns in the double-rook ending.

18 Bxc7 bxc3 19 Qxc3 g4 (Diagram 5)

The best chance to randomize things. The attack isn't really that dangerous, but White has to be careful.

20 hxg4 f2+ 21 Kh1

After the 'oversight' 21 Rxf2? Black has 21...Qxf2+ 22 Kxf2 Ne4+, though even here White is probably better; e.g. 23 Ke3 Nxc3+ 24 Kd3 Ne4 25 Rf1 with a huge pawn mass for the rook.

21...Nxg4 22 Qf3 Qh5+ 23 Qh3 Qg6 24 Qh4

Alternatively he could hurry to get rid of the f-pawn with 24 Bg3 Re3 25 Qh4 Re4 26 Bxf2 Ne3 27 Qh3 Nxf1 28 Rxf1 and despite losing the exchange, White is still much better.

24...Qf5 25 Bd6

Taking the exchange while it is on offer.

25...Kh8 26 Bxf8 Rxf8 27 d6 Rg8 28 d7 Qxd7 29 Rxf2

Finally eliminating the pesky f-pawn.

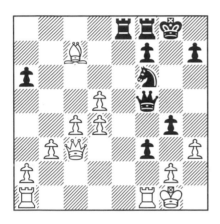

Diagram 5 (W)

Trying to randomize

Diagram 6 (W)

The Latvian Gambit

29...Qxd4 30 Raf1 Rg6!?

Otherwise 30...Nxf2+ gets all but a pawn back, but even so the prospects for Black are not good; e.g. 31 Qxf2 Qg4 32 Qf3 Qh4+ 33 Kg1 Rg7 34 Qa8+ Rg8 35 Qd5 etc.

31 Rf4! Qg7?

31...Qd6 is a better try, though White would still have more than one way to win; for example, 32 c5 Qd2 33 Qe1 Qd5 34 Rf5 Qc6 (threatening ...Rh6+, ...Rh1+, ...Qh6+ and ...Qh2 mate!) 35 Qc3+ Kg8 36 Qf3 and White has everything under control as 36...Ne3!? is busted by 37 Rg5!.

32 Rxf7 Rh6 33 Rf8+ 1-0

Latvian Gambit

Game 55
☐ N.Huschenbeth ■ J.Schlenker
German Championship, Bad Wörishofen 2008

1 e4 e5 2 Nf3 f5 (Diagram 6)

In 2001 Tony Kosten published a book *The Latvian Gambit Lives!* – but most GMs wouldn't agree with that! Black compromises his defences, rarely gets to use the f-file, and as will become clear below, isn't able to create enough play elsewhere either.

3 Nxe5 Qf6

Hitting the knight. The alternative 3...Nc6 can be defused by 4 Nxc6 dxc6 5 Nc3 Bc5 6 d3 Nf6 7 Be2 0-0 8 0-0 fxe4 9 Nxe4 Nxe4 10 dxe4 Qh4 11 Be3! (recommended by Kosten and Khalifman) 11...Bxe3 12 Bc4+ Kh8 13 fxe3 Bg4 14 Qd4, as in G.Legemaat-E.Van de Velden, correspondence 1996, when White is an e-pawn or two to the good which should constitute a winning advantage.

4 Nc4!

The most precise as now White can use his d-pawn to attack a future black centre. However, 4 d4 d6 5 Nc4 fxe4 6 Nc3 Qg6 7 f3 exf3 8 Qxf3 Nf6 9 Bd3 Qf7 10 0-0 Be7 11 Ne3 wasn't bad either, with a small edge for White in L.Guidarelli-J.P.Le Roux, Val d'Isère 2002.

4...fxe4 5 Nc3 Qf7

If 5...Qg6, after the normal-looking continuation 6 d3 Bb4 7 Bd2 Bxc3 8 Bxc3 Nf6 9 Bxf6 gxf6 10 Ne3 Black has serious problems, P.Hrabe-D.Holemar, Valtice 1991.

6 Ne3 c6 7 d3!

Obtaining the initiative is a more pragmatic try for ordinary mortals than the main alternative which involves grabbing a pawn: 7 Nxe4 d5 8 Ng5 Qf6 9 Nf3 Bd6 10 d4 Ne7 11 c4 0-0 when matters are less clear as Black obtains a lead in development and some open lines.

7...exd3

7...d5 8 dxe4 dxe4 9 Nxe4 gives Black less than nothing for his pawn.

8 Bxd3 d5 9 0-0 (Diagram 7)

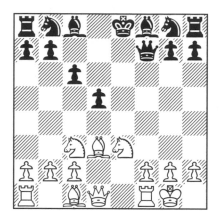

Diagram 7 (B)	Diagram 8 (B)
Black has no pieces out	Breaking things open

Analysts and correspondence players have spent a great deal of time trying to find a way to make this line playable for Black, but alas in vain. It seems that all lines lead him into trouble – which is hardly surprising if we glance at the position. White has developed three pieces and has castled as well, whereas Black has only brought out his queen. Such a lag in development cannot go unpunished!

9...Bc5

Other moves are equally difficult for the second player:

a) 9...Bb4 10 Ncxd5! cxd5 11 Nxd5 Bc5 12 Bf4 yields White a strong attack.

b) 9...d4 10 Bc4 Qd7 11 Qh5+ Kd8 12 Rd1 Nf6 13 Qh4 c5 14 b4 b6 15 bxc5 bxc5 16 Ne4 Be7 17 Ng5 with a crushing position, L.Diepstraten-P.Alloin, correspondence 1983.

c) 9...Bd6 10 Re1 Ne7 11 Nexd5! cxd5 12 Nb5 0-0 (or 12...Bf4 13 Bxf4 Qxf4 14 g3 Qf6 15 Nc7+ Kd8 16 Nxa8 b6 17 c4 Bb7 18 Nxb6 axb6 19 cxd5 led to a White win in H.Tiemann-A.Kosten, correspondence 2001) 13 Nxd6 Qxf2+ 14 Kh1 Bg4 15 Qd2 Qh4 16 b4 (or perhaps 16 Qe3 Nbc6 17 Nxb7 with a clear advantage, as pointed out by Khalifman) 16...Nbc6 17 Bb2 Rad8 18 Qc3 Qg5 19 Nxb7 Rb8 20 b5! and again White obtains the advantage, this time according to Kosten.

10 Na4 Bd6

Dropping back further is possible, but it's like choosing between the devil and the deep blue sea; e.g. 10...Be7 11 c4 Nf6 12 cxd5 cxd5 13 Nc3 Be6 (or 13...d4 14 Nb5 dxe3 15 Nc7+ Kf8 16 Bxe3 and Black is in even more trouble) 14 Bf5 Bxf5 15 Nxf5 Nc6 16 Nxe7 Kxe7 17 Be3 Kf8 18 Qa4 Kg8 19 Rad1, when the defender's badly-placed king and inferior structure ensure that White has a clear advantage.

11 c4 d4

If 11...Ne7 12 Nc3 Be6 13 cxd5 cxd5 14 Nb5 Nc8 15 f4! (or more simply 15 Nxd6+ Nxd6 16 Qc2) 15...0-0 16 f5 Bd7 17 Nxd6 Nxd6 18 b3 and Black is in hot water again, A.Kosten-J.Elburg, correspondence 2001.

12 Nc2 c5 13 b4! (Diagram 8) 13...cxb4

After 13...b6 White can force matters with 14 Be4 Bb7 15 Bxb7 Qxb7 16 bxc5 bxc5 17 Nxc5! Bxh2+ 18 Kxh2 Qc7+ 19 Kg1 Qxc5 20 Re1+ Ne7 21 Ba3 and wins, V.Kozlov-Jackson, correspondence 1991.

14 Nxd4 Nc6

Or if 14...Ne7, White has 15 Nb5 Be5 16 f4 Bxa1 17 Nd6+ Kf8 18 Nxf7 Bd4+ 19 Kh1 Kxf7 20 f5 with a continuing attack, as pointed out by Khalifman.

15 Nb5

15 Nxc6 bxc6 16 Be4 Qc7 17 Qf3 Ne7 18 Re1 is also very strong.

15...Bb8 16 c5 Nf6

After 16...Nge7, then 17 Nd6+ Bxd6 18 cxd6 Nf5 19 Re1+ is even stronger than in the game.

17 Re1+ Kf8 18 Nd6 Bxd6 19 cxd6

White's advantage is self-evident as he has the bishop pair, while Black's development is messed up with neither rook ready to enter the fray.

19...Ng4

19...Qd5 20 Bf1 Qxd1 21 Rxd1 Bg4 22 f3 Bf5 23 Nc5 is also miserable.

20 f3 Nge5 21 Be4 Bf5 22 Nc5 b6 23 Bd5

Black never seems to get a respite, so his king and rooks can't sort themselves out.

23...Qg6 24 Bf4 (Diagram 9) 24...bxc5?

Losing material, but the defence was already problematic; for example, 24...Re8 25 d7 Nxd7 26 Nxd7+ Bxd7 27 Be4 Qf7 28 Qd6+ Ne7 29 Qxd7 Qxf4 30 Bc6 isn't particularly joyful for Black either!

25 Bxe5 Nxe5 26 Bxa8 Nd3 27 Qe2 Qf7 28 Bd5 Qd7 29 Qe7+ Qxe7 30 dxe7+ Ke8 31 Bc6+ Bd7 32 Bxd7+ Kxd7 33 Rad1 c4 34 Re4 Rc8 35 e8Q+ 1-0

If Black insists on continuing with 35...Rxe8 then 36 Rxc4 Re1+ 37 Rxe1 Nxe1 38 Kf1 Nd3 39 Rd4+ tidies up.

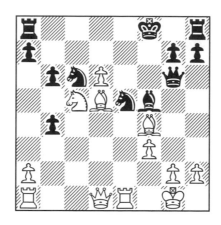

Diagram 9 (B)

No rest for the wicked

 TIP: As a general rule my recommendation is not to play unsound openings at all. It is better to spend one's time and effort getting to grips with correct openings and then choosing appropriate plans that meet the demands of a position. This enables one to improve over time, whereas playing for tricks in dubious variations is a recipe for stagnation!

Summary

If White knows his stuff, Black gets into difficulties in both the Elephant and the Latvian Gambits.

Chapter Eleven
Philidor's Defence

Introduction

1 e4 e5 2 Nf3 d6 (Diagram 1)

 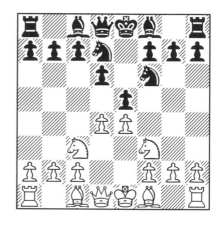

Diagram 1 (W)

Philidor's Defence

Diagram 2 (W)

The Hanham Variation

In Philidor's Defence Black defends the e5-pawn in the most solid way and keeps all options open as to the positioning of his queen's knight. The obvious downside to 2...d6 is that the king's bishop won't be developing to the active squares c5 or b4 in a hurry, and indeed in most variations the passivity of this piece is an issue.

One reason many are attracted to this essentially solid opening is that Black avoids many tricky systems that might be thrown at him and is able, to some extent, to dictate the type of positions that arise. If Black can stabilize matters, he may then have the time to prepare counterplay, though this often comes later than in many Open Games. This is because Black may have to stay on the defensive in the early part of the game and play with great accuracy to get close to equalizing.

In modern times, the tabiya after...

3 d4 Nf6 4 Nc3 Nbd7 (Diagram 2)

...known as the Hanham Variation, is most frequently reached via an alternative move order, emanating from the Pirc Defence: 1 e4 d6 2 d4 Nf6 3 Nc3 e5 (as in the first three games below) 4 Nf3 Nbd7 – this series of moves is actually known as the Lion. As will become evident, the Lion gives Black a solid Philidor while avoiding some promising options for White, such as 4 dxe5! (see the notes to Game 57).

Hanham Variation

Game 56
□ T.L.Petrosian ■ Art.Minasian
Armenian Championship, Yerevan 2008

1 e4 d6 2 d4 Nf6 3 Nc3 e5 4 Nf3

The usual reply and the most relevant one here (since this is a book on Open Games, not the Lion!), although 4 Nge2!? also features in Game 59. The simplifying 4 dxe5 dxe5 5 Qxd8+ Kxd8 is known, but doesn't really cause Black too many headaches.

4...Nbd7 5 Bc4 Be7 (Diagram 3)

 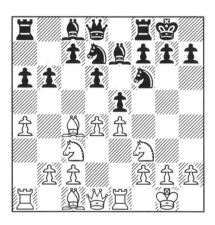

Diagram 3 (W)
Position after 5...Be7

Diagram 4 (W)
An alternative Black set-up

In the Hanham Variation Black maintains his hold on e5 and continues his attempt at solid development. He has less space and thus is slightly cramped, but if given time he can gradually harmonize his forces.

6 0-0

One way that White can try and upset Black's plan is to play for complications involving Bxf7+, though experience suggests that this is risky:

a) 6 Bxf7+? Kxf7 7 Ng5+ Kg8 8 Ne6 (the attack on the queen forces Black to shed material, but...) 8...Qe8 9 Nxc7 Qg6 10 Nxa8 (10 0-0 Rb8 11 f4 Nxe4 is a lesser evil, though White's prospects are still uninspiring) 10...Qxg2 11 Rf1 exd4 12 Qxd4 Ne5 left Black with a strong initiative in W.Heidenfeld-J.Wolpert, Johannesburg 1955.

b) 6 dxe5 is a better try, although after 6...dxe5 (6...Nxe5!? is also possible) 7 Bxf7+ Kxf7 8 Ng5+ Kg6 9 f4 exf4 10 Ne6 Qg8 11 Nxc7?! (11 Nd5! Bd8! is less clear-cut) 11...Ne5! 12 Nxa8 Bg4 13 Qd4 Nc6 14 Qf2, I.Shaymuratov-B.Sattarov, Navbahor 2009, and now 14...Qc4! Black has excellent compensation.

c) 6 Ng5 0-0 7 Bxf7+ is the best of the bunch and leads to chances for both sides; e.g. 7...Rxf7 8 Ne6 Qe8 9 Nxc7 Qd8 10 Nxa8 b6 11 dxe5 dxe5 12 Nd5 Bc5 13 Be3 (but not 13 Nxf6+? Qxf6 14 0-0 Ba6 15 Nc7 Bxf1 16 Qxf1 Qh4 with a quick Black win in V.Rasulov-G.Bagaturov, Urumia 2008) 13...Nxe4 14 Qe2 Ndf6 15 Nxf6+ Nxf6 16 Bxc5 bxc5 17 0-0 e4! with approximate equality according to Bauer.

6...0-0 7 Re1 c6

It's less well known for Black to delay (or even omit) this 'standard' move, but as White has yet to show anything convincing against it, there is no pressing need to vary from the beaten track. I suppose it comes down to a question of taste. For instance, after 7...a6!? 8 a4 b6 **(Diagram 4)**, White has tried the following:

a) 9 d5 Kh8 10 a5?! b5 11 Bf1 Bb7 12 b4 Rc8 13 Bb2 c6 14 dxc6 Rxc6 15 Bd3 Rc7 16 Qd2 Qa8 and Black had a dynamic position, R.Leitao-M.Bezold, Bermuda 1998.

b) 9 Bg5 Bb7 10 d5 Kh8 11 Nd2 Ng8 (with the centre closed Black can play this manoeuvre) 12 Be3 g6 13 Nf1 (Kuzmin prefers 13 g3 Bg5 14 f4 Bh6 which he gives as unclear) 13...Bg5 14 Qd2 Bxe3 15 Nxe3 f5 with adequate counterplay, A.Areshchenko-M.Sebenik, European Ch., Plovdiv 2008.

c) 9 b3 Bb7 10 Bb2 c6 11 Bd3 g6! (a clever move order as 12 Ne2?! runs into 12...exd4 13 Bxd4 c5 and White has to give up his important bishop in order to save the e-pawn) 12 Qd2 Re8 13 Rad1 Bf8 14 h3 b5 15 axb5 axb5 16 Ne2 exd4 17 Nexd4 Bg7 and Black was fine in A.Timofeev-D.Bocharov, European Ch., Plovdiv 2008.

This looks like quite a good idea, setting different problems for White.

8 a4 b6 9 b3

A practical choice: the bishop will be well placed on the long diagonal, so White is able to organize his pieces and obtain harmonious development. The main alternative, 9 d5, is examined in Game 57.

9...a6 10 Bd3 Re8 11 Bb2 Bf8 12 Ne2 Bb7 13 Ng3 g6 (Diagram 5)

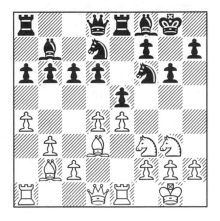 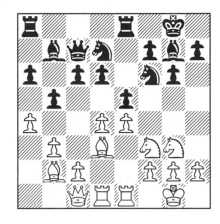

Diagram 5 (W)	**Diagram 6 (W)**
The move order is flexible	A standard pawn break

14 Qd2

The move order is quite flexible, so ideas and manoeuvres should be compared to analogous positions before making any definitive assessments.

Here 14 c4!? is interesting, to gain more space and limit the possibilities of ...b6-b5 and ...d6-d5, though after 14...exd4 15 Bxd4 Bg7 16 Qd2 Ne5 Black seems to have nullified White's opening initiative; e.g. 17 Rad1 Nxf3+ 18 gxf3 d5 19 cxd5 cxd5 20 e5 Nd7 21 f4 Qh4 22 Bf1 and a draw was agreed in P.Svidler-S.Movsesian, San Sebastian 2009. Note that 17 Nxe5 dxe5 18 Bc3 isn't favourable for White since the c4-pawn is rather in the way (compare Arutinian-Movsesian in the next note where the pawn was more favourably placed on c2).

14...Bg7

D.Arutinian-S.Movsesian, Pardubice (rapid) 2009, saw 14...exd4 15 Nxd4 c5 16 Nf3 Ne5 17 Nxe5 dxe5 18 Qe2 (White's forces are slightly more active so he keeps a pull, as long as he avoids counterplay) 18...Qc7 19 Rad1 h5 20 Bc1 Be7 21 Nf1 Red8 22 f3 h4 23 Bc4 Nh5 24 g3 and White kept his nose ahead.

Instead, after 14...Qc7, White tried 15 c4!? in N.Kosintseva-N.Khurtsidze, European Club Cup, Ohrid 2009, and the game continued in her favour with 15...a5 (Black should prefer Movsesian's recipe, 15...exd4 16 Bxd4 Ne5, to force the exchange of at least one pair of minor pieces) 16 Bc2 Rad8 17 Rad1 Bg7 18 h3 exd4? (losing patience) 19 Nxd4 Bc8 (19...Ne5 is now well met by 20 f4, while after 19...Nc5 20 Ngf5! is still very strong; e.g. 20...gxf5 21 Nxf5 Nfxe4 22 Bxe4 Nxe4 23 Rxe4 Rxe4 24 Bxg7 and White wins) 20 Ngf5! Bh8 (20...gxf5 is also bad: 21 Nxf5 Re5 22 Bxe5 dxe5 23 Qg5 Ne8 24 Re3 or 22...Nxe5 23 Nxg7 Kxg7 24 f4 Ng6 25 f5 with a winning position) 21 Qg5 Nc5? (21...Bb7 is a lesser evil since there is no killer blow... for now!) 22 Nxc6! Bxf5 23 exf5 Qxc6 24 Bxf6 and White won easily.

15 Rad1

15 c4 exd4! 16 Nxd4 Ne5 would return to Svidler-Movsesian above.

15...Qc7

Or immediately 15...b5, since 16 axb5 axb5 17 Ra1 didn't worry Black in J.P.Boudre-B.Badea, Marseille 2003.

16 Qc1 b5 (Diagram 6)

With everything apparently under control, this break seems appropriate.

17 c4 bxc4 18 Bxc4 Nb6 19 dxe5!

The idea is to leave Black with split pawns.

19...dxe5

But not 19...Nxc4? 20 exf6 Nxb2 21 Qxb2, when White keeps an extra pawn and the more promising position.

20 Bf1 a5 21 Qc2 Nfd7 22 Ba3 Bf8 23 Bxf8 Nxf8 24 Qc3

The fight for the dark squares continues, with the queen eyeing the somewhat vulnerable pawns on a5 and e5.

24...f6

The best way to prepare a challenge on the d-file.

25 Rd2 Red8 26 Red1 Rxd2 27 Nxd2 Kg7! 28 Nc4 Nxc4 29 Bxc4 Rd8 (Diagram 7)

Exchanges have eased Black's game, and he no longer seems to have any particular problems as his queenside weaknesses can easily be defended.

30 Rc1!? Qb6 31 h4

Trying to demonstrate that White is still calling the shots...

31...Bc8 32 h5 Ne6

...but with the knight coming to d4, Black is fine.

33 Bf1

33 Bxe6 Bxe6 34 Qxc6 Qxc6 (or 34...Rd1+ 35 Kh2 Qxc6 36 Rxc6 Bxb3) 35 Rxc6 Bxb3 is also equal.

33...Nd4 34 Qe3?!

White is drifting at this point; offering to repeat with 34 Bc4 is probably best here.

34...Be6 35 h6+ Kf7 36 Ne2 Qxb3 37 Nxd4 exd4 38 Qf4 Qb8!

After 38...Qb7 39 Bd3 it would be difficult for Black to reorganize, so instead he gives White a choice.

39 Qf3

Avoiding 39 Qxb8 Rxb8 40 Rxc6 Rb1 which would favour Black.

39...Qd6 40 e5?!

Seeking activity isn't always the way to save pawn-down positions. I prefer the blockading 40 Bd3 c5 41 Qe2 Rc8 42 Bc4.

40...Qxe5 41 Qxc6 d3 42 Rd1 d2 43 Qc2 Qf4 44 Bd3 (Diagram 8) 44...Bf5?!

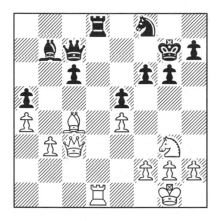

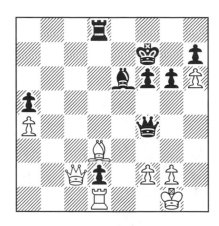

Diagram 7 (W)

Black has no problems

Diagram 8 (B)

...and has chances to win

Instead, 44...Qxh6 45 Rxd2 Kg7 was possible, still with an extra pawn and some advantage; whereas the natural-looking move played in the game just falls short.

45 Qb3+ Kf8 46 Bxf5 Qxf5 47 Qc3

Hitting a5, d2 and f6.

47...Qe6

Otherwise 47...Qe5 48 Qxe5 fxe5 49 Kf1 Rd4 50 Ke2 is distinctly drawish.

48 Qxa5 Rd7 49 Qb4+ Kf7 50 Kf1 Qd5 51 Qb5 Qd4 52 Qb3+ Rd5!?

A dramatic last winning attempt, since White is already past the worst.

53 a5 g5 54 a6 Kg6 55 a7 Rf5 56 Qg8+ Kxh6 57 Qf8+ Kg6 58 Qg8+ Kh6 59 Qf8+ Kh5 60 Qe8+ Kh6

60...Kh4?? 61 g3+ Kg4 62 Qe2+ would win for White.

61 Qf8+ Kg6 ½-½

Game 57
□ G.Kasparov ■ Z.Azmaiparashvili
1st matchgame (rapid), Crete 2003

1 e4 d6

Another strong GM heads for the Philidor via the Lion – in fact they all do these days! If we examine the 'official' move order more closely, we'll perhaps understand why...

After 1 e4 e5 2 Nf3 d6 3 d4 Nf6, White can play 4 dxe5! (instead of the docile 4 Nc3, which allows the Hanham with 4...Nbd7) 4...Nxe4 5 Qd5 Nc5 6 Bg5 **(Diagram 9)**, when Black faces a difficult choice.

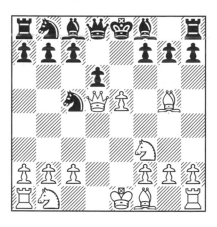

Diagram 9 (B)	**Diagram 10 (B)**
The critical 4 dxe5! line	A sharp White try

In each of the segments that follow, the scenario is the same: Black has an uphill task (some would say a mountain to climb!) in his quest for an acceptable game and anything resembling equality.

a) 6...Be7 7 exd6 Qxd6 8 Nc3 Qe6+ (no better is 8...c6 9 Qxd6 Bxd6 10 0-0-0 Bc7 11 Be3 Ne6 12 Ne4 0-0 13 Nd6 Bxd6 14 Rxd6 Nd7 15 Bc4 Nf6 16 Ne5 with the bishops plus pressure, J.Howell-J.Shaw, Oakham 1994) 9 Be3 c6 10 Qd4 0-0 11 Bc4 Qg4 12 0-0-0 b5 13 Qe5! and White was on top, S.Rublevsky-B.Abramovic, Yugoslav Team Ch. 1994.

b) 6...Qd7 7 exd6 Bxd6 8 Nc3 0-0 (after 8...Qe6+ 9 Be3 Qxd5 10 Nxd5 Ne6 11 0-0-0 Nc6 12 Nd2 Bd7 13 Ne4 Be7 14 Be2 0-0-0 15 Bxa7! White had stolen a pawn, M.Chandler-B.Gulko, Reykjavik 1991) 9 0-0-0 a6 10 Be3 Qc6 11 Ne5 Qxd5 12 Nxd5 Ne6 13 Nc4 and the bishop pair ensure White a definite edge, M.Larrea-J.Cueto Chajtur, Turin Olympiad 2006.

On a good day a diligent defender might be able to hold, but the general perception is that White can obtain an opening advantage with 4 dxe5; hence the reticence of the elite to enter a Philidor by the direct move order.

Black can try varying (after 1 e4 e5 2 Nf3 d6 3 d4) with 3...Nd7!? (the non-Hanham continuations 3...exd4 and 3...f5?! are examined in the next game), intending to answer 4 Nc3 by 4...Ngf6 and the house is in order. Unfortunately, White has the promising sequence 4 Bc4 c6 5 0-0 Be7 6 dxe5 dxe5 (6...Nxe5? is bad as 7 Nxe5 dxe5 8 Qh5 wins a pawn) 7 Ng5! Bxg5 8 Qh5 Qe7 9 Bxg5 Ngf6 10 Qe2, as in A.Gipslis-I.Csom, Budapest 1977, with a nice positional edge, thanks again to his two bishops.

In all these lines Black's only aim will be to avoid losing, whereas with the Lion move order he is able to obtain a playable position (and hopes of outplaying his opponent) without there being any troublesome deviations.

2 d4 Nf6 3 Nc3 e5 4 Nf3 Nbd7 5 Bc4

Here 5 g4!? **(Diagram 10)** is a sharp and unclear try which looks slightly random at first sight, but with White scoring 67%(!) it is evidently not that easy to meet. When first faced with this move Azmaiparashvili took the pawn, while in a later game he decided to ignore it.

a) 5...Nxg4 6 Rg1 Ngf6 7 Bc4 h6 8 Be3 c6 9 Qd3 Qc7 10 0-0-0 b5 11 Bxb5 cxb5 12 dxe5 dxe5 13 Nxb5 Qa5 14 Qc4 Rb8 15 a4 Qb4 16 Nxe5 Qxc4 17 Nxc4 gave White enough compensation, A.Shirov-Z.Azmaiparashvili, European Team Ch., Plovdiv 2003.

b) 5...g6 6 g5 Nh5 7 Be3 Bg7 8 Qd2 0-0 9 0-0-0 f5 10 exf5 Rxf5 11 dxe5 Nxe5 (not 11...Rxf3? 12 Qd5+ Rf7 13 e6 and wins) 12 Nxe5 Bxe5 13 Bc4+ Kh8 14 Kb1 with an interesting middlegame in prospect, A.Lastin-Z.Azmaiparashvili, FIDE World Ch., Tripoli 2004.

WARNING: Don't make the same mistake as many others and underestimate this line. It's better to have a good look at what type of position suits you and prepare your answer *before* you suffer at the hands of 5 g4 in practice.

5...Be7 6 0-0 0-0 7 Re1

7 Qe2 c6 8 a4 b6 9 Rd1 Qc7 10 d5 is similar to the main game, except that Qe2 and Rd1 has cost White an additional tempo for no obvious benefit. 10...cxd5 (10...c5?! is less appropriate due to 11 a5! bxa5 12 Nb5 Qb6 13 Bd2, or 11...Bb7 12 a6 Bc8 13 Bb5 with the better chances for White) 11 Nxd5 Nxd5 12 Bxd5 Bb7 is best, when White has nothing special, S.Brady-M.Orr, Irish Ch., Dublin 2003.

7...c6 8 a4 b6 9 d5 (Diagram 11)

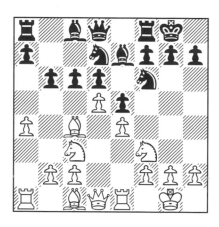

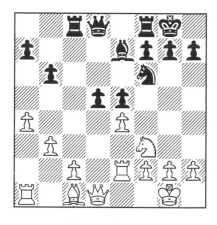

Diagram 11 (B)	**Diagram 12 (W)**
Fixing the pawn structure	A blow for freedom

This time White fixes the pawn structure, rather than keeping the tension as in the previous game.

9...cxd5

Again 9...c5 10 a5! doesn't give Black an easy choice. For example, 10...Rb8 11 Qd3 leaves White well in control; while 10...bxa5 accepts a slightly worse structure, and Black suffered in A.Miles-T.Gelashvili, St Vincent 2000: 11 Nd2 (with the positional threat of N-b3xa5, so Black returns the pawn immediately) 11...Nb6 12 Rxa5 Nxc4 13 Nxc4 Ne8 14 f4 exf4 15 Bxf4 f6 16 Qd2 Rf7 17 Rea1 with intense pressure.

Nor could Black have been satisfied with his game after 9...Bb7 10 dxc6 Bxc6 11

Bg5 a6 12 Bxf6 Nxf6 13 Nd5 Nxd5 14 Bxd5, V.Jansa-K.Mokry, Trnava 1987, when he faced a tricky 'good knight vs. bad bishop' scenario.

10 Nxd5

Other recaptures are inferior: after 10 Bxd5 Nxd5 11 Nxd5 Bb7, followed by ...Nf6, White is unable to maintain his central bind; while 10 exd5?! blocks his own pieces and even becomes a target for Black's counterplay; e.g. 10...Bb7 11 b3 Ne8 12 Bb2 a6 13 Nd2 Nc7, K.Spraggett-C.Bauer, French Team Ch. 2001, saw White resorting to 14 Ndb1 f5 15 Na3 in order to prevent ...b6-b5.

10...Bb7

Experience has shown that this is Black's best; whereas 10...Nxd5?! 11 Bxd5 Rb8 12 Qd3 Nf6 13 Bb3 h6 14 Bd2 Bb7 15 Rad1 Qc7 16 Nh4 d5 17 Nf5 gives White a strong attack, V.Jansa-P.Hesse, German League 1991.

11 b3

11 Bg5?! allows Black to release all the tension by 11...Nxd5 12 Bxd5 Bxd5 13 Bxe7 Qxe7 14 Qxd5 Rac8 with equality, A.Rodriguez Cespedes-V.Jansa, Andorra 1996.

11...Rc8 12 Re2

Defending the c2-square so that White can keep recapturing with pieces on d5.

12...Nxd5

Neither 12...Rc5 13 Ba3, nor 12...Nc5 13 Nxf6+ Bxf6 14 Bd5 can be considered as improvements for Black.

13 Bxd5 Bxd5

If Black tries 13...Ba6 to keep his 'good' bishop, then 14 c4 retains a bind; e.g. 14...Nf6 15 Ba3 Qd7 16 h3 Rc7 17 Ne1 Bc8 18 Nc2 g6 19 Ne3 Nh5 20 Rd2 Nf4 21 Ba8! and White was much better in C.Balogh-L.Seres, Budapest 2001. The threat to his d-pawn causes serious problems for Black.

14 Qxd5 Nf6 15 Qd1

After 15 Qd2, the break 15...d5! liberates; e.g. 16 exd5 e4 17 Ng5 Nxd5! as in S.Novikov-I.Akimov, St Petersburg 2005, when White can only avoid a disadvantage if he follows up with 18 Nxe4 f5 19 Nd6! Qxd6 20 Ba3 (Blatny).

15...d5 (Diagram 12)

Again this freeing move, but now things are less clear.

16 exd5 Qxd5

'Azmai' has also tried 16...e4 here but it is not certain that this is a better equalizing attempt; e.g. 17 Ng5 Qxd5 (if now 17...Nxd5?! 18 Nxe4 f5, then White has 19 Rd2!) 18 Qxd5 Nxd5 19 Nxe4 f5 20 c4 fxe4 (20...Nb4 21 Bg5! proved inadequate for Black in A.Khamatgaleev-C.Philippe, Budapest 1999) 21 cxd5 Bc5 22 h3 (or 22 Be3

Bxe3 23 Rxe3 Rc2 24 Rf1 Rd8 25 Rxe4 Rxd5 26 Re7 Rb2 27 Rxa7 Rxb3 28 Re1 h6 – Huzman) 22...Rf5 23 Be3 Bxe3 24 Rxe3 Rc2 25 Rf1 Rxd5 26 Rxe4 h6, when his active rooks enabled him to hold on for a draw in B.Macieja-Z.Azmaiparashvili, European Team Ch., Plovdiv 2003.

17 Qxd5 Nxd5 18 Nxe5

After 18 c4 Nc3 19 Re3 Nd1! (rather than 19...e4 20 Bb2 Bc5 21 Rxc3 exf3 22 Rxf3 Rcd8 23 Bc3, which was good for White in K.Asrian-Z.Azmaiparashvili, Greek Team Ch. 2005) 20 Re1 Rfd8 it seems that Black is again favourite to hold on; e.g. 21 Nxe5 Bb4 22 Bd2 Rxd2 23 Raxd1 Rb2 24 Re3 Bc5 25 Rf3 Re8 26 Nd3 Rxb3 27 Nxc5 Rxf3 28 gxf3 bxc5 29 Rd5 Rc8 30 Rd7 g6 31 Rxa7 Rb8 32 Rc7 Rb4 33 Rxc5 Rxa4 and the rook endgame is drawish according to Bauer.

18...Rfe8 19 c4 Bd6

The wily Georgian managed to modify his play a couple of years later with greater success; i.e. 19...Nc3 20 Re1 Bd6 21 Nf3 Rxe1+ 22 Nxe1 Be5 23 Kf1 Rd8 24 a5?! (surely 24 Bg5 is stronger, with chances for an advantage after 24...f6 25 Nf3, or 24...Ne4 25 Bxd8 Bxa1 26 Ke2 Nc5 27 b4 Nxa4 28 Nd3 when Black has to be careful) 24...Ne2 25 Rb1 Nc3 26 Ra1 Ne2 27 Rb1 Nc3 28 Ra1 drawing by repetition, V.Nevednichy-Z.Azmaiparashvili, Nova Gorica 2005.

20 Bb2 Nf4 21 Ree1 Bb4 22 Red1 Ne2+ 23 Kf1 Nc3 24 Rd3 Ne4 25 Rad1

Here 25 Bd4 Nd2+ 26 Kg1 f6 27 Be3 was more accurate, when White has a significant advantage according to Bauer.

25...Bc5 26 Rf3 Rcd8 27 Rxd8 Rxd8 28 Rd3

Giving the pawn back in order to snuff out Black's activity.

28...Rxd3 29 Nxd3 Nd2+ 30 Ke2 Nxb3 31 Be5 (Diagram 13)

White is still nominally better here, with his superior king and some pressure against Black's queenside.

31...f6 32 Bb8 Nd4+ 33 Kd2 Nc6 34 Nxc5 Nxb8

Of course not 34...bxc5? 35 Bd6 Na5 36 Kd3 etc.

35 Nd3 Kf7 36 Kc3 Ke6 37 c5 Kd5 38 cxb6 axb6 39 Kb4 Kc6 40 Kc4

In knight endings, just as in king and pawn endings, even a slightly more active disposition of forces can create serious problems for the defender.

40...Na6

40...Nd7 41 Nb4+ Kd6 42 Kb5 also leaves White with some pressure.

41 Nb4+ Nxb4 42 Kxb4 h5 43 f4 g6 44 Kc4 Kd6 45 Kb5 Kc7 46 Ka6 (Diagram 14) 46...Kc6?

Black probably didn't have time to calculate and so had to guess which way was best here. Unfortunately this wasn't it.

Instead, he could have saved the game with 46...h4! 47 Ka7 f5! (but not 47...g5? 48 fxg5 fxg5 49 h3 Kc6 50 Kb8 Kc5 51 Kc7 and wins) 48 h3 Kc6 49 Kb8 Kc5 50 Kc7 Kb4 51 Kxb6 Kxa4 52 Kc5 Kb3 53 Kd4 Kc2 54 Ke5 Kd3 55 Kf6 Ke4 56 Kxg6 Kxf4 57 Kf6 Ke4! 58 Kg5 Ke5 59 Kxh4 Kf4 60 g4 Ke5! 61 g5 f4 62 Kg4 Ke4 63 g6 f3 64 Kg3 Ke3 65 g7 f2 66 g8Q f1Q and the queen ending is a book draw; e.g. 67 Qe6+ Kd2 68 Qd5+ Kc1 69 Qc5+ Kb1 70 Qb6+ Ka1, though White can still try for a while!

47 h4 f5 48 g3 Kc5 49 Kb7 1-0

Now it's easily won; e.g. 49...Kb4 50 Kxb6 Kxa4 51 Kc5 Kb3 52 Kd4 Kc2 53 Ke5 Kd3 54 Kf6 Ke4 55 Kxg6 Kf3 56 Kxf5 Kxg3 57 Kg5 etc.

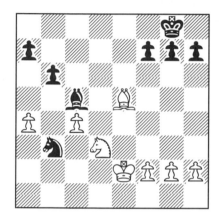

Diagram 13 (B)
White is nominally better

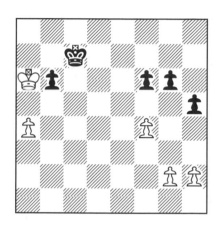

Diagram 14 (B)
Black could still draw

Larsen Variation

Game 58
□ **O.Korneev** ■ **P.Garcia Castro**
Pontevedra 2003

1 e4 e5 2 Nf3 d6

Finally we have a game with the traditional move order!

3 d4

Some players opt for 3 Bc4 here, when 3...Be7 4 0-0 Nf6 5 Re1 0-0 6 c3 Nbd7 is a solid practical system for Black. For example, 7 d3 c6 is very much like some lines of the Bishop's Opening (see Game 51, note to Black's fourth move), while 7 d4 exd4 8 cxd4 d5 leads to simplified equality after 9 Bxd5 Nxd5 10 exd5 Nb6 11 Nc3 Bb4 12 Qb3 Bxc3 13 bxc3 Qxd5 14 Ba3 Rd8, L.Yudasin-Z.Franco Ocampos, Pamplona 1994.

If a more tense struggle is sought, then one could (instead of 7...exd4) keep things closed by 7...c6 8 Bb3 Qc7, intending ...h7-h6, ...Re8, ...Nf8 with heavy manoeuvring in prospect. White has more space, but Black is highly flexible. Of course this resembles a Hanham formation, except that White has a pawn on c3, and so his knight will perhaps have to hop from b1 to d2 to f1 and then on to g3.

3...exd4

Occasionally 3...f5?! inspires some gamblers and can lead to sharp play; but if White knows his stuff he will reply 4 Nc3! and obtain the better game; for example, 4...fxe4 5 Nxe4 d5 6 Neg5 h6 7 Nf7! Kxf7 8 Nxe5+ Ke7 (8...Ke6 is refuted by 9 Qg4+ Ke7 10 Ng6+ Ke8 11 Qe2+ Ne7 12 Nxh8 etc – Bauer) 9 Bd3! (there is no need to be overly materialistic as Black's development is in such disarray) 9...Qe8 10 0-0 Be6 11 Re1 Nc6 12 Ng6+ Kd7 13 Nf4! Bd6 14 Nxe6 Qf7 15 Qg4 1-0 M.Pavlovic-D.Van Dooren, Cappelle la Grande 2006.

4 Nxd4 g6 (Diagram 15)

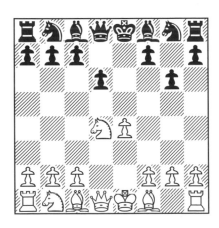

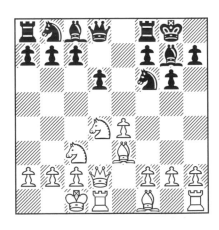

Diagram 15 (W)

The Larsen Variation

Diagram 16 (B)

A good Dragon for White

The kingside fianchetto initiates Larsen's System, which is outwardly attractive – Black gets potential for action along the long diagonal or down the e-file – but in the real world turns out to be probably too slow.

 WARNING: Appearances can be deceptive!

5 Nc3 Bg7 6 Be3 Nf6 7 Qd2

White plays as if in a Sicilian Dragon, Yugoslav Attack – except that in that famous variation Black has a pawn on e7 rather than on c7, the consequence being that, unlike in the Sicilian, there is no counter-attack along the c-file. This means that White's king will be relatively safe on the queenside, giving him the necessary foundation to launch an attack, either on the kingside or, if Black weakens the d-pawn, even in the centre.

7...0-0 8 0-0-0 (Diagram 16) 8...Nc6

8...Re8 is a significant alternative, but this only forces White to make a move he was probably going to play anyway, and unless (or until) White pushes his king-side pawns (including the f-pawn) to gain space, there isn't much doing on the e-file. So 8...Re8 is met by 9 f3 Nc6 (after 9...a6 White just gets on with his kingside attack: 10 g4 b5 11 Bh6 etc) 10 g4 and then:

a) 10...Nxd4 11 Bxd4 Be6 12 g5 Nh5 13 Bxg7 Nxg7 14 h4 Qe7 15 f4 c6 16 Be2! Rad8 17 Bf3 f6 18 h5 with a strong attack, M.Rodin-Y.Meister, Russian Team Ch. 1992.

b) 10...Ne5 11 Be2 a6 12 g5 Nh5 13 f4 Ng4 14 Bg1 c5 15 Nb3 Bxc3 16 bxc3 Rxe4 (the rook gets to capture the e-pawn...) 17 h3 Ng3 18 Bf3 Ra4 19 Bxc5 Nxh1 20 Bxh1 Rxa2 (...and the a-pawn!) 21 Kb1 Ra4, M.Rytshagov-V.Meijers, Mezezers 2000, and here Bauer's 22 Qxd6 Qxd6 23 Rxd6 was the simplest win.

c) 10...a6 11 h4 h5 12 g5 Nd7 13 f4 Nb6 14 Nxc6 bxc6 15 Bxb6 (15 Bd4 is solid and good, but the move played in the game is even better) 15...cxb6 16 Qxd6 Qxd6 17 Rxd6 Bxc3 18 bxc3 Rxe4 19 Bg2 with a big advantage for White, M.Krysztofiak-V.Bogdanov, Rowy Jantar 2000.

9 f3 Nxd4 10 Bxd4 Be6 11 g4

As White threatens to make rapid progress on the kingside, Black needs to do something dramatic elsewhere.

The same could be said about 11 h4, so there too Black would be wise to lash out with 11...c5; for example, 12 Be3 (12 Bxf6?! Qxf6 13 Qxd6 leaves too many holes on the dark squares and allows Black excellent play) 12...Qa5 13 a3 (after 13 Qxd6, Black has the strong rejoinder 13...Nxe4! 14 fxe4 Bxc3 as pointed out by Bauer, who also mentions that 13 Kb1 Rfd8 14 Nd5 Qxd2 15 Nxf6+ Bxf6 16 Rxd2 d5 leads to equality) 13...Rfd8 14 Bg5 a6 15 g4 b5, intending ...b5-b4 with dangerous counterplay, A.Petrushin-R.Kimelfeld, USSR 1979.

11...c5 12 Be3 Qa5 (Diagram 17)

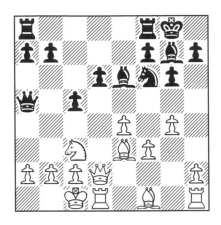

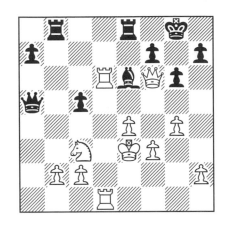

Diagram 17 (W)
Time for action

Diagram 18 (B)
The white king runs off

13 Bh6!

13 Kb1 is somewhat slow, so that 13...b5 14 Nd5 Qa6 is fine for Black. D.Doncevic-B.Ivkov, Cannes 1988, is an indication of why Black should then be happy in the middlegame: 15 Bh6 Bxd5 16 exd5 Bxh6 17 Qxh6 Rfe8 18 h4 c4 19 h5 Qb7 20 hxg6 fxg6 21 g5 Nxd5 22 a3 Re7 23 Rd4? Re1+ 24 Ka2 Nb4+ 0-1.

White could consider 13 a3 Rfd8 14 Bh6 (after 14 g5 Ne8 15 Nd5 Qa4! 16 c3 Bxd5 17 Qxd5 b5 Black has adequate counterplay, as in A.Shimanov-G.Nagibin, Russian Team Ch. 2008) 14...Bh8 15 Bg5 with pressure, I.Glek-P.Mijnheer, Bussum 1995.

13...Bxh6

The difficulties faced in the Larsen are also illustrated by 13...Rfd8 14 Bxg7 Kxg7 15 h4 h5 16 gxh5 Nxh5 17 Rg1 b5 18 Qg5 b4 19 Nb1, when Black was in serious trouble, L.Yurtaev-B.Gulko, Frunze 1985.

14 Qxh6 b5

A valiant attempt to get things moving – Black has to do something with the threat of White just pushing his h-pawn. After 14...Bxa2 (snatching a pawn near White's king, but wasting time) 15 h4 Be6 16 h5 Qc7 (or if 16...c4 17 hxg6 fxg6 18 g5 Nh5 then 19 Rxh5 is very strong) 17 Nb5 Qe7 18 Nxd6, White was well on top in M.Hennigan-H.Westerinen, Gausdal 1995.

15 Bxb5 Rab8

Unfortunately, Black's position doesn't quite work, though White still needs to be precise.

16 Qf4 Ne8 17 Bxe8 Rfxe8 18 Rxd6!

Stronger than 18 Qf6 Qb4 19 Ne2 Bxa2 20 Nf4 Re5 21 Nd3 Qd4 22 Nxe5 Qxb2+ 23 Kd2 dxe5, as Black would then have compensation for his small material deficit (Bauer).

18...Bxa2

Or 18...Rxb2 19 Kxb2 Qb4+ 20 Kc1 Qxc3 21 Rhd1 and, despite the complications and a slightly exposed king, White is clearly better; e.g. 21...c4 22 e5 h5 23 Qd4 Qxf3 24 gxh5 etc.

19 Qf6 Be6 20 Rhd1 Qa1+

A check is only a check. The white king can walk to safety.

21 Kd2 Qa5 22 Ke3! (Diagram 18) 22...Rxb2?

22...c4 is more resilient, but White should still win, as V.Tseshkovsky-V.Vorotnikov, Aktjubinsk 1985, would seem to indicate: 23 h4 Rxb2 24 Kf4 Rb6 25 Rd8 Rb8 26 Rxb8 Rxb8 27 h5 gxh5 28 gxh5 Re8 29 h6 Kf8 30 Rg1 Qc7+ 31 e5 1-0, since the threat of Rg8+ is decisive.

23 Rxe6! 1-0

Now it's all over, as both 23...fxe6 24 Rd7 and 23...Rxe6 24 Rd8+ are terminal.

Antoshin Variation

Game 59
□ **A.Moiseenko** ■ **M.Kazhgaleyev**
Moscow 2006

1 d4 d6 2 e4 Nf6 3 Nc3 e5 4 Nge2!? exd4 5 Nxd4 Be7 (Diagram 19)

The Antoshin Variation, which historically arises via 1 e4 e5 2 Nf3 d6 3 d4 exd4 4 Nxd4 Nf6 5 Nc3 Be7.

6 Be2

This move, aiming for natural development, is the most popular, but perhaps not the most challenging one at White's disposal. In fact he has a wide choice here:

a) 6 Bf4 (aiming to castle long) 6...0-0 7 Qd2 Nc6 8 0-0-0; e.g. 8...Nxd4 9 Qxd4 Be6 10 f3 Nd7 11 Qe3 (after 11 Nd5 Bxd5 12 Qxd5 Bf6 Black is very solid, although White has a nominal edge due to the bishop pair) 11...Bf6 12 g4 Qe7 13 h4 Be5 with a reasonable position for Black, K.Kulaots-M.Kazhgaleyev, Dresden Olympiad 2008.

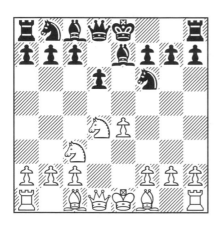

Diagram 19 (W)

The Antoshin Variation

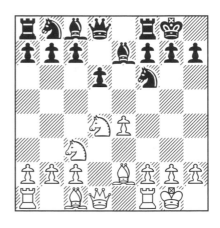

Diagram 20 (B)

A standard continuation

b) 6 g3 (to fianchetto his king's bishop) 6...d5 7 e5 Ng4 8 Bg2 and then:

b1) 8...Nxe5 9 Qe2 Nec6 10 Be3 Nxd4 11 Bxd4 0-0 12 Nxd5 Bb4+ (12...Bd6 13 0-0-0 Nc6 14 Bc3 Bf5 15 Qb5 left White with pressure in C.Lutz-J.Hickl, German League 2009) 13 Nxb4 Qxd4 14 c3 Qd8 15 Rd1 Nd7 16 0-0 c6 was K.Landa-D.Fridman, Dutch Team Ch. 2005, and now with 17 Rfe1! Bauer emphasizes that White is still the more active.

b2) 8...c6!? was recommended by Bauer; e.g. 9 f4 Qb6!? or 9...c5!? with decent chances for counterplay. Instead, 9...Nh6 10 0-0 Qc7 was too passive and after 11 f5! Qxe5 12 Bxh6 Black was already in trouble in M.Carlsen-E.Bacrot, World Blitz Ch., Moscow 2007.

c) 6 Bc4 (placing the bishop on its most active square) 6...0-0 7 0-0 a6 8 a4 Nxe4 (aiming to eliminate White's centre, which is in contrast to 8...Nc6 9 Re1 Nb4 10 Nd5 Nbxd5 11 exd5 Ng4 12 h3 Ne5 13 Bb3 Bf6 14 Be3 Re8, where White maintained a slight edge due to his extra space, E.Dervishi-G.Wall, Genoa 1999) 9 Nxe4 d5 10 Bd3 dxe4 11 Bxe4 Bf6 frees Black from the bind, but 12 Be3 Nd7 13 c3 Re8 14

Qc2 g6 15 Rfe1 Bg7 16 Rad1 c5 17 Ne2 Qc7 still left White with the more active pieces and thus a slight pull in L.Yudasin-M.Adams, Dos Hermanas 1993.

Even if Black cannot fully equalize in these lines, his disadvantage is deemed to be manageable, which explains the popularity of the Antoshin.

6...0-0 7 0-0 (Diagram 20) 7...Re8

Here the ambitious 7...c5!? is plausible, gaining space while pushing the white knight from the influential d4-square. The cost is having to live with a backward d-pawn, but evidence suggests that Black can get away with this daring idea; e.g. 8 Nb3 Nc6 9 Be3 (alternatives include 9 Bf4 Be6 10 Bg3 d5 11 e5 Ne8 12 Bf3 Nc7 13 Ne2 Qd7 14 Re1 Rad8 15 Nf4 Bf5, R.Zelcic-M.Tratar, Salzburg 2004; and 9 f4 a5 10 a4 Nb4 11 Bf3 Qb6 12 Nb5 Be6, T.Sakelsek-M.Sebenik, Slovenian Ch., Maribor 2004) 9...a5 10 Nc1 Re8 11 Bb5 Be6 12 Nd3 Qb6 13 a4 Red8 14 Nf4 Nd4, I.Smirin-H.Stevic, Croatian Team Ch. 2004, and in each case Black obtained a satisfactory position.

Another idea is the 'freeing' 7...d5, though here after 8 exd5 Nxd5 9 Nxd5 Qxd5 10 Bf3 Qc4 11 c3 Bf6 12 Bf4 White can count on a small edge, V.Ivanov-E.Egorov, Voronezh 2001.

8 Re1

8 f4 has been played more often, but after 8...Bf8 9 Bf3 c5! White has been unable to demonstrate a convincing way to gain an advantage; for example, 10 Nde2 Nc6 11 h3 Bd7 12 Be3 b5!? and Black was happy enough in K.Lahno-R.Tischbierek, Stepanakert 2005.

8...Bf8 9 Bf1 Nbd7 10 Bg5

If White develops more slowly with 10 b3 Nc5 11 f3, Black might be induced to counter with 11...d5; e.g. 12 exd5 (or 12 e5 Nfd7 13 f4 c6 14 Bb2 Ne6 15 Nxe6 Rxe6 16 Kh1 Rh6 17 Qf3 Nc5 18 f5 Qh4 with complications, Wang Hao-B.Predojevic, Calvia Olympiad 2004) 12...Rxe1 13 Qxe1 Nxd5 14 Nxd5 Qxd5 15 Bb2 Bd7 16 Rd1 Qh5 17 Ne2 Bd6 and Black had equalized, M.Adams-E.Bacrot, Internet 2003.

10...h6

Or 10...c6 11 Qd2 Ne5 12 f3 h6 13 Bh4 Ng6 14 Bf2 and Black equalized again with 14...d5 in V.Anand-E.Bacrot, Mainz (rapid) 2007.

11 Bh4 c6 12 a4 (Diagram 21)

12 Qd2 Ne5 13 h3 Ng6 14 Bg3 Qb6 15 Na4 Qc7 16 Nc3 Qb6 with a draw by repetition, M.Perunovic-V.Nevednichy, Serbian Team Ch. 2003, was rather uninspiring, but it does show the problems White has to keep any sort of an edge.

12...Ne5!?

Black also has a good score with the prudent 12...a5, which prevents White from gaining space with a4-a5, as well as the knight from manoeuvring via a4; e.g. 13 Bc4 g6!? 14 Ba2 Bg7 15 Qd2 Qb6 16 Nf3 g5!? 17 Bg3 Ne5 18 Nxe5 dxe5 19 Nd1 Bf8 and White was never able to make use of the f5-square, D.Stojanovic-M.Kobalia, Bosnian Team Ch. 2002.

13 a5 a6 14 h3 Bd7

In I.Smirin-T.Gelashvili, Athens 2008, Black played ambitiously with 14...Ng6 15 Bg3 h5!? 16 Qd2 h4 17 Bh2 Nh5 18 Na4 Qf6 19 Nb6 Rb8 20 Ra3 Ne5 21 Be2 Qg6 22 Re3 Nf6 23 Bf1 c5 24 Nb3 Nxe4 and the outcome was far from clear, although White eventually won.

15 Qd2 Ng6 16 Bg3 Nh5 17 Bh2 Qf6 18 Na4 Rad8 19 Nb6 Nhf4

Now White obtains the potential long-term advantage of the bishop pair. In return Black's active knights and solid position offer him a certain security, but he will have to be vigilant about his lack of space.

20 Nxd7 Rxd7 21 Qc3 d5! (Diagram 22)

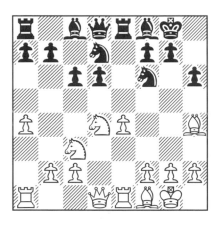 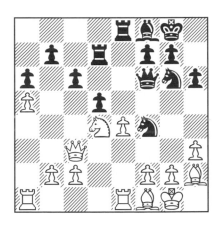

Diagram 21 (B)	**Diagram 22 (W)**
Position after 12 a4	Liberating Black's position

This liberates Black's position without really enabling White's bishops to become dangerous.

22 exd5 Nxd5 23 Qc4 Rxe1 24 Rxe1 Ndf4 25 Nb3 Rd5 26 Re8 Re5 27 Rxe5

I wonder what Murtas intended after 27 Rb8 Re1 28 Rxb7. For instance, 28...Nxg2 is well met by 29 Rxf7! Qxf7 30 Kxg2, and 28...Ne2+ by 29 Qxe2 Rxe2 30 Bxe2 Qxb2 31 Bxa6 Qxc2 32 Bf1. So perhaps he would just have played 28...Bd6!? to enhance his initiative on the kingside.

27...Qxe5 28 Qd4 Ne2+ 29 Bxe2 Qxe2 30 Qd2 Qe4 31 Bg3 h5!

The centralized queen, combined with pushing the h-pawn, gives Black slight pressure.

32 Qd3 Qe1+

Kazhgaleyev obviously wants more than 32...Qxd3, splitting White's pawns but offering limited winning chances.

33 Qf1 Qe6 34 Qd1 h4 35 Bc7 Qe7 36 Bb6

I prefer 36 Bb8!?, staying on the b8-h2 diagonal.

36...Qe4 37 Nc5

After 37 Bc7 Nf4 38 Bxf4 Qxf4 39 Qd2 Qe5, Black threatens ...Bd6.

37...Bxc5 38 Bxc5 f6 (Diagram 23)

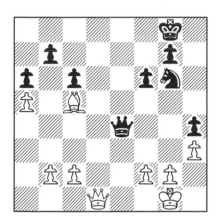

Diagram 23 (W)

Threatening ...Nf4

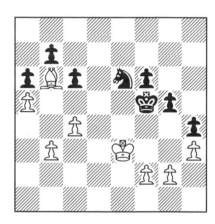

Diagram 24 (B)

Now Black can win

The immediate 38...Nf4?! would fail to 39 Qd8+ Kh7 40 Qxh4+, but now ...Nf4 really is threatened.

39 Be3 Ne7!?

Rather than 39...Ne5 40 b3, when Black cannot do very much and a draw would be likely.

40 Qd8+ Kh7 41 Qe8!

The pin keeps Black restrained.

41...Qe5 42 c4!? Ng6 43 Qxe5 Nxe5 44 b3

The bishop is at least equal to the knight in the ending, as there is likely to be action on both fronts and Black's pawns are more vulnerable.

44...Kg6 45 Kf1 Kf5 46 Ke2 g5 47 Bc5 Ng6

If 47...Ke4 48 Be7 Nd7 49 Bd8 Kd4 50 Kd2 and Black will have to give ground.

48 Kf3 Nf4 49 Bb6?!

This is inaccurate, whereas after 49 Bd6! Black would have to be careful; e.g. 49...Nd3 50 Ke3 Ne1 51 g4+! or 49...Ne6 50 Ke3 Ng7 51 g4+! with some winning chances for White.

49...Ne6 50 Ke3? (Diagram 24)

50 Be3 was absolutely necessary, when White shouldn't be worse. But now Kazhgaleyev has some inspiration...

50...g4! 51 hxg4+ Kxg4

Suddenly things are happening and White's bishop is not at hand to help out.

52 Ke2 f5 53 Kf1 c5

Further humiliation for the bishop.

54 Kg1 f4 55 Kh2 f3

Creating an outside passed pawn, which will cost White time and ultimately the game.

56 gxf3+ Kxf3 57 Kh3 Kxf2 58 Kxh4 Ke3 59 Kg4 Ke4 60 Ba7 Nd4 61 Bxc5 Nxb3 62 Bb6 Kd3 63 c5 Kc4 64 Kf5 Kb5 65 Ke6 Nxa5 66 Kd6 Nb3 67 Kd5 a5 0-1

Summary

I consider the main line of the Hanham to be quite difficult for both sides, but an error by Black has more serious consequences. It may be that the Lion move order gives him an easier time and, indeed, at a high level the Open Games move order has been superseded by that of the Lion, so this version of the 'Philidor' is now almost a hybrid system.

The best line arising uniquely from the Philidor move order is the Antoshin Variation, where, despite having a quiet bishop on e7, Black doesn't seem to have any great difficulty in obtaining a playable game.

Chapter Twelve
Petroff's Defence

Introduction

1 e4 e5 2 Nf3 Nf6 (Diagram 1)

 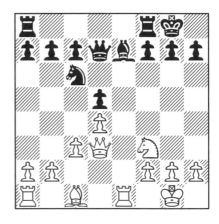

Diagram 1 (W)

Petroff's Defence

Diagram 2 (W)

A very dull position

In Petroff's Defence Black develops his king's knight and threatens the white e-pawn, while leaving his own to its fate. Black thus offers the exchange of e-pawns, something that frequently occurs throughout this chapter. One of the reasons many club players spurn this defence is the assumption that, once these pawns come off, it will be hard to generate winning chances with either colour.

Strong GMs, however, are attracted to its erstwhile solidity and the Petroff has become very popular in recent years. White's opening advantage with a symmetric pawn structure often comes down to a mere tempo in development, a temporary plus that requires vigorous action if it is to lead to anything concrete. So in fact the opening has paradoxically become very sharp, even double-edged, in recent years – at least when White tries the critical lines.

If you are tempted to follow the elite and switch to the Petroff, I should warn you that winning with Black is a problematic exercise if White doesn't do anything special. A typical example is...

3 Nxe5 d6 4 Nf3 Nxe4

...and now the distinctly dry continuation 5 Qe2 Qe7 (forced, as otherwise Black has e-file problems) 6 d3 Nf6 7 Bg5 Qxe2+ 8 Bxe2 Be7 9 Nc3 c6. There are close to a thousand games with this position in the database and three quarters of them ended in draws, most of them within 10 more moves (as, for example, in Game 60).

Also, you may not know it, but the first head-to-head meeting between Kasparov and Karpov (USSR Team Ch. 1981) was in fact a Petroff. The opening in that game won't exactly be an inspiration to those who seek sharp action either...

5 d4 Be7 6 Bd3 d5 7 0-0 Nc6 8 Re1 Bf5

8...Bg4 is more usual, as in Games 66 and 67.

9 Nbd2 Nxd2 10 Qxd2 Bxd3 11 Qxd3 0-0 12 c3 Qd7 (Diagram 2)

...with a position that one could describe as about as exciting as an Exchange French, although Kasparov, playing White, actually got close to winning.

 NOTE: The Petroff is a practical option if your first priority is not to lose, or against certain opponents who may get frustrated, but not when you need to win at all cost!

Strategy

White obtains a slight lead in development, but before this fizzles out, he needs to create some pressure. In lines where both d2-d4 and ...d7-d5 have been played, White often aims to do this with an early c2-c4. Another trend is to challenge a black knight on e4 with an early Nb1-c3, allowing doubled pawns so as to open lines and exploit his more active pieces to seek an edge.

Black's primary strategy is to take the sting out of White's opening advantage. Later Black usually gets some choice as to his piece deployment and can sometimes provoke complications, but generally White dictates the pace.

Theoretical

At the higher echelons the Petroff has become very theoretical, but club players tend to rely on rudimentary knowledge and generally avoid the critical lines.

We start with the sort of game that many associate with the Petroff...

Game 60
□ **J.Timman** ■ **L.Bruzon Bautista**
5th matchgame, Curaçao 2005

---

1 e4 e5 2 Nf3 Nf6 3 Nxe5

The most common move. Instead, 3 d4 is examined in the next section below, while 3 Nc3 Nf6 transposes to the Four Knights Game in Chapter Four (as indeed occurred in Game 27).

3...d6

Some players have experimented with 3...Nxe4?!, but in that case 4 Qe2! is both required and strong, as after 4...Qe7 5 Qxe4 d6 6 d4 dxe5 7 dxe5 Nc6 8 Bb5 Black struggles to equalize.

4 Nf3 Nxe4 5 Qe2 (Diagram 3)

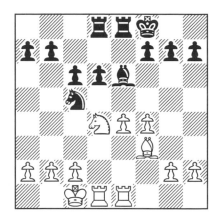

Diagram 3 (B)

Another boring variation

Diagram 4 (W)

The game is very equal

When an inexperienced player faces the Petroff for the first time, this modest move often appears on the board. White can't really expect much out of the opening, but also there is little risk of anything going wrong.

The more testing lines with 5 Nc3 and 5 d4 are examined in Games 63-68.

5...Qe7 6 d3 Nf6

There is no particular tension, nor any pawn breaks in view, and piece play by itself can rarely make much headway.

7 Bg5

White tried another plan in F.Vallejo Pons-V.Ivanchuk, Linares/Morelia 2006: 7 Nc3 Qxe2+ 8 Bxe2 Be7 9 0-0 0-0 10 Nd4!? Nbd7 11 Bf4 Ne5 12 h3 Bd7 13 Rae1 Rfe8 14 Bd1 Nc6, but had no advantage to show for it.

7...Qxe2+ 8 Bxe2 Be7 9 Nc3 c6 10 Ne4

The immediate 10 0-0-0 is the most common move here, though the percentage of draws is just as high! Nevertheless, in an earlier game Timman was able to obtain some advantage after an imprecision from his opponent: 10...Na6 11 Rhe1 Nc7 12 Ne4 Nxe4 13 dxe4 Bxg5+ 14 Nxg5 f6?! (the correct move is 14...Ke7, which has achieved 40 draws in 43 outings in my database; e.g. 15 f4 Ne6 16 Nxe6 Bxe6 with solid equality) 15 Nf3 Ke7 16 Nd4 Be6 17 f4 Rad8 18 Bf3 Rhe8 19 Rd2 Kf8 20 Red1 Bf7 21 Nf5 d5 22 c4 with some pressure, leading to a rare win for White in J.Timman-J.Piket, Wijk aan Zee 1995.

10...Nbd7 11 0-0-0 Nxe4 12 dxe4 Nc5

The main difference to the previous note is that Black's knight is on c5, which frankly doesn't change the nature of the position very much.

13 Bxe7 Kxe7 14 Rhe1 Be6 15 Nd4 Rad8

Black could probably snatch the pawn here – 15...Nxe4 16 Bh5 (or 16 Bg4 Bxg4 17 Rxe4+ Be6 18 Nf5+ Kf6 19 Nxd6 Bd5) 16...d5 17 f3 Nc5 18 b4 Nd7 19 Bxf7 Kxf7 20 Rxe6 Rhe8 – but Bruzon isn't tempted. Why take any unnecessary risks on the way to equalizing?

16 f4 Rhe8 17 Bf3 Kf8 (Diagram 4) 18 e5

Capturing on e6 would give White the theoretical advantage of bishop vs. knight, but after 18 Nxe6+ Nxe6 19 g3 a5! the noble steed is assured access to c5, from which point it can press down on e4. White cannot create any pressure when his e-pawn requires constant attention.

18...Bc8 19 Nb3 Nxb3+ ½-½

20 axb3 dxe5 21 Rxd8 Rxd8 22 Rxe5 is as equal as it can get!

White plays 3 d4

Game 61
☐ V.Ivanchuk ■ G.Kamsky
Linares 1994

1 e4 e5 2 Nf3 Nf6 3 d4 exd4!? (Diagram 5)

The main line with 3...Nxe4 is covered in the next game.

4 e5

Here 4 Bc4!? transposes to Urusov's Gambit, mentioned at the beginning of Chapter Six. My advice there is for Black to reply 4...Nc6, returning to the Two Knights Defence in Chapter Two.

4...Ne4 5 Qxd4 d5 6 exd6 Nxd6 7 Nc3

The symmetrical structure may suit Black in his quest to equalize, but White retains a slight lead in development and, in particular, following...

7...Nc6 8 Qf4 (Diagram 6)

Diagram 5 (W)

Black plays 3...exd4!?

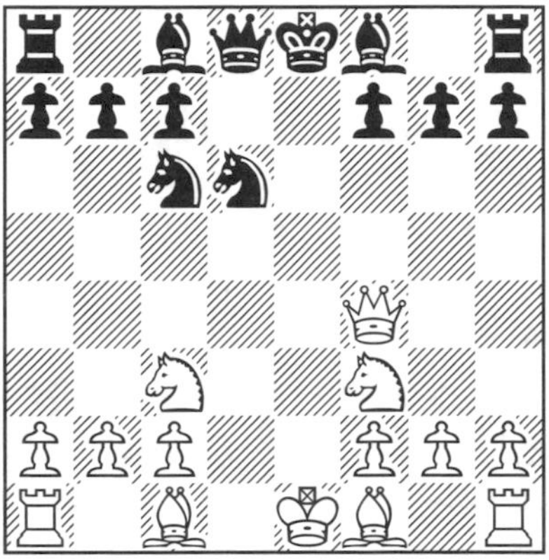

Diagram 6 (B)

An active queen

...his queen takes up an active posting. It's an unusual square for a royal lady so early in the game, but one that denies her counterpart a positive role for the time being.

8...g6

Black has a couple of other tries here:

a) 8...Nf5 (spending a valuable tempo, but planning to regain it by directing the bishop to d6) 9 Bb5 Bd6 10 Qe4+ Qe7 11 0-0 0-0 12 Re1 Qxe4 13 Nxe4 Ne5 14 Nxe5 Bxe5 15 Ng5 (Black is denied the time to get himself fully organized) 15...Bf6 16 c3 Nd6 17 Bd3 g6 18 Bf4 Bd7 19 Bxd6 cxd6 20 Ne4 Be7 with a persistent edge for White, R.Zelcic-I.Leventic, Croatian Team Ch. 2006.

b) 8...Bf5 9 Bb5! (the most challenging) 9...Qe7+ 10 Be3 Nxb5 11 Nxb5 Qb4+ (trading off White's more active queen) 12 Qxb4 Bxb4+ 13 c3 and despite the simplification White has a good score from here; e.g. 13...Bd6 14 Nxd6+ cxd6 15 0-0-0 Be6 16 b3 d5 17 Rhe1 with a small but evident pull for White, M.Rudolf-V.Tichy, Prague 2005.

9 Bd2

It's a moot point whether White should place the bishop on d2 or e3. Here's an example of the latter: 9 Be3 Bg7 10 0-0-0 0-0 11 h4 h6 12 Bc5 Be6 13 Bb5 Qf6 14 Qxf6 Bxf6 15 Bxc6 bxc6 16 Bd4 with an edge in J.Tomczak-M.Mingachev, World Junior Ch., Belfort 2005.

9...Qe7+

Black's other principal plan involves castling short, when the resulting positions are reminiscent of 4...g6 versus the Centre Game (see Chapter Nine); i.e. after 9...Bg7 10 0-0-0 and then:

a) 10...Be6 11 Ng5 (if 11 Bd3 0-0 12 h4 Qf6 13 Qh2 Ne5 and Black was fine in I.Boleslavsky-V.Alatortsev, USSR Ch., Moscow 1945) 11...0-0 12 Nxe6 fxe6 13 Qg4 with a small pull for White, J.Dubiel-M.Bartosik, Bytom 1994.

b) 10...0-0 11 h4 h6 (11...Qf6?! 12 Qxf6 Bxf6 13 Nd5 Bd8 14 Bh6 Re8 15 Bg5 Be6 16 Bxd8 Bxd5 17 Bxc7 Bxf3 18 gxf3 Nf5 19 Bd3 and White had won a pawn, V.Anand-Zoefel/Boehme, Frankfurt simul 1994) 12 Nd5 Be6 13 Bc3 Bxd5 14 Rxd5 and again Black hasn't quite equalized, E.Gufeld-B.Rabar, Moscow 1961.

10 Be2 Be6 11 0-0-0 Bg7 (Diagram 7)

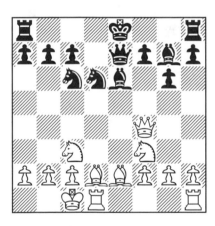

Diagram 7 (W)

Position after 11...Bg7

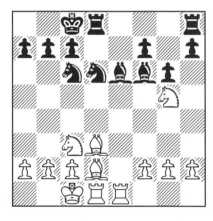

Diagram 8 (B)

White's best chance

12 Rhe1

In a battle between two legends, E.Geller-V.Smyslov, Moscow 1991, the preliminary moves 12 h4 h6 were played before 13 Rhe1. This had favourable consequences for White, as after 13...0-0-0 14 Bd3 Qf6 15 Qxf6 Bxf6 he was able to play 16 Bxg6! Rhg8 17 h5 Bg4 (17...Bxc3 18 Bxc3 Bxa2 19 Bd3 Be6 was possible, but ceding the bishop pair is a concession) 18 Bh7 Rh8 19 Bd3 Bxh5 20 Be2 Bg6 21 Nd5 Bg7 22 Bc3 Bxc3 23 Nxc3 with a small edge due to Black's ragged structure.

12...0-0-0 13 Bd3

In N.Sousa-A.Pinheiro, Portuguese Ch., Barreiro 2000, White won a pawn after 13 Qa4 h6 14 Nb5 Kb8 15 Be3 Nxb5? 16 Bxb5 Qb4 17 Bxa7+!, but 15...Nc8! would have neutralized his aggression.

Alternatively, 13 Ng5 Be5 14 Qa4 (again this move) 14...Bxc3 15 bxc3 Bd7 16 Bf3 Qf6 was seen in V.Stika-M.Volf, correspondence 2003, when *ECO* gives 17 Bxc6 Bxc6 18 Qxa7 and claims an edge for White, although the further 18...b6 19 f3 Bb7 20 Qa4 h6 looks pretty equal to me.

13...Qf6 14 Qxf6

Here 14 Ng5 can be met by 14...Bf5 15 Bxf5+ Nxf5 with equality.

14...Bxf6 15 Bg5

In my opinion 15 Ng5! **(Diagram 8)** offers the best chance of an edge; for example:

a) 15...Bc4 (the computer move) is risky: 16 Bxc4 Nxc4 17 Nxf7 Rxd2 18 Nxh8 Rxd1+ 19 Nxd1 Nd6 20 Nxg6 hxg6 21 Re6 and White is better.

b) 15...Bd7 (the human move) is less compromising: 16 Nce4 Nxe4 17 Nxe4 Be7 (if 17...Bg7 18 Bg5 Rde8 19 Bf6 Bxf6 20 Nxf6 Rxe1 21 Rxe1 Be6 22 a3 yields continuing pressure) 18 Bc3 f5 19 Nf6 Rhf8 20 Nxd7 Rxd7 21 Bc4 and the bishop pair ensures that White has something to work with.

15...Bxc3! 16 Bxd8 Bxe1 17 Bf6 Re8 18 Nxe1 Nb4

As is often the case, 18...Bxa2?? would be foolhardy due to 19 b3 trapping the bishop.

19 a3 Nxd3+ 20 Nxd3 Bf5 (Diagram 9)

Given the presence of opposite-coloured bishops, Black's adequate development and lack of weaknesses, a draw looks on the cards already.

21 Nf4 Ne4 22 Bd4 b6 23 f3 Nd6 24 b3 h5 25 a4 Kb7 26 Bf2 Bd7 27 Re1 Rxe1+ 28 Bxe1 Nf5 29 Kd2 a6 30 Bf2 a5 31 Nd5 Be6 32 Nf4 Bd7 33 Nd5 Be6 34 Nf4 Bd7 ½-½

It was noticeable to me that in just about all the game references (in the notes above) Black was able to hold his slightly worse endgames.

NOTE: It is typical of the quieter lines of the Petroff that Black doesn't fully equalize, but is not really in danger of losing either!

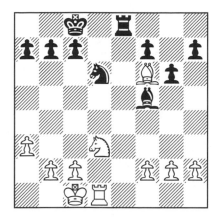

Diagram 9 (W)

A draw is on the cards

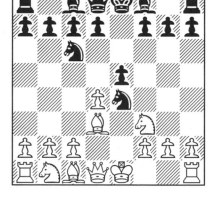

Diagram 10 (W)

Leaving the knight en prise

Game 62
□ A.Shirov ■ M.Adams
6th matchgame, Elista 2007

---

1 e4 e5 2 Nf3 Nf6 3 d4 Nxe4 4 Bd3 d5

I was actually present when Jakob Murey uncorked the remarkable 4...Nc6!? **(Diagram 10)** against Jan Timman in 1993.

As in that game, after 5 Bxe4 d5 6 Bg5 Qd7 7 Bd3 Black regains his piece with 7...e4, when his position isn't that bad. White's strongest line hasn't yet become clear, though he scores better with other fifth moves, such as 5 dxe5 and then:

a) 5...Nc5 6 Nc3 Nxd3+ (6...d5!) 7 Qxd3 d6 8 Bf4 dxe5 9 Nxe5 Qxd3?! 10 Nxd3 Bd6 11 Nb5! with a clear advantage, S.Rublevsky-V.Iordachescu, FIDE World Ch., Tripoli 2004.

b) 5...d5 6 exd6 (otherwise 6 0-0 transposes to 4...d5 5 dxe5 Nc6!? – see the note to Black's fifth move) 6...Nxd6 7 Nc3 Be7 8 Bf4 Be6 9 Qd2 Qd7 10 0-0-0 0-0-0 11 Qe3 Qe8 12 Nd4 Bf6 13 Nxe6 Qxe6 14 Qxe6+ fxe6 15 Ne4, when the two bishops and weak e6-pawn also gave White an edge, B.Socko-L.Kritz, German League 2005.

Although 4...Nc6 isn't bad (it scores about the same percentage as the main line) and can indeed transpose, 4...d5 is played about six times more often.

5 dxe5

Historically, 5 Nxe5 **(Diagram 11)** has been the usual move here (and by a ratio of 9:1), but the text is becoming increasingly popular, especially at a higher level. Despite the 'French Defence, Exchange Variation' pawn structure, 5 Nxe5 actually leads to some very forcing lines. The point is that if White is somewhat pedestrian with his development, then his half-tempo advantage will disappear, so White has to play the forcing lines in order to seek any advantage.

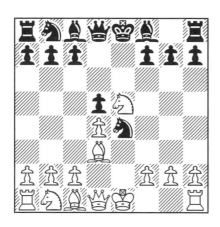

Diagram 11 (B)	**Diagram 12 (W)**
White plays 5 Nxe5	Slow play won't suffice

In response Black can choose between:

a) 5...Bd6 6 0-0 0-0 7 c4 Bxe5 (this whole line is under a cloud) 8 dxe5 Nc6 9 cxd5 Qxd5 10 Qc2 Nb4 11 Bxe4 Nxc2 12 Bxd5 Bf5 13 g4 Bxg4 14 Be4 Nxa1 15 Bf4 f5 16 Bd5+ Kh8 17 Rc1 c6 (critical; if 17...Rad8 18 Nc3 c6 19 Bg2 h6 20 h4 and White consolidated his advantage, M.Parligras-I.Karkanaque, Sozina 2004) 18 Bg2 Rfd8 19 Nd2 Rxd2 20 Bxd2 Rd8 21 Bc3 Rd1+ 22 Rxd1 Bxd1 23 Bf1! Kg8 24 Bc4+ Kf8 25 b4! Nc2 26 Bb3 seems to be better for White, A.Voyna-B.Rumiancevas, correspondence 1995.

b) 5...Nd7 (the best move) 6 Nxd7 Bxd7 7 0-0 Bd6 and now:

b1) 8 Qh5 Qf6!? (more solid is 8...Nf6 9 Re1+ Kf8 10 Qe2 Ng4 11 h3 Qh4 12 Qf3 Nf6 13 Nc3 c6 14 Ne2 Ne8 15 Bf4 Qf6 16 Bxd6+ Nxd6 17 Qxf6 gxf6 and Black held his slightly inferior ending, F.Caruana-A.Motylev, European Ch., Plovdiv 2008) 9 Nc3

Qxd4 10 Be3 (or 10 Nxd5 Bc6 11 Ne3 g6 with equality, *Deep Fritz*-V.Kramnik, 4th matchgame, Bonn 2006) 10...Qe5 11 Qxe5+ Bxe5 12 Nxd5 Nf6 13 Rae1 Nxd5 14 Bd2 f6 15 f4 Nxf4 16 Bxf4 0-0 led to a quick draw in M.Palac-A.Saric, Zagreb 2008.

b2) 8 c4 c6 9 cxd5 cxd5 **(Diagram 12)**.

White has struggled to obtain anything significant from this position by slow means and so has found it necessary to grab the d-pawn; e.g. 10 Qh5 (or 10 Nc3 Nxc3 11 bxc3 0-0 12 Qh5 g6 13 Qxd5 Qc7 14 Qf3 Qxc3 15 Bh6 Rfe8 16 Qf6 Bf8 17 Bxf8 Rxf8 18 Be4 Bc6 19 Rac1 Qb4 20 Bxc6 bxc6 21 Rxc6 Rad8 22 Rd1 Qa4 and a draw was soon agreed in S.Rublevsky-V.Kramnik, Russian Ch., Moscow 2005) 10...0-0 11 Qxd5 Bc6 12 Qh5 g6 13 Qh3 Ng5 14 Qg4 Ne6 15 Bh6 Re8 16 Nc3 Nxd4 17 Rad1 Be5 18 f4 f5 19 Qg3 Bf6 and Black had a comfortable game, M.Oleksienko-I.Hera, European Ch., Dresden 2007.

5...Be7

Of the three main moves this has been the least successful recently. The other two options are:

a) 5...Nc5 6 0-0 Be7 **(Diagram 13)** (6...Nxd3 seems natural, but this allows White to get his c2-c4 lever in rather easily; e.g. 7 Qxd3 Be7 8 Rd1 c6 9 c4 dxc4 10 Qc2 Qc7 11 Nbd2 0-0 12 Nxc4 Bg4, D.Pavasovic-M.Ilincic, Hungarian Team Ch. 2007, and now 13 Qe4 gives White a slight pull), when the question to the d3-bishop is 'should he stay or should he go?':

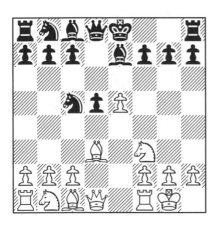

Diagram 13 (W)

Decision time for the d3-bishop

Diagram 14 (B)

Decision time for the f8-bishop

a1) 7 Nc3 (stay) 7...Nxd3 8 Qxd3 c6 9 Nd4 0-0 10 f4 f5 (limiting the potential for

White's kingside majority to expand) 11 Nb3 (after 11 Rd1 Na6 12 Nb3 Nc7 13 Be3, Z.Hracek-A.Motylev, European Ch., Dresden 2007, Black should play 13...b6!) 11...Na6 12 Be3 Nc7 13 Ne2 b6 14 Nbd4 Ba6 15 Qd2 Qe8 16 c3 c5 and Black wasn't worse, D.Navara-V.Kramnik, 2nd matchgame, Prague (rapid) 2008.

a2) 7 Be2 (go) 7...0-0 8 Be3 Nc6 9 Nc3 Be6 10 Nb5 Nd7 11 Bf4 a6 12 Nbd4 Nxd4 13 Nxd4 c5 14 Nxe6 fxe6 15 Bg3 c4 16 Bg4 Nc5 17 b4 cxb3 18 axb3 a5 with equality, A.Shirov-B.Gelfand, European Club Cup, Kallithea 2008. So 5...Nc5 certainly seems to be holding up at the moment.

b) 5...Nc6 6 0-0 Bg4 7 Nc3 Nxc3 8 bxc3 **(Diagram 14)** and then:

b1) 8...Be7 (acceptable) 9 Re1 (or 9 Bf4 Qd7 10 Rb1 Nd8 11 h3 and White retained the initiative, P.Svidler-A.Karpov, San Sebastian 2009) 9...0-0 10 h3 Be6 11 Rb1 Rb8 12 Qd2 Qd7 13 Qf4 f6 14 Qg3 and White managed to keep some pressure in V.Bologan-A.Saric, Bosnian Team Ch. 2008.

b2) 8...Bc5!? (I prefer this active move) 9 Re1 (or 9 Bf4 0-0 10 h3 Bh5 11 Rb1 Rb8 12 g4 Bg6 13 Bf5 Ne7 14 Qd3 Qe8 15 Bxg6 fxg6 16 Bg3 Qa4 with counterplay, B.Predojevic-D.Fridman, Philadelphia 2007) 9...0-0 10 h3 Bh5 11 Rb1 b6!? 12 Bf5 Kh8 13 g4 Bg6 14 Bxg6 fxg6 15 Be3 Be7 16 Rb5 Rxf3!? (one of the points behind his recapture with the f-pawn) 17 Qxf3 Nxe5 18 Qg3 Nc4 and Black had enough compensation, E.Bacrot-Wang Yue, FIDE Grand Prix, Baku 2008.

6 0-0 Bg4!? (Diagram 15)

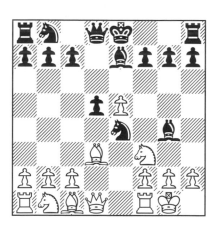

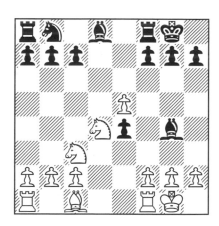

Diagram 15 (W)	**Diagram 16 (B)**
Position after 6...Bg4!?	What now for Black?

Black could consider 6...Nc6, when 7 Nc3 Nxc3 8 bxc3 Bg4 transposes to the previous note – though as I mention there, the bishop would be more active on c5.

On the other hand, after 6...0-0 White would normally try 7 c4, and then 7...Nc6, with ideas of ...Nb4, seems fine for Black. For example, 8 Bc2 (after 8 cxd5 Qxd5 9 Qc2?! Nb4 10 Bxe4 Nxc2 11 Bxd5 Nxa1, A.Garrido-R.Rodriguez, Asturias 1992, Black is better off than in the analogous 5 Nxe5 Bd6 variation, as he still has his dark-squared bishop) 8...Nb4 9 cxd5 Nxc2 10 Qxc2 Qxd5 11 Rd1 Qc6 12 Qxc6 bxc6 13 Be3 c5! (controlling the d4-square; Black shouldn't allow the white knights too much leeway) 14 Nbd2 Nxd2 15 Nxd2 Be6 16 Rdc1 Rfd8 17 Nb3 Bxb3 18 axb3 Rd5 and Black was able to hold in D.Jakovenko-P.Harikrishna, Russian Team Ch. 2008.

7 Bxe4

Giving up the 'minor exchange' leaves Black with a vulnerable pawn on e4, but it shouldn't be enough to worry him.

Instead, 7 h3 is the most testing; e.g. 7...Bh5 8 Re1 Nc6 9 Nc3 Bg6 (the consequences of 9...Nxc3 10 bxc3 can be seen in the notes above – Black doesn't have that easy a time) 10 Bd2 Nxd2 11 Qxd2 d4 12 Ne4 0-0 13 a3 Qd5 14 Qf4 Rfe8 15 Re2 Bf8 16 Ng3 and White managed to use his space to maintain an advantage and went on to win in G.Kamsky-M.Carlsen, World Chess Cup, Khanty-Mansiysk 2007.

7...dxe4 8 Qxd8+ Bxd8 9 Nd4 0-0 10 Nc3 (Diagram 16) 10...Nd7

Here 10...f6! has been suggested and may even equalize; e.g. 11 Bf4 (if 11 exf6 Bxf6 12 Be3 Rd8, or equally after 11 Nxe4 fxe5 12 Nb3 Nc6 13 f3 Bf5, Black seems to be okay) 11...fxe5 12 Bxe5 Nd7 13 Bg3 Nc5 and I can't see any advantage for White.

11 h3 Bh5 12 e6 fxe6?!

This turns out to be inferior, so Black should have opted for 12...Nc5! 13 exf7+ Bxf7, when the bishop pair compensates for the weak e-pawn.

13 Nxe6 Re8 14 Nxd8 Raxd8 15 Bg5

White retains some pressure despite the opposite-coloured bishops.

15...Nf6 16 Rfe1 (Diagram 17) 16...Bg6?!

The difference is subtle, but 16...Rd4! was a better try, as after 17 g4 Bg6 18 Rad1 Rxd1 19 Rxd1 Kf7 Black would have more chances to hold than in the game; e.g. 20 Bxf6 gxf6 21 Rd7+ (21 Nb5 can be met by 21...e3! with counterplay against White's weakened kingside) 21...Re7 22 Rxe7+ Kxe7 23 Nd5+ Kd6 24 Nxf6 Ke6 25 Ng8 e3 26 fxe3 Bxc2 27 Kf2 Kf7 28 Nh6+ Kg6 29 Ng8 Kf7 with a draw.

17 Rad1 Kf8?!

Now if 17...Rxd1 18 Rxd1 Kf7 19 Bxf6 gxf6, unlike in the previous note, 20 Nb5! would be particularly annoying.

18 Bxf6 gxf6 19 Nd5

Forking two pawns, so Black must give up something.

19...e3 20 Nxe3 c5 21 Kf1

21 g4 is probably more precise, though it doesn't change matters a great deal.

21...Rd4 22 c3 Bd3+ 23 Kg1 Rd6 24 Rd2 b5 25 Nc2 Red8 26 Red1 Ke7 27 Ne1 Be4 28 Rxd6 Rxd6 29 Rxd6 Kxd6

White's plan is to bring up his king while making the minimum of concessions with his structure. Meantime Black will try and chastise him on the queenside.

30 Kf1 Kd5 31 Ke2 Bb1 32 a3 Kc4 33 Kd2 (Diagram 18) 33...Be4?

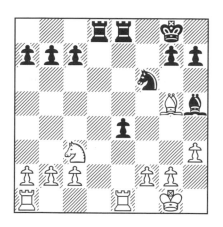

Diagram 17 (B)

White retains some pressure

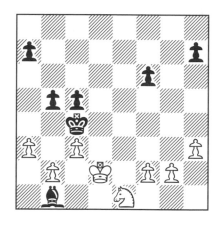

Diagram 18 (B)

All is not lost yet

Overlooking White's 35th move. It seems that, despite being a pawn down, all was perhaps not lost! There was one last chance with 33...Kb3! 34 Kc1 Bg6 35 Nf3 b4 36 Nd2+ (or 36 axb4 cxb4 37 cxb4 Kxb4) 36...Ka4 37 axb4 cxb4 38 g4 (nor does 38 c4 b3 39 c5 Kb5 40 Nxb3 Kc4 41 Nd2+ Kxc5 convince me that White can win) 38...bxc3 39 bxc3 Ka3! 40 f4 Bd3 and Black should still be able to draw, thanks to his superior piece, the long-range bishop.

34 f3 Bg6 35 b4! Kb3

Otherwise 35...cxb4 36 axb4 would just lead to a technical win, as Black has no targets for counterplay.

36 bxc5 Kxa3 37 c6 Ka4 38 g4 Be8 39 c7 Bd7 40 Nd3 Ka5 41 Nc5 Bc8 42 Ne4 Kb6 43 Nxf6 Kxc7 44 Nxh7 Kd6 45 h4 a5 46 h5 Ke7 47 Ng5 Bb7 48 h6 Kf6 49 f4 1-0

Adams was in no mood to continue the agony; 49...Bd5 50 f5 Bc4 51 h7 Kg7 52 f6+ Kh8 53 f7 Bxf7 54 Nxf7+ Kxh7 55 Nd6 is clear enough.

Nimzowitsch Attack

Game 63
□ P.Leko ■ V.Kramnik
Wijk aan Zee 2008

1 e4 e5 2 Nf3 Nf6 3 Nxe5 d6 4 Nf3 Nxe4 5 Nc3 (Diagram 19)

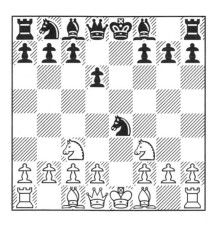

Diagram 19 (B)

The Nimzowitsch Attack

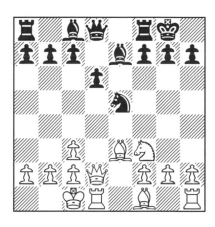

Diagram 20 (W)

The 7 Be3 variation

This popular line is known as the Nimzowitsch Attack. White aims to accelerate his development and castle queenside, and then will rely largely on piece play to create problems for his opponent.

5...Nxc3 6 dxc3 Be7 7 Bf4

7 Be3 is a major alternative, whereupon Black's knight heads for e5 rather than c5; i.e. 7...Nd7 8 Qd2 Ne5 9 0-0-0 0-0 **(Diagram 20)** (considered best, as after 9...Nxf3 10 gxf3 White's damaged structure is less of an issue than his ability to create pressure along the open lines; e.g. 10...Be6 11 Rg1 Bf6 12 Bd4 Kf8 13 Be3! – coming back now that Black's king gets in the way of his rooks – 13...a5 14 a4 b6 15 Bd3 Rb8 16 b3 d5 17 f4 Qd6 18 Rg3 and Black's pieces continue to lack co-ordination, A.Motylev-V.Bologan, Moscow 2006), and then:

a) 10 Nd4 can be countered in gambit-style by 10...c5! 11 Nb5 Be6 12 Nxd6 Qb6 13 b4 Rad8! (improving on the older 13...Bxd6 14 Qxd6 Qxd6 15 Rxd6 cxb4 16 cxb4 Bxa2 which offers White a small pull) 14 Bxc5 Qc7 15 Nb5 Qc6 with excellent play, K.Landa-V.Kosyrev, Internet 2005.

b) 10 h4!? Bg4 11 Be2 Qc8 (the start of an unusual adventure) 12 h5 Re8 13 Nxe5 dxe5 14 Bxg4 Qxg4 15 Qd5 Qa4 16 Kb1 Bd6 17 c4 b6 18 g4 Qd7 19 Qe4 Qe6 and Black has everything covered, D.Jakovenko-A.Shirov, Moscow 2007.

c) 10 Kb1 b6 (or 10...Nxf3 11 gxf3 Bf5 12 h4 Qd7 13 h5 Bf6 14 h6 g6 15 Bd4 Qd8 16 Rg1 c5 and White couldn't break through, A.David-A.Brun, European Club Cup, Kallithea 2008) 11 Nd4 Bb7 12 h3 a6 13 f4 Nd7 14 Nf5 Re8 15 Rg1 Nc5 proved to be equal in M.Adams-E.Bacrot, Wijk aan Zee 2006.

7...0-0

In Game 64 Black organizes his development differently: 7...Nc6 8 Qd2 Be6, with the plan of castling long.

8 Qd2 Nd7 9 0-0-0 Nc5 (Diagram 21)

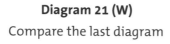

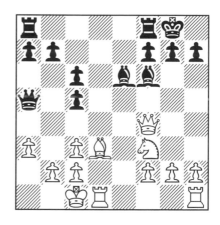

Diagram 21 (W)	Diagram 22 (W)
Compare the last diagram	White has some chances

10 Be3

Despite many recent high-level games it isn't yet evident which is White's best:

a) 10 Nd4 Re8 11 f3 Ne6 12 Be3 Bg5 13 f4 Nxd4 14 fxg5 Nc6 15 h4 Bg4 16 Re1 Qd7 seemed fine for Black in M.Adams-V.Kramnik, Wijk aan Zee 2008.

b) 10 h4 Bf6 (rather than 10...c6 11 Bxd6 Qxd6 12 Qxd6 Bxd6 13 Rxd6 Ne4 14 Rd4 Nxf2 15 Rg1 Ng4 16 a4 Be6 17 Ng5 Bf5 18 Bd3 Bxd3 19 cxd3 Nf6 and White somehow used his extra space to squeeze out a win, Z.Efimenko-A.Khalifman, Russian Team Ch. 2006) 11 Ng5 h6 12 f3 (or 12 Bd3 Nxd3+ 13 Qxd3 g6 14 Nf3, V.Topalov-E.Bacrot, Wijk aan Zee 2006, when 14...Bg7 15 Qd2 Kh7 keeps the kingside solid enough) 12...Rb8 13 g4 b5 14 Bd3 Re8 was double-edged in S.Rublevsky-A.Shirov, Russian Team Ch. 2006.

c) 10 Kb1 Re8 11 Be3 c6 12 Qc1 Qc7 13 Nd4 a5 14 c4 a4 15 a3 Bd7 16 Be2 Rab8 17 g4 Bf8 with equality, M.Vachier Lagrave-D.Jakovenko, French Team Ch. 2008.

The text move distinguishes itself from the others in that White gives himself the option of Bxc5.

10...c6

There has been serious interest in 10...Re8. For example, 11 Bc4 Be6 12 Bxe6 Nxe6 13 h4 Qd7 14 Qd5 (or 14 Qd3 Qc6 15 Qf5 transposing; whereas 15 Rh3?! Nc5 16 Qc4 Qe4 17 Qf1 Bf6 18 h5 h6 didn't really worry Black, K.Lahno-D.Frolyanov, Moscow 2005) 14...Qc6 15 Qf5 Qc4 16 Kb1 (or 16 Ng5 Bxg5 17 hxg5 Nf8 18 Kb1 Re5 with equality, S.Karjakin-V.Kramnik, Wijk aan Zee 2007, as White can't use the open h-file to cause any damage) 16...g6 17 Qh3 h5 18 Nd2 Qe2 19 Rde1 Qg4 (several games have reached this position) 20 Qh2 d5 21 f3 Qa4 22 g4 Bd6 23 Qg1 Nf4 24 c4 Rxe3! and the simplification led to a draw in R.Ponomariov-B.Gelfand, Moscow 2008.

11 Bxc5

After 11 Kb1 Re8 12 Nd4 Ne4 13 Qc1 d5 14 f3 Nd6 15 g4 Bd7 16 Bf4 b5 17 h4 Qb6 18 h5 c5 Black obtained reasonable counterplay, V.Popov-D.Frolyanov, Russian Team Ch. 2006.

11...dxc5 12 Qf4 Qa5 13 Bd3 Be6

13...c4? is dubious, as after 14 Bxc4 Qf5 15 Qxf5 Bxf5 16 Rhe1 Bf6 17 Ne5 Rac8 18 h3 Rc7 19 g4 Bc8 20 f4, the bishop pair is not enough for the half-pawn deficit with Black being so passive, M.Vachier Lagrave-V.Gashimov, Lausanne 2006.

14 a3 Bf6 (Diagram 22) 15 h4?!

This proves insufficient for an advantage. 15 Ng5! is more promising; e.g. 15...Bxg5 (now 15...c4? is just bad due to 16 Bxh7+ Kh8 17 h4!) 16 Qxg5 Rfd8 (or 16...Rad8 17 Rhe1 with a pull, though Black might try 17...Qb6 18 Qh4 g6, intending ...c5-c4) 17 Rhe1 Qc7 18 Qxc5 Qxh2 19 Qe3 Qh6 20 Qxh6 gxh6 21 Re3 and the ending was better for White, S.Fedorchuk-K.Landa, Paris 2006.

15...c4 16 Be4 Bxc3! 17 bxc3 Qxa3+ 18 Kb1

But not 18 Kd2? f5 19 Ng5 Rae8 20 Ra1 fxe4, when Black is clearly better.

18...f5

After this virtually all the remaining moves are forced. Here 18...Qxc3!?, with three pawns and an exposed white king for the piece, might be a way to try for more than half the spoils.

19 Ng5 fxe4 20 Qxe4 Bf5 21 Qxc4+ Kh8 22 Nf7+ Rxf7 23 Qxf7 Qxc3! (Diagram 23)

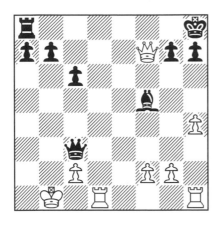

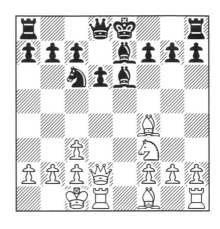

Diagram 23 (W)	**Diagram 24 (B)**
Heading for a draw	Can Black take the a2-pawn?

24 Qxf5

Allowing the draw is a sensible decision. After 24 Qa2 Re8 25 Qb2 Qa5 why should White be better?

24...Qb4+ 25 Ka2 Qa4+ 26 Kb2 Qb4+ 27 Kc1 Qa3+ 28 Kb1 ½-½

Going the other way would only be dangerous for White; i.e. 28 Kd2?! Rd8+ 29 Ke2 Qe7+ 30 Kf3 Rf8 and Black certainly shouldn't be worse.

> ## Game 64
> ## □ V.Kramnik ■ M.Adams
> ### Dortmund 2006

1 e4 e5 2 Nf3 Nf6 3 Nxe5 d6 4 Nf3 Nxe4 5 Nc3 Nxc3 6 dxc3 Be7 7 Bf4 Nc6 8 Qd2 Be6 9 0-0-0 (Diagram 24) 9...Qd7

This time Black prepares to castle long.

Surprisingly, he can also try the daring 9...Bxa2!? here, which is both sharp and far from clear; e.g. 10 b3 a5 11 Kb2 a4 12 Kxa2 (playing the devil's advocate looks critical; instead after 12 Ra1 axb3 13 cxb3 Bxb3 14 Rxa8 Qxa8 15 Kxb3 Qa1 Black had plenty of compensation in C.Kleijn-M.Van Delft, Dutch Team Ch. 2008) 12...axb3+ 13 Kxb3 Ra5 14 Kb2 Qa8 15 Bc4 d5 16 Bxc7 (16 Bb3 Ba3+! 17 Kb1 Be7 18 Kb2 Ba3+ is just a draw, S.Sjugirov-K.Maslak, Ulan Ude 2009) 16...0-0! 17 Bxa5 Nxa5 18 Ne5 Ba3+ 19 Kb1 Nxc4 20 Nxc4 dxc4 21 Qd7 b5, K.Berbatov-J.Lampert, European Junior Ch. 2008, with a complicated position requiring further tests.

10 Kb1 a6

A slight concession, since after castling queenside Black will have to be careful about a bishop sacrifice on a6.

Instead, the no-nonsense 10...0-0-0 may be the most precise, as 11 Bb5 is probably nothing to worry about; e.g. 11...a6 12 Ba4 Bf6 13 Bg5 Bxg5 14 Qxg5 b5 15 Bb3 f6 16 Bxe6 Qxe6 17 Qf4 h5 18 h3 g5 was equal in V.Ivanchuk-V.Kramnik, Moscow 2008. White could try 11 Ng5 Bxg5 12 Bxg5 f6 13 Be3 as in the main game, but then if ...a7-a6 can be avoided, Black may have an extra tempo to play with.

11 Ng5

The sequence 11 Bd3 h6 12 Rhe1 0-0-0 13 Qe2 Rhe8 14 Be3 (the immediate 14 Bxa6 is thwarted by 14...Bg5!, when 15 Bxb7+ Kxb7 16 Qb5+ only leads to a draw) 14...Kb8 15 Bxa6! bxa6 16 Qxa6 (intending c3-c4, Rd3 etc) is the sort of thing that Black has to be careful about. So maybe he should save a tempo by playing 11...0-0-0 straight away.

On the other hand, 11 Nd4 Nxd4 12 cxd4 d5 13 Bd3 Bd6 14 Rhe1 0-0-0 15 Bg3 Bxg3 16 hxg3 Bf5 17 Bxf5 Qxf5 18 Re7 Rhe8 19 Rde1 Rxe7 20 Rxe7 gave White a nagging pull in Z.Almasi-A.Motylev, Wijk aan Zee 2006.

11...Bxg5 12 Bxg5 f6 13 Be3 0-0-0 (Diagram 25) 14 b3

Similarly, 14 h3 Rhe8 15 b3 Bf5 16 f3 Kb8 17 g3 Re7 18 Bg2 Rde8 19 Rde1 h5 20 g4 Bg6 was dead equal in V.Bologan-V.Gashimov, Poikovsky 2008.

14...Rhe8 15 f3 h5 16 Bf2 Bf5 17 Be2 Re7 18 Rhe1 Rde8 19 Bf1

White's bishop pair is not really putting Black under any pressure, but the defender still needs to stay vigilant.

 WARNING: When your opponent is trying to squeeze a win out of virtually nothing, stay focused on the job in hand and keep trying to find the best moves. Don't be distracted by considerations such as: 'this is boring', 'why is he wasting our time?', 'I'll have White tomorrow and I'm sure it will be a more lively game', or even 'where shall I go for a few drinks tonight, this dry position is giving me a thirst!'. Sometimes the only reason the stronger player wins is because his opponent loses concentration.

19...Rxe1 20 Bxe1 Re7 21 Bf2 Qe8 22 c4 a5 23 a3 b6 24 Qc3 Nb8 25 Kb2 Qc6 26 Qd2 Nd7 27 Qd5 Ne5 28 Re1 Be6 (Diagram 26) 29 Qd2

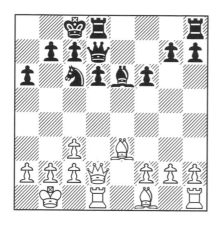

Diagram 25 (W)

Black goes long this time

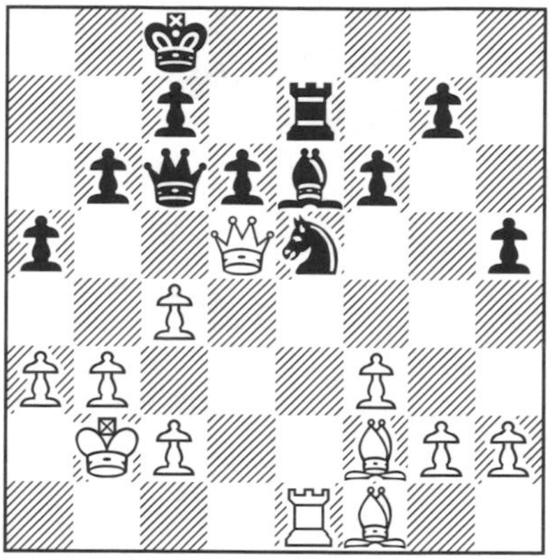

Diagram 26 (W)

Not fearing exchanges

Black is not afraid of exchanges. For instance, after 29 Qxc6 Nxc6 30 g3 Ne5 31 Bg2 Kd7 32 f4 Ng4 33 Bg1 Bf5 34 Rxe7+ (or 34 Bc6+ Kd8 35 Rxe7 Kxe7) 34...Kxe7 35 h3 Nh6, I don't see how White can make progress.

29...Qe8 30 f4 Nc6 31 Bd3 Bf7 32 Rxe7 Qxe7 33 Qd1 Kb8 34 Qf3 Nd8 35 Be4 f5 36 Bd3 g6 37 g3 Be8 38 Qe3 Qxe3 39 Bxe3 Ne6 40 b4 axb4 41 axb4 c5 ½-½

3 Nxe5 Main Lines

Game 65
□ **A.Sokolov** ■ **L.Oll**
USSR Championship, Odessa 1989

1 e4 e5 2 Nf3 Nf6 3 Nxe5 d6 4 Nf3 Nxe4 5 d4 d5 6 Bd3 Bd6

The main lines with 6...Nc6 7 0-0 Be7 are examined in Games 66-68.

7 0-0 0-0 8 c4 (Diagram 27)

The pawn structure is symmetrical, as for that matter are the disposition of the pieces, but White has the privilege of moving first and his last move obliges Black to make a slightly defensive reply.

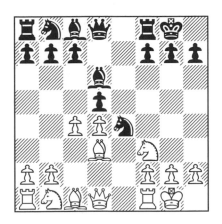

Diagram 27 (B)	**Diagram 28 (W)**
White sets the pace	Should White take on b7?

8...c6 9 Nc3

White has two noteworthy alternatives:

a) 9 Qc2 Na6 10 a3 Bg4 (Black has another reasonable approach in 10...f5 11 Nc3 Nc7 12 Ne2 Ne6 13 b4 Bd7 14 Bb2 a5 with a complex struggle in prospect, A.Grischuk-A.Morozevich, Prague rapid 2002) 11 Ne5 Bxe5 12 dxe5 Nac5 13 f3 Nxd3 14 Qxd3 Nc5 15 Qd4 (sharp and critical) 15...Nb3 16 Qxg4 Nxa1 17 Bh6 g6 18 Nc3 (after 18 Bxf8 Qxf8 19 cxd5 Qc5+ 20 Kh1 Nc2 21 Qd7 Ne3 22 e6 Nxf1, White took the draw in A.Timofeev-Wang Hao, Nizhnij Novgorod 2007) 18...Qb6+ 19 Rf2 (or if 19 Kh1!? Qxb2 20 Qf4, as in D.Jakovenko-V.Kramnik, Dortmund 2009, then 20...f5! 21 Na4 Qe2 22 Rxa1 Rfe8 with mutual chances according to Fier) 19...Rfe8 20 Qf4 Qc7 21 Re2 Re6 22 Kf1 d4! (Black had been struggling in this line until Alekseev showed the way) 23 Qxd4, and as Black gains a tempo for the retreat of his knight (thus achieving a satisfactory position), White proposed a draw which was accepted in V.Ivanchuk-E.Alekseev, Moscow 2008.

b) 9 cxd5 cxd5 10 Nc3 Nxc3 11 bxc3 Bg4 12 Rb1 Nd7 13 h3 Bh5 **(Diagram 28)** and now White has to decide what to do with his rook – the fact that 14 Rb5 has scored 63% for White as opposed to only 50% for 14 Rxb7 may be of some relevance:

b1) 14 Rxb7 Nb6 15 Qc2 Bxf3! (15...Bg6 16 Bxg6 hxg6 17 Ng5 Qc8 18 Rxf7 Rxf7 19

Qxg6 Qf5 20 Qxd6 Rf6 21 Qe7 favours White slightly, V.Gashimov-P.Harikrishna, Spanish Team Ch. 2007) 16 Bxh7+ Kh8 17 gxf3 Qh4! 18 Bf5 g6 19 Bg4 f5 20 f4 Rae8 21 Bf3 g5 22 Bg2 gxf4 23 Qd3 Rg8 24 Qf3 (24 Kh1? gets into hot water after 24...Rxg2! 25 Kxg2 Qh5 26 Rh1 f3+ 27 Kf1 Re2 28 Rxa7 Qe8, when Black is clearly better, B.Bournival-D.Ippolito, Peabody 2007) 24...Qg5 25 Rxa7 Rc8 26 Bd2 (26 c4!?) 26...Nc4 27 Bc1 Nb6 28 Bd2 Nc4 29 Bc1 Nb6, drawing by repetition in N.De Firmian-D.Ippolito, Bermuda 2009.

b2) 14 Rb5! Nb6 15 c4 Bxf3 (after 15...Nxc4 16 Rxd5 Bh2+ 17 Nxh2 Qxd5 18 Bxc4 Qxc4 19 Qxh5 White has a big score, suggesting that the two pieces are more important than the rook and pawn; e.g. 19...Rfd8 20 Nf3 Qxa2 21 Re1 Re8 22 Rxe8+ Rxe8 23 Bf4 Qb1+ 24 Kh2 Qe4 25 Bg3 Qg6 26 Qc5 and White was clearly on top, D.Brandeburg-S.Ernst, Dieren 2008) 16 Qxf3 dxc4 17 Bc2 Qd7 18 a4 **(Diagram 29)** (White has the bishop pair and light-square pressure for the pawn, while Black pins his hopes on the c-pawn)

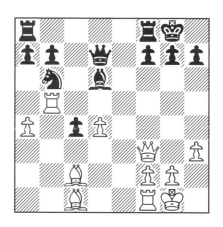

Diagram 29 (B)

Both sides have chances

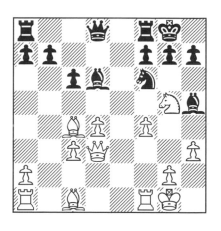

Diagram 30 (B)

Position after 15 f4

18...g6 19 Be3 Rac8 20 Rfb1 c3 21 a5 Nc4 22 Rxb7 Qe6 23 Bb3 (or 23 Ra1 Rc7 24 a6 Nxe3 25 fxe3 Kg7 26 e4 f6 27 Qxc3 Rff7 and Black defended successfully, V.Topalov-A.Shirov, Wijk aan Zee 2004) 23...Qf5! 24 Qxf5 gxf5 25 Ra1 was A.Grischuk-A.Shirov, FIDE World Ch., New Delhi 2000. In his notes Grischuk gave 25...Nd2! 26 g3 Nxb3 27 Rxb3 c2 28 Rc1 Rc4 29 Kf1 Rfc8 30 Ke2 a6 as equal, which was later played out in P.Petran-M.Galyas, Budapest 2001, at which point a draw was agreed!

9...Nxc3 10 bxc3 dxc4

Or 10...Bg4 11 cxd5 cxd5, transposing to line 'b' in the previous note.

11 Bxc4 Bg4 12 Qd3

Chasing the bishop is also possible: 12 h3 Bh5 13 g4 Bg6 14 Ne5 Nd7 15 Nxg6 hxg6 and White has the two bishops, but Black is solid; e.g. 16 Qf3 Qf6 17 Kg2 Qxf3+ 18 Kxf3 b5 19 Bd3 Nb6 and Black held firm, D.Stellwagen-Wang Hao, World Junior Ch., Yerevan 2007.

12...Nd7

Or 12...Bh5 13 Ne5 (less testing is 13 Ng5 Bg6 14 Qh3 Qd7 15 Re1 Qxh3 16 Nxh3 Nd7 with equality, A.Deshmukh-D.Barua, Commonwealth Ch., Bikaner 1999) 13...b5 14 Qh3 bxc4 15 Qxh5 Qa5 16 Bd2 Qd5 17 Qe2 as in M.Agopov-E.Solozhenkin, Helsinki 2000, and now in his notes Solozhenkin gave 17...Bxe5 as equal, though after 18 Qxe5 Nd7 19 Qxd5 cxd5 20 Bf4 I prefer White slightly.

13 Ng5

After 13 Bg5 Qa5 14 Bh4 Nb6 15 Bb3 Qh5 16 Bg3 Rad8 17 Rfe1 Bxf3 a draw was agreed in E.Chevelevitch-R.Rabiega, German League 2008. Presumably the players decided that the position was again about equal.

13...Nf6 14 h3 Bh5 15 f4 (Diagram 30)

Otherwise Black plays ...Bg6 with a comfortable game.

15...h6

Sometimes Black flicks in 15...b5 16 Bb3 before playing 16...h6, though it makes little difference.

16 g4

This sharp move requires Black to play very accurately to earn a draw. The quieter 16 Nf3 Bxf3 17 Rxf3 Re8 18 Be3 Bc7 19 Raf1 Qd6 20 Bf2 Re4 21 Bh4 Rae8 led to comfortable equality in G.Kamsky-E.Bareev, Linares 1993.

16...hxg5 17 fxg5 b5!?

The timing of this move doesn't seem to be that important; for example, 17...Nxg4 18 hxg4 Qd7 19 gxh5 Qg4+ 20 Kf2 Rae8 21 Rg1 Qh4+ 22 Kg2 and even at this late stage 22...b5 23 Bb3 transposes to the game.

18 Bb3 Nxg4 19 hxg4 Qd7!

There is no need for Black to chance his arm with 19...Bxg4?! 20 g6! Be6 21 Rxf7! (21 gxf7+ Bxf7 22 Rxf7 Rxf7 23 Qg6 is well met by 23...Qf6! 24 Bxf7+ Qxf7 25 Qxd6 Rf8 – Nunn) 21...Bxb3! (but not 21...Qe8? 22 Qh3! Rxf7 23 Qh7+ Kf8 24 Bg5 1-0 A.Garrido-E.Palacios, Asturias 1992) 22 Qh3 Rxf7 23 Qh7+ Kf8 24 Qh8+ Ke7 25 Bg5+ Rf6!, even if there is no obvious win for White after 26 Qxg7+ Ke6! 27 Bxf6 Qg8 28

Re1+ Kf5 29 Rf1+ Bf4 or 26 Re1+ Kd7 27 Qxg7+ Rf7! 28 gxf6 Qf8.

20 gxh5

20 Qf5 is another try, but Black's defences are more than adequate: 20...Bxg4 21 Qxd7 Bxd7 22 Rxf7 Rxf7 23 g6 Be8 (J.Nunn-V.Salov, Brussels 1988) 24 Bg5! a5 25 Kg2?! (Salov's 25 Rf1 Raa7 26 Rf3! leads to equality according to Nunn) 25...a4 26 Be6 Kf8 27 Rh1 Rf6! 28 Bxf6 gxf6 29 Bf5 Kg8 30 Rh7 Bxg6 31 Bxg6 Bf4 soon led to a draw in H.Hamdouchi-J.P.Le Roux, Belfort 2003, as Black couldn't make anything of his nominal advantage.

20...Qg4+ 21 Kf2 Rae8 22 Rg1 Qh4+ 23 Kg2 (Diagram 31)

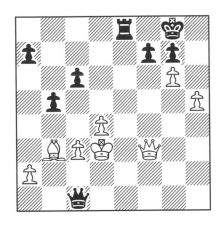

Diagram 31 (B)

How should Black continue?

Diagram 32 (B)

Perpetual check ensues

For the sacrificed piece Black obviously has attacking chances against the exposed white king, but what should he play here?

23...Qh2+!

This check is the most reliable. Instead:

a) 23...c5?? 24 Rh1 was the end of the game in N.Short-R.Hübner, Tilburg 1988, as Black resigned.

b) 23...Re4?! 24 Qf3! Bh2 25 Rh1! (Short suggested 25 Bd2 Rg4+ 26 Qxg4 Qxg4+ 27 Kxh2 Qh4+ 28 Kg2 Qe4+ 29 Kf2 Qf5+ 30 Ke2, although 30...c5! is not entirely clear) 25...Rg4+ 26 Kf1 Rg3 creates a weird position where it is easy for humans to go wrong; e.g. 27 Qxc6?? Qh3+ 28 Kf2 Qf5+ 29 Ke1 Rc8?? (29...Bg1! wins for Black) 30 Be6! 1-0 L.Psakhis-A.Mikhalchishin, Klaipeda 1988. However, after 27 Qf5! Qxh5 28 Qe4 Qh3+ 29 Kf2 Rg4 30 Qxc6 Black may not have enough compensation.

24 Kf1 Bf4!

Excellent. Oll avoids 24...Re1+? 25 Kxe1 Qxg1+ 26 Kd2, when the white king runs away to safety.

25 Qf3!

25 Bxf4? would be wrong, since 25...Qxf4+ 26 Kg2 Re3! wins the queen and probably the game for Black.

25...Re1+ 26 Kxe1 Qxg1+ 27 Ke2 Bxc1 28 Rxc1!

Not 28 Kd3? due to 28...Qxg5 and Black is better.

28...Qxc1 29 g6 Re8+ 30 Kd3 (Diagram 32) 30...Qb1+

Black elects to force the draw. If instead 30...Re7!? 31 gxf7+ Kf8 32 Qh3! Qb1+ 33 Bc2 Qxa2 34 Qc8+ Kxf7 35 Qf5+ White is the one who has perpetual check, as pointed out by Oll.

31 Kd2 Qe1+ 32 Kd3 Qb1+ 33 Kd2 Qe1+ ½-½

1 e4 e5 2 Nf3 Nf6 3 Nxe5 d6 4 Nf3 Nxe4 5 d4 d5 6 Bd3 Nc6 7 0-0 Be7 (Diagram 33)

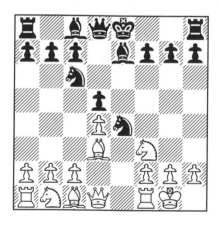

Diagram 33 (W)
Black plays ...Be7

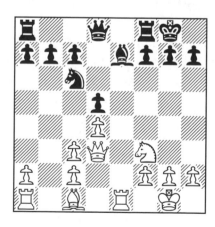

Diagram 34 (W)
The 8 Nc3 Bf5 variation

8 Re1

8 Nc3 is an interesting try, getting Black to make a decision before castling. Then 8...Nxc3 9 bxc3 Bg4 10 Re1 0-0 11 Bf4 Bd6 12 Bxd6 Bxf3 13 Qxf3 Qxd6 14 Re3 Rae8 15 Rae1 Rxe3 16 Rxe3, P.Leko-R.Kasimdzhanov, Nalchik 2009; and 8...f5!? 9 Ne2 0-0 10 c4 Be6 11 Nf4 Bf7 12 cxd5 Bxd5, A.Grischuk-B.Gelfand, Bastia (rapid) 2003, 13 Ne5!, are both somewhat better for White.

Instead, 8...Bf5 is Black's best scoring move, after which 9 Re1 forces the release of central tension: 9...Nxc3 10 bxc3 Bxd3 11 Qxd3 0-0 **(Diagram 34)**, and then the question is whether White wants to relieve his compromised pawn structure or not.

a) First of all, the natural 'structural-improvement strategy' 12 c4 dxc4 13 Qxc4 is not completely equal for Black. It's true that there isn't very much in it for White, especially if he plays slowly, since he can't really launch a direct attack now that two pairs of minor pieces have been exchanged. However, he can still aim to exploit his lead in development; e.g. 13...Bf6 (or if 13...Bd6 14 Bg5 Qd7, R.Edouard-A.Neumann, Bad Wiessee 2008, then 15 Rab1 with a pull) 14 Ba3 Re8 15 Rxe8+ Qxe8 16 Re1 Qd7 17 d5 Ne7 (if 17...Na5 the continuation 18 Qd3 b5 19 Nd2 c6 20 d6 Nb7 21 Ne4 favours White somewhat) 18 Ne5 Bxe5 19 Rxe5 Ng6 20 Re4, R.Edouard-D.Frolyanov, Differdange 2008, and now I suggest 20...Rd8! 21 Qb3 b6 22 c4 h6 with only a tiny edge to White.

b) The direct 12 Bf4 Bd6 13 Ng5 g6 14 Qh3 h5 15 Qg3 (slightly more dangerous than 15 Bxd6 Qxd6 16 Qf3 Qd7 17 Re3 Rae8, which was only equal in P.Svidler-B.Gelfand, Turin Olympiad 2006) 15...Bxf4 16 Qxf4 Qd7 17 Nf3 Kg7 obliges Black to defend accurately, but shouldn't offer White more than a nominal edge, E.Bacrot-R.Kasimdzhanov, Jermuk 2009.

c) The distracting 12 Rb1!? Na5 13 Qf5 Re8 14 Bf4 g6 15 Qh3 can be met in more than one way. For example, 15...Nc4 16 Ne5 (16 Rxb7 Bd6 enables Black to seize the initiative) 16...Bd6 17 Nxc4 Bxf4 18 Rxe8+ Qxe8 19 Qf3 dxc4 20 Qxf4 Qe2 with equality, M.Adams-J.Polgar, Wijk aan Zee 2008; while 15...c6 16 Ne5 Bf6 17 Re3 Bxe5 18 dxe5, as in I.Cheparinov-M.Roiz, Kemer 2007, and now 18...Nc4! (Roiz) and if 19 Rxb7 Rb8! (Marin) also gives Black an adequate game.

8...Bg4 9 c3

White supports his centre while making way for his queen to probe the queenside. For the alternative plan involving 9 c4, see Game 67.

9...f5 (Diagram 35)

This move is the standard reply, and yet is clearly ambitious as Black takes positional risks with his structure in order to seize the initiative on the kingside.

10 Nbd2 0-0 11 Qb3 Na5

Black can also offer up his b-pawn to accelerate his counterplay: 11...Kh8!? 12 Qxb7 Rf6, but after 13 Qb3 Rb8 (if 13...Rg6 White has scored heavily with 14 Bb5! forcing a concession) 14 Qc2 Bd6 15 h3 Bh5 16 Bf1 Rg6 17 Qd3 Qf6 18 b4 Black has nothing convincing for his pawn, I.Smirin-T.Balogh, Belgrade 1998.

So there is a suspicion that 11...Kh8 is a bit dubious, and certainly the top players have all been opting for the game move in recent years.

12 Qc2 Nc6 13 Qb3

Repeating so as to save time on the clock for later.

13...Na5 14 Qc2 (Diagram 36) 14...Nc6

Diagram 35 (W)

Black plays ambitiously

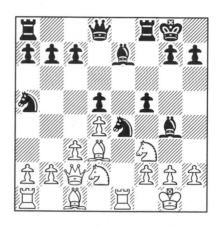

Diagram 36 (B)

Does Black want a draw?

Having done its job in driving the queen from b3, the knight returns once more to its central position – although this allows White, should he so wish, to take a draw by repetition with 15 Qb3.

Instead, Black has an important alternative in 14...Bd6; e.g. 15 Ne5 Bh5 and then:

a) 16 b4 Nc6 17 Ndf3 Re8 18 Bb2 Qf6 19 Qb3 Kh8 20 Be2 Rxe5! 21 dxe5 Nxe5 was an interesting exchange sacrifice in P.Leko-V.Anand, Linares 2005, and White couldn't find anything better than allowing a perpetual check after 22 Nxe5 Bxe5 23 Bxh5 Bxh2+ 24 Kxh2 Qh4+ 25 Kg1 Qxf2+ 26 Kh2 ½-½.

b) 16 Ndf3 c5 17 dxc5 Bxc5 18 Be3 was D.Stellwagen-K.Lahno, Wijk aan Zee 2006, when Black should have played 18...Bxe3! 19 Rxe3 Qc7 20 Qa4 Nc6! 21 Nxc6 bxc6, bolstering her centre sufficiently to claim that chances are equal.

15 b4 a6 16 Rb1

The main alternative is the immediate 16 a4; e.g. 16...Bd6 17 Ba3 (after 17 Rb1 Nxd2 18 Nxd2 Qh4 19 Nf1 Ne7 20 Bd2 f4 21 f3 Bd7, A.Shirov-V.Kramnik, French Team Ch. 2005, a draw was agreed as Black already had a comfortable game) 17...Kh8 18 b5 axb5 19 Bxd6 cxd6 20 axb5 Na5 with unclear play, R.Ponomariov-M.Adams, Wijk aan Zee 2005.

16...b5!

Slowing down White's queenside play in this way seems to give Black a satisfactory position.

17 a4 Rb8 18 axb5 axb5 19 Ne5?

Vacating the f3-square in order to play f2-f3 is tempting, but it turns out to be weak. Instead, White should probably settle for something more modest such as 19 h3 Bh5 20 Be2 Bh4 21 Rf1 Re8 22 Nxe4 fxe4 23 Nxh4 but this offers only equality, as was the case in L.Bruzon Bautista-P.H.Nielsen, Havana 2007.

19...Nxe5 20 dxe5 (Diagram 37)

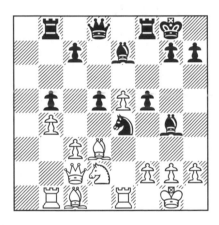

Diagram 37 (B)

Time to sacrifice

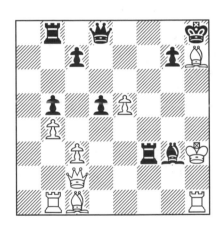

Diagram 38 (B)

The final mistake

20...Nxf2!

A delightful sacrifice to open up White's king. Alternatively, 20...c5 21 f3 Qb6 22 Bxe4 fxe4 23 fxg4 cxb4+ 24 Kh1 Qf2 also gave Black more than enough for his piece, F.Amonatov-V.Kunin, Moscow 2009.

21 Kxf2 Bh4+ 22 g3

If 22 Kf1, the continuation 22...Bxe1 23 Kxe1 Qh4+ 24 g3 Qxh2 25 Nf1 Qxc2 26 Bxc2 Rbe8 favours Black, D.Howell-V.Kramnik, London 2009.

22...f4! 23 Kg2 fxg3 24 hxg3 Bh3+?!

Here 24...Bxg3! 25 Kxg3 Qg5 was the correct way forward; e.g. 26 Ne4 Rf3+ 27 Kg2 Qxe5 28 Nf6+ Qxf6 29 Bxh7+ Kf7 and Black's attack gives him the advantage.

25 Kxh3 Bxg3 26 Bxh7+?

White could perhaps escape at this point with 26 Nf3! Rxf3 27 Kg2 Bxe1 28 Kxf3 Qh4 29 Ke2, since after the further moves 29...Rf8 30 Kd1 Qh1 31 Qe2 Bg3+ 32 Kc2 Rf2 the resource 33 Bd2! saves the queen. With variations such as this one it is understandable that neither side was able to play these wild complications precisely!

26...Kh8 27 Nf3 Rxf3 28 Rh1? (Diagram 38)

Although 28 Kg2 was the last chance to resist according to Fridman, the direct 28...Bxe1 29 Kxf3 Qh4 followed by ...Rf8 looks very good for Black in any case. From now on Black just keeps giving checks until the flagging resistance is broken.

28...Bf4+ 29 Kg2 Qg5+ 30 Kxf3 Qg3+ 31 Ke2 Qg2+ 32 Kd3

After 32 Ke1 Black seems to win with 32...Bg3+ 33 Kd1 Qxh1+ 34 Ke2 Qh5+ 35 Ke3 Re8.

32...Qf3+ 33 Kd4 Bxe5+ 34 Kc5 Bd6+ 35 Kd4 c5+ 36 bxc5 Be5+ 37 Kxe5 Qf6+ 38 Kxd5 Rd8+ 39 Ke4 Re8+ 40 Kd5 Qe6+ 0-1

It is mate next move.

Game 67
□ A.Naiditsch ■ V.Kramnik
Dortmund 2008

1 e4 e5 2 Nf3 Nf6 3 Nxe5 d6 4 Nf3 Nxe4 5 d4 d5 6 Bd3 Nc6 7 0-0 Be7

Black sometimes plays 7...Bg4 which may transpose below or, if not, then still involves similar themes: 8 c4 (8 Re1 Be7 transposes) 8...Nf6 9 Nc3 Bxf3 10 Qxf3 Nxd4 11 Qh3! (a high scoring move for White) 11...dxc4 12 Bxc4 Be7 (12...Qc8!? 13 Re1+ Be7 14 Rxe7+!? Kxe7 15 Qe3+ Ne6 16 f4 Qd7 was very messy in R.Fontaine-J.R.Koch, French Team Ch. 2009, and perhaps requires a deeper probe) 13 Bg5 Qc8 14 Qd3! Ne6 **(Diagram 39)** and then:

a) 15 Bxe6 fxe6 16 Rfe1 (after Ponomariov's 16 Qc4!? Qd7 17 Rad1 Qc6 18 Qxc6+ bxc6 19 Rfe1, simply 19...Kf7! is fine for Black) 16...Qd7 17 Qc4 0-0-0 18 Rxe6 Nd5

19 Bxe7 Qxe6 20 Bxd8 Rxd8 21 g3 (as in R.Ponomariov-M.Turov, Kharkov 2001), and now 21...Qg8! was a precise equalizer, L.Dominguez-A.Hernandez, Cuban Ch. 2003.

b) 15 Bxf6! Bxf6 16 Nd5 Bd8 (not 16...Bxb2? due to 17 Rae1 Kf8 18 Rxe6 fxe6 19 Nf4 e5 20 Qd5 and wins, V.Akopian-A.Ramaswamy, Gibraltar 2007; or if 16...Qd8 17 Nxf6+ Qxf6 18 Bxe6 fxe6 19 Qb5+ c6 20 Qxb7 White has the edge due to his superior pawn structure) 17 Qa3 c6 18 Rfe1 b5 19 Bd3 Qd7 20 Nf4 Be7 21 Nxe6 Bxa3 22 Nc5+ Qe7 23 bxa3, when the two pieces were better than the rook and pawn, R.Hovhannisyan-A.Nasri, World Junior Ch., Yerevan 2007.

8 Re1 Bg4 9 c4 Nf6 10 Nc3 (Diagram 40) 10...Bxf3

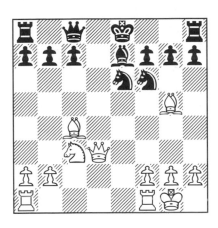

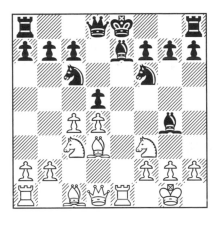

Diagram 39 (W)	**Diagram 40 (B)**
White scores well here	Position after 10 Nc3

The beginning of a long forcing sequence. If this whole variation creaks a little for Black lower down, then here is perhaps the place to look for a practical alternative:

a) 10...0-0 11 cxd5 Nxd5 12 Be4 Be6 is probably wrong as Black has lost a tempo (...Bg4-e6) compared to an analogous variation. All the same, his position remains solid.

b) 10...dxc4 11 Bxc4 0-0 12 d5 Na5 13 Bd3 c6 14 h3 Bh5 15 Re5 Bg6 16 Bg5 (Kasparov later gave 16 Bxg6 hxg6 17 d6 Bxd6 18 Rxa5 Qxa5 19 Qxd6 as a simpler way to an advantage) 16...Bd6 17 Re2 Bb4 18 Bxf6 gxf6 19 Rc1 has been under a cloud since G.Kasparov-J.Timman, Amsterdam 1994, as White has at least a small plus and maybe more.

c) 10...Nxd4!? is more interesting: 11 cxd5 Bxf3 (11...Nxf3+ 12 gxf3 Bh5 13 Bb5+ Kf8 was successful for Black in T.Nedev-M.Bakalarz, Dresden Olympiad 2008, but this needs testing by the elite) 12 gxf3 c5 13 dxc6 (13 d6!? Qxd6 14 Nb5 was successful in E.Sutovsky-E.Inarkiev, Poikovsky 2009, but the pawn sacrifice isn't at all clear after 14...Nxb5 15 Bxb5+ Kf8) 13...Nxc6 14 Bb5 0-0 15 Qxd8 Bxd8 16 Be3 Ba5 with equality, T.Radjabov-V.Gashimov, FIDE Grand Prix, Sochi 2008.

11 Qxf3 Nxd4 12 Qd1 Ne6 13 cxd5 Nxd5 14 Bb5+ c6 15 Nxd5 cxb5 (Diagram 41)

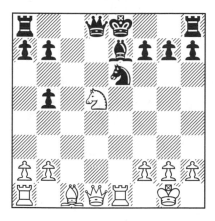

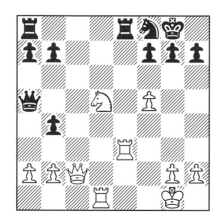

Diagram 41 (W)

The end of the sequence

Diagram 42 (W)

White has a dangerous initiative

16 Bf4

White has a couple of other ideas here:

a) 16 Qh5 0-0 17 Nxe7+ Qxe7 18 Qxb5, when having a bishop in the open position offers him a nominal edge, although after 18...Rfd8 19 Be3 a6 20 Qb3 Rac8 21 h3 h6 22 Rad1, V.Ivanchuk-V.Kramnik, Dortmund 2008, and now 22...b5, Black is near enough to equality.

b) 16 Qb3 0-0 17 Be3 (17 Nxe7 Qxe7 18 Qxb5 transposes to line 'a') 17...Bc5 18 Rad1 Bxe3 19 Rxe3 Qa5 20 Qc2 Rfe8 21 f4 b4 22 f5 Nf8 **(Diagram 42)** when Black's extra pawn is hardly relevant, whereas White's more active pieces give him a dangerous initiative. Gelfand has been tested three times in this position...

The second and third games continued 23 Ne7+ Kh8 24 Qc4 Ne6! 25 Nd5, when 25...Qc5 26 Qxb4 Qxb4 27 Nxb4 Nc5 (T.Radjabov-B.Gelfand, Bazna 2009), and 25...Rad8! 26 Ree1 Qc5+ 27 Qxc5 Nxc5 (P.Svidler-B.Gelfand, Moscow 2009), both led to quick draws.

However, in the earlier game (P.Leko-B.Gelfand, FIDE Grand Prix, Nalchik 2009), 23

Red3 caused Black lots of problems, and after 23...Nd7 24 Qc7! Qc5+ 25 Kf1 Qb5 26 Qg3! Leko judges the position to be 'practically lost' for Black, due to the threats of Nc7 and f5-f6. So it seems that Black needs to find an improvement earlier – and Gelfand had presumably found one. For example, 23...b3! 24 axb3 Re1+ 25 Kf2 Rxd1 (exchanging a pair of rooks reduces White's pressure) 26 Rxd1 Re8 27 f6 is described by Leko as 'practically unpleasant' for Black, but analysis engines suggest that 27...Re5! is fine, as White's kingside 'attack' is an illusion.

The top players would be aware of all this, so Radjabov and Svidler both varied – it's an illustration of how deep opening preparation can be for the highest echelon.

 TIP: Whether a variation involves long-forcing lines or quiet manoeuvring, don't try and learn things parrot-fashion. Aim to understand the reason behind each move and then you'll find it so much easier to play analogous lines over the board.

16...Nxf4 17 Rxe7+ Kf8 18 Re5 Qd6 19 Qd2! (Diagram 43)

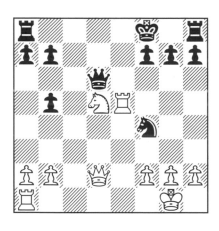

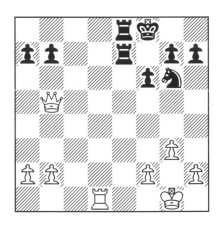

Diagram 43 (B)	Diagram 44 (B)
A shocking novelty	White comes out on top

This novelty came as a complete shock to Kramnik who then spent an hour trying to find a solution to his problems! White audaciously leaves a rook *en prise* and calmly continues development!

Previous practice had seen 19 Rf5 Rd8 20 Ne3 Qxd1+ 21 Rxd1 Rxd1+ 22 Nxd1 Ne6 23 Rxb5 b6 24 Nc3 Ke7 with complete equality and ½-½ in R.Kasimdzhanov-A.Yusupov, Essen 2001.

19...Ng6?!

The critical line runs 19...Qxe5 20 Qb4+ Ke8 (not 20...Kg8?? 21 Ne7+ Kf8 22 Ng6+ and 23 Nxe5) 21 Qxb5+ Kd8 22 Rd1 Ne2+! (after 22...Qxd5 23 Rxd5+ Nxd5 24 Qxd5+ Ke7 25 Qxb7+ Kf6 26 Qf3+ Ke6 27 Qe4+ Kf6 28 g4, the queen was stronger than the two rooks in Z.Stanojoski-T.Sammalvuo, Dresden Olympiad 2008) 23 Kh1 Nd4 24 Qxb7 Rc8 25 h3, which was given as unclear by Naiditsch.

Frankly, while a rook is a big investment, Black's king looks highly precarious and I wouldn't want to play this position with Black – though someone has tried: 25...Rc5 (25...g5!? has been analysed as leading to equality, but this certainly needs testing) 26 Ne3 Re8 27 Nf5 Rc7? (here 27...Qe1+ 28 Kh2 Qxd1 29 Qb8+ Kd7 30 Qd6+ Kc8 31 Qxc5+ Kb8 32 Nxd4 Qa4 33 b4 Qd7 34 Nc6+ Ka8 35 b5 would only leave White with a slight pull according to Golubev) 28 Qb8+ Kd7 29 Rxd4+ Kc6 30 Qb3 and White won in P.Smirnov-D.Neelotpal, Pardubice 2008.

20 Ree1 f6 21 Rad1 Kf7 22 Qe3!

White's wonderfully centralized pieces offer him more than a mere pawn's worth of play. Black has difficulty finding a sensible move.

22...Rhe8

If 22...Rhd8 23 Ne7 Qxd1 24 Qe6+ and mate next move.

23 Ne7!

The threats on the a2-g8 diagonal force Black to surrender his queen.

23...Qxe7

Or if 23...Rxe7 24 Rxd6 Rxe3 25 Rxe3 with a winning endgame.

24 Qb3+ Kf8 25 Rxe7 Rxe7 26 Qxb5 Rae8 27 g3 (Diagram 44)

The dust settles and Black has only rook and knight for the queen. Naiditsch demonstrates exemplary technique to convert his advantage.

27...Ne5 28 Kg2 Nc6 29 b4

Pressing on the queenside.

29...a6 30 Qb6 h6 31 a4 Ne5 32 Qc5 Kg8 33 b5

Denying Black the c6-square.

33...axb5 34 axb5 Nf7 35 h4 Kh8 36 Rd2 Kg8 37 Kh3 Kh8 38 f4

Further restricting the knight.

38...Kg8 39 h5 Kh8 40 Qf5 Nd8 41 Rd7 Ne6 42 Qd5 1-0

Black loses more material and so resigns.

Game 68
□ V.Akopian ■ R.Kasimdzhanov
FIDE Grand Prix, Nalchik 2009

1 e4 e5 2 Nf3 Nf6 3 Nxe5 d6 4 Nf3 Nxe4 5 d4 d5 6 Bd3 Nc6 7 0-0 Be7 8 c4 (Diagram 45)

This could perhaps be considered as the main line of the whole Petroff.

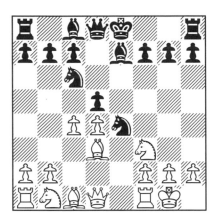

Diagram 45 (B)

The main line Petroff

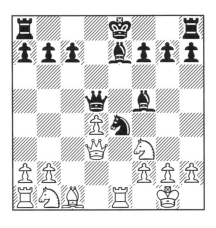

Diagram 46 (W)

A critical position

8...Nb4

Taking the opportunity to hit the light-squared bishop, which will normally withdraw to e2.

Black sometimes opts for the prudent retreat 8...Nf6 (despite being about as fifth as common, it achieves about the same percentage), when he prepares to recapture on d5 with his knight. Then after 9 Nc3 there is another dichotomy:

a) 9...Be6 10 cxd5 (after 10 c5 Bg4 11 Bb5 0-0 12 Bxc6 bxc6 13 h3 Bxf3 14 Qxf3 Re8 15 Re1 Nd7 16 Bf4 Bf6 17 Rxe8+ Qxe8 18 Qd3 Nf8! Black's knight was able to come to e6 offering him a satisfactory game, G.Milos-P.Zarnicki, São Paulo 2002) 10...Nxd5 11 Re1 0-0 12 a3 Bf6 13 Be4 h6 14 Bc2 (now that Black has played ...h7-h6, White intends to construct a battery on the b1-h7 diagonal) 14...Nde7 15 Be3 Nf5 16 Ne2 Re8 17 Qd3 g6 18 Qd2 Nxe3 19 fxe3 Bg4 with a complex position,

A.Grischuk-B.Gelfand, Russian Team Ch. 2006.

b) 9...0-0 10 h3 (stopping any ideas of ...Bg4, whereas 10 cxd5 Nxd5 11 Re1 Be6 transposes to line 'a') 10...Nb4 11 Be2 dxc4 12 Bxc4 Nbd5 13 Re1 c6 (with a typical IQP scenario) 14 Bg5 Be6 15 Qb3 Rb8 16 Bh4 h6 17 Bg3 Bd6 18 Be5 Nxc3 19 Bxe6 Ncd5 20 Bf5 Re8 21 g3 Qc7 22 Re2 Re7 23 Rae1 Rbe8 and Black was very solid, P.Svidler-B.Gelfand, European Club Cup, Fuegen 2006.

These sample lines suggest that 8...Nf6 can be considered a playable alternative.

9 Be2

With 9 cxd5!? White saves time for development but cedes the bishop pair, and his score goes down to 53% (compared to 60% for the bishop retreat). Indeed, Black's bishops seem to give him reasonable prospects, though he has to play very carefully, especially as his king tends to stay in the centre for quite a while. The critical position occurs after 9...Nxd3 10 Qxd3 Qxd5 11 Re1 Bf5 **(Diagram 46)** when there are three tries, but as is so common in the Petroff, nothing particularly convincing has been found for White:

a) 12 g4 Bg6 13 Nc3 Nxc3 14 Qxc3 f6 15 Bf4 (15 Qxc7 0-0! 16 Rxe7 Qxf3 was fine for Black in V.Anand-I.Sokolov, Dortmund 1999) 15...Kf7 16 h4 h5 17 Qxc7 Rhe8 18 Ng5+ fxg5 19 Bxg5 Kg8 20 Bxe7 Qxd4 and Black had enough activity, T.Radjabov-V.Kramnik, Nice (rapid) 2009.

b) 12 Nc3 Nxc3 13 Qxc3 Be6 (13...c6? gets into hot water after 14 Bh6! due to latent threats along the long diagonal; e.g. 14...gxh6 15 Re5 Qd7 16 Rae1 Be6 17 d5! cxd5 18 Rxe6 and wins, A.Kovacevic-A.Csonka, Hungarian Team Ch. 2006) 14 Re5 Qc6 15 Qa5 Rd8 16 Bf4 0-0 17 Rc1 Qb6 18 Rb5 Qxa5 19 Rxa5 Ra8 20 d5 Bd7 21 Ne5 Bd6 and Black had successfully equalized in A.Naiditsch-V.Kramnik, Dresden Olympiad 2008.

c) 12 Ne5 0-0-0 13 Qf3 g6 14 g4 Bb4!? (14...Bh4 15 Nc3 Nxc3 16 bxc3 Be6 17 g5 Rhe8 18 c4 Qxd4 19 Rb1 c6 20 Nxc6 Qxf2+ led to a draw in A.Volokitin-H.Koneru, Cap d'Agde rapid 2006) 15 Re2?! Bxg4 16 Nxg4 (or 16 Qxg4+ f5 17 Qf3 Qxd4 with excellent compensation) 16...Nc3! 17 Qxd5 Nxe2+ 18 Kf1 Rxd5 19 Kxe2 Rxd4 and Black was clearly better, M.Adams-J.Smeets, London 2009.

9...0-0 10 a3

Instead, 10 Nc3 **(Diagram 47)** often transposes, though not always:

a) 10...Bf5 11 a3 Nxc3 12 bxc3 Nc6 13 Re1 (maintaining the tension; otherwise 13 cxd5 Qxd5 leads back to the main line) 13...Re8 14 Bf4 (more dangerous than 14 Qa4!?, after which 14...a6 15 Be3 dxc4 16 Qxc4 Bd6 17 Qa2 Qf6 18 Rad1 h6 19 c4 Be4 20 c5 Bf8 21 d5 Bxf3 22 Bxf3 Nd4! gave Black a good game in V.Ivanchuk-V.Kramnik, Moscow 2007) 14...dxc4 15 Bxc4 Bd6 16 Rxe8+ Qxe8 (a key line; Black has held firm here) 17 Bxd6 cxd6 18 Ng5 Bg6 19 h4 Qe7! 20 Qg4 h6 21 h5!? (or 21 Nh3 when Black has 21...Qe4 22 Nf4 Ne5!) 22...Bxh5 22 Qxh5 hxg5 23 Rd1 Rf8! 24 Rd3 Qe1+ 25 Kh2 Qxf2 26 Rh3 Qf4+ 27 g3 Qd2+ 28 Kg1 Qc1+ with perpetual check, L.Dominguez Perez-P.Leko, Dresden Olympiad 2008.

b) 10...Be6 is a way for Black to vary, but experience suggests that it may not be quite as trustworthy; e.g. 11 Ne5 f6 12 Nf3 (investing two whole tempi to induce Black into playing a loosening move) 12...Kh8 13 a3 Nxc3 14 bxc3 Nc6 15 Nd2 dxc4 (after 15...Na5 16 cxd5 Bxd5 17 c4 Bf7 18 Bb2 f5 19 Bc3 c5 20 d5 Bf6 21 Qc2 White was successful in R.Kasimdzhanov-M.Adams, FIDE World Ch., Tripoli 2004) 16 Nxc4 Qd7 17 Bf4 Rad8 18 Re1 Bg8 19 h3 Bd6 20 Nxd6 cxd6 21 c4 and White could always lay claim to a pull, even if Black eventually held in R.Kasimdzhanov-A.Shirov, Leon (rapid) 2005.

10...Nc6 11 cxd5 Qxd5 12 Nc3 Nxc3 13 bxc3 Bf5 14 Re1 Rfe8 15 Bf4 Rac8 (Diagram 48) 16 h3

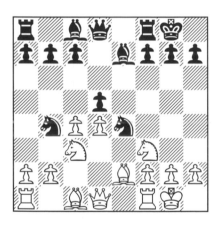

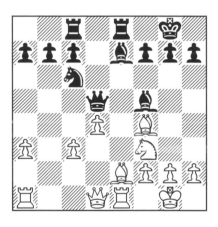

Diagram 47 (B)

White plays 10 Nc3

Diagram 48 (W)

Further down the main line

This move has emerged as the main line. Many leading players have been striving to eke something out of this for White, but the defenders have generally been able to find a route to equality. Here is a selection of White's most important alternatives:

a) 16 Bd3 Qd7 17 Rb1 Bxd3 18 Qxd3 b6 19 d5 Bf6 (or the adventurous 19...Bxa3 20 Ng5 g6 21 Ne4 Be7 22 Rbd1 f5, D.Jakovenko-V.Kramnik, Moscow 2007) 20 c4 h6 21 h4 Ne7 22 Rbd1 (22 h5 can be met by 22...b5!) 22...Ng6 23 Bg3 h5 was equal in J.Polgar-V.Anand, Wijk aan Zee 2005.

b) 16 Bg3 Bd6 17 Nd2 Bxg3 18 hxg3 Na5 19 Qa4 Bd7 20 Qc2 gave White nothing in M.Adams-V.Anand, Sofia 2005.

c) 16 Qa4 Bd7 17 Qc2 Qf5 18 Qxf5 Bxf5 19 Bb5 Bd7 20 d5 Ne5 21 Bxd7 Nxd7 with equality, V.Anand-V.Kramnik, World Ch. Tournament, Mexico City 2007.

d) 16 c4 Qe4 17 Be3 Qc2 (if 17...Bf6 then 18 Ra2! b6 19 h3 Na5 20 Bd2 yields White a slight pull, V.Kotronias-S.Marjanovic, Greek Team Ch. 2003) 18 c5!? (or 18 d5 Na5 19 Nd4 Qxd1 20 Rexd1 Bd7 21 Bd2 Bf6 22 Bxa5 Bxd4 23 Rxd4 Rxe2 ½-½ P.Leko-V.Kramnik, 3rd matchgame, Brissago 2004) 18...Na5 19 Qxc2 Bxc2 20 Rac1 Be4 leaves White with a very small edge according to Kotronias (2005). However, top players (as White) haven't tested this analysis in practice, which suggests that Black doesn't have any particular problems here.

16...h6 (Diagram 49)

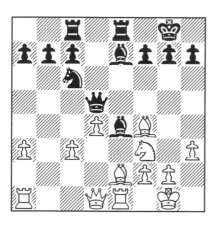

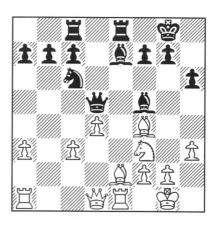

Diagram 49 (W)
Black plays 16...h6

Diagram 50 (W)
Black plays 16...Be4

Here again, a simple semi-waiting move has become the preferred choice amongst the elite. Otherwise there are two bishop moves that require some attention:

a) 16...Bf6 is not considered as sufficient for equality and so has been abandoned, due essentially to White's annoying plan of hitting this bishop with Nh2-g4; e.g. 17 Nh2 Qa5 18 Bd2 Ne7 (or 18...Rcd8 19 Bf3 h6 20 Ng4 Bxg4 21 hxg4 Bg5 22 Bxg5 hxg5, V.Kramnik-V.Anand, Wijk aan Zee 2003, when Kramnik suggested 23 Qc1 Rxe1+ 24 Qxe1 intending Rb1; e.g. 24...Kf8 25 Rb1 Re8 26 Qc1 with a clear advantage – Huzman) 19 Bf3 Rcd8 20 Ng4 Bxg4 21 hxg4 h6 22 Rb1 (22 Bxb7!? could be even better) 22...b6 23 a4 c6 24 Qc2 Qa6 25 Re4 Qc8 26 Rbe1 with an edge, A.Shirov-V.Bologan, Wijk aan Zee 2004.

b) 16...Be4 **(Diagram 50)** has also dropped out of favour. There doesn't seem to be anything particularly wrong with it, though one or two lines leave Black navigating on a knife-edge:

b1) 17 Bd3 Bxf3 18 Qxf3 Qxf3 19 gxf3 Bd6 with equality, V.Akopian-E.Bacrot, European Club Cup, St Vincent 2005.

b2) 17 Be3 Na5 18 Nd2 (instead 18 c4 Nxc4 19 Bxc4 Qxc4 20 Nd2 Qd5 21 Nxe4 Qxe4 22 Bg5 Qxe1+ 23 Qxe1 Bxg5 24 Qa5 Bf6 25 Qxa7 c5 was at least equal for Black, P.Leko-V.Kramnik, 1st matchgame, Brissago 2004) 18...Bf5 19 c4 Qd7 20 Nf3 Bf6 21 Rc1 c5 22 dxc5 Qxd1 23 Rcxd1 Nb3 24 c6 Rxc6 25 Bxa7 Bc3 26 Rf1 Ra6 with equality, V.Ivanchuk-V.Kramnik, Wijk aan Zee 2008.

b3) 17 Qa4 Qf5 18 Bg3 Bc2 19 Qb5 Qxb5 20 Bxb5 a6 21 Bxc6 bxc6 22 Re5 (after 22 Ra2 Ba4 23 c4 Bb3 24 Rae2 Kf8 25 c5 Bd5 White kept a pull in A.Grischuk-A.Volokitin, Foros 2006, though 23...c5 looks like an improvement) 22...c5 23 Rae1 Kf8 24 dxc5 f6 25 Rd5 Bb3 26 Rd7 Ba4 27 Rd4 Bc6 was equal in A.Shirov-B.Gelfand, Moscow 2007.

b4) 17 a4 Bf6 (or 17...Bd6 18 Be3 Na5 19 Nd2 Bf5 20 c4 Qe6 21 c5 Bf8 22 Rc1 b6 23 Nf3 Qb3 and Black held firm in T.Radjabov-Wang Yue, FIDE Grand Prix, Baku 2008) 18 Nd2 Bxg2 19 Bg4 Bh1 20 f3 Bh4 21 Rxe8+ Rxe8 22 Qb3 Ne7 23 Be5 Qxb3 24 Nxb3 f5 25 Bxf5 Nxf5 26 Kxh1 Bg3 27 f4 g5!? (27...Kf7 looks simpler) 28 fxg5 Kf7 with a complicated endgame, K.Asrian-Wang Yue, Taiyuan 2007.

b5) 17 Nd2 Bxg2 18 Bg4 Bh1! 19 f3 Bh4 20 Rxe8+ (better than 20 Rf1?! f5 21 Bh5 g6 22 Kxh1 gxh5, when Black was at least equal, P.Leko-V.Anand, FIDE World Ch., San Luis 2005) 20...Rxe8 21 Qb3 (C.Van Oosterom-H.Wellen, German League 2009) and now 21...Ne7! (Huzman) would be unclear (compare Asrian-Wang Yue above where White has the additional move a3-a4).

17 Nd2

There is no consensus at this point either, which perhaps reflects White's difficulty in finding a way to really test Black:

a) 17 Qc1 was tried in a later game between the same two combatants, but after 17...Bf6 18 Qb2 Na5 19 Be5 Qd8 20 Rad1 b6 21 Bb5 c6 22 Ba6 Ra8 23 c4 Bxe5 24 Nxe5 Bc8 White's slight space advantage came to nothing, V.Akopian-R.Kasimdzhanov, FIDE Grand Prix, Jermuk 2009.

b) 17 c4 has also been tried (compare this with 16 c4, where neither player has touched their h-pawn); for example, 17...Qe4 18 Bg3!? (bearing down on c7 makes sense, though presumably 18 Be3 is also possible, as in the analogous line 'd' in the note to White's 16th move) 18...Bf6 (here 18...Qc2 19 Qxc2 Bxc2 20 d5 Na5 21 Nd4 Ba4 22 Bg4 Ra8 23 Bxc7 Nxc4 24 Rac1 Nxa3 25 d6 proved to be good for White, P.Svidler-K.Landa, German League 2005) 19 Bf1 Qc2 20 Qxc2 Bxc2 21 Rxe8+ Rxe8 22 Rc1 Ba4 23 d5 Ne5 24 Nd2 Bd8 25 c5 c6 26 Ne4 cxd5 27 Nd6 Re7 28 Nxb7 Rxb7 29 Bxe5 Bc6 was level in A.Shomoev-K.Landa, Russian Team Ch. 2006. It seems that Landa had decided that 18...Bf6 is better at this point than 18...Qc2.

c) 17 g4!? is a double-edged try, but 17...Bg6 18 Bf1 Bd6 19 Rxe8+ Rxe8 20 c4 Qe4 21 Be3 Rd8! 22 Bg2 Qe7 proved to be fine for Black in A.Grischuk-V.Ivanchuk, Linares 2009.

17...Na5

17...Qd7 is also playable; e.g. 18 Nc4 Bd6 19 Qd2 Bxf4 20 Qxf4 Re4 21 Qg3 Rce8 22 Ne3 R4e7 23 Bb5 a6 24 Bc4, G.Kasparov-A.Motylev, Russian Ch., Moscow 2004, when Huzman suggested 24...b5!? 25 Ba2 Be4 as the simplest way of equalizing.

18 Bf3

If 18 Nf1, then 18...Qb3! 19 Ne3 Qxd1 20 Bd1 Bd7 21 Nd5 Bd6 nullifies White's pressure, T.Gharamian-D.Fridman, German League 2008.

18...Qd7 19 Ne4 Rcd8 20 Ng3 Bg6 21 Bh5! (Diagram 51)

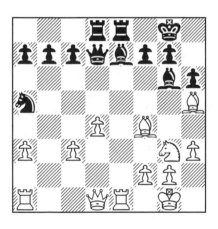
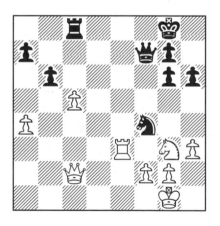

Diagram 51 (B)
Setting Black some problems

Diagram 52 (W)
Now Black is slightly better

At least setting some practical problems. For instance, after 21...Bxh5 22 Qxh5 b6 23 Nf5 White has dangerous play on the kingside. Instead, Kasimdzhanov decides to deny White access to the f5-square, even if that means living with a compromised pawn structure.

21...Bd6! 22 Bxd6 Rxe1+ 23 Qxe1 cxd6!

Trying to keep his pawns intact with 23...Qxd6 24 Bxg6 Qxg6 would be inferior due to 25 Qe5.

24 Bxg6 fxg6 25 Qe4 Qf7

Black's pawns have indeed been degraded, but the exchange of the bishops has simplified his defensive task. In fact White, who also has a far from ideal structure, doesn't seem to have any pressure at all.

26 Re1 Rf8 27 Re2 Nc4 28 a4 Nb6 29 Qc2 Nd5 30 c4?!

If instead 30 Qb3, rather than 30...Nb6?! 31 Qxf7+ Kxf7 32 Ne4 Rd8 33 Rb2 when White has the better chances, 30...b6 is probably best; e.g. 31 Ne4 Nf4 32 Qxf7+ Rxf7 33 Re3 d5 with equality.

30...Nf4 31 Re3 Rc8! 32 c5 dxc5 33 dxc5 b6! (Diagram 52)

Now Black is slightly better, since 34 c6 is met by 34...Qd5! 35 Qe4 Qxe4 36 Rxe4 Nd5 37 Rd4 Ne7 38 Rd7 Nxc6 with an extra pawn, even if converting it might be quite difficult.

34 Ne4 bxc5 35 Rf3

35 Nd6? is again well parried by 35...Qd5!.

35...Rf8

Settling for equality. Otherwise Black could play for more by holding onto the c-pawn; for example, 35...Kh8!? (35...Qf5 also looks plausible, as 36 Rc3 Qd5 37 Rc4 Nd3 38 f3 obliges White to go on the defensive) 36 Nd6 (36 g3 Nxh3+ 37 Kg2 Qe6 is murky, but if White doesn't have anything he is just a couple of pawns light) 36...Qe6 37 Rxf4 (37 Nxc8? loses to 37...Qe1+ 38 Kh2 Ne2) 37...Qxd6 38 Rf7 a6 would be a tough technical test.

36 Nxc5 Qd5 37 Qb3 Qxb3 38 Rxb3 Rc8 39 Nd3 Nxd3 40 Rxd3 Rc4 41 Rd6 Rxa4 ½-½

Summary

As the illustrative games bear witness, the Petroff can be very exciting. There are many new ideas coming to light all the time, due mainly to strong interest at the highest level, which have woven the opening into a rich tapestry of complex variations. On the other hand, it can also be extremely boring if your opponent doesn't know much theory, or has no particular desire for a fight.

Index of Variations

2. Two Knights Defence: 2 Nf3 Nc6 3 Bc4 Nf6

4 Ng5 d5 5 exd5 Na5 6 Bb5+ c6 7 dxc6 bxc6

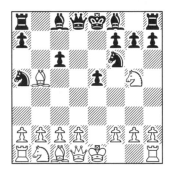

      8 Qf3 – *40;* 8 Bd3 – *43*

      8 Be2 h6

          9 Nh3 – *43*

          9 Nf3 e4 10 Ne5 Bd6 – *45, 47*

4 d4 exd4

      5 Ng5 – *49*

      5 e5 – *52, 56*

      5 0-0

          5...Bc5 – *59, 63*

          5...Nxe4 – *65*

3. Evans Gambit and Giuoco Piano: 2 Nf3 Nc6 3 Bc4 Bc5

4 b4

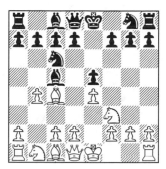

4...Bb6 – *72*
4...Bxb4 – *75, 79*

4 c3

4...Bb6 5 d4 Qe7 – *81*
4...Nf6 5 d4 exd4

6 e5 – *86*
6 cxd4 Bb4+
    7 Bd2 – *88*
    7 Nc3 Nxe4 8 0-0 Bxc3 9 d5 – *91, 95*

4. Four Knights Game: 2 Nf3 Nc6 3 Nc3 Nf6

4 d4 exd4 5 Nxd4 Bb4 6 Nxc6 bxc6 7 Bd3 d5

– 103, 105

4 Bb5

4...Bb4 – *108, 112*

4...Nd4 – *115*

4...Bd6 – *119*

5. Scotch Game: 2 Nf3 Nc6 3 d4 exd4 4 Nxd4

4...Bc5

5 Nxc6 – *125*

5 Be3 – *130, 134*

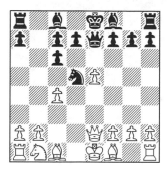
6. Central Gambits

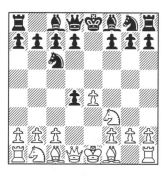

7. King's Gambit: 2 f4

2...Bc5 – *183*
2...exf4 3 Nf3

 3...g5 4 h4 g4 5 Ne5 – *168, 171*
 3...d6 – *174*
 3...d5 – *178*

8. Vienna Game: 2 Nc3

2...Nc6 3 f4 – *210*
2...Nf6

 3 f4 d5 4 fxe5 Nxe4 – *193, 197*
 3 g3 – *201*
 3 Bc4 – *205*

9. Other White Systems

10. Black Avoids 2...Nc6 – Introduction: 2 Nf3

11. Philidor's Defence: 2 Nf3 d6 3 d4

3...Nf6

    4 dxe5! – *252*
    4 Nc3 Nbd7 5 Bc4 Be7 – *247, 253*

3...exd4 4 Nxd4

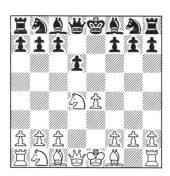

    4...g6 – *258*
    4...Nf6 5 Nc3 Be7 – *261*

12. Petroff's Defence: 2 Nf3 Nf6

3 d4

3 Nxe5 d6 4 Nf3 Nxe4

5 d4 d5 6 Bd3

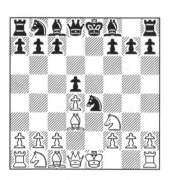

Index of Complete Games